PERGAMON INTERNATIONAL LIBRARY
of Science, Technology, Engineering and Social Studies

*The 1000-volume original paperback library in aid of education,
industrial training and the enjoyment of leisure*

Publisher: Robert Maxwell, M.C.

D1046073

Cross-
Cultural
Encounters

(PGPS-94)

THE PERGAMON TEXTBOOK
INSPECTION COPY SERVICE

An inspection copy of any book published in the Pergamon International Library
will gladly be sent to academic staff without obligation for their consideration for
course adoption or recommendation. Copies may be retained for a period of 60 days
from receipt and returned if not suitable. When a particular title is adopted or
recommended for adoption for class use and the recommendation results in a sale
of 12 or more copies the inspection copy may be retained with our compliments.
The Publishers will be pleased to receive suggestions for revised editions and new
titles to be published in this important international Library.

Pergamon Titles of Related Interest

Giles/Robinson/Smith   *LANGUAGE: Social Psychological Perspectives*

Giles/Saint-Jacques   *LANGUAGE AND ETHNIC RELATIONS*

Krasner   *ENVIRONMENTAL DESIGN AND HUMAN BEHAVIOR: A Psychology of the Individual in Society*

Marsella/Pedersen   *CROSS-CULTURAL COUNSELING AND PSYCHOTHERAPY*

Morris   *SAYING AND MEANING IN PUERTO RICO: Some Problems in the Ethnography of Discourse*

Newmark   *WOMEN'S ROLES: A CROSS-CULTURAL PERSPECTIVE*

Tamir   *COMMUNICATION AND THE AGING PROCESS: Interaction Throughout the Life Cycle*

Related Journals*

INTERNATIONAL JOURNAL OF INTERCULTURAL RELATIONS

TECHNOLOGY IN SOCIETY

WOMEN'S STUDIES INTERNATIONAL QUARTERLY

WORLD DEVELOPMENT

*Free specimen copies available upon request.

CROSS-CULTURAL ENCOUNTERS

Face-to-Face Interaction

Richard W. Brislin
Culture Learning Institute
East-West Center

Pergamon Press
New York   Oxford   Toronto   Sydney   Paris   Frankfurt

Pergamon Press Offices:

U.S.A.	Pergamon Press Inc., Maxwell House, Fairview Park, Elmsford, New York 10523, U.S.A.
U.K.	Pergamon Press Ltd., Headington Hill Hall, Oxford OX3 0BW, England
CANADA	Pergamon Canada Ltd., Suite 104, 150 Consumers Road, Willowdale, Ontario M2J 1P9, Canada
AUSTRALIA	Pergamon Press (Aust.) Pty. Ltd., P.O. Box 544, Potts Point, NSW 2011, Australia
FRANCE	Pergamon Press SARL, 24 rue des Ecoles, 75240 Paris, Cedex 05, France
FEDERAL REPUBLIC OF GERMANY	Pergamon Press GmbH, Hammerweg 6, Postfach 1305, 6242 Kronberg/Taunus, Federal Republic of Germany

Library of Congress Cataloging in Publication Data

Brislin, Richard W   1945-
    Cross-cultural encounters, face-to-face inter-
action.

    (Pergamon general psychology series ; no. 94)
    Includes index.
    1. Intercultural communication.   2.   Ethno-
psychology.   3.   Social interaction.   I.   Title.
GN496.B74   302   80-20202
ISBN 0-08-026313-5
ISBN 0-08-026312-7 (pbk.)

Printed in the United States of America

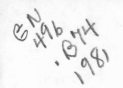
Contents

Preface ix

Chapter

1. Introduction 1
   Cross-cultural contact: A growth area
   Some basic issues
   Some reasons for the difficulties
   Types of cross-cultural contact
   General factors to be used in organizing research and analysis
   Some cautions
   Are these concepts a hodgepodge of pigeonholes?

2. History: The Background for People's Current Behavior 18
   Introduction
   Historical ideas
   Historical events in the lives of individuals
   Summary

3. Individual's Attitudes, Traits, and Skills 40
   Attitudes toward out-groups: prejudices and stereotypes
   Interpersonal cruelty
   The authoritarian personality syndrome
   An introduction to traits and skills
   The importance of traits in cross-cultural contact
   The importance of skills in cross-cultural contact
   Summary and conclusions

4. An Individual's Thought and Attribution Processes 72
   The formation of categories
   The consequences of categorization
   Attribution
   Orientation programs dealing with attribution
   Summary and conclusions

5.   Membership and Reference Groups   109
        Membership groups
        Reference groups
        Membership groups and adjustment
        Confrontation between old and new reference groups
        The process of reference group change
        Factors influencing the development of new reference groups
        The development of deviance
        The consequences of shifting reference groups: positive aspects
        The consequences of shifting reference groups: negative aspects
        How much preparation?
        Summary and conclusions

6.   The Analysis of Situations   138
        Introduction
        A general explanation and two examples
        The difficulty of analyzing situations
        Research examples: anonymous vs. face-to-face rejection
        Research examples: individuation vs. anonymity
        Key situational factors
        Familiarity: confronting cultural differences
        Coping with unfamiliar situations: culture shock
        The role of situations in determining favorable attributions
        The influence of situations in determining task productivity
        Summary and conclusions

7.   Groups in Situations: Managing Cross-Cultural Contact   171
        Introduction
        Some caveats
        The background factors or givens which face the administrator
        Factors under the control of administrators
        The changes which may follow intergroup contact
        Summary and conclusions

8.   Sojourners' Task Assignments   200
        Problems faced by all sojourners
        The move from less to more industrialized societies
        The move from more to less industrialized societies
        Summary and conclusions

9.   Organizations   228
        Case studies of organizational difficulties
        Organizational factors which help or hinder sojourners

Factors which must be faced by organizations
Benefits stemming from successful organizations
Summary

10.   The Processes of Adjustment   271
Processes in short-term adjustment
Processes in long-term adjustment
Adjustment in pluralistic societies
Effects of a sojourn, and research difficulties
Recommendations for increasing sojourner satisfaction
Summary

11.   Speculations About Cross-Cultural Interaction   308
Future research
Application of research findings
Disseminating research findings
Motives, and lessons from success stories
Summary

References   333

Author Index   355

Subject Index   361

About the Author   373

Preface

Large numbers of programs exist which encourage face-to-face interaction among people from different cultural backgrounds. Some of the programs have received widespread publicity while others exist in relative anonymity. Refugees are integrated into a community through voluntary organizations; adolescents are given opportunities to spend a year or summer abroad while living with members of a host country family; diplomats are assigned to various embassies, some of which could be the target of terrorist activities; students pay their own way or are given scholarships to study abroad; businessmen take various assignments as part of their work in multinational organizations; researchers take sabbaticals in other countries; and court orders require that children attend classes with age mates from various ethnic groups.

Are there any commonalities in the experiences of these diverse people? If so, is there enough material of interest to develop a worthwhile study area centered on cross-cultural, face-to-face interaction? I believe that the answer to both questions is "yes," and the major purpose of this book is to explain and to defend this position. Integration of the diverse research literatures and accumulated insights of experienced practitioners follows nine general themes:

1. historical ideas with which people are familiar;
2. people's attitudes, traits, and skills;
3. their ways of thinking about themselves and others;
4. the groups they join;
5. the situations they face;
6. the manner in which they manage specific contact situations involving various groups;
7. the tasks people want to accomplish;
8. the organizations in which they work;
9. and the adjustment processes they experience while living in another culture.

If the goal of documenting commonalities across people's various cross-cultural experiences can be achieved, then professionals concerned with *different* programs will have concepts which they can share. Further, they can benefit from each other's insights rather than labor in the belief that would-be colleagues are doing irrelevant studies and analyses. The ideals of "professionalism" and "identification with a valued area of study" should also increase in strength as researchers, educators, and practitioners pool their knowledge. Consequently, professionals will be better able to prepare people for their cross-cultural experiences, to point out how the positive benefits can be increased and the difficulties decreased, and to increase the probability that people will be able to accomplish their goals during their sojourn in another country.

Over the years I have been working on this project, I have been the beneficiary of assistance offered by colleagues and friends. The most pleasant aspect of the project is thanking them for their help, support, and critical insights. Members of the Culture Learning Institute, East-West Center have long lent support: Verner Bickley, Michael Hamnett, Norman Dinges, and Kathleen Wilson. During the 1978–79 academic year, I took a sabbatical at Georgetown University under the sponsorship of the School of Foreign Service and the Society for Intercultural Education, Training, and Research. The profitable stay was made possible by the efforts of Peter Krogh, Diane Zeller, Harold Bradley, Patricia Dooley, and Sally Cranston. A number of these people, plus Richard Detweiller and Jacqueline Wasilewski, read and critiqued early drafts of each chapter. Thirty-five juniors, seniors, and graduate students at the School of Foreign Service took a course on intercultural communication which I offered, and they provided useful feedback regarding some of the ideas in this book. My family, including two preschool children, was tolerant during the times I had to read materials on intercultural interaction rather than stories of wizards, magic animals, and trains attempting to reach heretofore unattained heights.

Postscript

Shortly after the manuscript was sent to the publisher for copy editing, my father passed away. I would like to dedicate this book to his memory. His job assignments provided me with my first opportunities for cross-cultural interaction. He was always encouraging and supportive toward my research activities. His own work was a model of independence and honesty in his pursuit of positive, constructive relations among people from very different backgrounds. Several of the ideas in this book developed during conversations with him. He will be long remembered by the people who knew, loved, and were influenced by him.

1
Introduction

CROSS-CULTURAL CONTACT: A GROWTH AREA

Predictions about future day-to-day living in various parts of the world include greater amounts of face-to-face contact among people from very different cultural backgrounds. Even if people would prefer otherwise, increasing numbers of airplanes bring tourists and investors from other countries, legal requirements restrict free choice in selecting neighbors, and liberal immigration laws bring refugees into already overburdened school systems. To cope with everyday problems in the work, school, and neighborhood settings, people will have to deal effectively with others who may once have been the targets of discrimination. The major goal of this book is to organize and to explain a large number of concepts which can provide a basis for understanding and, perhaps, improving intergroup interaction. Further, ideas will be suggested which should prove useful to professionals who are responsible for programs which encourage face-to-face contact among people from different groups. The programs include those that are required because of legislation, as in desegregated schools, and those that are selected voluntarily, as in opportunities to study in another country.

The reasons for increased face-to-face contact yield a now familiar litany. Technological factors include increased travel both between and within nations and greater exposure of various cultural groups through the mass media. Social factors include developments in civil rights and affirmative action leading to more frequent contact among groups in educational, work, public housing, social service, and health care settings. Economic factors include dependence on other countries for precious commodities such as oil, and for foreign students in an era of declining enrollments among a country's own potential student population. Political factors include the growing awareness that since the world is so complex and demands so much interdependence, hegemony is no longer a realistic alternative. A combination of these factors is present in intergovernmental organizations, multinational corporations, and complex investment pro-

1

grams for wealthy individuals from oil-producing countries who buy controlling stock in various corporations. Current campus humor includes recommendations for mandatory Arabic for all incoming freshmen to better prepare them for interaction with their most probable sources of future employment.

A major assumption to be defended throughout the book is that research findings and the wisdom of accumulated experience from one type of intergroup contact can be helpful in analyzing others. Currently, the analysis of intergroup interaction centers on various *types of contact* which are designated by commonly accepted labels. Examples of such categories are the overseas scholar, technical assistance adviser, diplomat, student in a recently integrated school, worker in a multinational corporation, or immigrant to a country. "Experiences" refer to the accumulated set of events, and people's reactions to them, which are common for the participants in any one type of contact. Examples of such experiences are becoming accustomed to the local method of determining grades for overseas students and establishing relationships with host country counterparts for technical assistance workers. If the assumption is true, then more information becomes available concerning any one type of contact. Borrowing from research on various types of contact becomes possible, for example, adjustment over time to life in another country whether a person is a foreign student, diplomat, technical assistance advisor, businessperson, or immigrant (chapter 10). Further, research on these types of international contact may yield insights applicable to intergroup interaction *within* any one country. For instance, there is also adjustment over time experienced by children attending desegregated schools and by people forced to integrate their neighborhoods.

Even though the borrowing of insights is possible, intergroup interaction will always be a complex phenomenon to study. In addition to the many types of contact, there are many types of groups. The "backgrounds" of people who form the different groups can be due to racial categorizations, ethnic loyalties, nationalities, social classes, and minority status within a country dominated by another group whose members hold power. For convenience, "cultural group" or "culture" will be the terms used throughout this book, and these will be defined later in this introductory chapter. For now, a culture can be explained as an identifiable group with shared beliefs and experiences, feelings of worth and value attached to those experiences, and a shared interest in a common historical background.

SOME BASIC ISSUES

The issues to be investigated in this book include the following:

1. What happens to people when they engage in various forms of cross-cultural contact? More specifically, what happens in those situations involving face-to-face interactions, whether they involve relations with friends, co-workers, or hosts in another country when people live abroad. The question will be examined by looking at a variety of concepts from psychology, sociology, anthropology, education, political science, and other disciplines.

2. Can a common language of solid, useful concepts be suggested which will facilitate communication among people interested in different types of cross-cultural experiences? Currently, people involved in the analysis of cross-cultural contact identify with one or a few types. They subscribe to journals likely to carry articles about their specialty and they go to professional meetings at which seminars dealing with one or a few types of experiences are to be given. There is little enrichment across investigators and practitioners concerned with different types of cross-cultural contact. One reason may be that the people use different *terms* for what might be similar aspects of cross-cultural contact and, hence, come to believe that they are dealing with different *phenomena*. For instance, while technical assistance workers must form good relations with host country co-workers, participants in other types of contact must also form supportive friendship networks with host nationals (chapter 5). A broader concept, then, such as "support group," might be a useful tool that will aid in the analysis of these and other cross-cultural encounters. The thesis to be presented here is that a good deal of commonality exists across people's experiences in different types of contact and that a limited, manageable set of concepts can be suggested which will aid in the analysis of all cross-cultural encounters. A hope is that the analysis of cross-cultural contact will become more sophisticated given such a set of concepts. A general framework which permits organization of the concepts will be introduced later in this chapter. Detailed analyses are presented in chapters 2 through 11.

3. Can the advantages of cross-cultural interaction be better specified? In addition to understanding the changes in people's lives brought about by the social, technological, and economic factors mentioned earlier, there are other reasons for studying cross-cultural contact. If people learn a great deal from their experiences, as will be argued in different parts of this book, then knowledge of the learning process can be used in program planning. Administrators in charge of arranged cross-cultural encounters

can design programs which increase the probability of positive outcomes. Just one of many learning possibilities (Bochner, 1977) is that program participants can observe how members of another culture attempt to cope with problems of pollution, inflation, and unemployment, all of which are faced by people in different parts of the world. In bringing together the diverse solutions, and by valuing such diversity, a solution may be found which has not been previously attempted in a given culture.

Another learning possibility is that by studying the stresses and strains of such contact, and by analyzing how people overcome their problems, a greater understanding of aggressive and nonaggressive reactions to stress may occur. Possibly, administrators can then intervene to minimize the former and maximize the latter. Contact between members of different cultural groups does not necessarily have positive benefits. This generalization is supported both by the research literature (chapter 7) and by people's everyday experience with cross-cultural interaction on the job, in desegregated schools, in neighborhoods, and while living in another country. Indeed, the outcomes *may* be negative in many cases. Further, almost all contact involves a period of stress during which the probability of aggressive reactions is increased (chapter 10). Some contact experiences, however, seem to yield more *long-term* positive outcomes than others, and do seem to lead eventually to nonaggressive, cordial relations among people. Another hope, then, is that knowledge of these stresses and strains will indicate the stages at which aggressive reactions are likely, the advantages of preparation for such problems, and a greater understanding of the factors which administrators might introduce to minimize long-term difficulties.

SOME REASONS FOR THE DIFFICULTIES

Why are there problems when people come into contact with different cultures? Why can't people just get along with each other no matter what their backgrounds? There are many answers to these questions, some of which will be treated in later chapters. Here, a preliminary treatment allows the introduction of a definition of "culture" and some indications of its importance in determining behavior toward people from another culture.

For the analysis of cross-cultural contact, "culture" can be defined in two ways: (a) the actual unfamiliar people with whom an individual interacts, or, (b) as a more abstract concept, focusing on people's characteristic behavior, ideas, and values. The former is easier to conceptualize: in cross-cultural contact, individuals will interact with people who have a different skin color, speak a different language, claim a different ethnic heritage, acknowledge allegiance to a different government, or who possess two or three of these indicators. The more abstract definitions are also helpful since they allow an analysis on how culture affects the behavior of its members, and an analysis of how subsequent contact with others (affected by a different culture) can be problematic.

There are many abstract definitions of culture, most of which have been suggested by anthropologists. The two which are most often cited in cross-cultural research are those of Kroeber and Kluckhohn (1952) and Triandis (1972, 1977b). After reviewing over 150 definitions, Kroeber and Kluckhohn (1952) concluded that the "following central idea is now formulated by most scientists. . . ."

> Culture consists of patterns, explicit and implicit, of and for behavior acquired and transmitted by symbols, constituting the distinctive achievements of human groups, including their embodiments in artifacts; the essential core of culture consists of traditional (i.e., historically derived and selected) ideas and especially their attached value; culture systems may, on the one hand, be considered as products of action, on the other as conditioning elements of further action [p. 180].

Triandis (1977b) adds the concept of subjective culture, by which he means people's response to the "man-made part of the environment, or to a group's characteristic way of perceiving its social environment [p. 423]."

For the purposes of analyzing cross-cultural contact, any of a number of abstract definitions are equally useful. All suggest that, in any given culture, a large number of everyday behaviors, traits of people, standards (e.g., of physical beauty, success, intelligence), and recommended norms for morality are considered good, proper, or correct. People become very comfortable with these elements of their culture. However, they also become intolerant of people both from within and outside the culture who deviate in some way. Socialization of children into a community often uses negative models who are either on the fringes of a culture or who are outsiders. My father remembers that, in the community where he was raised, there was a one-armed man named Hook Jackson who cleaned up the streets after the horse-drawn carts and carriages passed by. My father's teachers would say to him, "If you don't do your homework, you'll end up like Hook Jackson." In chapter 4, research will be reviewed that indicates the powerful effects such vivid images and stories have on people's thinking. The point to be made here is that, in using a negative model in this story, the teachers were reinforcing certain personal ambitions, levels of employment, and class membership which were valued in the culture. Incidentally, my father recently mused, "I wonder if Hook knew how many indolent students were threatening his job?" Of course, even though my father told this story in a humorous way, similar conclusions regarding what is desirable and undesirable were drawn by *his* children.

Examples of difficulties in cross-cultural interaction

The product of a culture's influence, then, is a residue of behaviors, ideas, and beliefs with which people are comfortable and which they consider "proper" or "the right way." In intercultural contact, however, people interact with others who also consider certain behaviors desirable. Often, the same behavior is considered desirable to people from one culture and distasteful to people from the other. Any limited number of examples will be unrepresentative, but a few should be given. All readers are surely familiar with people who are so committed to a certain religion, political posture, or set of beliefs about race that they have a difficult time interacting with others who hold different views. Instead, they constantly interact with people who possess similar views and who reinforce their beliefs.

A few examples of everyday behavior are useful in communicating the abstract point about a culture's influence on people's beliefs concerning what is proper. In many Asian countries, people who dine at another family's home leave after the last dish is served. If they do not leave, the message is taken to be, "We haven't had enough to eat." In most parts of North America, the same behavior would be considered rude since the message is taken by the hosts as, "They only want our food, not our company." The difficulties that might arise when North Americans entertain Asians, or vice versa, are obvious.

In Greece, Americans are often upset by questions which, according to their standards, are overly personal. Shortly after Americans accept employment in a Greek company, for instance, their co-workers might ask questions about religion, political views, or salary earned, all of which are considered rude by the Americans. The difference lies in what Greeks and Americans consider an "in-group." An in-group refers to people who are readily accepted by an individual and with whom the individual interacts freely. An out-group refers to people who are excluded or ignored. In the United States, the in-group consists only of people an individual knows well, for instance, family members and old friends. In Greece, the in-group consists of family, close friends, *and* visitors to the country. Since personal questions are quite appropriate among members of the in-group, Greeks do not consider themselves rude in asking them (Triandis, 1972).

These two examples bring up another point which will be addressed throughout the book, especially in chapter 9. In thinking about the examples of everyday behavior involving Asians, Americans, and Greeks, a major assumption held by people who work and who do research on intercultural contact is that people can be prepared for such encounters. Short-term training programs are very frequently held, organized by administrators in charge of programs involving cross-cultural contact, either in the home country just before departure, or in the host country shortly after arrival (Brislin & Pedersen, 1976). Explanations similar to those presented here can be offered to people, and the assumption is that greater understanding of the other culture and lesser probability of ending interpersonal relationships are likely. Treatments of concepts to help increase an understanding of cross-cultural contact, as will be presented throughout this book, will hopefully aid in the choice of content for such programs.

The In-Group/Out-Group Distinction. The example of interaction between Greeks and Americans introduces a central concept, the in-group/outgroup distinction, which will be addressed in many chapters. Part of every individual's socialization involves relations between members of various groups within a given country. Individuals are taught that certain people should be avoided on the basis of their color, religion, social status, ethnic heritage, occupation, parentage, or perceived state of mental health. Indeed, such a division of people into one's own in-group and a set of outgroups has been posited as a universal among humans (Brewer & Campbell, 1976). This in-group/out-group distinction is of central importance for individuals because it allows them to find an identity as to who they are and who they are not. Further, if individuals have out-groups whom they can blame for troubles, the in-group is then solidified since there is a common goal—dislike of the out-groups—around which to rally. The most notorious historical example was the use of the Jewish people as scapegoats and shared enemy among Germans during the rise of the Third Reich. Solidification of the in-group is useful since it provides many basic needs, such as friendship, opportunities for employment, and potential marriage partners. Individuals, then, become accustomed to reacting in terms of in-groups and out-groups. They continue to use such distinctions when interacting with people from other cultures whom they do not know.

TYPES OF CROSS-CULTURAL CONTACT

As mentioned earlier, research and analysis into the nature of crosscultural interactions has centered around types of contact, each involving a number of participants. Put another way, analysis has been centered on categories of individuals who are grouped together because they are likely to have had similar experiences. These are listed below. Published works on each type of contact are shelved in different parts of libraries and are the concerns of different agencies and professional organizations. Many valuable results, helpful for policy formation regarding each type of contact, have emanated from such research and analysis. Many of the findings and recommendations will be reviewed in later chapters. This approach, however, has heretofore not led to communication among specialists who are each concerned with a specific type of contact even though, as will be argued throughout this book, they could benefit from each other's work. Another consequence is that the specialists have not identified with a larger universe of co-workers who are involved with various types of contact. This state of affairs leads to a lack of professional identity and, consequently, an absence of support for others doing similar work. In very practical terms, this lack of identity means that some specialists do not attempt to disseminate their work widely since they do not perceive enough interest outside their own organization. For this reason, a high percentage of the existing materials consists of limited distribution reports which are mimeographed or photocopied rather than widely circulated, catalogued, and easily accessible books, monographs, and journal articles. In lighter moments, these materials are referred to as the "underground or phantom press in cross-cultural studies." When people obtain an item, they feel that it is due to luck rather than to their efforts to stay abreast of goings-on.

Another consequence stemming from this absence of communication is that specialists in some fields feel that there is little relevant work on which to draw. However, if they identified with the broad range of cross-cultural experiences, they would have a great deal of material to consult for helpful suggestions applicable to their specific case. One purpose of this book is to persuade specialists that the study of a wide body of literature could be fruitful.

The goal, then, is to develop concepts which are useful in the analysis of all forms of cross-cultural interaction. The source materials for this task are presently organized around the following fourteen types of cross-cultural contact. Ten of these involve moving to a country other than the one in which a person holds citizenship. The term frequently used to refer to people who spend a significant length of time in another country is "sojourners." The other four types involve contact among different cultural groups within any one country. The citations refer to important research studies concerned with each type of contact.

1. Overseas students studying at the college level in a country other than the one in which they received their elementary and secondary education (Klineberg & Hull, 1979; Spaulding & Flack, 1976).
2. Businessmen on assignment in a country other than the one in which they hold citizenship. Usually, the businessmen are employed in multinational corporations (Cleveland, Mangone, & Adams, 1960; Harris & Moran, 1979).
3. Diplomats and other members of an embassy who represent one country while stationed in another (Harmon, 1971; Nicolson, 1960; Reychler, 1978).

4. Language interpreters who work in permanent international organizations or in short-term, ad hoc, multinational conferences. Their major task is to allow communication among people who do not speak the same language. Often, they make inferences based on the cultural background of the speakers and/or the audience and use these in their choice of wording and intonation for their translation into the other language(s) (Gerver & Sinaiko, 1978).

5. Technical assistance personnel assigned to overseas posts, usually working under contracts and funding from a governmental agency (Arensberg & Niehoff, 1971; Goodenough, 1964).

6. Participants in organized programs emphasizing contact with people in the receiving (host) country, and living accommodations and salary levels more similar to the host than the sender country. The Peace Corps is the program of this type which has received the most attention (Textor, 1966a).

7. Military personnel assigned as advisers to governments and/or to defense units in other countries (Guthrie, 1966).

8. Emigrants who move from one country and then attempt to establish citizenship in another. This category includes both people who are forced from their native country ("pushed") and those who voluntarily leave ("pulled") for ideological reasons or for better opportunities for themselves and their families (Taft, 1973).

9. Researchers who do work in cultures other than their own. Potential difficulties include understanding the point of view of members of another culture and meeting problems of acceptance in places where research methods (e.g., interviewing, testing) are unfamiliar (Brislin, 1979b; Finley, 1979).

10. Tourists, who engage in short-term stays in another culture, on vacation, and who have the primary purpose of obtaining enjoyment from their trip. The experiences of hosts or others within the culture who deal with many tourists are also important (Hiller, 1977). Longer tours of three or four months can have impacts similar to those found among overseas students (Pool, 1965; Steinkalk & Taft, 1979). Programs for adolescents are offered by organizations such as Youth for Understanding or the Experiment in International Living (Watt & Walker, 1977). In almost all cases, the adolescents are involved in the programs for periods of time ranging from one month to one year.

11. Members of a certain ethnic group, within a country, who interact with members of other ethnic groups or with members of the dominant majority group. Examples are interactions among blacks, Chicanos, Native Americans, and whites in the United States (Ehrlich, 1973). Most of the research has centered on four settings in which interaction among people takes place: in civilian work/job settings (Triandis,

1977a); among members of a country's military services (Akter & Pasinski, 1973; Stouffer, Lumsdaine, Lumsdaine, Williams, Smith, Janis, Star, & Cottrell, 1949); in educational institutions—research has centered on desegregation and bilingual education (Gerard & Miller, 1973); and in people's home environments within their neighborhoods (Deutsch & Collins, 1951).

12. People participating in "arranged interethnic contact," such as legally desegregated schools, interracial summer camps, government-funded housing projects, military units composed of ethnically diverse personnel, or experiments created by behavioral and social scientists designed to examine specific hypotheses that might aid in understanding such contact. Category 9, above, is similar, but this category includes those situations in which the official norm or purpose is to increase ethnic or racial tolerance. There is also an administrator who, together with members of a staff, is in charge of making the program effective in both its task-oriented goal (e.g., good education, military capability) and in its human-relations goal (i.e., increased interethnic harmony: Amir, 1969).

13. Members of ethnic groups who are required by authorities to move from one area of a country to another ("forced relocation": Dinges & Brandon, 1977; Kiste, 1974; Leighton, 1945).

14. Students who, as part of their education, live and work with members (usually a family) or an ethnic group other than their own. This is called the "home stay" program at some colleges which offer it (Baty & Dold, 1977).[1]

The results of research and analysis concerning these types of experience will be reviewed throughout the book. But these categories will not form the basis of the review's organization. Instead, a number of conceptual factors, or broad categories which include a number of more specific concepts, will be suggested. These should lead to a more integrated analysis than one based on types of experience.

GENERAL FACTORS TO BE USED IN ORGANIZING RESEARCH AND ANALYSIS

There are six basic factors which will be used for the purposes of integrating the existing empirical research, the commentary of individuals who have had a great deal of cross-cultural experience, and my own analyses. The six factors deal with history or background; the individuals who are involved; groups; situations; tasks to be completed; and the organizations with which the individuals must deal. In addition, two combinations of factors will be examined which seem especially important: the special problems faced by groups of people from different cultural backgrounds, who are expected or required to interact in specific situations; and the nature of adjustment to another culture, which involves coping with groups, situations, tasks, and organizations. The examples provided under each explanation of the general factors will be dealt with more thoroughly in later chapters. The headings presented below, in summary, are the general categories which provide the basis for integrating more specific concepts useful in analyzing face-to-face cross-cultural interaction.

History or background

There are socially imposed limits to intergroup relations which are well established in all cultures over which individual members have little or no control. These include, for instance, the history of race relations within a country, and the long-established norms governing what is acceptable and not acceptable regarding contact among people from the different races. "History" can refer both to the society as a whole and to individuals. A factor in an individual's history is the manner in which (s)he was disciplined as a child. Children have little control over the manner in which parents discipline them; research (e.g., Adorno, Frenkel-Brunswick, Levinson, & Sanford, 1950; Ehrlich, 1973) has demonstrated the effects of parental discipline on the acquisition of rigid versus tolerant attitudes toward people from out-groups. Another more speculative possibility is that the language people speak predisposes them to look at out-group members in a certain way. This is a derivation of the Sapir-Whorf hypothesis (Miller & McNeil, 1969; Whorf, 1956) which suggests that the language(s) a person learns provides a set of concepts and organizing principles around which information from the environment is processed.

History, then, refers to aspects of a people's world which they are "born into" and which they are expected to learn or accept in order to become a normal, functioning member of society.

Individual factors

The broad category of individual factors includes variables commonly studied by psychologists in their efforts to understand human behavior. Applied to intergroup relations, these factors include those personality traits and skills that have been found useful in analyzing the negative and positive experiences of people during cross-cultural contact. Since this category also incorporates people's attitudes and opinions about other groups, it must include a treatment of prejudice and stereotyping. Another valuable method of analysis is to look upon the individual as an active processor of information. A basic premise is that people cannot deal with each and every piece of information that competes for their attention. What factors influence the many everyday decisions concerning what should be attended to and what should be ignored? With respect to the very different types of people one is likely to meet during cross-cultural encounters, how do individuals decide who is "good," "bad," "right," and "wrong?" A major research area to be examined is called "attribution" (Harvey, Ickes, & Kidd, 1976; Jones, Kanouse, Kelley, Nisbet, Valins, & Weiner, 1972); its concern is how and why people employ certain perceived motives, traits, and explanations in analyzing other people's behavior as well as their own.

Group factors

Even though there will always be a few hermits, almost all people want to form relationships with others that involve frequent interaction in mutually developed activities and affective ties such that individuals look after one another and are concerned with each others' feelings (general definition of "group" from Homans, 1950). Group-level factors, then, deal with the development of support networks and the integration of new people into well-established groups. An important topic is the analysis of a group's norms, or the way things are "properly" done, and the relation between people's acceptance of the norms and their feelings of success or failure in their contact experience. Another important topic is the establishment of broadened and overlapping group ties through which people develop close affective feelings toward others who were previously categorized as out-group members. From such relationships, the possibility exists that people with cross-cultural experience may become mediators for others who belong to one group but who are somehow blocked in their attempts to interact with members of a second group. As a simpler example, but one which involves important efforts for the people involved, American academics who have done research in a country other than their own have helped certain of its citizens gain admittance to institutions of higher learning in the United States or Canada. Mediation may take the form of explaining the other country's grading procedures so that transcripts can be evaluated, or sending out the specific information a candidate desires rather than the general brochure provided by the institution's admissions office.

 ## Situational factors

Situational factors, probably the most difficult to conceptualize, consist of aspects of the cross-cultural experience that individuals must face and deal with in some way. These factors are external to the individual: they are those aspects of the environment that must be dealt with to maximize the positive aspects of a sojourn. The clearest example is probably a contrast between overseas students who find a respected position in a community within the host country and those who are unable to do so. Ritterband (1969), for instance, has shown how Israeli students are readily accepted into Jewish communities in the United States since they are able to teach Hebrew and the Old Testament to children. They have a "niche" into which they fit; in the language of this review, the niche is a situational variable which allows a relatively easy adaptation for the sojourner.

Other situations include the inevitable set of circumstances which virtually every individual must face during a sojourn. "Culture shock" (Oberg, 1958) is the most frequently mentioned. In brief, culture shock is a summary term which refers to the accumulated stresses and strains which stem from being forced to meet one's everyday needs (e.g. food, cleanliness, companionship) in unfamiliar ways. The difference between "situational" and "history/background" factors is that the former are malleable. Individuals are faced with a set of circumstances, but they can behave in certain ways to modify the situation to their benefit. For instance, individuals can strive to find a supportive niche and can prepare themselves so that the negative effects of culture shock are minimized (Brislin & Pedersen, 1976). In fact, they can look upon culture shock as a positive experience which motivates them to learn about the other culture, and to learn about their own culture by comparing it with the one to which they are adjusting (Adler, 1975).

Task factors

Many people are expected to work on a certain project while interacting in other cultures. Examples are the obtaining of a degree for overseas students, the completion of a piece of research for academics, the negotiation of agreements among diplomats, and the acquisition of a permanent job among adult immigrants. Important factors include the clarity of the task, people's preparation for completing it, the varying standards people in different cultures have for considering certain job performance as "acceptable," and the possibility for contributions to joint efforts. Many people are sent to another country with little preparation other than information regarding the tasks to be completed. Consequently, they are often unprepared for problems stemming from cross-cultural human relations, even though these can affect success or failure in their work (Fahvar & Milton, 1972).

Organizational factors

Most cross-cultural contact involves organizations which provide opportunities, administrative help, and the possibility of continual attention to complex projects. Examples are the foreign student adviser's office present on many university campuses, or the administrative bureaucracy in charge of seeing to the needs of people forced to leave their homes as part of relocation. Further, much contact is explicitly part of a large institutional structure, such as businessmen in multinational organizations, diplomats and their staff at the United Nations, or language interpreters at multinational conferences.

Influential variables include the level of funding available to the organization, qualities of administrators (e.g., their training, experience), for effective cross-cultural relations versus other aspects of job performance, and the sorts of orientation programs provided by the organization prior to people's cross-cultural experiences. A potential advantage of organizations which deal with cross-cultural contact is that staff members, as a result of their everyday work, might develop broad, global viewpoints. They may be able to take into account both the needs of the country in which they hold citizenship *and* the needs of others (Alger, 1965).

Groups in situations

Many contact experiences take place in situations involving the presence of distinct groups. The groups have different norms regarding acceptable and appropriate behaviors and sometimes are forced to compete for scarce resources. Interaction among individuals which transcends membership in the different groups is uncomfortable, suspect, or forbidden. Further, individuals owe loyalties to one of the groups and so are likely to accept its norms regarding interaction with members of the other. As discussed in the early pages of this chapter, however, a number of societal changes are requiring interaction. Examples are legal requirements demanding school integration (Gerard & Miller, 1973) and the integration of housing patterns within neighborhoods (Deutsch & Collins, 1951). Political settlements have required contact among former enemies, as in the case of Arabs and Israelis along the West Bank of the Jordan River (Amir, Rivner, Bizman, & Ben-Ari, 1980).

Studies which have been carried out among such groups coming into contact are numerous and now constitute one of the more sophisticated and helpful research literatures. Key variables include the intensity of precontact attitudes held by group members; opportunities for intimate contact; the relative status of the groups; and the opportunities to establish superordinate goals valued by members of both groups (Amir, 1969).

Many of the concepts have been applied in carefully designed programs whose goal is to maximize the positive outcomes of the contact (Cook, 1970).

Cross-cultural adjustment

With an understanding of the individual, situational, group, task, and organizational factors which must be faced, the long-term adjustment of people can be considered. As already mentioned, people are active processors of information and do not simply surrender themselves to the situations they encounter. Rather, they modify their behavior to cope with the sorts of new problems they will inevitably encounter as part of their cross-cultural experience. Important variables include people's reactions to stress; the changes in attitudes and values which sometimes occur as a function of the sojourn (Taft, 1977); people's adjustment over time, which includes the ups and downs in feelings of satisfaction with cross-cultural contact (Gullahorn & Gullahorn, 1963); and the types of adjustment patterns people adopt, such as the contrast between the complete rejection and the tolerance of differences concerning the behavior of people in the host culture. Research has also been concerned with the advantages of cross-cultural contact, such as increased self-reliance, ability to take the point of view of others, and the ability to develop workable rather than overly idealistic policies.

SOME CAUTIONS

In attempting to develop concepts useful in the analysis of all types of cross-cultural contact, conclusions from individual research studies will be examined in the hope of drawing more general implications. For instance, the experiences of technical assistance advisers might be examined, followed by a similar treatment of students attending a recently desegregated school. Hopefully, of course, the transitions will be smooth and the arguments clear. At times, however, the technique of weaving back and forth between types of experiences may become maddening. During these frustrating periods, the reader is asked to "bear with" the author as a point is being developed.

To develop arguments without a frustrating number of clumsy phrases, only a few terms for the actual participants in cross-cultural encounters should be used. For convenience, "sojourners" will be used whenever reference is made to people living in a country other than their own. In a few cases, use of the term will be strained. For instance, immigrants are technically not sojourners but they will occasionally be designated by this term. In the case of intergroup contact within a country, no one term is available. Consequently, more specific designators will be used, such as "resident of an integrated neighborhood."

Any consideration of generalizability demands discussion of the countries in which research has been done. Unfortunately, since most of the published literature has been carried out in the United States, a strict interpretation would limit generalizability to cross-cultural contact involving people from this one country. Attempts have been made to incorporate research done elsewhere wherever possible. Excellent research, for instance, exists concerning immigrants in Australia (Taft, 1973), overseas students after they return to Turkey (Kagitcibasi, 1978) and Brazil (Gama & Pedersen, 1977), and diplomats from various countries who have worked in many different parts of the world (Alger, 1965; Reychler, 1978). In those cases where generalization is unwarranted, note will be made of the fact. Even when the specific examples are not directly applicable, however, the *concept* suggested by the examples should be useful in analyzing cross-cultural contact any place in the world. For instance, the influence of parental discipline on a child's intergroup attitudes will be reviewed in chapter 2. Examples will be drawn from research carried out in the United States. Even though the specific types of discipline may not be found in another country under investigation, the concept that child-rearing practices has effects on intergroup relations remains a useful idea.

ARE THESE CONCEPTS A HODGEPODGE OF PIGEONHOLES?

There are two other dangers in developing concepts for the analysis of cross-cultural contact. One is that the concepts will be so numerous and varied that the final product will be as amorphous as the current organization of the field centered around different types of experience. The second is that the concepts will be treated as pigeonholes which encourage people to ignore the important interrelationships among them.

There are only partial solutions to these problems. There are always dangers that key variables based upon overlaps among the suggested concepts will be missed. Nevertheless, the advantages of providing *some* organization of the heretofore scattered research and analysis outweigh the disadvantages. If the final set of concepts is useful, future efforts can center on complex interrelationships. In fact, this is one way a scholarly field develops as more and more people become involved in it.

The problem of number and variety is partially addressed by examining the concepts as they apply to the experiences of the individual. Thus, "individual" factors are those which stem from the traits, skills, and attitudes of the people themselves. The "group, task, situational, background, and organizational" factors all have the common element of affecting the behavior of individuals. Examples are how group norms affect individual members or how an organization's structure helps or hinders the individual's adjustment. The common element, then, is that the analysis of the various concepts helps in understanding what happens to people during their intercultural experience. Hopefully, a greater understanding will lead to principles which can be applied by program administrators such that the cross-cultural experience will be more beneficial to the people involved. Further, the concepts may be useful to people who wish to gain insights into their own cross-cultural experiences. Often, people complain that their experiences constitute an uninterpretable jumble of unrelated events. With the availability of concepts to pinpoint self-analyses, greater insight into the consequences of cross-cultural contact is possible.

NOTE

1. A few other types of contact might have been considered. The experiences of missionaries (Ziffer, 1969), migrant workers, and guest workers were not reviewed since limited amounts of research have been done. In the case of missionaries, some analyses have been done relevant to their goal of seeking religious converts, but this work has limited use for the broader purposes of this book. Research on guest and migrant workers has focused largely on economic implications rather than on their experiences in coping with life in another culture. Categories overlap in some cases. When missionaries do not have the goal of seeking religious converts and, instead, participate in community development, their work resembles that of technical assistance advisers (category 5) or people who live in a style similar to that of hosts (category 6). When migrant and guest workers seek permanent residence in another country, their experiences resemble those of immigrants (category 8). While research on intercultural marriage (Tseng, McDermott, & Maretzki, 1977) and intercultural adoption (Simon & Alstein, 1977) could have been considered, my judgment is that generalizations from these lifelong and very intimate relations must be done with caution. Fearing inappropriate borrowing, I decided to draw from this extensive literature only on a few occasions. Future research could examine the similarities and differences between the cross-cultural experiences considered in this book and intercultural marriage and adoption.

2

History: The Background for People's Current Behavior

INTRODUCTION

People are born into cultures in which certain ideas and behaviors are valued because they have contributed to the functioning of society. Often, the ideas form a set of romantic myths, knowledge of which is one measure of patriotism. While not completely untrue, the myths stretch facts to emphasize the positive aspects of a society and to downplay the negative. Further, people are exposed to the valued ideas and are sheltered from alternatives through the society's media of communication. These can include oral transmission through the efforts of storytellers, books, radio, movies, and television depending, of course, on the society's level of technological development. Finally, a society's members develop attitudes and values because of the parental discipline which they received. Collectively, these contributions to an adult's personality, attitudes, and typical ways of behaving are called "history" or "background." The argument presented in this chapter is that these history/background factors have a major influence on people's reactions to out-group members. Much as knowledge of a society's history is necessary to understand current events, knowledge of an individual's history is important to understanding current behavior. All too often, these background factors are ignored in treatments of cross-cultural interaction.

Since individuals have very different histories, no one chapter can include principles which are directly applicable to everyone. By studying a set of historical ideas commonly shared by members of a specific society, however, the usefulness of the analysis may become clear. The case to be examined is the white, middle-class American. Arguments will be made that exposure to a common set of historical ideas encouraged the development of individualism, a distrust of foreign alliances, a "melting pot" ideal for immigrants, the acceptability of imposing one's own point of view on others, and defense of the status quo concerning race relations.

Even though the picture to be developed does not describe any one person's exposure to the ideas in an exact manner, I believe there is a familiarity with the ideas shared by members of the society in question.

This chapter also discusses the possibility that the language people speak provides them with a set of perceptual filters which limit their opportunities for effective cross-cultural interaction. As with historical myths they are expected to learn and the manner in which they were disciplined as children, people have little control over the language(s) they are expected to learn. The common thread of this chapter is that, because of their socialization into a culture, people bring a set of ideas and predispositions concerning other groups to any cross-cultural encounter. To have any chance of improving cross-cultural relations, these ideas and predispositions must be better understood.

HISTORICAL IDEAS

Almost every schoolchild in the United States is exposed to ideas about settlement of the country, relations with other countries in the struggle for independence, and the westward movement. The current concern with individual achievement and individual rights are manifestations of these historical ideas.

The development of individualism

Upon arrival in the new country, settlers had to engage in a tremendous struggle to survive. Status markers carried from the countries they left, such as titles and studied mannerisms typical of higher classes, had little function in a wilderness which had to be cleared so that houses could be built and crops planted. Hard work became valued and was expected of everyone. The demand of hard work became a great equalizer, breaking down previous class distinctions. This development is summarized in a story learned by every modern schoolchild. In the early 1600s the Jamestown settlement leader, John Smith, allegedly said that if people did not do their share of the work, they would not eat. Once settlements were secure and people had learned the skills necessary for survival in the new environment, many headed West and claimed land as their own. People who are now folk heroes (e.g., Daniel Boone) are said to have made a point of moving further West as soon as they could see smoke from the chimney of a neighbor two or three miles away. Presumably, the mere threat of frequent contact with others was seen as providing unacceptable constraints on behavior. Both the development of settlements and the movement of people away from them led to a set of valued behaviors that collectively is called "individualism." People relied upon their own initiative and hard work if for no other reason than the scarcity of other people upon whom they might depend. People developed status because of the success shown in their work, not because of some accident of birth which happened to give them a title or an inheritance.

This quality of rugged individualism is still highly valued in the United States.[1] It is particularly noticed by outsiders. When multicultural groups meet to discuss the values held by members of various cultures, they inevitably mention the independent streak which almost all citizens of the United States possess (Ho, 1979). An overseas student from Japan once told me: "It's fun being able to do what you want in the United States. But since everyone is doing what they want, there's no one to do things with." This value has certainly been functional in contributing to the development of the United States, but it may leave citizens ill prepared for the current demands resulting from the interdependence among nations. For instance, problems stemming from the distribution of oil, the settlement of refugees, and the emergence of new and independent nations all demand dependence on others.

The distrust of foreign and a concern with internal affairs

A concept related to individualism is the distrust of alliances or even contact with different cultures and the subsequent "turning inside" which distrust entails. In the 1600s and 1700s, some people emigrated to the American colonies to avoid religious persecution. After settling in America, they simply wanted to be left alone so that they could live and worship as they pleased. Other groups with well-established sets of religious beliefs were not persecuted in countries such as the Netherlands, but their adult members were upset upon seeing children learn and behave according to the norms of a dominant group. The elders feared that the children would change due to their exposure to bad influences and would reject the religious beliefs of the minority community. For this reason, groups like the Puritans went to New England. By establishing communities in a desolate wilderness, they all but eliminated external influence since there were few outsiders with whom they came into contact. The establishment of some communities, then, was based on a distrust of contact with others.

Another major historical event (really a series of interconnected events occurring over a number of years) was the struggle for independence from Britain. Perceptions of betrayal, misunderstanding, and lack of support on the part of the British government led to a desire for independence. In developing a new government, certain aspects of the British system were considered but then discarded, especially when these aspects were reminiscent of the monarchy. The miseries of the war for independence also led to a distrust of alliances with other countries since there was a justifiable fear that such alliances would require participation in other people's wars. The sheer distance and lack of speedy travel and communication between the United States and European countries during the late eighteenth century contributed to the resulting isolationism. This distrust of alliances, distance, and the demands of time and effort in developing a new country all contributed to a "turning inward." The affairs at home became the target of attention. As with the valued trait of rugged individualism, a turning inward is functional in many ways, but it does not encourage the development of traits, skills, and attitudes which ease the stresses of cross-cultural contact.

An elite to deal with foreign relations

The factors already mentioned did not lead to a complete absence of contact with other cultures. The necessity of international trade, for instance, prevented complete isolationism. However, such contact became the province of a highly select elite (Nicolson, 1960). Policymaking with other countries was negotiated by this diplomatic elite without input from the voting public. One reason for this lack of consultation was simply that the majority of Americans did not know or care much about other countries (Rosenberg, 1965). Many presidents have enjoyed the foreign policy arena because they could make decisions unencumbered by pressures from political constituencies and other interest groups. These and other interrelated factors kept the making of foreign policy out of the public's concern. Potential policymakers were selected from a very small set of schools on the east coast of the United States (Thayer, 1959), precluding a better representation of citizens. Further, policymakers rarely felt compelled to communicate the reasons for their decisions to the public.

As with most areas that involve intercultural contact, this state of affairs is changing. The Vietnam War is often cited as a reason for more concern on the part of the average citizen with international matters. If cherished family members are to be killed or permanently handicapped and inflation fueled due to a war now questioned for its usefulness and wisdom, then people feel they have a right to have a voice in policy decisions. In addition, the long, ghastly gas station lines in 1973 and 1979 forced people to think about the relation of the United States to other parts of the world. As will be discussed more fully in the chapters on individual factors, vivid, personalized incidents are tremendously effective in attracting the attention of people.

While the history of the United States has seen little citizen participation in foreign policy decision making, more recent events lead to a prediction of greater involvement in the future. There are going to be tremendous problems in the transition. The lack of preparation and experience in international affairs on the part of the average citizen, for instance, has prevented people from acquiring much sophistication in even talking about foreign relations. Interviews on television with the "person on the street" yield little besides slogans such as, "Get tough with the Arabs to get their oil," or "the Russians will cheat on Arms Limitations agreements if given any chance at all." Hearing such comments, policymakers become reinforced in their beliefs that their time would be poorly spent in seeking input from members of the voting public.

Feelings of commitment to the new country

After 1800, the population of the United States increased due to the arrival of immigrants, most of whom left homes in various European nations. Many factors led to a breaking of ties with the home country. Leaving home, with the realization that many kinsmen and friends would never be seen again, involved a major commitment on the part of people who could only guess what awaited them in America. The distance between Europe and the United States and the lack of opportunities for communication meant that very little news was received from home. The amount of time and effort necessary to earn a living wage, during an era when 12- to 14-hour workdays and 6- to 7-day workweeks were common, meant that little energy remained which could be spent on maintaining contact with the home country. Yet, many immigrants felt they had a better life in the United States, a major difference being the relative lack of religious and political oppression. Even economic opportunities seemed better among farmers who formerly could not grow crops on overworked land and in the face of a blight.

Severed relations, distance, hard work, and opportunity might be called factors that had a direct relation to a greater commitment to the new country. Other factors led to the same commitment in a more indirect way which might, at first glance, seem to contradict common sense. For instance, values which were functional in the old country came under pressure. Handlin (1951) suggests that the time spent in traveling to America was influential. Old values of courtesy, patience, and concern for others had little function in overcrowded, squalid ships. An aggressive pushiness to secure the most desirable location on ship for one's family was the type of behavior that yielded the most rewards. Another value which changed was the self-sufficiency of many families and the accompanying status markers, such as the father as unquestioned head of the family. The immigrants settled into a society where, especially in cities, labor was becoming increasingly specialized. As Zubrzycki (1966) points out, in the new country

. . . the family does not constitute the basic unit of the social division of labor and the individual is expected to perform many social roles independently of his role and status within the family. The process of adjustment in these circumstances must necessarily transform the internal structure of the family. The members of the family tend to react differently because of their different roles in the new society. . . . Such influences can cause members of the family to pull in different directions [p. 66].

Children, in some cases, obtained jobs which paid a higher salary than their fathers earned, causing obvious difficulties in traditional families.

Empirical research has been carried out in this type of value conflict. Studies by social psychologists (Collins & Hoyt, 1972; Festinger, 1957) indicate that when people engage in behavior discrepant with what they think is right or correct, they reduce the discrepancy by reevaluating their behavior. In this case, the reevaluation would lead to greater commitment to the immigrants' goal, a life in America. In effect, people say to themselves that if they have to experience the value conflicts, then the reason for the conflicts, life in America, must be worth the trouble. Consequently, commitment to the new country becomes stronger.

The children of immigrants had additional experiences which led to an even greater commitment to the United States. A major experience often cited by scholars concerned with immigration (e.g., Murillo-Rohde, 1976; Taft, 1976) is the interrelationships among parents, children, the school, and the children's peers. Many parents wanted to maintain certain old-world customs, such as the language spoken in the home and deferential behavior toward elders, but children saw little use for them. Children were spending time in schools, when they were able to avoid sweatshops, where the *lingua franca* was English. Success in school was dependent on learning English, as was the development of relations with peers whose parents came from other countries. The site of the great melting pot was the school. Children would come home and hear the old-country language spoken, but would look upon its use as quaint, archaic, and certainly of not much practical benefit. The normal tendency among adolescents which demands acceptance from age peers led to a more-than-usual distance from parents. Adolescents, in effect, socialized each other since they spent so much time together in order to avoid what they considered "fossils" at home. The norms they accepted were those of the new country. Often, the adolescent groups cut across the cultural backgrounds of members. The networks which developed allowed contact with many types of people, including potential marriage partners. Marriage among members of different cultures, of course, led to a further breakdown of influence flowing from the first generation of immigrants to their children.

A more speculative possibility (Leighton, 1945) is that the adolescents, by spending so much time with each other, developed support groups which continued into their adulthood. Support might take the form of mutual investments in each others' businesses or political patronage. The resulting networks of people, in institutions central to the functioning of the new country, assured participants' assimilation into it. When members of this second generation married, their children had even less commitment to the old world since it was primarily seen in the behavior of grandparents, surely an influence with little impact.

The important point for an understanding of intercultural relations is that the rejection of old-country behavior, and the commitment to the new country, led to the same sort of turning inward that has already been discussed. The answer to the common-sense question, "Shouldn't people in a nation made up of descendants of immigrants be more concerned with other countries?," for the reasons suggested above, is "not necessarily." A positive trend in the 1960s and 1970s is that adults and children are relearning the languages, music, and food preparation techniques of their ethnic heritage. This trend, hopefully, consists of more than holiday and once-a-year festivals/parades that people participate in to fill leisure time. Can this trend be channeled into a greater and more sophisticated concern with the relations between the United States and other countries? There is no clear answer to this question at the present time. Intercultural relations would benefit if some of our best minds attempted to answer it.

The "right" to impose one's way: The Westward movement

The settlement of the new country was dependent upon people moving Southwest and West into sparsely populated land. Often, the general term "westward movement" is used to encompass all such settlement. The idea of a "manifest destiny" grew, a vision that the United States should and must extend from the Atlantic to the Pacific. Northern and Southern borders would also have to be determined, with the major criterion resulting in sizeable incursions into present-day Mexico and Canada. The concept of manifest destiny as a motivational force and rallying point should not be downplayed: it was a major theme in the 1800s that attracted great enthusiasm and support (Walsh, 1979). The end state, a large nation, was seen as justifying the means to obtain it. So what happened when Westward-moving settlers encountered Native Americans or Mexicans? The settlers, as part of their perceived rights, were convinced that they *should* take the land and do away with those who stood in their path. The settlers imposed their demands on others and made no effort to understand or to accommodate the needs of other people. At all times, there were courageous individuals who pointed to the inhumanity of these policies, but there was never a large audience which was willing to listen. For instance, the American bison was almost exterminated as settlers moved West. Workers on the transcontinental railroad needed food, and hunters were able to secure an income by supplying it. Little or no thought was given to the effects on those American Indians who used the bison for food, clothing, and housing.

The history of treaties with American Indians, as is now widely acknowledged (e.g., DeLoria, 1969), is deplorable. The Native Americans were moved from reservation A to reservation B as some kind of value was found in A. Indian cultures based on hunting were devastated by confinement to small reservations and by the absence of game. A general program of massive governmental interference prevented the Indians from living in ways which were familiar to and valued by them. Instead of a proud, independent Indian culture, the interference led to an expensive, distrustful dependence which continues to plague the United States.

Treaties with Mexico were also imposed and, in some cases, were illegal (Walsh, 1979). The bitterness present-day Mexicans feel about these treaties, and about the bloodshed which preceded them, is real. The fact that the United States dictated unfair terms, not open to serious negotiation or compromise, has long contributed to the poor relations which exist even today. Policymakers in the United States, over the years, have not looked upon Mexico as a neighbor deserving of special attention and favored treatment. This background of poor relations has resulted in the absence of effective channels of open communication, solidified by many years of good will, for the negotiation of present-day issues. Because Mexico is now developing its oil and natural gas resources, suddenly the United States is interested in Mexico. Past ill-treatment, however, will take its toll on negotiations for the sale of these commodities.

As indicated briefly under the discussion on commitment to a new country, the immoral behavior on the part of people in the United States had to be justified *to themselves*. Justification took the form of viewing the Westward movement as a noble goal, carried out by people who should be honored as heroes. Those who stood in the path of these heroes could thus be viewed as enemies, or as members of an out-group not deserving of the considerations given to in-group members. In addition, the out-group people were viewed as uncivilized and ignorant, better off under the protection of the United States than left on their own. This view has been disseminated through the treatments of history to which every schoolchild is exposed, as well as by the entertainment industry which has long used American Indians and Mexicans as stock characters. Later in this chapter, the effects of ideas encountered in schools and through the mass media will be given a more extensive treatment.

The important point for intercultural communication is that people in the United States became accustomed to imposing their demands on others without their active participation in decisions that affected their lives. Familiarity and feelings of comfortableness with such an approach is poor preparation for developing effective relationships with other countries in today's world. Small nations want their views considered: if they become unhappy with the treatment received from one superpower, they can ally themselves with another. Balance of power can be influenced since these small nations have raw materials, potential sites for strategically placed military bases, and votes in the United Nations which can be withheld from countries considered unfriendly or domineering.

The "right" to impose one's way: Slavery and its heritage

In addition to a movement westward, the development of the United States as a major nation was dependent upon establishing a solid economic base. This meant the development of agriculture and industry for which labor was perceived as essential. The slave trade developed to fill the need (Davis, 1966).

There are few more pernicious examples of people from one nation imposing a policy on another. Men, women, and children were forcefully taken from their homes in Africa, placed on overcrowded ships that led to the death of a significant number, and sold to the highest bidder in the United States. Families were broken up and couplings of males and females arranged to meet the demands of the white landowners. Slaves were denied the rights of citizens, such as protection by the courts or the right to vote. Slaves were not owned only by red-necked bigots who might be dismissed as unrepresentative of citizens of the United States. A number of America's founders and heroes, such as George Washington and Thomas Jefferson, owned slaves (Brodie, 1974). A civil war had to be fought before blacks could legally have freedom from ownership and control by others (the 1860s). There is a difference, of course, between what is "legal" and what is "right" in the minds of people. Blacks struggled for a century before the Civil Rights Act of 1964 guaranteed (again, only in the legal sense) basic rights. Today, vestiges of discrimination (some would use stronger terms than "vestiges") can be seen in housing patterns, inner-city schools, and unemployment statistics.

The American dilemma (Myrdal, 1944) is that, while the United States is supposedly devoted to the principle that "all men are created equal," it has allowed blacks to be treated so hideously. Some sort of naive justification is necessary so that people can explain their behavior to themselves and to their children. The major part of the justification is most unpleasant to discuss: whites viewed blacks as less than human, not really part of the category our founders had in mind when they wrote about the equality of men. Moreover, the Constitution of the United States gives official sanction to such a view in the admittedly perverse sort of thinking which has always marked white treatment of blacks. A black was counted as 3/5 of a white in determining the population of a state for the purpose of apportioning representatives to Congress.

There has always been a difference in the opportunities given to descendants of European immigrants and to the descendants of black slaves. The "melting pot ideal" was that, if immigrants blended into the United States by learning its language and becoming involved in its institutions, they would have the opportunity to pursue a decent living. But blacks were denied this opportunity; they were set aside as a unique group deserving of discriminatory treatment. The exact reasons for the special discrimination are hard to understand even today, but the following were undoubtedly influential. The first, and probably the most important to many whites, is the difference in physical features. Whites have standards of physical beauty which they apply in judging others, and blacks do not meet these. Recently, Berscheid and Walster (1974) have documented the effects of physical attractiveness on a wide variety of social behaviors. People judged as attractive, in contrast to the less attractive, were thought to have more social presence, competence in job performance, intelligence, and a *lesser* degree of culpability for a misdemeanor. Physical attractiveness seems to be a major determinant in how people are treated by others, and so there is a likelihood of discrimination at the first instant of contact between whites and blacks. F. Scott Fitzgerald said that the rich are different from you and me—they have more money. Similarly, the physically attractive are different from you and me—they are better looking and are given more opportunities.

A second reason has already been briefly mentioned. There still is the belief, on the part of many whites, that the black is from an inferior race. There seems to be no awareness on the part of whites that they have created a vicious circle. Historically, whites did not allow blacks the opportunity for advancement, and in many cases they forcefully denied blacks any exit from poverty. Thus, blacks were seen only in positions of subservience and were only allowed work which demanded few skills. The whites justified this state of affairs by solidifying their belief that blacks were capable and deserving of no more.

Although I am very uncomfortable citing the following quotes, they are important for an understanding of intercultural contact. Little purpose will be served by depositing such quotes under a rug since they are still representative of the feelings many people have. Jones (1972) has analyzed interviews with white Americans that were collected between 1940 and 1946 by the Social Science Institute at Fisk University (1946). Some excerpts from three of these interviews concerning white perceptions of blacks involve the themes of physical characteristics and innate capabilities of an inferior people.

(1) . . . The Negro is a black and kinky-haired person from whose body comes a not entirely pleasant odor. He is always regarded as an inferior person and race, mentally and morally, destined by birth and circumstances to serve the white people. . . .

(2) . . . A Negro is different from other people in that he is an unfortunate branch of the human family who hasn't had the opportunity, who hasn't been able to make out of himself all that he is capable of. . . .

(3) . . . Negroes have their own characteristics. First their utter lack of responsibility. They have an inborn sense of rhythm and music. As a race, they are not honest. . . . They are not a very stable race: they are here today and there tomorrow [pp. 30–31].

These sentiments have been passed along by whites from generation to generation, giving them a certain strength due simply to the amount of time they have been in existence. There is good evidence that such intense racial feelings have declined in recent years. The number of people holding these views has decreased, indicating hope for even more improvement (Watson, 1973a; chapter 7 of this volume). I think it would be dangerous, however, to dismiss such quotes as quaint reminders of a past which has been overcome. A person has only to read the newspaper accounts of the latest Ku Klux Klan rally to be reminded of the current existence of racial hatred. In addition, many people have been exposed to these sentiments during childhood. To their credit, they may have ignored them to a great extent as adults. However, in times of stress, people often resort to older, more negative beliefs from their past. For instance, people may seek a scapegoat during financially difficult times, and blacks still provide a safe target in many parts of the country. Or, blacks may provide a convenient reason to "explain" difficulties whites have in obtaining desired jobs or housing (McConahay & Hough, 1976).

A third reason for the discriminatory treatment is that blacks have always been kept in a position of subservience. Whites possessed all power, defined broadly as their ability to control the behavior of others (French, 1956). Recent research (Kipnis, 1976) has indicated that people in power lose respect for those in subordinate positions. People in power tend to belittle the ability of others and to take credit for any good work which is performed by others. The research data provided by Kipnis provide support for the common belief that power is corrupting. People in power become "heady" and arrogant, ignoring the feelings and accomplishments of those in subordinate roles. My guess is that most readers have experienced the situation in which a former co-worker was promoted into a position of greater authority vis-a-vis others, and that this person subsequently adopted behaviors that could be called arrogant or "credit taking." Historically, since whites forced blacks into subservient roles, they saw them in no other way. Consequently, they derogated the importance and worth of blacks.

Comfort with people in their place

A product of these historical developments was that whites became comfortable with having their will accepted and with keeping blacks, as well as Indians and Mexican-Americans, in a subservient position. This type of relationship became the norm, the "correct" way of doing things, passed on from generation to generation with the consequent unquestioning acceptance which longevity entails. The norm had a number of facets, including people's roles. Social psychologists explain that *"Role,* a term borrowed directly from the theater, is a metaphor intended to denote that conduct adheres to certain 'parts' (or positions) rather than to the players who read or recite them [Sarbin & Allen, 1968, p. 489]." For example, certain behaviors are expected from the role of policeman or stenographer, no matter who occupies the position. The behaviors involved in the performance of roles involve such issues as the following:

1. Is the conduct appropriate to the social position granted to or attained by the actor?
2. Is the enactment proper? That is, does the overt behavior meet the normative standards which serve as valuational criteria for observers?
3. Is the enactment convincing? That is, does the enactment lead the observer to declare unequivocally that the incumbent is legitimately occupying the position [Sarbin & Allen, 1968, p. 490]?

Black-white relations took place according to well-defined roles which whites considered normative. Contact took place according to master-servant roles, landowner-sharecropper, homeowner-maid, giver of orders-receiver of orders, and informal address ("Jack" or "boy")—formal address ("Mr. Smith" or "sir"). Black and white children were not allowed to play together; adolescent and adult males could visit black women at night for sexual contact, but last night's partners could not speak during the day. In the early or mid-1900s, limitations in the amount of contact were enforced by Jim Crow laws: front of the bus-back of the bus; orchestra-balcony; our school-your school; our restaurant-outsiders not allowed.

Whites, then, became accustomed to limited contact according to widely accepted role expectations. One of the major adjustments to the civil rights movements of the 1950s and 1960s was white acceptance of new roles with which they had no experience and for which they had no historical guidance. These new roles, demanding adjustment even today, include neighbor, co-worker, and child's school chum. Research (reviewed by Ehrlich, 1973) indicates that negative attitudes developed through experiences with one group, blacks, leads to negative attitudes toward other out-groups. The important point for the broad arena of intercultural communication is that Americans are unaccustomed to diverse types of interaction with people from different backgrounds. Rather, Americans are more comfortable with limited amounts of interaction according to well-defined roles. Consequently, they are somewhat inept at accepting people from other cultures as equals with a viewpoint worthy of attention. This ineptness, the product of history, has to be overcome if Americans are to interact effectively in today's interdependent world.

HISTORICAL EVENTS IN THE LIVES OF INDIVIDUALS

The use of the broad term "history" in this treatment of intercultural contact includes both a society's past and the individual's past. The latter refers to people's exposure to concepts, as well as to their treatment by others, over which they have little control. Three topic areas will be considered here: the language people are expected to learn; the way in which children are disciplined, with the prediction that certain forms of discipline lead to certain traits that are still identifiable when the children reach adulthood; and the influence of education and the mass media on the perception of outgroups.

The relation between language and interaction with others

A speculative possibility is that the language people learn as children presents them with concepts, structures, and vocabulary which form a basis for reacting to out-group members and/or strangers. If this is true, then people unknowingly have certain limits put on their range of possibilities regarding interaction with others. This position, which has been studied by linguists, psychologists, and anthropologists, is an aspect of the so-called "Sapir-Whorf" hypothesis (Miller & McNeil, 1969; Whorf, 1956). In its broadest terms, the hypothesis states that "the difference between . . . languages suggests that people speaking different languages must experience the world in different ways. It appears that 'culture' includes, in addition to values and technology and religious practices, a particular cognitive structure. Children acquiring their first language learn more than a set of vocal skills; they take on the world view of their group [Brown &

Lenneberg, 1965, pp. 244–245]." For our present purposes, only those aspects of language which might involve relations with out-group people will be examined. The English language will be used in most examples, and one feature which is possibly found in all languages (a universal) will also be analyzed.

Ehrlich (1973) has suggested that "National language systems, at least of the Indo-European variety, have three structural characteristics that facilitate the development [p. 21]" of concepts that have an effect on how outsiders are perceived. His first suggestion is that words used to describe individuals may also be used to describe groups. People can say that "Charlie is ambitious" and also that "Americans are ambitious." This feature of the language allows ease in expressing generalizations from observations of one person to all members of that person's group. This feature of languages means that it is easy to form and to think in terms of stereotypes (see also chapters 4 and 5).

The second feature "is that the use of collective nouns without qualification unambiguously encompasses the collectivity. The statement 'Atheists are cynical,' may be correctly transliterated *'All* atheists are cynical' [Ehrlich, 1973, p. 21]." As another example, suppose an individual has a good deal of contact with a group of exchange students from India (Lambert & Bressler, 1956). The person might say that "the Indians are conscious of their status," a generalization which may be true of those Indians who were able to participate in the exchange program. But the feature of language Ehrlich identifies allows others who overhear the original statement to say, "All Indians are concerned with their status." Again this feature of languages contributes to stereotypes or generalizations about people which mask individual variations.

The third feature is that any qualification of a general statement about people, such as those used as examples in the previous two paragraphs, demands more verbosity and more complex grammatical constructions. It simply is easier (much less effort has to be expended) to talk about groups in the same way one would talk about individuals, and to do so according to categories that listeners are certain to understand. The following statement might be the best summary of a person's experience: "Based on the group of people from India with whom I interacted who were interested in coming to the campus at which I worked, my impression is that they were concerned with their status." Such statements tend to bore listeners, however, demand more verbal skills than many people have, and involve more effort than many people are willing to expend. The easier and more pithy "the Indians were concerned with their status" is the likely verbalization.

Erhlich also reviewed research on the connotation of colors. Studies have suggested that certain words widely used to label skin color ("black" especially) have negative connotations in English (Gergen, 1967) and in many other languages (Osgood, 1977). The argument is that the color words have connotations which children learn as a natural part of language acquisition and that the children transfer the connotation to people who have skin color described by the same words. Gergen (1967) summarized the connotations of "black."

> After careful study of color symbolism in the Western tradition, Matthew Luckiesh lists the following as most commonly associated with black: woe, gloom, darkness, dread, death, terror, horror, wickedness, curse, mourning, and mortification. . . . From his studies, Faber Birren concludes that "despair" is the major association elicited by black. Such attributes stand in marked contrast to those associated with white: triumph, light, innocence, joy, divine power, purity, regeneration, happiness, gaiety, peace, chastity, truth, modesty, femininity, and delicacy. Studies of color symbolism in the Bible, the works of Chaucer, Milton, Hawthorne, Poe, and Melville also reveal a major tendency to use white in expressing forms of goodness, and black in connoting evil [p. 397].

Just one manifestation of these connotations is that among dark-skinned people, those whose skin is somewhat *less* dark are considered more attractive and are looked upon as more desirable marriage partners.

Another feature, analyzed by Klineberg (1964), is that vocabulary items are introduced into languages which use the names of different culture groups. The "use of common expressions with an ethnic referent may contribute to the tendency to attribute specific characteristics to ethnic groups. English appears to be particularly rich in such expressions [p. 36]." Examples are to "Jew him down" in business dealings, or a "Chinese puzzle" to describe a complex problem. Expressions like these may reinforce stereotypes which discourage interaction with out-group members. Jewish people may be avoided because they are seen as schemers, and the Chinese may be rejected because they are perceived as inscrutable. Klineberg also gives examples from two other languages:

> Italians say "fare il portughese," to do what the Portuguese do, when they refer to slipping into a theater or onto a streetcar without paying the price of admission, or otherwise "getting away with it." A Frenchman who prefaces his remarks by the statement "Je suis un paysan du Danube" (I am a peasant from the Danube) means that he is ignorant of the subject of which he is about to speak [p. 37].

The final feature to be examined here is the (possibly) universal system of affective connotation which exists in all languages. Some introduction is necessary before examples from intercultural communication can be considered. A major attempt has been made in recent years to measure the affective qualities of human communication, the work being led by Charles Osgood. The most influential publication emanating from the research has been *The Measurement of Meaning* (Osgood, Suci, & Tannenbaum, 1957). A concise and readable summary of key findings is available (Osgood, 1971). After painstaking analysis, Osgood concluded that the connotation of words can be analyzed and summarized according to three dimensions of meaning. Each of the three dimensions can be measured by a series of seven point scales, with the ends of scales marked by bipolar adjectives. The three dimensions are evaluation, potency, and activity. Examples of scales for measuring each are as follows:

Evaluation
good ____ ____ ____ ____ ____ ____ ____ bad
unfavorable ____ ____ ____ ____ ____ ____ ____ favorable
like ____ ____ ____ ____ ____ ____ ____ dislike

Potency
strong ____ ____ ____ ____ ____ ____ ____ weak
soft ____ ____ ____ ____ ____ ____ ____ hard
little ____ ____ ____ ____ ____ ____ ____ big

Activity
fast ____ ____ ____ ____ ____ ____ ____ slow
noisy ____ ____ ____ ____ ____ ____ ____ quiet
dead ____ ____ ____ ____ ____ ____ ____ alive

An especially impressive body of research supervised by Osgood (1965; Osgood, May, and Miron, 1975) has shown that people from many different cultures (over 30 languages have been studied) scattered all over the world use these same dimensions when explaining the meaning of concepts. These dimensions have been posited as cultural universals. Rating scales have been developed in over 30 languages so that the dimensions can be analyzed as they apply to any concept. Some examples of English and French scales for the evaluative dimension are:

English	*French*
likable-repugnant	sympathique-antipathique
happy-sad	gai-triste
nice-awful	gentil-méchant

While these are not exact translation equivalents, there is an "evaluative feeling tone" (Osgood, 1965, p. 102) which is common to the English and French scales. It is the total feeling tone which would be used in the comparison of meaning across cultures.

This set of findings probably seems rather tame. How does it have a bearing on intercultural relations? The general thrust of my arguments follows Osgood (1971, pp. 37–38), although the examples involving inter-group contact are different. If people react to concepts in terms of evalua-tion, potency, and activity, then they react to out-groups in this manner since "out-group" is a concept. A survival mechanism may be built into reactions according to the three dimensions. Osgood (1971) speculates, "What is important to us now, as it was way back in the age of the Neanderthal Man, about the sign of a thing is: First, does it refer to some-thing *good* or *bad* for me . . . [p. 37]." For instance, is the "thing" a person I know and trust who is bringing good, or is it a stranger who may be bringing harm. Second, does the person seem strong or weak compared to me: is it a powerful or a frail person? Third, with respect to my behavior, do the actions of the other person demand activity or passivity: does the person demand that I interact in some way, or can the person be safely ignored? Such thoughts may go through people's minds today when they meet out-group members since the three dimensions provide an easily available framework for analysis. The natural tendency to react in terms of evaluation, potency, and activity may put limits on the sorts of interaction people attempt with out-group members.

A few more findings from the research program led by Osgood are worth considering. It has already been mentioned that, in many of the world's languages, "black" has a negative connotation on the evaluation dimension. However, it is also considered potent by people in many cultures (Osgood, 1977, p. 443). If the argument is accepted that con-notations of the concept "black" play a part in white people's reactions to black people, then the following generalization may be warranted. The combination of a negative evaluation (bad) and potency (strong, pos-sible danger) may lead to a forcing of black people into a subservient position out of which they cannot move. Keeping blacks powerless re-moves any danger. The subservient position, however, invites negative evaluations. Osgood (1979) gives evidence that strength is evaluated more positively than weakness, and activity is evaluated more positively than passivity. The forceful maintenance of a system in which blacks were inactive and weak, as in their bondage of slavery, invited the negative evaluation on the part of whites. The vicious circle continues: blacks are kept in a weak position and are then negatively evaluated because they appear weak.

Negative views of out-groups: Parental discipline

The relationship children have with their parents, and the type of discipline parents choose to use in socializing their children, have effects on attitudes toward out-groups. The end products of both tolerant and intolerant attitudes will be reviewed in chapter 3. Here, the individual's history will be examined to see if factors can be identified which lead to negative out-group evaluations.

In retrospective reports, adults express the opinion that they acquired attitudes about out-groups from their parents (Rosenblith, 1949). Acquisition can stem from a number of factors, e.g., parents have some control over access to out-groups. They might prevent children from coming into contact with outsiders. Another type of parental behavior which is especially influential is marked by punitive disciplinary tactics, strong demands for obedience, acceptance of traditional and conservative norms, and little encouragement of the child in individual self-development (Harris, Gough, & Martin, 1950). In a study which examined both adults' views of out-groups and reports on how they were raised (gathered from the parents of the adults), Dickens and Hobart (1959; reviewed by Ehrlich, 1973) identified two factors which are similar to those found by other investigators (Harding, Proshansky, Kutner, & Chein, 1969; Pushkin and Veness, 1973). "Dominance" refers to the child being put into a subservient role, with punishment assured if (s)he does not conform to the parents' wishes. "Ignoring" refers to behaviors which keep the child from becoming an important part of the family and which disregard the individual needs of children. The views which mothers of intolerant adults endorsed included feelings that quiet children are more desirable than talkative ones; and that the needs of children are not important in planning family activities.

It should be pointed out that, although these relations between parental discipline and adult intolerance are valid, there is not a single explanation of the facts which is widely accepted by specialists who have studied the issues (Harding et al., 1969). One explanation is that a disciplined and harsh family setting provides experience which leads to a rigid, intolerant, out-group-rejecting adult personality. That is, adults experience certain treatments by others as children, acquire the point of view that such treatment is normal and expected, and so treat out-group members accordingly (Adorno et al., 1950). A second explanation is that education affects both measures: adults with little formal education use harsh disciplinary techniques, and poorly educated adults have intolerant attitudes. The third explanation is that children naturally identify with their parents and acquire attitudes through this process. Children "take over" the attitudes of their parents regarding out-groups, just as they do many other attitudes toward occupations, political preferences, religion, discipline, and necessities for an adequate standard of living.

Education certainly is influential: it will be examined for its effects on intercultural attitudes in chapter 7. Other research, however, indicates that when the amount of education is taken into account, the relation between disciplinary methods and adult attitudes remains (Roberts & Rokeach, 1956). The discipline vs. identification issue is certainly an important area for further investigation. While I feel that the arguments for the effects of discipline are persuasive, the debate is not of central importance to the present analysis of intercultural contact. All arguments include the fact that parents affect their children, and that rigid parents engender intolerance in their children. The product of a background which involves harsh discipline, then, is an adult ill suited to effective intercultural contact.

Negative views of out-groups: Education and the mass media

At least two features of children's experience in school affect views of out-groups. As a direct extension of research on parental discipline, Stephan and Rosenfield (1978) suggest that "It is reasonable to speculate that school systems with excessively authoritarian rules and highly punitive disciplinary practices may also promote negative racial attitudes [p. 802]."

The second aspect of education is the content children are expected to master, or at least the materials which they are expected to read (Ehrlich, 1973). As with parental discipline, the premise is that children have little influence on what school materials administrators decide to use. Following on the themes of "turning inward" and a lack of interest in other nations discussed earlier, Klineberg (1963) pointed out that these are reinforced in children's readers encountered in school. Based on an analysis of 15 books widely adopted for classroom use, he concluded:

> . . . life in the United States as it is portrayed in the children's readers is in a general way easy and comfortable, frustrations are rare and usually overcome quite easily, people (all White, mostly blond and "North European" in origin) are almost invariably kind and generous. There are other kinds of people in the world, but they live in far-off countries or in days gone by; they evidently have no place on the American scene [p. 77].

Similar findings have been reported by others. The research of Blom, Waite, and Zimet (1967) and Waite (1968), based on texts published in the mid 1960s, indicates that very few attempts were made to include people from different ethnic groups as figures in the books. Those stories which *did* include characters from other groups were unrealistic; for instance, blacks were typically depicted as members of a single family in a prosperous and pleasant part of white suburbia. While the civil rights movement encouraged the development of more "ethnically integrated" textbooks in the 1970s, past errors could not be erased. Since today's adults were exposed to the sort of texts Klineberg described, unrealistic stereotypes reinforced in school continued to plague organized attempts (reviewed in chapter 7) to increase intergroup tolerance.

Ideally, even if the children receive a lackluster introduction to the nature of intercultural contact in school, they would be exposed to realistic treatments at home. After all, isn't one of the century's greatest achievements the television, a vehicle by which the most learned can instruct us, the most witty entertain us, and the most experienced guide us? Anyone who has watched more than 15 minutes of American commercial television recently knows the answer. Much too often, television reinforces the same stereotypes and unrealistic out-group attitudes found in school readers. Apparently, television and other mass media vehicles become more important as children grow older. In a study of 11 national and cultural groups, Lambert and Klineberg (1967) found that six-year-old children report a primary dependenec on their parents for attitudes about other ethnic groups. Children of ten and older, however, report a greater dependence on television and reading material. The label "influential" is given to school texts but, interestingly, not to the teachers who introduce the materials. A recent complaint about television's treatment of other cultures concerns the Arabs. Characters are either wealthy stumblebums in situation comedies or unprincipled terrorists in so-called dramas. No mention is made of their contributions to the arts and sciences. The widely syndicated columnist Meg Greenfield (1977) points out that

> There is a dehumanizing circular process at work here. The caricature dehumanizes. But it is inspired and made acceptable by an earlier dehumanizing influence, namely, an absence of feeling for who the Arabs are and where they have been [p. 110].

In addition to the content of television programs, movies, and short stories in magazines, the structure adopted by the mass media for the presentation of material has had a major effect. Issues are oversimplified so that they can be covered in a short amount of time or in a small amount of space. Characters are overdrawn so that there are clear "heroes" and "villains." (Note how easily the color symbolism of "white hats" and "black hats" would have fit into the previous sentence). Happy endings are common, problems are solved, and loose ends are wrapped up in a nice bow. Current statistics indicate that children spend more time watching TV than any other activity except sleep. The constant, oversimplified view of the world provided by TV must take its toll. However, life is not so easy to analyze: heroes and villains overlap in complex issues like school integration, the assignment of technical assistance workers overseas, and the treatment of foreign students in the United States. Similarly, issues aren't perfectly clear-cut and problems can't be solved to everyone's satisfaction. An oversimplified view of reality is as dangerous as the intolerant content of attitudes toward out-groups.

While bemoaning the fact that there is not as much research on the issues as would be desirable, Ehrlich (1973) concludes that "The primary contexts for the diffusion of knowledge of ethnic stereotypes, and for the legitimation of such knowledge, are the family and the school. . . . Consensual ethnic stereotypes are copied in the mass media of communication and the media of mass education [p. 32]."

SUMMARY

The ideas to which people are exposed concerning their country's history have an influence on their attitudes and values. Many of the ideas concern relations with people from indigenous subcultures. Examples are black-white relations in the United States and parts of Africa; white-aboriginal relations in Australia; and Catholic-Protestant relations in Northern Ireland. The ideas also deal with relations between countries: Israel-Egypt, the United States-Great Britain, and Japan-China. To develop this broad generalization, the specific case of the white, middle-class United States was chosen to exemplify how historical analyses might yield insights into current problems of intergroup interaction.

The history of the United States, which provides a set of norms which individuals are expected to learn, as well as the experience of individuals during their early years, encourages the adoption of negative attitudes toward out-groups. To use some vernacular, individuals are in sad shape to meet the current demands of greater intercultural interaction. Many Americans are:

1. exposed to concepts of individualism which do not involve concerns about others,
2. distrustful of alliances with other countries,
3. deferent to an elite in matters concerning foreign policy,
4. familiar with imposing their point of view,
5. comfortable with well-defined roles during periods of contact with others,
6. likely to use features of the language(s) they have learned in reacting to out-groups,
7. accustomed to treating others in certain ways based on the type of discipline they received as children,
8. exposed to negative, oversimplified treatments of out-groups through school texts and the mass media.

A throwing up of one's hands in frustration is an understandable reaction. However, some people *do* interact effectively with members of other cultures; their traits and special abilities have been identified. Some organizations *are* influential in encouraging people to improve intercultural relations. My argument is that people's history makes good intercultural relations difficult, but that the past can be overcome. The remaining chapters review what has and what might be done to improve on what history has given us.

NOTE

1. The emphasis on individualism does not mean that Americans are incapable of collective action or have no loyalty toward groups. The argument is that, in comparison to people in other cultures, Americans are very much concerned with individual achievement and individual privileges. In comparing the United States and China, Ho (1979) makes the point clearly.

> . . . studies . . . point to a remarkably consistent pattern of differences between Chinese and Americans (who as a group may be taken most suitably to be representative of the individualist orientation) in their attitudes, values, and personality characteristics. These differences reflect the fundamental contrast in cultural orientations between the two groups on the collectivist–individualist dimension [p. 148].

> It would be of interest to refer to some observations made by a group of development psychologists [from the United States] who made a visit to the People's Republic of China in 1973 (Kessen, 1975). What impressed these psychologists the most was the near absence of antisocial, disruptive, or aggressive behavior, and the conspicuously prosocial behavior of Chinese children. They also raised a question of central concern to all those who cherish individualist values; but at what cost to individual variation are these achieved [p. 147]?

3

Individual's Attitudes, Traits, and Skills

Largely through the sorts of experiences covered in chapter 2, people develop certain attitudes, traits, and skills which play a major part in determining the amount and success of intercultural interaction. Many researchers have been active in investigating these individual-level variables, and their combined efforts have led to a good deal of insight. Beginning with the general concept of attitudes, this chapter moves toward a discussion of prejudicial attitudes, or people's preconceived feelings about out-groups. Analysis will center on the forms which prejudice takes and the functions it serves for people. Although "stereotypes" once was a neutral term referring to people's thought processes, the link between prejudice and stereotypes has become very strong over the last 30 years. When prejudice is so intense that out-group members are dehumanized, interpersonal cruelty is a probable outcome. Arguments are made that the basic element of a willingness to inflict pain on others is present in historical atrocities such as Nazi concentration camps and in current problem areas such as prisons and fraternity initiations. Insights into especially strong prejudicial attitudes, which are manifested in many aspects of people's lives, can be gained through analyzing the authoritarian personality syndrome.

Two other concepts used to describe people are "traits" and "skills." Although the existence and importance of traits is currently a debated topic among psychologists, the argument presented here is that trait analysis is one of several useful approaches in understanding cross-cultural interaction. The importance of various traits such as tolerance, sociability, and task orientation is discussed. Skills are more modifiable than traits and are usually acquired during a person's formal education or through job experience. Skills considered especially important in cross-cultural interaction include knowledge of subject matter, and ability to follow up on opportunities and to use one's talents in a given culture. A common element underlying many traits and skills is sensitivity to the viewpoints of people in other cultures.

ATTITUDES TOWARD OUT-GROUPS: PREJUDICES AND STEREOTYPES

In broad terms, attitudes refer to people's reactions toward a concept or, in everyday language, their feelings, beliefs, and readiness to act. The concept can be a person, group, event, object, or abstraction. Attitudes are commonly analyzed according to three components (McGuire, 1969): affective, cognitive, and conative. The affective component refers to people's emotional reactions, to their "gut feelings," and a common way of measuring it is to use the evaluative dimension from Osgood's (1971) research, already reviewed. Hence, the affective component is summarized by people's subjective feelings of goodness or badness. The cognitive component refers to people's belief and information about the object. These may be totally correct from a person's own viewpoint but absolutely bizarre from an observer's perspective. The conative component refers to people's behavioral intentions toward the object. These might include a desire to form friendships or a willingness to spend several years in another culture.

Often, beliefs have affective overtones, and the combination of the cognitive and the affective is a good example of the interrelationships among the components. The *cognition* that a certain group is lazy involves *affect* since "lazy" is an emotionally laden adjective. Although, typically, there is consistency among the components, there are certainly exceptions, especially when actual behavior is considered. In intercultural relations, people may have positive feelings about an out-group but may not behave in a friendly manner. Reasons for this might be perceived in-group pressures to maintain social distance, or simply a lack of knowledge concerning how to approach and interact with people from a different background. An understanding of these three components helps elucidate the differences among prejudice, discrimination, and stereotyping. Prejudice refers to a person's emotional reactions and, thus, represents the affective component. Discrimination refers to a person's behavior which puts out-group members at a disadvantage and, consequently, represents the conative component. Stereotypes most frequently refer to a person's beliefs about out-group members and, consequently, are a manifestation of the cognitive component.

When considering the concept of intercultural contact, "prejudice" is the word often used when people's attitudes are analyzed. The word appears frequently when interracial relations within a country are discussed. It is less frequently used in discussing relations between citizens of different nations. Yet, clearly, the same sorts of attitudes are involved when problems of foreign student acceptance in another country or the development of working relations between host country nationals and overseas businessmen are analyzed. A thorough understanding of prejudice is necessary, and I believe the best way to analyze the concept is to examine the functions it serves for people and to analyze the forms it takes (Brislin, 1978).

Prejudice: Its function

When people react negatively to others on an emotional basis, with an absence of direct contact or factual material about the others, the people are said to behave according to prejudice. One of the conclusions from the large body of research on this concept is that "prejudice" is far more complex than would be judged from the way the word is used in ordinary, everyday usage. This complexity has to be understood if the problems stemming from prejudice are to be addressed effectively.

An understanding of prejudice can begin if its functions are analyzed. In the past, the majority of research on this topic has dealt with interpersonal contact within countries, especially black-white and Gentile-Jewish relations. Katz (1960) has written the clearest presentation of the functions of various attitudes which people hold, and these can be applied to the more specific case of prejudicial attitudes. Functions refer to the uses of attitudes, or to what they *do* for people.

The four functions which attitudes serve are:

1. The utilitarian or adjustment function. People hold certain prejudices because such attitudes lead to rewards and to the avoidance of punishment in their culture. For instance, people want to be well liked by others. If such esteem is dependent upon rejecting members of a certain group, as was discussed previously in analyzing black-white relations, then it is likely that the people will, indeed, reject members of the out-group. Or, if jobs are scarce and if people from a certain group want those jobs, it is adjustive to believe that out-group members have no responsibility in work settings. Thus there will be less competition for the desired employment. Another very common example of the adjustment function stems from people's familiarity with a well-established circle of friends, topics of conversation with which they are comfortable, and ways of behaving toward in-group members which are considered part of good etiquette. Much effort is demanded when interacting with people who are not familiar with the same ways of doing things, who have to stumble in an unfamiliar language, and who may seem ill at ease in one's company. Hence, it is adjustive simply not to go through the discomfort which stems from reaching out to people from different backgrounds and, instead, to stick with one's own group.

2. The ego-defensive function. People hold certain prejudices because they do not want to admit uncomfortable things about themselves. Holding the prejudice protects the people from a harsh reality. For instance, if a person is unsuccessful in the business world, (s)he may believe that members of a certain successful group are a scheming bunch of cheaters. This belief protects the individual from the self-admission that (s)he has inadequacies. Another example involves the facts about socialization reviewed in chapter 1. People believe, as part of the basic feelings of self-esteem, that they have grown up in a society where proper behavior is practiced. These people may look down upon members of other cultures (or social classes within a culture) who do not behave "correctly." This prejudicial attitude, then, serves the function of protecting people's self-esteem.

3. The value-expressive function. People hold certain prejudices because they want to express the aspects of life which they highly prize. Such aspects include basic values of people concerning religion, government, society, and aesthetics. Katz (1960) emphasizes that this function is related to an individual's "notion of the sort of person he sees himself to be [p. 173]." For example, people who discriminate against members of a certain religious group may do so because they see themselves as standing up for the one true God (as defined by their religion). As a more intense example, people have engaged in atrocities toward out-group members to retain the supposed values of a pure racial stock (again, their own).

4. The knowledge function. People hold certain prejudices because such attitudes allow individuals to organize and to structure their world in a way that makes sense to them. People have a need to know about various aspects of their culture so that they can interact effectively in it. But the aspects of culture are so numerous that various discrete stimuli must be categorized together for efficient organization. People then behave according to the category they have organized, *not* according to the discrete stimuli (Triandis, 1977). Often, these categories are stereotypes which do not allow for variation within a category. For instance, if people believe that members of a certain cultural group are childlike and cannot be given any responsibility, they may employ that stereotype upon meeting a member of that group. Given a set of stereotypes, people do not have to think about each individual they meet. They can then spend time on the many other matters that compete for their attention during an average day. The prejudicial stereotypes thus provide "knowledge" about the world which individuals use in going about their everyday lives. The problem, of course, is that the stereotypes may be wrong and are always overdrawn.

Stereotypes should be discussed in more detail at this point. Use of the term "prejudicial stereotypes" in the preceding paragraph does not mean that stereotypes and prejudice are one and the same. Some stereotypes stem from prejudicial attitudes, and only these are considered in this treatment of the knowledge function of attitudes. More generally, stereotypes refer to any categorization of individual elements *concerned with people* which mask differences among those elements. Stereotypes are absolutely necessary for thinking and communicating since people cannot respond individually to the millions of isolated elements they perceive each day (Duijker & Frijda, 1960). They must group elements together into categories and then respond to the categories. Stereotypes are a form of generalization which involve the name(s) of some group of people and statements about that group. Thus, when we speak of "conservatives" or "Marxists" or "academics" or "sojourners," we are using stereotypical categories that mask individual differences within these categories. Stereotypes will always be a factor in any sort of communication, a fact which must be realized in any analysis of interaction between individuals from different backgrounds. A refusal to deal with them means a refusal to deal with one of the most basic aspects of thinking and communication.[1]

It is useful to distinguish between stereotypes and prejudicial stereotypes. The latter refer to generalizations about other groups which are negative, often hostile, and not based on firsthand contact. Often, they are repetitions of "conventional wisdom," untested by the people who use the prejudicial stereotypes in their everyday conversation. These types of stereotypes can be changed through educational programs and through intercultural contact, as will be discussed in chapter 7. In addition, people can be made aware of the strong tendency to stereotype, and can be encouraged to avoid decisions based solely on stereotypes. Educational programs and contact experiences which have the goal of reducing prejudicial stereotypes and decisions based on stereotypes have a chance of success. Programs which have the goal of obliterating stereotypes as a method of thinking and communication are bound to fail.

Returning to the functions of attitudes, certain prejudices can have several uses particularly when an individual's entire life span is considered. Young children develop a prejudice to please their parents (adjustment), continue to hold it because of what they learn in school (knowledge), and behave according to the prejudice since they wish to express their view of themselves (value). Programs to change prejudice often fail because the most important function, or functions, are not recognized. Most change-oriented programs are concerned with presenting well-established facts about the targets of prejudice. But such a program will only change people's attitudes which serve the knowledge function. Much more work has to be done on finding ways to change prejudices that serve the other three functions.

Prejudice: Its forms

In addition to an understanding of the functions of prejudice, it is also important to consider various forms which prejudice takes in its expression. The range of expression is large.

1. Red-neck racism. Certain people believe that members of a given cultural group are so inferior, according to some imagined standard, that the group members are not worthy of decent treatment. The term "red-neck" comes from the Southern United States[2] where world attention was focused on the white majority's treatment of blacks during political demonstrations prior to the Civil Rights Act of 1964. The type of prejudice summarized by the term "red-neck," however, is found all over the world. This extreme form of prejudice has most often been assessed by asking people to agree or disagree with statements like this (from scales analyzed by Ashmore, 1970): "The many faults, and the general inability to get along, of (*insert name of group*), who have recently flooded our community, prove that we ought to send them back where they came from as soon as conditions permit." "(Insert name of group) can never advance to the standard of living and civilization of our country due mainly to their innate dirtiness, laziness, and general backwardness."

Whereas all of us cringe at the thought of such tasteless, abhorrent sentiments, we all know that such prejudices exist. All of us can give many examples from the countries in which we have lived. Formal education has had a significant influence on lowering the incidence of red-neck racism. Research has shown that, as the number of years of formal education increases, the incidence of racism decreases. However, to combat further this extreme form of prejudice, accurate figures on the number of people who hold such views are needed. Only large-scale surveys can provide this information. The questions that would have to be asked of people, however, mean that the survey would generate hostility on the part of those being interviewed. The resulting non-cooperation between interviewer and interviewee would invalidate the results. Consequently, program planners are in a bind: they want to establish programs to reduce red-neck racism, but the content of the attitudes prevents their assessment, especially in an era when many people hide these intense attitudes. Program planners, like readers of a book such as this one, probably underestimate the current levels of red-neck racism since they do not normally interact with people who hold such views.

2. Symbolic racism. Certain people have negative feelings about a given group because they feel that the group is interfering with aspects of their culture with which they have become familiar. The people do not dislike the group per se and do not hold sentiments which are indicative of red-

neck racism. Symbolic racism (McConahay & Hough, 1976) is expressed in terms of threats to people's basic values and to the status quo. When directly questioned, people will assert that members of a certain group are "moving too fast" and are making illegitimate demands in their quest for a place in society. Put another way, the people have nothing against members of the out-group: they just don't want any interference with their plans for employment, housing, or schooling for their children. Symbolic racism is expressed by responses to questions like these (the answer indicative of symbolic racism is noted in parentheses):

> "Over the past few years, (*insert name of group*) have gotten more economically than they deserve." (agree)
> "People in this country should support _____ in their struggle against discrimination and segregation." (disagree)
> "_____ are getting too demanding in their push for equal rights." (agree)

Sentiments like these are probably more widespread than red-neck feelings among members of the affluent middle-class in various countries. Again, however, the unavailability of exact figures hampers intelligent planning for programs to deal with this form of prejudice. It is important to understand the differences between red-neck and symbolic racism. Since people who hold symbolic sentiments do not view themselves as red-necks, programs aimed at changing extreme racist views (such programs are presently most common) are doomed to failure. McConahay and Hough (1976) are correct when they state that current change programs seem incomprehensible to holders of symbolic views "and they do not understand what all the fuss is about. This enables racism to be considered 'somebody else's' problem while holders of symbolic views concentrate upon their own private lives [p. 44]."

3. Tokenism. Some people harbor negative feelings about a given group but do not want to admit this fact to themselves. Such people definitely do not view themselves as prejudiced and do not perceive themselves as discriminatory in their behavior. One way that they reinforce this view of themselves is to engage in unimportant, but positive, intergroup behaviors. By engaging in such unimportant behaviors people can persuade themselves that they are unprejudiced, and thus they can refuse to perform more important intergroup behaviors. For instance, Dutton (1976) found that, if people gave a small amount of money to an out-group, they were less willing to later donate a large amount of their time to a "Brotherhood Week" campaign emphasizing intergroup relations and goodwill. Other people in the Dutton study donated time to the Brotherhood Week if they had previously not been asked to give the small sum of money. Similarly,

I once discussed this research finding with a person in charge of administering a large educational exchange program. She noted that people who gave money during a fund raising campaign later declined to have a foreign student in their homes as a guest. In both cases, the small amount of money was a token which seemed to allow some people to persuade themselves that they were unprejudiced and so did not have to prove themselves by engaging in the more important, time-consuming behavior.[3]

4. Arm's length prejudice. Certain people engage in friendly, positive behavior toward out-group members in certain situations but hold those same out-group members at an "arm's length" in other situations. The difference across situations seems to be along a dimension of perceived intimacy of behaviors (Triandis & Davis, 1965). For semiformal behaviors—e.g., casual friendships at a place of employment, interactions between speaker and audience at a lecture, or interactions at a catered dinner party—people who harbor an arm's length prejudice will act in a friendly, positive manner. But for more intimate behaviors—e.g., dating, interactions during an informal dinner held at someone's home, or relations between neighbors—people will interact in a tense, sometimes hostile manner. Frankly, I have observed this sort of arm's length prejudice at places where such behavior would ideally not be expected, as at various institutions devoted to international education and to the exchange of people from various countries for the purpose of intercultural understanding. I have observed a Caucasian social psychologist (who has long lectured on the dysfunctional consequences of prejudice), during a visit to my home, become noncommunicative and ultimately rude when my Chinese-American neighbor unexpectedly dropped in for a visit. This form of prejudice is difficult to detect since people who engage in it seem to be tolerant of out-group members much of the time.

5. Real likes and dislikes. Certain people harbor negative feelings about a given group because members of the group engage in behaviors that the people dislike. This fifth category is derived more from common sense than the scholarly literature, and it represents an expression of my feelings that not all forms of prejudice should be looked upon as an indication of some sickness or flaw (Watson, 1973b). People *do* have real likes and dislikes. No one person is so saintly as to be tolerant and forgiving toward all who engage in behaviors (s)he dislikes. For instance, I very much dislike the practice of littering, and there are certain groups more likely to leave their trash on the ground after a picnic. Sometimes they are from cultures where servants or laborers are expected to do such cleanup. However, my realization of the group's backgound does not lessen my dislike of litter. Seeing members of a certain group engage in disliked behaviors, I am less likely to interact pleasantly (or to seek out interaction) with other members of that group in the future. My recom-

mendation is that more attention be given to this common, but heretofore neglected, type of everyday prejudice.

6. The familiar and the unfamiliar. This form of prejudice is one manifestation of the adjustive function of attitudes discussed earlier. People who are socialized into a culture are likely to become familiar and comfortable with various aspects of that culture. These people, when interacting with members of out-groups, are likely to experience behaviors or ideas which are unfamiliar and, hence, they are likely to feel uncomfortable. Consequently, the people are likely to prefer to interact with members of their own cultural group. What might seem like intense prejudice and discrimination to an onlooker, then, may be simply a reflection of people's preference for what is comfortable and nonstressful. In a study of everyday interaction among members of nine ethnic groups on Guam (Brislin, 1971), I found that informants were able to verbalize this reason for people's choice of friends. An informant from the Marshall Islands wrote: "Culture makes these groups stick together. Somebody might not get along with one from another country. He likes to find some friends who have the same beliefs he has, and he could only find these characteristics with the people from his own country [p. 177]." And a resident of Truk wrote about the type of strained conversation that can arise when members of different groups interact. In my opinion, the discomfort stemming from strained conversations is a major reason why people do not seek out subsequent intercultural interaction.

A Trukese that has never experienced the cold winter of the U.S. could not comprehend and intelligently appreciate a Statesider telling him the terrible winter they had in Albany anymore than a person from Albuquerque that has never seen an atoll could visualize the smallness of the islets that make up such an atoll. [Truk, of course, is an atoll.]

I believe that this sort of mild prejudice based on what is familiar and unfamiliar is the phenomenon recently referred to by the former United States Ambassador to the United Nations, Andrew Young (*Playboy,* July 1977; *Newsweek,* June 20, 1977). In mid-1977, Young labeled a number of people as "racists," but in explaining his use of the term he was clearly referring to a lack of understanding and an insensitivity regarding other cultural groups. When questioned by the press, Young had to admit that he himself was a "racist" according to this sense of the term, which he eventually labeled as an "unfortunate" use. My feeling is that much insensitivity and misunderstanding stems from unfamiliarity. People are unfamiliar with out-groups; they don't interact because they don't know how; and so they are unable to develop any sensitivity and understanding. As with the form of prejudice described under "real likes and dislikes," this everyday type of behavior deserves more attention from behavioral scientists than it has heretofore received.

INTERPERSONAL CRUELTY

Although uncomfortable to admit, people involved in intercultural contact have to be aware of the intense negative behaviors of which humans are capable. Recent research, carried out both in specially designed research settings and through retrospective analysis of historical cases, has shown that ordinary individuals who are respected members of their community will engage in atrocious behavior if they feel that the situation warrants such behavior. People will administer extremely painful shocks to another person, as part of their role as "teacher," if they feel that a visible authority figure will take the blame for any harm done (Milgram, 1974). People, when assigned the role of prison guards, will engage in sadistic behavior toward others who are role-playing prisoners (Zimbardo, 1973).

Retrospective analyses of Nazi concentration camp murders have found that very normal, mentally stable, and untroubled individuals engaged in the persecution of the Jewish people because they believed that the war efforts and their government required the extreme action. My own feeling is that these examples of interpersonal cruelty are much more common than people would like to admit. For instance, I hypothesize that on the *individual level,* the types of interpersonal cruelty that go on during fraternity initiations and hazings are no different than the behaviors in the other three examples. It should be remembered that fraternity initiations still lead to deaths (*New York Times,* January 20, 1975; September 19, 1975). Humans have a willingness, as individuals, to inflict severe pain on others. The underlying commonality in the examples is that individuals are willing to watch a person endure pain over which they have some control. And, they are unwilling to challenge the authority which gives them the "right" to administer the pain. The social system in which individuals find themselves, then, determines the degree of the interpersonal cruelty. Orientation programs meant to prepare people for life and work in another culture do not deal with this aspect of human behavior. To deal fully with issues in intercultural relations, however, such behavior must be given a great deal of attention rather than ignored for fear of offending people.

To complicate matters, individuals are capable of great kindnesses and other forms of altruistic behavior (Wispe, 1972). They volunteer large amounts of free time in behalf of others; they risk injury in going to the aid of others in danger; they give up food and possessions so that the more needy will not go hungry and will have protection from the elements.

I agree with Klineberg (1964) that the capacities for cruelty and altruism are both part of the human personality. The relation between the capacities is not completely understood, although the in-group (altruism more likely) vs. out-group (cruelty easier) is a helpful starting point. A major determinant seems to be the situational pressures people perceive. These will be covered in chapter 6.

THE AUTHORITARIAN PERSONALITY SYNDROME

Combining some concepts from the present chapter and the discussion of people's history, there is a type of parent-child relation which fosters prejudicial attitudes, too-frequent and facile stereotypes, and interpersonal cruelty. Research on these interrelationships was first brought together in the classic book by Adorno, Frenkel-Brunswick, Levinson, and Sanford (1950). The findings reported here are those that have stood up well in research done subsequent to 1950 and are not simply artifacts of the measurement problems which troubled the earlier research (as reviewed by Ashmore, 1970; Christie & Cook, 1958).

Authoritorian parental behaviors include harsh physical punishment, expressions of love dependent upon the child's "good" behavior, an easily recognized and enforced hierarchy of authority within the family, and an importance placed on status. Parents comfortable with these norms in family life have a number of traits which lead to the rejection of out-groups. They tend to be rigid; are comfortable with the conventional values of their culture and are not willing to accept deviation from them; reject any feelings which might be construed as a weakness, such as fear; show little self-insight, and so have difficulties examining their feelings regarding aggression and sex; and are comfortable with interpersonal relations defined according to clear status markers (Harding et al., 1969). The relation among parental attitudes/behaviors and personality development/attitude formation in children is summarized by the term, "authoritarian personality" syndrome. In the words of the original set of researchers (Adorno et al., 1950):

> . . . the political, economic, and social convictions of an individual often form a broad and coherent pattern, as if bound together by a "mentality" or "spirit," and . . . this pattern is an expression of deep-lying trends in his personality [p. 1].

Children tend to adopt these personality traits and the accompanying prejudices. An important point to remember is that people who behave according to this syndrome enjoy both using their authority and accepting it from others who are higher in status. The expression of authority on both levels leads to an unquestioning acceptance of the commands a person receives and passes on, and an acceptance of the system which permits the communication of orders. If the orders are unreasonable, there is no readily available means to challenge them. In originally contemplating their work, Adorno and his colleagues (1950) wanted to gain insight into German atrocities toward the Jewish people during World War II. They asked whether or not there is a personality syndrome which would lead to an unquestioning acceptance of the hideous orders to remove Jews from their homes, transport them like cattle, starve them, use selected women as prostitutes, and put six million of them to death. They answered their own question in the affirmative. However, there is absolutely no evidence that the authoritarian personality syndrome is found in only a few parts of the world. Manifestations of it can be seen in many countries, as can the atrocities which the syndrome encourages. Treatment of blacks and American Indians in the United States has already been reviewed. The 1960s and 1970s have given us the examples of My Lai, Vietnam; Northern Ireland; Uganda; Cyprus; Iran; and Afghanistan. I am not, of course, saying that the authoritarian personality syndrome causes these tragedies. I am suggesting, however, that these travesties can take place when people accept a syndrome which does not permit a questioning of unreasonable orders, which readily allows the rejection of out-groups, and which uses out-groups as negative models who are in their place because they are not "like us."

AN INTRODUCTION TO TRAITS AND SKILLS

The previous discussion of prejudice and stereotypes has allowed an analysis of those manifestations of people's attitudes which are most relevant to cross-cultural interaction. In addition to attitudes, people's traits and skills play a prominent part in determining the amount and type of interaction. Traits refer to qualities of an individual which, in everyday language, answer the question: "What sort of personality does (s)he have?" In answering, people use words like "sociable," "hard-working," "dependent upon others," and so forth. Traits are products of a person's unique experiences within a culture and they are possibly also affected by an individual's heredity. They are central to the research area known as "individual differences." Personality traits are, in a sense, a complement to the study of culture. "Culture" refers to those aspects of a society that all its members share, are familiar with, and pass on to the next generation. "Personality" refers to unique combinations of traits (which all people in a culture know about, even though a given trait does not describe a given person) which differentiate individuals within a culture. For instance, even though all people in a culture may be exposed to a capitalistic economy, some will be more oriented than others to the individual accumulation of personal wealth.

A current controversial topic in personality research centers around the consistency of traits. Are traits consistent across different stages of a person's life and across different situations in which people find themselves (Mischel, 1973)? If the answer is "no," then traits are less than perfect predictors of behavior. Everyday experience gives examples which bear upon the question. The same people *do* behave differently at a formal embassy reception than at a student's post-dissertation defense get-together which is held over a keg of beer. Or, the same person may behave in a deferential manner in a situation involving unfamiliar people, but in a dominating manner in a situation where all others are well known. Do these differences suggest that traits are not useful as units of analysis? Should the interaction of traits and situations be the focus of inquiry? Should traits be described in somewhat more specific terms, e.g., dominant in familiar but not unfamiliar situations? These are the current research questions asked by specialists (Endler & Magnusson, 1976). Well replicated research findings add fuel to the controversy. The relation between measured personality traits and observable behavior is not strong: the research findings can be summarized in terms of correlations in the range of plus or minus .30 (Mischel, 1973). The cross-cultural contact literature leads to the same conclusion: measured traits are not a good predictor of success in a long-term sojourn. The greatest amount of research on this topic has been done with Peace Corps volunteers (Guthrie & Zektick, 1967; Harris, 1977).

My opinions about the usefulness of traits will be discussed in the next few paragraphs. Some of my conclusions are based on relevant cross-cultural research and others are based on methodological considerations.[4] First, the existence of traits which transcend multiple (not necessarily all) situations will be assumed. In other words, I accept the proposition that people are affiliative, or power seeking, or achievement-motivated in a number of situations. Recent research and analysis has been based on the development of personality measures which are meant to analyze the special nature of cross-cultural contact (Ruben & Kealey, 1979). The problem with published, standardized personality tests is that because they were designed to measure traits in a variety of situations, there is the risk that they may not be effective in the unfamiliar and unique cross-cultural settings already described. In addition, standardized tests were developed in one country. In chapter 2, the development of valued behaviors and traits within a culture and how these are often irrelevant for cross-cultural interaction were discussed. Consequently, the standardized tests (designed to measure such traits) may be ineffective in the analysis of cross-cultural contact for this additional reason. My second assumption, then, is that research based on personality measures specifically designed for cross-cultural studies should be reviewed.

However, an acceptance of the usefulness of traits does not rule out the possibility that situational pressures have an effect. People actively seek out information about the situations in which they find themselves, and use that information in deciding how to behave. In effect, they combine information about the situation with knowledge about their own traits. The resulting behavior, then, is a combination of traits and situations. A rigid, intolerant person, for instance, may behave politely toward out-group members in church but would not even consider entertaining them at home. Or, overseas businessmen may be very individualistic in the United States but may work through groups on assignment to Japan, realizing the importance of groups in the latter country. In these two examples, the fact that situational variables have an effect does not mean that rigidity/intolerance and individualism are nonexistent. My third assumption, then, is that the study of the interaction between individuals and situations is a fruitful approach.

Finally, my fourth assumption is that traits are *not* the only concepts which should be analyzed. Like all other concepts in the behavioral and social sciences, they have limited usefulness. If a knowledge of traits alone provided adequate understanding of cross-cultural contact, this book would be concerned solely with them. The fact that concepts dealing with history, groups, situations, tasks, and organizations also must be covered means that knowledge of traits has to be combined with knowledge of the other categories. Likewise, knowledge about any *one* of the other categories provides an incomplete picture since information about other concepts has not been integrated.

The usefulness of traits has demanded this lengthy introduction because it is a hotly debated topic at the present time. The importance of analyzing skills is not so controversial. Skills refer to those behaviors, or patterns of behavior, which are acquired through experience, apprenticeship, study, or training. Second-language skills necessary for deep involvement in another culture are obvious examples. Task-related skills, and knowledge of appropriate behavior in a given culture are others. The basic difference between traits and skills is that the latter are more learnable. Because of the modifier "more," one researcher's list of traits will overlap with another's list of skills. For instance, most behavioral scientists consider "need for achievement" a trait, although McClelland and Winter (1971) present evidence that it can be developed in people (given time and effort) much like a skill. My list of skills will be based largely on the sorts of behaviors I have seen successfully modified in orientation and training programs designed to prepare people to live and work in another culture (Brislin & Pedersen, 1976).

THE IMPORTANCE OF TRAITS IN
CROSS-CULTURAL CONTACT

A few concepts have been analyzed in detail by investigators involved in *different* forms of cross-cultural contact. One is the traits people have *prior* to their cross-cultural contact experience which lead to a successful or unsuccessful sojourn. Research or analysis by highly experienced participants has been carried out with respect to: members of the Peace Corps (Benson, 1978; J. Harris, 1973); overseas students (Klein, 1977; Spaulding & Flack, 1976); children in recently desegregated schools (Stephan & Rosenfield, 1978); diplomats (Nicolson, 1960; Thayer, 1959); overseas businessmen (Cleveland, Mangone, & Adams, 1960); technical assistance advisers (Ruben & Kealey, 1979); researchers who work in cultures other than their own (Finley, 1979; Kashoki, 1978); and immigrants (Taft, 1977).

In the majority of these studies, an analysis of the cross-cultural sojourn was made together with an analysis of traits which would affect the sojourn. As discussed previously, this is probably a better approach than the practice of interrelating scores on existing personality trait inventories with aspects of a sojourn. Traits which have a relation to different types of sojourns have been analyzed by others, notably Taft (1977) and Hammer, Gudykunst, and Wiseman (1978). The organization of the diverse findings which follows is not drawn directly from them, although it is influenced by their work. Traits can be grouped according to six types: indicators of a tolerant personality, the strength of one's personality, relations with other people, intelligence, task orientation, and potential for benefiting from the novel cross-cultural experience.

The meaning of "success" in a sojourn must be defined. A three-part analysis based on, but not directly borrowed from, the work of Ruben and Kealey (1979) will be used. An assumption behind this analysis is that in almost all sojourns the participants have a specific goal above and beyond the pleasure to be gained from traveling. Foreign students want to obtain a degree; technical assistance advisers have projects to complete; immigrants must establish homes and find jobs. The three aspects are:

- psychological adjustment, which refers to general feelings of well being, satisfaction with the sojourn, feelings of comfort in the new environment (allowing a reasonable period of time to cope with the stresses which

accompany any major change in life), and feelings that the time devoted to the sojourn is well spent.
• interaction effectiveness, defined as the ability to develop warm, cordial relations with people from other cultures; participation with host-culture people in their everyday activities; development of a respect for those activities; and feelings *on the part of the host-country people* that the sojourner values the interaction and activities.
• task effectiveness, defined as the ability to fulfill one's goals in the host country, to overcome obstacles which block the attainment of goals, and (where relevant) to assure that there will be follow up on projects after a person's sojourn is completed.

Some research projects have been designed with enough care to specify when a certain trait is related to only one or two of these aspects. Where possible, such findings will be reviewed.

Tolerant personality traits

In discussing prejudice, stereotypes, and authoritarianism, the opposite of the tolerant personality was described. In contrast to the rigid person who has many prejudices and who thinks in terms of very simple stereotypes, some people are tolerant of others different from themselves and are able to appreciate the fact that others have a legitimate point of view. The traits leading to tolerance include multidimensionality, or the ability to use several factors in thinking about an issue. For instance, some people can integrate information on the economic, social, and political ramifications of a proposal, while others can think in terms of only one.

Analysis of the trait called "openness-closedness" of stereotypes (Harvey, Hunt, & Schroder, 1961) begins with two assumptions: all people use stereotypes, but some people are more aware than others that any stereotype should be open to modification. According to Scott (1965):

> An image is "closed" to the extent that the person regards the attributes included in it as completely defining the object. . . . The more "open" the image, the more is the person willing to entertain the possibility that essential features of the object have not yet been recognized by him, and that these additional attributes would reveal new similarities and differences in relation to other objects [p. 81].

Tolerance for ambiguity means an ability to think about problems and issues even though all facts and probable effects of decisions are not known. A person who has this trait realizes that, especially with respect to important problems, decisions cannot be made which will address all ramifications and please everyone. Still, the person is able to live and work in such an ambiguous situation. Applied specifically to life and work in another culture, Ruben and Kealey (1979) suggest that:

> The ability to react to new and ambiguous situations with minimal discomfort has long been thought to be an important asset when adjusting to a new culture. Excessive discomfort resulting from being placed in a new or different environment—or from finding the familiar environment altered in some critical ways—can lead to confusion, frustration, and interpersonal hostility. Some people seem better able than others to adapt well in new environments and adjust quickly to the demands of a changing milieu [p. 19].

With respect to the work of diplomats, Nicolson (1960) indicates that international-oriented policymaking is an uncertain venture, and the people involved must be able to tolerate the fact that not all decisions they make will be the best ones possible (because of conflicting pressures). In my experience, another ambiguity is that since people sometimes do not see the effects of their decisions for years to come, they receive little feedback so that they might improve their decision-making skills.

The common sense, everyday concept of "patience" is also relevant. Especially in cross-cultural settings where the (not completely understood) feelings of others and procedures of bureaucracies have to be taken into account, things do not get accomplished as quickly as one might like. Patience is a manifestation of tolerance for the intricacies of other cultures.

An interesting trait related to tolerance is "category width" (Detweiler, 1980). As previously discussed in the context of stereotypes, people group the millions of stimuli to which they are exposed into categories. However, some people have wider categories than others; for instance, turtles, grasshoppers, dogs, cattle, horses, and legumes might be potential sources of food for a broad categorizer, but not for a narrow categorizer.

> The width of one's categories would seem to be particularly crucial in an intercultural context. It is hypothesized that the narrow categorizer would categorize (i.e., give meaning to) behavior narrowly using his/her own cultural values and would be unaccepting of the idea that a behavior or situation might have different meanings. Little variation would be allowable within the "normal" or desirable categories—hence negative inferences and inappropriate expectations would be common. Contrarily, it is hypothesized that the broad categorizer would [give meaning to] behavior in a more general way and would be more accepting of the idea that a behavior or situation might have different meanings. . . . Since intercultural interaction is typified by cues which have new or different meaning, the width of one's categories should have a major impact on the process [Detweiler, 1980].

The tolerant personality, then, can use many dimensions in thinking about an issue; realizes that stereotypes should be open to change; is comfortable even though all aspects of a situation are not perfectly clear; is patient in dealing with others; and takes a broad point of view when thinking about concepts, probably realizing that narrow conceptualizations can lead to an imposition of one's own values. These traits relate to various aspects of a sojourn. Detweiler found that broad categorizers were less likely to terminate prematurely their Peace Corps assignment on a remote island in the Pacific. Apparently, broad categorizers found it easier to accept the many everyday differences between the United States and the Pacific island. Ruben and Kealey (1979) found that technical assistance advisers who scored highly on a measure of tolerance for ambiguity were successful in their task assignment. The assignment involved both establishing projects *and* sharing needed skills with host country personnel. Most likely, then, the tolerance for ambiguity measure was related to a *combination* of task effectiveness and interaction effectiveness.

Strength of personality

First used by J. Harris (1973) in his analysis of Peace Corps volunteers, "strength of personality" may seem like a quaint term in an era which has contributed the "I'm O.K., you're O.K., we're all O.K." approach to popular thinking about people's traits. The most central part of personality strength, positive self-concept or self-esteem, has been analyzed by many researchers (e.g., Hare, 1977; Klein, 1977; Stephan & Rosenfield, 1978). Self-concept refers to positive feelings about oneself, a sense of worthiness, and feelings that one deserves to be respected by others. In cross-cultural contact, people will inevitably meet stresses and strains as they attempt to complete their work and to form relationships with others. People with low self-esteem have a tendency to blame difficulties on themselves too frequently and with too much vigor: "Since I am not worthy of respect, people are ignoring me or are purposefully making things hard for me."

In analyzing the changes of white junior high school students stemming from their experiences in a desegregated school, Stephan and Rosenfield (1978) found that students who showed an increase in self-esteem developed more favorable attitudes toward black-white interaction. Further, Ehrlich (1973) concluded that people with high self-esteem have more positive feelings toward *many* out-groups than do people with lower self-esteem. In an analysis of legislative voting records, Robinson and Snyder (1965) cited the unpublished work of Hermann (1963) and concluded that United States congressmen with a high degree of personal security have more internationally oriented voting records.

Other personality strength factors are related to self-esteem. In cross-cultural research, many host country scholars are somewhat deferent in putting forth their own ideas (Kashoki, 1978; Kumar, 1979b) in the company of sojourners from countries with a long tradition of research (e.g., United States, Western European nations). My guess is that this is partially due to problems of self-esteem and that efforts to increase feelings of worth toward people's original ideas will alleviate the difficulties. On a sojourn, many people feel that they are representative of their country and that slights toward their country are also insults to them. I have found this to be especially true at the East-West Center, an organization which hosts sojourners from Asian and Pacific nations. This is a hard point to communicate to citizens of the United States since they *don't* often view themselves as representatives. However, forgetting the point can cause serious difficulties. In one of the first studies of sojourners, Lambert and Bressler (1956) identified the issue and its potential negative effects. They found that people from India enjoyed their sojourn less if they felt that their country was not accorded a high degree of status.

In analyzing the work of diplomats, Nicolson (1960) and Thayer (1959) indicated that integrity, loyalty, and courage are key factors in representing one's country during international negotiations. Very recently, I had the uncomfortable experience of hearing horselaughs upon present-ing these ideas to potential foreign service officers. I suppose that the reception was due to colorful recent events involving dishonesty which fill a percentage of the column inches and television time of the media. Unfortunately, such vivid stories (see chapter 4) are more interesting than the day-to-day integrity of thousands of dedicated diplomats and their staffs. The prime negotiating tool of diplomats is their reputation for honesty. A person may be able to cajole one favorable treaty through devious means, but chicanery eventually becomes public and a second opportunity for negotiation becomes impossible (Nicolson, 1960). The work of diplomats also demands an interesting mix of loyalty and courage. Loyalty to one's country demands that key information be communicated clearly and promptly. Courage demands that the information be com-municated even though recipients may not want to hear it (e.g., the in-formation does not mesh well with conventional wisdom, or it is politically controversial). Courageous diplomats put their thoughts forward even at the risk of danger to their careers. A solid sense of self-esteem is a key ingredient in such decisions.

Relations with other people

A number of personality traits affect the ease by which sojourners can establish warm, cordial relations with host country people. The most frequently cited trait is empathy (Finley, 1979; Ruben, 1977; Stagner, 1977; Taft, 1977; White, 1965). Empathetic people are able to understand the feelings of others, or to place themselves in the position of the others and to sense how they are reacting. The old American Indian advice to "walk in their moccasins to understand them" is also a helpful example. In cross-cultural settings, it is especially useful for an individual to understand how (s)he is being perceived by others. Empathetic people have an advantage since they can judge from the others' point of view and can modify their own behavior accordingly. Empathetic people are also able to personalize knowledge. Much cross-cultural contact involves communicating with people who do not share the same types of information. People who personalize knowledge are able to judge the amount of information the other person possesses and are able to communicate their knowledge through appropriate examples based on the background which the other person brings to the learning situation. In my experience, much goodwill is fostered through this type of communication.

Sociability is another trait. Some people are warm, make others feel comfortable in their presence through choice of topics for conversation, are able to communicate an interest in people, and are considerate enough to listen to others rather than to talk at them. Related traits are respect for others with different points of view, an interest in topics to which a person may not have been exposed but which are important to others, a willingness to sacrifice one's own desires in favor of someone else's (selflessness), and an ability to be nonjudgmental when observing unfamiliar behaviors or hearing different opinions. In cross-cultural contact situations, sojourners are unfamiliar with many aspects of the culture and are groping for appropriate behaviors. If host country people act in a judgmental manner (you're right or wrong!) toward the gropings, sojourners become self-conscious and uncomfortable. Even if the judgments might be perceived by the originator as positive ("You speak our language without an accent!"), they can be interpreted as patronizing.

Although they are unpleasant to consider, a number of factors over which an individual has little control affect the quantity and quality of interpersonal relations. In a general sense, these factors, which are trivial in any deep, long-lasting relationship, are influential in "first impressions" since they are valued by host society members in early stages of interaction. In the United States, for instance, people who are physically attractive, have money and are willing to spend it, and who have a pleasant patter are likely to have more opportunities than people who lack these social entrées. In other countries, the factors would include the power and status of one's patron, political affiliation, and luck in the genetic draw, also known as one's "family."

Role shifting is a trait which contributes to the successful completion of tasks, especially when close collaboration with host country nationals is required. The most extensive analysis of its effects has been concerned with the work of researchers in unfamiliar cultures (Brislin, 1979b; Finley, 1979). Many sojourners who have money for research come from economically well-developed countries. When working in countries where research budgets are small, there is a tendency to place host-country scholars in subordinate positions. Subsequently, understandable tensions arise between the hosts and visitors. A person with the ability to shift roles can, for instance, be a leader or follower depending upon the situation. If the research project demands interviewing, even a recognized expert on survey techniques would be wise to listen to host country researchers. Norms as to when question-asking and question-answering are appropriate vary tremendously from culture to culture (Frey, 1970). In addition to obtaining necessary information, listening carefully to people also accords them status.

Intelligence

Most behavioral scientists agree that intelligence stems from a combination of genetic and environmental influences, although disagreement exists regarding the relative strength of each class of factors (Nurcombe, 1974). For the purposes of this book, no absolute definition of intelligence can be given since different demands are made on people in different cultures (Berry, 1972). However, one aspect of cross-cultural contact is that problems have to be solved and adjustments made during an individual's sojourn. An aspect of intelligence which seems useful is the ability to solve problems, the exact form of which a person has not seen before. Only this sense of the broad concept "intelligence" will be used in the following discussion.

Although Ehrlich (1973, p. 149) analyzed three reasons why intelligence is useful in lessening the probability of prejudice, his analysis can be more generally applied. People with a high degree of intelligence may resist acquiring certain stereotypes because they see no use for them. That is, people reject the stereotypes because they have no function in problem solving. Second, intelligent people will be able to look beneath the surface and see the nontruths which are especially prevalent in prejudicial stereotypes. Third, the intelligent individual may be better able to see similarities among people. This last possibility stems from the principle that seeing similarities is a more demanding intellectual task than seeing differences. Perceiving similarities leads to a basis for interaction; perceiving differences leads to a basis for out-group rejection. In a study of children's views of people from other nations, Lambert and Klineberg (1967) concluded:

. . . for ten of the eleven cultures examined, the 6-year-olds view foreign peoples as different from their own group reliably more frequently than do 10- or 14-year-olds. This general age trend corresponds to one aspect of the normal intellectual development of children. . . .

It may be therefore that similarities are basically more difficult for young children to grasp than differences, in the sense that contrasting or coordinate categories of thought are more easily used than are superordinate ones [p. 185].

Since a high degree of intelligence in the work of diplomats, technical assistance workers, foreign students, or any person completing an important task is obviously useful, no further discussion seems necessary.

Task orientation

Many researchers have pointed out that some people are especially good at maintaining positive social relations and some are good at completing tasks competently and on schedule (Fiedler, 1967). While the ability to do one does not rule out the ability to do the other, some people are quite clearly better at maintaining relations than completing tasks, and vice versa. The reader may want to think about answers to these questions:

1. If you wanted help on your income tax computations, who would you ask?
2. If you needed help on a report due within two weeks, who would you select to prepare it?
3. If you were to have a cocktail party, who is the first person you would invite?
4. If an out-of-town business client was visiting your firm, who would you select to entertain the guest after work hours?

Are the people listed for (1) and (2) different from those listed for (3) and (4)? If so, the task-social distinction is reflected.

Task-oriented people identify with their work and judge the success of their sojourn in large part on whether or not they successfully completed their assigned projects. They are precise in their efforts (Finley, 1979) which helps others who might follow since precision leads to clarity. They have industry (Nicolson, 1960), an old-fashioned term which connotes diligence and persistent effort applied to overcoming difficulties. They are reliable (Benson, 1978), a trait which refers to their dependability. In the words of a Peace Corps administrator I once interviewed, "You can ask certain people to do something once, they agree, and you just know that the job will get done."

The task aspect of people's sojourns will be covered in more detail in chapters 8 and 9. A major finding should be previewed now, however. The people who are most skillful at task completion may not be the best in developing interpersonal relations. Too much of a task orientation can interfere with the interpersonal: an individual may want to be successful at work regardless of others' feelings. In a study of technical assistance advisers (Ruben & Kealey, 1979), people's task and social skills had a complex relationship. Some people completed their projects but were not able to share their knowledge with host-country co-workers. The consequent danger is that there will not be needed follow-up in the areas of maintenance and expansion. Other advisers, perhaps not as technically skilled, completed their work and were able to transfer their skills to co-workers. Ruben and Kealey (1979) made recommendations for the selection of future advisers:

> Perhaps individuals who are excessively task-oriented, for example, are not the best candidates to work with nationals in developing countries, [even though this orientation] would be ideal for positions in more technologically-oriented cultures.[5]

Potential for benefit

Some people are more open than others to benefiting from a cross-cultural experience. Two factors are openness to change itself and the ability to perceive and use feedback (Taft, 1977). Some people realize that they may have to change to gain maximum benefit (e.g., learning about other people, expanding one's point of view). Old, habitual patterns of behavior might not be functional in another culture whose members do not value "foreign practices." People able to perceive feedback from hosts are likely to obtain the necessary information so that they can modify their behavior as appropriate. Often, norms of politeness in other cultures mean that feedback is not obvious. Slight shrugs of the shoulders, gaze aversion, lack of follow-up to a perceived commitment, and absence of an invitation to a desired event are more common than a direct, "Your behavior is inappropriate!" Since some people do not perceive such feedback as a message, they have no basis for an informed decision about possible changes.

The opposite of "openness to change" is a rigid belief that a person's life has been fine up to now and that no additional learning is necessary. Such people have no motive to interact with host country nationals and, instead, establish support groups among fellow nationals who are also sojourning abroad. When there are many sojourners from the same country, designated areas develop (e.g., little America) in which people live, socialize, and buy all necessities of life.

THE IMPORTANCE OF SKILLS IN CROSS-CULTURAL CONTACT

There are several differences between traits and skills. Traits, which are products of a person's unique heredity and experience, are acquired without formal training. Skills are more modifiable, and are usually acquired through some sort of formal education, such as a training program, or through long experience on a job. Many skills can be introduced during orientation programs designed to prepare people for life and work overseas. To be sure, traits and skills overlap. The skill shown by use of a second language, for instance, is easier to acquire for intelligent people who have a desire for interaction with native speakers of that language (Lambert & Tucker, 1972). There is no intention to draw a hard and fast line between traits and skills. Use of the two categories, however, is an aid in thinking about cross-cultural contact. Especially helpful studies and reviews include those by Benson (1978) among Peace Corps volunteers and overseas military personnel; and by Hammer, Gudykunst, and Wiseman (1978) among American students who have studied in an overseas university. Skills appear to be of six types: knowledge of the subject matter, language, communication skills, taking advantage of opportunities, ability to use traits in a given culture, and ability to complete one's task in a given culture.

Knowledge of subject matter

People put a tremendous amount of energy into learning job-related skills and/or complex subject matter, and many identify themselves with others who share the same level of ability. This sharing is one reason for the existence of interest groups which allow people to come together and to learn about recent developments in their fields of specialization. A common finding from research carried out in the Peace Corps was that volunteers who were able to use their skills were happier during their sojourn and were rated as more successful by supervisors (Ezekiel, 1968; Textor, 1966a). For instance, volunteers who had specialized in teaching English as a second language had a more successful sojourn if they were able to use those skills. In contrast, English teachers who spent their sojourn on community development projects were less successful. One of the major changes in the Peace Corps since its inception in 1961 is that specialists are currently being recruited and selected to a much greater extent. The "classic" early 1960s image (almost a cliché/stereotype) of the young liberal arts major assigned to the development of sanitary facilities is no longer operative in the early 1980s. No one reason can explain the change, but a contributing factor was surely the lesser satisfaction by people who did not use their specialty.

Language

Many people take a sojourn without the ability to speak the host-country language. Some have a successful experience *if* they interact with hosts who speak the sojourner's language or if they can afford interpreters. Even in these cases, however, people put limits on the benefits they can gain from their sojourn. They can only interact with a limited number of others, and these are unrepresentative of all host-country members. A more abstract point is that people unable to use a certain language are not exposed to important concepts and ways of thinking about the world which are reflected in that language. This lacuna means that limits are put on the development of interpersonal relations.

Many observers have noted that efforts to speak another language, even imperfectly, are appreciated by host-country people. Efforts to learn show concern and interest. There may be a few exceptions: the stereotype of French people not wanting to hear their language spoken less than perfectly may have a grain of truth. It may be, however, that the French appreciate the effort made to learn their language as long as they don't have to listen to the effort's products.

Common sense indicates that, in some cases, a lack of language skills can be debilitating. Immigrants are especially vulnerable to discrimination if they do not have language skills enabling them to learn about and to express their rights guaranteed by law. Based on work done among Puerto Ricans living in New York City, Murillo-Rohde (1976) indicated that a lack of facility in the English language leads to discrimination by the white American majority, thereby thwarting their upward mobility. In chapter 2, the concept that people give respect to those who "fight back" was discussed. If people don't have the language skills to fight back, or to advance themselves, there is a dangerous tendency for the majority group to conclude that the immigrants deserve their current place in society.

Communication skills

A number of skills relate to the ability to communicate with others from different backgrounds. Again, such skills are directly related to traits:

empathetic people, for instance, will develop communication skills faster and easier than nonempathetic people. My assumption, however, is that the skills to be discussed are modifiable: if people want to improve, they can do so.

A basic necessity in communication is to understand the meaning of any utterance emitted by others. In a cross-cultural context, understanding is harder to achieve since people bring different backgrounds, needs, and values to the communication setting. Assume that people are involved in negotiations concerning the future status of a program involving cross-cultural contact. Rogers (1952; also Sawyer & Guetzkow, 1965) suggests that, to insure there is communication rather than a series of misunderstood speeches, a person should state the position of the other to the latter individual's satisfaction. Negotiations would not continue until both parties agreed that the meaning of a given statement was communicated. Undoubtedly, the ability to perceive meaning accurately in cross-cultural communication is a skill which improves with practice.

Another desideratum in communication is "conversational currency." In early encounters between people, there are a number of topics which are considered proper subject matter for conversation. These differ from culture to culture. In one, a proper topic might be the weather; in another, the progress of key rugby teams. People with "conversational currency" have an easier time interacting with others since there are not likely to be inappropriately long periods of silence during initial encounters. Orientation programs designed for people about to live in a given culture can include treatments on what topics are considered proper for discussion as well as information about each topic.

Much communication is based on nonverbal cues. In recent years an extensive research literature analyzing nonverbal behavior has developed, greatly influenced by the work of Edward Hall (1959; 1966). Behaviors that have been analyzed include the use of space, gestures, clothing, amount of eye contact, facial displays, positioning of the body during interaction with others, control of body odors, and timing of input into conversations. Well-known examples of specific behaviors include the greater proximity which Latin Americans maintain during conversations, a distance which North Americans find uncomfortable. Another is the amount of touching among males in some Southeast Asian countries, a sign of friendship there but a sign of (traditionally) deviant behavior in North America. Unfortunately, the literature is so vast that it cannot be adequately reviewed in one book. Several recent reviews have appeared (Harper, Wiens & Matarazzo, 1978; LaFrance & Mayo, 1978) which provide a guide to important nonverbal behaviors which might be incorporated into orientation programs. A number of researchers have concluded that knowledge of other nonverbal styles, and the ability to use them as appropriate, hastens the development of positive interpersonal relationships. LaFrance and Mayo (1978) conclude:

> Nonverbal styles that are similar to one's own group are perceived as pleasing, while dissimilar styles receive less positive response. As an example of this, a recent study found that white subjects were much more favorable toward a Black when she spoke standard English than when she spoke in Black dialect (Bishop, 1976). . . . One way of coping with communication style differences is to use the other style. Subcultural groups learn to communicate with the dominant culture by code switching and this includes being bi-nonverbal as well as being bilingual. For example, Cuban Americans engage in one conversation style when speaking Spanish and switch to another when conversing in English (Gallois & Markel, 1975) [p. 84].

Taking advantage of opportunities

Much can be learned during a sojourn, but some people are better than others at taking advantage of available opportunities. A drawback for many people is that they do not know how to get around in other countries: they are not mobile. Fortunately, information about transportation, curfews, and opportunities for movement out of tourist traps can be incorporated into orientation programs. In addition, anxieties about moving from familiar, secure, but unrepresentative places in a culture can be treated (Higginbotham, in Brislin, 1979a). As specialists in intercultural communication ponder abstract concepts such as the relation of prejudices to traits, they easily forget that people sojourning in another culture are stymied in their desire to learn if they don't have the necessary skills to move about as they wish. In some cases, instruction in host-country mobility and other important skills can have astounding consequences. Harding and Looney (1977) found that many displaced adolescents from Vietnam, while at refugee camps in California, were depressed, suffered from sleep loss, were antisocial, and withdrew from contact with others. When instruction in mobility skills (e.g., how to use the bus system) and occupational activities was provided, symptoms significantly decreased.

Another important skill is finding enjoyable, reinforcing activities in the host country. If people like the folk music of their own country, for instance, they might enjoy learning about the music of the host country. In the orientation programs he designed, K. David (1972) incorporated training in this skill. His method involved asking people to list the activities they found enjoyable in their own country, and to then study the culture hosting their sojourn. People would then indicate how they might go about following up their interests in the host country. In a similar exercise, people listed what they disliked and then studied the host culture to see how these could be avoided. Benson (1978) feels that the ability to find reinforcing activities is predictive of a successful sojourn:

> Adjusted individuals have been shown to participate in a wide variety of behaviors. [In efforts to aid sojourners] attention should be given to determining both the transfer of U.S. activities to the host country and the willingness to participate in activities distinctive to the host country [p. 33].

In my own experience, adult sojourners unable to participate in host country experiences sometimes turn to alcohol as a solace. Many sojourns take place in remote settings: the familiar stimulations of symphonies, discos, libraries, and television are unavailable. Some people bury themselves in their work and this may be adjustive for them. Others become interested in aspects of the host culture such as its sports, dance, or medicine, sometimes acquiring the expertise of a professional anthropologist. Still others develop close interpersonal relations which live far beyond the date ending the sojourn. But without activities to fill time not spent in sleeping, the probability of dysfunctional adaptation is increased.

Ability to use traits in a given culture

A person may have traits which are predictive of a successful sojourn, such as empathy, but may not know how to use the traits in a given culture. The knowledge necessary to use traits demands very specific information about another culture. For instance, Gumperz (1978) analyzed in detail a conversation between a female from Great Britain and an immigrant to England who had previously lived in India and who was a native speaker of Punjabi. The conversation dealt with the Indian's wish to enroll in a college course; but the host, a native speaker of English, had to report that the course was designed for certain categories of people and that the Indian did not fit into any of the categories. The discussion became heated and resulted in ill feelings. During a subsequent interview, the host mentioned that she could not understand what led the visitor to express agreement and disagreement, and she felt that he was rude at times. There was no question concerning the host's empathy or desire to help. The problem was an inability to use these traits during the conversation. The host interpreted "yes" and "no" as agreement and disagreement, while the Indian meant them as conversation fillers: "I heard you." The host interpreted shouting as rudeness, while the sojourner was simply using increased pitch and loudness as a way of indicating a desire to speak. The Indian's use of these concepts reflects a direct application of cues from the

Punjabi language. To use her desirable traits, then, the host would have to know these conventions. Gumperz (1978) feels that these conversational cues are not easily taught. He gives a hint on how teaching can be improved, however, when he indicates that the cues "are best learned through practice in actual interaction where errors can be good-naturedly corrected, such as peer or family relations [p. 30]." People assigned to help sojourners could strive to create orientation programs with a supportive atmosphere in which such good-natured correction of mistakes could take place.

Ability to complete one's task in a given culture

Arguments regarding the ability to complete one's task in a specific culture are similar to those regarding the use of traits. Specific knowledge is necessary so that people skillful at task completion in their own culture can achieve the same level of success in another. Peace Corps workers have had difficulties applying their knowledge in other countries. In the Philippines (Szanton, 1966), American teachers would suggest methods by which the curriculum could be improved during meetings with Filipino colleagues. The Americans would then be surprised that, even though there seemed to be agreement, the suggestions never received a follow-up. In this case, Americans were unsuccessful because they were unaware of the tremendous sensitivity Filipinos have concerning embarrassing others in public. Any suggestion from an American was taken as an implied criticism of the Filipino currently in charge of the curriculum, hence other Filipinos would ignore it as soon as possible so that their colleague would not be embarrassed. But, since they did not want to embarrass their American colleagues, they were polite during the time the suggestion was put forward. The practice of initial politeness and subsequent inattention toward suggestions was the solution which embarrassed the fewest people. Americans were more effective when they learned such norms and made their suggestions in accordance with them. For instance, they might quietly work with the curriculum designers "behind the scenes." Eventually, the designers themselves might introduce the ideas at faculty meetings.

SUMMARY AND CONCLUSIONS

Before beginning a sojourn, people bring a set of attitudes, traits, and skills which have an influence on the success or failure of their stay in another country. Attitudes refer to people's feelings, beliefs, and readiness for action with respect to various social objects. Prejudice refers to those attitudes directed at out-groups that are both negative and based on prevailing "wisdom" within a culture rather than first-hand contact. Prejudices serve a number of functions for people, such as (a) solidifying the in-group; (b) allowing people to blame problems on others; (c) expressing values, as in the acceptance of one true God or one great race; and (d) organizing their knowledge about the world. Prejudices can be expressed in a variety of forms, from vicious red-neck racism through more symbolic feelings of interference with familiar life styles, to deeply felt disapproval of behaviors which out-group members practice. An understanding of forms and functions is necessary since, too often, prejudice is examined with a very narrow perspective. It is commonly viewed as hostile, rigid, overt, and name-calling behavior (red-neck racism) which could be changed if people would come into contact and learn more about each other (knowledge function). This terrible oversimplification has plagued organized attempts to reduce prejudice.

Stereotypes are generalizations which involve thoughts about a group of people and comments about the group. Stereotypes are a form of categorization and are always used since people cannot respond to every individual piece of information. Rather, people form categories which allow an organization and a reduction of the isolated elements. Since stereotypes are categories, and since categories are basic to thinking, stereotypes will never cease to exist. However, people can be made aware of the tendency to stereotype, can demand more information before forming a category, and can be aware that stereotypes should always be open to modification (W. Scott, 1965) as more information becomes available.

If children are exposed to an authoritarian style of discipline from their parents, they are likely to develop intense prejudicial attitudes and to use many stereotypes which are not open to modification. The parental behaviors involve harsh discipline and insistence on a rigid, unquestioned hierarchy of authority within the family. People socialized into such families enjoy using authority as well as accepting it from others of higher status. The combination of intense prejudice and acceptance of authority means that when programs aimed at hostility toward out-groups are organized (e.g., massacres of innocents during wartime; the Holocaust; kidnapping of embassy employees), people are unlikely to question the order that they must participate.

A knowledge of prejudice, stereotypes, and the authoritarian syndrome provides a backdrop to the positive traits and skills which are desirable in cross-cultural contact. Traits are acquired by a person over a lifetime and are traditionally considered as enduring characteristics which distinguish one individual's personality from another's. Skills are the products of formal study. Researchers have been especially active in the analysis of how traits and skills relate to success in a wide variety of cross-cultural experiences. Success refers to psychological feelings of well-being, the establishment of cordial relations with host-country people, and the completion of one's task. Traits leading to success include:

1. tolerance toward points of view different from one's own.
2. strength of personality, largely centered around a positive self-concept.
3. ability to develop relations with others, which involves empathy, respect, and a willingness to shift between such roles as "leader" and "follower."
4. intelligence, which leads to a search for information beyond that easily available in stereotypes.
5. task orientation, or a desire to complete one's work. People who are extremely task oriented, however, may not be effective in situations demanding the involvement of host-country colleagues.
6. potential for benefit, which includes a willingness to receive and to use feedback from others so that the benefits of the sojourn can be maximized.

Skills leading to success include:

1. knowledge of subject matter, which has an obvious relation to task completion. Sojourners able to use their skills are likely to be more successful than colleagues assigned to tasks which do not involve their specialties.
2. language skills, which lead to increased opportunities for cross-cultural interaction.
3. communication skills, including knowledge of topics commonly discussed and key nonverbal behaviors which carry as much (or more) information as the spoken or written word.
4. taking advantage of opportunities, based on a knowledge of how to move about in another culture and an ability to pursue one's interests.
5. ability to use traits, which demands knowledge of everyday behavior in another culture. A person cannot be empathetic, for instance, without understanding how people show their feelings.
6. ability to complete one's task, again based on very specific knowledge of another culture. Tasks are completed within bureaucracies according to well-developed procedures which involve the sensitivities of many people.

Some administrators involved in selecting and training people for a sojourn take these findings into account. No one potential sojourner possesses all these desirable traits and skills, but the analysis of specific assignments can indicate which ones are critical. Ruben and Kealey

(1979), for instance, suggest that sojourners who are expected to teach skills to host-country colleagues must combine a task orientation with an interest in and respect for others. For people who are open to change and willing to consider their strengths and weaknesses without feeling threatened, the lists of traits and skills provide a good basis for self-examination.

Sojourners use their attitudes, traits, and skills in seeking out information about the host culture and in making judgments about their own behavior and that of others. The assumption is that people are not passive recipients of information that they receive by chance. Rather, they actively seek out information and interpret it according to their individual needs. For instance, they might pay attention to certain information if it is consonant with their attitudes or if it is useful in the application of their skills. The implications of this individualistic, active processing of information is considered in the next chapter.

NOTES

1. I emphasize the necessity of dealing directly with this issue because, recently, I have found difficulty in encouraging multicultural groups to discuss stereotypes since the link between prejudice and stereotypes has become so strong. Stereotypes have acquired a distasteful status (Bosmajian, 1974).

2. It is important to note that not all people from the southern United States are racists.

3. Interestingly, Freedman and Fraser (1966) found that obtaining small commitments from people allowed petitioners a "foot in the door" for the later commitment of larger resources. Worth-while research could examine the conditions under which the tokenism versus foot-in-door result is obtained. For instance, Dutton's request involved resource commitment to a clear out-group while Freedman and Fraser's did not.

4. People's everyday encounters with others certainly influence judgments about traits. In recent years, I have had the interesting experience of putting down journal articles which questioned the usefulness of traits, and then interacting with people I haven't seen in a few years. Those people seem to have the same stable traits they had years ago; and, they seem to show the same traits at work, in their homes, during their vacations, and so forth. Probably, a few traits are especially important for the understanding of a given individual, while a different set of a few traits are relevant to the understanding of another. Personality tests yielding scores which supposedly summarize profiles on many traits, however, may mask the importance of that smaller number.

5. Complexity is added to this issue when host countries expect and demand high levels of technical competence. In some cases, host country leaders want technical assistance and have no interest in human relations skills. A more precise statement, then, is that there should be a match between host country requests and assistance from sojourners. Ruben and Kealey (1979) seem to feel that the person with at least some social sensitivity will be more effective in the majority of cases.

4

An Individual's Thought
and Attribution Processes

A person brings attitudes, traits, and skills to a sojourn, and the success of the cross-cultural experience is influenced by them. In addition, a person brings an ability to think about the sojourn, to process information, to reflect upon experiences, and to respond after due consideration of alternatives. In recent years, psychologists have made advances in understanding people's thought processes, and they have taken as a starting point that people actively engage in thinking about their world. This contrasts with an older view that people are mere passive recipients of information who behave in ways which can be predicted by outsiders who have control over the information. Put another way, the traditional research approach has looked at S-R bonds: stimuli leading to responses. The newer approach looks at S-O-R bonds: stimuli are organized by people (or more generally, organisms), processed by them, and this mental activity contributes to the decision regarding their response. Very often, the processing of stimuli varies from person to person based on differences in attitudes, traits, skills, and interests. Many researchers interested in cross-cultural studies have adopted this approach (Brewer, 1979; Triandis, 1977a). To be sure, the processing of information is not always rational and the eventual response does not always appear desirable. Two people might respond to the same stimuli very differently: tolerant acceptance for one and hostile discrimination for the other.

A major assumption guiding the research and analysis to be reviewed is that people's thinking about out-groups and their members is not fundamentally different from any sort of thinking. Hence, an understanding of people's thinking, called "cognitive processes" by researchers, should be an aid in understanding cross-cultural interaction. For instance, Brewer (1977) feels that:

... the phenomena associated with intergroup perception can be adequately accounted for as natural consequences of a more general cog-

72

nitive process by which human beings structure, simplify, and give meaning to their physical and social environment [p. 24].

This point of view received a major impetus in Gordon Allport's (1954) classic analysis of prejudice (see also Bruner, Goodnow, & Austin, 1956; Taylor, Fiske, Etcoff, and Ruderman, 1978). It was reviewed in chapter 3 where arguments were made positing that stereotypes are one type of category which people use to organize, simplify, and respond to the massive amount of stimulation they receive each day.

The way in which people categorize will be covered in this chapter: examples will be based on how people react to cross-cultural contact. In addition, the consequences of categorization will be covered. What happens once an individual element, such as a person from another culture, is placed in a category? The discussion will deal with how categorization *increases* the amount of information available to a person, and how information is processed once a category is formed.

Categories are used in making judgments about one's own behavior and that of others. People want to know why others behave in a certain way, and they also feel the need to examine their own behavior, especially in unfamiliar situations. Researchers have been very active in studying how people judge themselves and others, and they have used the term "attributions" to refer to the thought processes involved (e.g., E. Jones, 1979; E. Jones, Kanouse, Kelley, Nisbett, Valins, & Weiner, 1972; Kelley, 1972). Put another way, researchers have been active in analyzing how and why people make attributions concerning the causes of various behaviors they perceive. Analyses have included the behaviors involved in cross-cultural contact (e.g., Malpass & Salancik, 1977).

Finally, this chapter will include a discussion on how cross-cultural contact can affect people's categorization and attribution processes. Consideration will be given to the possible broadening of categories and to the development of more complex cognitive processes, including greater sophistication in attributions about the causes of behavior. This treatment of how cross-cultural experiences can affect cognitive processes should complement the following analysis of how initial categorization affects cross-cultural interaction.

THE FORMATION OF CATEGORIES

People group individual stimuli into different categories for a number of reasons, eight of which will be reviewed here. Some of the reasons have clear functions, as in the reduction of highly complex information to manageable proportions or the maintenance of one's self-esteem. The reasons apply to the categorization of all sorts of elements: examples here will be drawn from people's reactions to information relevant to the cross-cultural contact in which they might participate or which they might avoid.

Conspicuous differences

The old saying, "first impressions are lasting," is often true if those first impressions are based on easily seen similarities and differences. The baselines against which judgments of similarity and difference are made, of course, are one's own set of traits, habits, physical features, and so forth. Similarities and differences are of central importance in forming the categories of in-group and out-group. LeVine (1965) summarized a great deal of research:

> . . . the images of an out-group that adults pass on to children are affected by the amount of direct experience the adults have had with members of the out-group and by the amount of conspicuous difference (in physical features, dress, language, and occupational specialization) between the in-group and the out-group [p. 49].

Triandis, Loh, and Levin (1966) found that the additional features of political beliefs and quality of a person's spoken language affected categorization. The "quality of language" feature is a good example of how one's own standards of what is similar and different are influential. Linguists are extremely hesitant to say that one person's use of a language is a "standard" which might be the basis for judging another person's language use. There is no doubt, however, that in everyday life people engage in such judgments: whether a person has a "pleasant" accent, uses "proper" grammar, or has an "educated" vocabulary. Based on the work of Ehrlich (1973), absolute and relative size of an out-group as well as cultural distinctiveness would be added. Various examples of the latter have been given throughout this book: cultural differences in the adaptation of modern technology or in the size of the typical family living in the same household are two other examples of distinctive information which could lead to placement in one category versus another.

Familiarity

Decisions regarding what is similar and different are based on both conspicuous criteria, discussed immediately above, and the degree of deviation from what is familiar. An individual gains satisfaction from the use of familiar categories since they lead to a predictable environment in which everyday needs can be satisfied. Because of their familiarity, a person is likely to use the categories in a variety of situations. According to Scott (1958):

> A particular frame of reference which the individual applies success- fully to adjustment within the realm of familiar events may, because of its rewarding character, find strong emotional attachment within the per- son and hence be applied indiscriminately to the interpretation of new events concerning which information is inadequate [p. 14].

For instance, people consider certain jobs acceptable and others unac- ceptable with respect to such criteria as cleanliness, opportunities for ad- vancement, and so forth. When out-group members find employment, they become "acceptable" or "unacceptable" according to the familiar job categorization. When societal norms prevent the out-group members from acquiring higher-status jobs, stereotypes about the capabilities of out- groups are likely to form (Hoffman, 1977).

Functional importance

Some categories are formed because they help people adjust to their world. Group labels such as ethnicity, sex, or religion are categories of this type. These boundaries which *might* separate groups are not rigid. Rather, they can be manipulated at will to serve one's needs and to attain one's goals. In one instance, it might be best to employ one's ethnic heritage, as when traveling to a country where one's ancestors were born. Many people, of course, can draw upon more than one such label because of the differing heritages of their grandparents and great-grandparents. In other instances, it may be best to draw upon one's religion if, for instance, people with whom interaction is necessary are deeply committed to the same religion. In most cases, such fluidity is not cold, callous, and scheming. It simply represents the application of one's thinking to best meet the de- mands of a specific situation. In applying the trait called "personalizing knowledge" while instructing others (chapter 2), for instance, people might draw from common experiences based on shared membership in the same national or gender group. At times, application of these fluid cate- gories will seem questionable. College scholarships are often available to people from a certain ethnic background. Some applicants discover their ethnic heritage after hearing about the availability of such desired com- modities.

Similar categories are used to maintain social distance among people. The function, then, is to control interaction among people according to well-established societal norms. Children are taught that certain people should be avoided on the basis of their occupation, income, class, family, or nationality (chapter 1). When interaction is not allowed among people from such well-defined categories, there is never an opportunity to acquire information about these people which might lead to a change in categorization.

Maximizing relative advantage of the in-group

The tendency to think in terms of one's in-group and out-groups is very strong. Turner (1975; also Brewer, 1979) has hypothesized that people have a strong desire to seek out ways which might maximize the advantage of their in-group relative to their out-groups. Interestingly, there is *not necessarily* a derogation of the out-group as long as the in-group is raised in one's own thinking. This motivated search leads to the manipulation of categories which put the in-group in a favorable light. If the in-group consistently loses in games of skill, then it still might have the perceived advantage of being more sportsmanlike. If the in-group shares its resources, it may be seen as generous; if the out-group does so, it may be seen as an example of irresponsibility (Brewer, 1979).

Eventually, people develop the habit of making judgments in terms of what is acceptable and beneficial to their in-group. This leads to ethnocentric thinking, the practice of centering judgments around standards which are acceptable in one's own culture. One benefit of a sojourn is that people can see how different approaches are functional in the solution of problems and how familiar methods from the sojourner's own culture might not be as effective.

Projection and externalization

Categories are formed to reduce one's troubles by projecting reasons for difficulties on an out-group. Projection, in this case, refers to a transfer of one's negative feelings from the in-group to an out-group. In a perceptive treatment of projection, Sanford (1973) wrote that an acceptable way of handling one's negative feelings

> . . . is to participate vicariously in the aggression of officials against people who have been [categorized] as morally low—usually, today, people of color. . . . This "fantasy," however, is not acted out except under special conditions, the most important of which are emotional excitement sufficient to impair the functioning of the higher mental processes and a barrage of propaganda depicting the people who become victims as less than human [p. 70].

To Sanford's criteria of who is an acceptable target for aggression, the lack of retaliation potential should be added. Out-group members who are unlikely to join together in protest, or who are prevented from doing so through institutionalized discrimination, are safe targets. Recently, the "target potential" of blacks in the United States has changed because of legal sanctions which make projection by whites less easy and safe.

Externalizing is a concept related to projections. Tajfel (1969) found that people externalize their own behavior to their in-group. That is, an individual expects in-group members to think and behave in the same way as (s)he does. This tendency is manifested when people talk in terms of how a certain group "thinks" when, in actuality, they have never spoken to in-group members about the issues under consideration. The tendency extends to thinking about other countries (Janis & Smith, 1965). If a person is suspicious of other people, then (s)he is likely to suspect the intentions of and motives behind the policies of other countries. Or, if people are generally happy and satisfied with their lives, they are likely to think in positive terms about other countries rather than in such negative terms as "hostile" or "backward."

Belief similarity

The most extensive study of ethnocentrism carried out by a single team of researchers led to both an extensive literature review (LeVine and Campbell, 1972) and to an empirical analysis (Brewer and Campbell, 1976). The main conclusion of the empirical research was that perceived similarity was the best predictor of positive attitudes. People who perceived an out-group as similar to their in-group were likely to think positively about the out-group and to welcome interaction with its members (Rokeach, 1960). Another basis of perceived similarity is a sense of common fate or shared experience (Rabbie and Horwitz, 1969; M. E. Smith, 1978). Similarity provides a basis for seeking common ground. Shared opinions give people a basis for discussion and, consequently, an opportunity to learn more about each other. Nothing is more damaging to the development of interpersonal relations than statements like, "We cannot agree! We have nothing in common—there is no basis for further discussion!"

In addition, if a person perceives that others have similar beliefs, (s)he is reinforced. Since one aspect of people's self-image is that they have a reasonable set of opinions about the world, they enjoy learning that those opinions and beliefs are shared. Further, the tendency to externalize suggests that if a person holds certain views, then others must be worthwhile if they are intelligent and perceptive enough to hold those same views.

Desirable and undesirable qualities

Some categories are based on qualities of people which lead to desirable and undesirable images. The in-group bias has already been discussed:

people are socialized to believe in the superiority of the groups of which they are members. Brewer (1979) has analyzed the content of the evaluation bias and has concluded that there are desirable qualities that people expect from members of their in-group. These qualities are trustworthiness, honesty, and loyalty. If in-group members share these traits, a person can be confident that group norms will be upheld, such as aid in time of need or accurate information when attempting to solve problems. During cross-cultural contact, misunderstandings occur because manifestations of in-group behavior may not happen as soon as a person might desire. During the first weeks of a sojourn, many people receive a warm welcome: foreign students in the United States often comment on the initial friendliness of Americans. From the Americans' point of view, however, the friendly welcome is simply polite behavior which is not meant as a promise of future interaction. Because of the welcome, the students often expect the Americans to demonstrate the loyalty of in-group members. When the expectation is not confirmed, they become disappointed.

In an analysis of the 123 words most commonly used in people's stereotypes of out-groups, Ehrlich (1973) summarized his research by suggesting that the words can be placed into fourteen categories. By far, the biggest category referred to words which label out-group members as people who should be kept at a distance and not sought out for the development of friendly relations. Examples of the exact words (Ehrlich, 1973, p. 26) are: arrogant, bitter, boastful, cynical, grasping, humorless, pessimistic, prejudiced, reserved, strange, suspicious, and talkative. Note that the tendency to label in-group members in a positive light, and out-group members in a negative manner, means that people are not likely to seek relationships outside their in-group. This is an example of "autistic hostility" (Newcomb, 1947; Newcomb, Turner, & Converse, 1965). An individual dislikes out-group members and so does not interact with them. But since there is no interaction, there is no opportunity to test whether or not the reasons for the ill feelings are warranted.

Salient information

In the late 1970s, "saliency" was a word very commonly used by researchers who discussed categorization and its consequences (Brewer, 1979; Taylor & Fiske, 1978). Saliency refers to the most colorful, or important, or interesting piece of information which confronts people at a specific time and place. Dictionary definitions of "standing out conspicuously, prominent, and striking," are helpful descriptors. Another explanatory device is to view a salient piece of information as overwhelming the situation and, hence, difficult to ignore. When a person is a stranger in another culture, stumbling around and unable to meet everyday needs, one of its members may volunteer assistance. This helpful person is then salient, and the sojourner is likely to generalize about the culture based on early experiences with this host. The potency of salient information helps explain the presence of taxi drivers in so many accounts of cross-cultural experiences. Visitors are tired upon arrival at airports and they usually do not know how to get to their first appointments. So the first host-country person contacted is a taxi driver and (s)he overwhelms the situation and becomes the focus of the visitor's attention.

Many factors contribute to saliency. Taft (1977) relates the concept to people's self-image, suggesting that some information will be more relevant to one person than another because of its appeal to valued aspects of one's personality. A person interested in autonomy, for instance, would be interested in discovering how to go about one's work without being dependent on others. An affiliative person would be interested in finding out places where host country people can be met. Very recent theoretical analyses have placed saliency at the top of a hierarchy of categorization mechanisms. Others, such as the seven reviewed in previous paragraphs, are considered as factors which might be salient in a certain situation. Brewer (1979) takes this position:

> Any of the situational factors found to be associated with enhancement of in-group bias can be subsumed under the effect of salience of the distinction between in-group and out-group. Factors such as interdependence, intergroup similarity, and shared fate all affect the probability that a respondent will be aware of a relevant basis for categorization into groups, which in turn determines the amount of in-group bias that is evidenced [p. 319].

It may be that an understanding of cross-cultural interaction is better achieved by viewing saliency as a high-level concept rather than as one of many bases for categorization. A decision about this can only be made on the basis of future research and by the experiences of practitioners who apply both approaches in the selection, training, and evaluation of sojourners.

THE CONSEQUENCES OF CATEGORIZATION

After people put discrete elements into categories, they use the categories in their thinking and tend to ignore the individual elements. Among category members, similarities are emphasized and differences tend to be ignored. Although there is certainly overlap in the sorts of ways in which people use the categories they adopt or create, exposition is aided by giving labels to types of thinking and by providing examples drawn from the experiences of sojourners.

Confirmation of thinking

If people are confronted by evidence which supports an already existing stereotype, they are likely to give more credence to that evidence than is deserved (Feldman & Hilterman, 1977, p. 37). In turn, the stereotype becomes stronger because the additional information is perceived as supporting it. Further, if certain elements belong to a category, such as "sportsmanlike" for the British, less information is needed about that trait to confirm the stereotype (Campbell, 1967). As with much thinking which involves stereotypical categories, a circular process develops. An example can be found in Kidder's (1977) analysis of American sojourners in India. The sheer numbers of Indians willing to work as servants for Americans means that a category of "fit for servants" will develop. When many applicants apply for a single opening, the stereotype is reinforced and the concept of "job-appropriateness" is given more credence than it deserves. Because the stereotype is held by influential Americans who might employ Indians in other work settings, the out-group members are not offered jobs involving greater responsibility and larger salaries. Consequently, they are seen in the role of servant, which further reinforces the category.

Increasing the available information

Once categories of people are formed, individuals met for the first time are likely to be put into one of the categories. In turn, new information becomes available since all "knowledge" from the category can be applied. Sojourners face this problem when they interact with host nationals. Once a person is labeled as an American, information is available from the corresponding stereotype, such as, "politically naive, likely to impose own point of view, materialistic, ambitious, and industrious." If the person is in a high-level position and earns a good salary, host country people wonder about C.I.A. connections so often that this feature has become part of the American stereotype. Hosts then behave according to the stereotype, not the individual qualities of the sojourner. One argument for the advisability of longer sojourns is that time is necessary for close interpersonal relationships to be established which might overcome the stereotype. Given time, hosts might react to individuals instead of categories; but, too often, a person's sojourn ends at about the time a close relationship has developed.

People use categories in making inferences about relevant traits because it is such an easy way of thinking. Summarizing an interesting research program on the use of stereotypes in predicting behavior, McCauley and Stitt (1978) wrote: "Perhaps stereotype predictions from category to trait are generally easier than predictions from trait to category [p. 933]." Almost all researchers are uncomfortable in using examples of stereotypes because of their possible misuse, but it is hard to communicate certain ideas without examples, such as the following. Knowing only that a person is studious and academically oriented, few people would assign the category of "Jewish religion and/or ethnic group." Knowing only the category of ethnicity, on the other hand, many people readily use the trait of studiousness in thinking about the Jewish individuals they meet.

Minimizing in-group differences; maximizing out-group differences

Once categories of in-group and out-group members are formed, people minimize differences within their group and maximize the differences between themselves and out-group members (Taylor et al., 1978). Sojourners tend to see themselves as a reasonable group of people who want only the best for themselves and others. The hosts, however, are perceived as being a cliquish and standoffish group which makes no attempt to welcome newcomers. In more abstract terms, differences among in-group members are seen as miniscule, and people behave as if one in-group member could speak for all others. Differences between in-group and out-group members become exaggerated. The position of the average out-group member, also seen as perfectly representative of the group, is perceived as more extreme than it really is. This phenomenon has been investigated in analyses of peace negotiations with other countries (White, 1965). Both the United States and the U.S.S.R. build nuclear weapons of similar capability. There is a tendency for people in the United States to view their missiles as defensive and to view themselves as peace loving. Russia's weapons are seen as offensive, and its citizens are viewed as hostile. The Russians make the predictable mirror image reversal in their own thinking. Especially in times of conflict, these differing perceptions can escalate so that aggressive action seems to be the most "reasonable" course of action.

Integrating new information

Categories are formed through experience, and in their initial development people can be very open, nonjudgmental, and might strive to take individual differences among people into account. Still, the pressures to categorize are so strong that generalizations about the individual elements are bound to form. Once established, new information is integrated into the category *without* the thought and concern which marked the initial formulation (Scott, 1965). Foreign student advisers almost inevitably succumb to this phenomenon. When working with the first group of sojourners from a certain country, they may treat students as individuals. But certain problems are likely to be experienced by several members of the first wave and so the whole group may be categorized. When a second group arrives, they will be labeled on the basis of the first. There is no insidiousness at work. Foreign student advisers work hard and have to use many resources to complete their duties, to look after the continuing program of the first group while orienting the second, and to fulfill their other roles as spouse, parent, and scholar. Since pressures of time force oversimplification of thinking, categories are formed.

As a specific example, assume that the foreign student adviser is expected to counsel sojourners on academic grading procedures. Three members of the first group run into problems involving plagiarism, a common occurrence among students from countries in which essay writing is not expected in school (Marr, 1979). Consequently, the adviser incorporates material on the plagiarism problem in orientation programs for the second group. Is the adviser misusing the experiences of three people, or is (s)he wisely using the best available information to form a category which will guide the treatment of future students?

The phenomenon of initial category formation and subsequent judgments also affects the work of cross-cultural researchers. The first wave of researchers working in another country is often welcomed since there is the belief that well-educated people can provide various types of help. If sojourners from that group are interested only in advancing their own careers and make no effort to contribute to the culture in some way, difficulties arise. The politeness of host-country people often means that the offending researchers will not be confronted with their errors. Instead, the next group will not be welcomed as warmly and sometimes will be denied permission to enter the culture. The categorization of people in this way means that researchers pay for the sins of their predecessors (Brislin, 1979b).

The principle of information integration has been applied to the thinking of major political figures. Based on a content analysis of the speeches and writings of John Foster Dulles, Holsti (1962) demonstrated that the former secretary of state had an image of the U.S.S.R. which included the descriptors "hostile," "aggressive," and "dynamic." Messages from Russia, whether firm or conciliatory, were integrated into this image. Rigid images of this sort force people into a rut out of which creative, innovative solutions are less likely to emerge.

Linking one's own and other cultures

In discussing two reasons for categorization, familiarity and projection/
externalization, a major use of categories was introduced. Categories provide a link between one's own culture and others in which a person might
sojourn. The dangers are that people will use unfamiliar categories in inappropriate places and might impose their own-culture categories on situations where host-country conceptualizations are far superior.

Recently, a number of researchers interested in cross-cultural interaction have given this problem a good deal of attention (Gudykunst, Hammer, & Wiseman, 1977; Malpass & Salancik, 1977). A promising approach
is to treat the problem in orientation programs by developing categories
which cut across one's own culture and those of other cultures. If people
could do this, they might be able to develop what is called an "intercultural perspective."

> This perspective is a psychological frame which aids the trainees in better
> understanding the unfamiliar situations that are encountered in a foreign
> culture. The psychological viewpoint is neither from the trainees' own
> culture nor from the host country. Rather, this perspective acts as the
> facilitating "psychological link" between the trainees' own cultural per-
> spective (i.e., assumptions, values, patterns of thought, learned behaviors,
> etc.) and the perspective of another culture. It is hypothesized that this
> intercultural perspective facilitates effective functioning in another cul-
> ture [Gudykunst, Hammer, & Wiseman, 1977, p. 106].

A number of approaches have been used to develop an intercultural perspective. The most successful, in my observations, has been use of the
emic-etic distinction, originally formulated for the design of cross-cultural
research projections (Berry, 1969; M. Harris, 1976).

If there is a piece of jargon which cross-cultural research specialists use,
at the risk of shutting off communication with the uninitiated, it is "emics
and etics." Any noncommunication is unfortunate since the terms summarize a very important conceptual and analytical tool (Brislin, 1976a;
Irwin, Klein, Engle, Yarbrough, & Nerlove, 1977). Before explaining the
concept, however, a problem which can be analyzed with the help of this
analytical tool will be posed. Then emics and etics will be introduced in
their abstract form, and subsequently applied to this specific problem
which is based on difficulties faced by a team of technical assistance advisers.

The problem involves drought and starvation in East Africa (Talbot,
1972). A group of European consultants recommended that development
projects be established to increase water availability and grasslands for the

Masai, an East African culture whose members had long been involved in raising cattle. Instead of leading to more healthy herds of cattle and better grazing areas, the development projects led to starvation for the cattle and eventually for some of the Masai. How can this be explained? The concepts of emics and etics are useful for such an analysis.

Emics and etics refer to the two goals of cross-cultural research. One is to document principles which are valid in all cultures and to establish theoretical frameworks useful in comparing human behavior in various cultures. This is the "etic" goal, and the term comes from phonetic analysis. In linguistics, a phonetic system is one which documents and analyzes all meaningful sounds which are present in all languages and integrates them into a general framework. The other goal of cross-cultural research is to document valid principles of behavior within any one culture, with attention given to what the people themselves value as important and what is familiar to them. Such an analysis has to reject the importation and imposition of frameworks from outside a culture since, by definition, a researcher cannot gain insight into emics by using foreign tools. The tools must be indigenous. This latter type of thinking constitutes an emic analysis, and the term comes from phonemics. In linguistics, a phonemic analysis documents sounds meaningful in a specific language.

An example from linguistics may be helpful. A phonetic system will have to include an initial "ng" sound, an initial "l" sound, and an initial "r" sound since these are important in at least one of the world's languages. In addition, these sounds can be integrated into a general framework based on such hierarchical concepts as activation of vocal chords and parts of the mouth used in making the sounds. An English phonemic system will have the "l" and "r" sounds, but not the initial "ng" sounds since the latter is not a part of the English language. The Japanese language does not have two phonemes, one for "l" and one for "r," a fact which leads to ethnic jokes when Americans and Japanese come into contact. English speakers have to put special effort into learning the initial "ng" sound, a task which was faced by many Peace Corps volunteers assigned to Pacific island cultures. Japanese studying in the United States have to work hard on the l-r distinction, as most teachers of English as a second language will testify. The "metaphor" of emics and etics for the analysis of cross-cultural interaction contains the elements drawn from work in linguistics: what is present and absent, what is meaningful, what has to be given special attention since it is common in one system but not another, and what can be systematized into integrative frameworks.

Cross-cultural researchers have attempted to deal with both emics and etics in their research: applications to the experiences of sojourners will be emphasized here. In orientation programs, sojourners would be encouraged to start their thinking by examining concepts which may have cross-cultural validity. In addition, they would be asked to keep in mind that not all aspects of those concepts will be the same in one's own country compared to the host country.

Returning to the example from the experiences of technical assistance advisers working in East Africa, Talbot (1972) analyzed the concept "uses and care of cattle" from the perspective of the Masai and from the perspective of people from Europe and North America in charge of rangeland development. Members of both cultures have similar conceptualizations about several core connotations, and these are the proposed etics: provision of milk, fertilizer, and demands placed on humans for the care of cattle. But, in addition to this etic core, there are differences which can be called the emics within each group.

North America, Europe Emics	*Masai Emics*
cattle for meat	cattle not primarily used for meat
cattle raised for sale	cattle not generally raised for sale
grazing over a large area	grazing in small areas (to protect from predators)
emphasis on quality as much as quantity	emphasis on quantity
other signs of wealth and prestige available besides cattle	cattle are a major sign of wealth and prestige
experience with conservation	always a struggle to maintain limited herds, so no opportunity to think about conservation when large numbers of cattle are present

The emphasis on quantity was a major problem in the rangeland development projects. Prior to European contact, since natural conditions such as droughts and fires effectively limited the size of herds, the intelligent practice was to always have as many cattle as possible. But when water and grasslands became more common after development, the Masai norm of "desirability of quantity," without a self-imposed norm of "desirability of limitations for the purpose of conservation" led to herds of unreasonable size. The cattle then overgrazed and destroyed the available rangeland. In turn, cattle died for lack of food and the Masai themselves were faced with starvation. This case is frequently cited as an example of failure of technology (rangeland development) due to ignorance of a human variable (norm of quantity).

In using such cases to encourage the development on an intercultural perspective among sojourners, the facilitator suggests a thought process which might be used when interacting in another culture. Sojourners would seek out those culture-common aspects of a concept (etics) since these provide a link between their own experience and the experience of host country people. But there is an explicit warning that this step is not sufficient. Sojourners must also seek out information on how aspects of the concept may be different in one culture compared to another (emics). A combination of the two categories, culture-common and culture-specific, is more likely to provide accurate information. An example introduced in chapter 1 can be reexamined here. In comparing the meaning of in-group and out-group for Greeks and Americans, the culture-common aspect refers to acceptance and rejection of people. The culture-specific aspect adds that for Greeks, but not Americans, the in-group consists of visitors to one's country. Unless both emics and etics are understood, sojourners will be uncomfortable in the company of Greeks.

If sojourners develop an intercultural perspective in terms of emics and etics, they will be able to meet reality "head-on." Rather than the frequent throwing up of arms, coupled with complaints that concepts mean different things in different cultures, sojourners can accept this fact as reality and then deal with it directly.

Avoiding stress

In thinking about complex problems, people who use categories experience less discomfort and stress. Using categories provides a means of organizing relevant issues, even though the categories might not be particularly accurate. Here, the relationship is in the direction of category use leading to a decrease in stress. The opposite direction is also important to consider. The use of people's familiar categories increases when they are under stress. As Pruitt (1965) explains it:

> . . . people tend to become rigid and repetitive under stress. They think up fewer new alternatives and are, therefore, more likely to persist in old, maladaptive approaches. Experimenters (for example, Driver, 1962) have also found that dimensionality of thinking reduces under stress, in other words, that individual objects (in Driver's thesis, other nations) seem less complicated the greater the stress. In addition, some authors have speculated that stress causes a reduction in the number of consequences considered in evaluating a potential course of action [pp. 395–396].

Relating this work to the specific case of face-to-face contact, Randolph, Landis, and Tzeng (1977) considered the timing of category formation. Sojourners, in the early stages of interaction with host country members, often have unpleasant experiences. A partial explanation is that the sojourners have not developed a set of categories which help provide an explanation for the hosts' behavior. If the experience is particularly stressful, such as the rejection of an offer of friendship, then sojourners are likely to fall back on old ways of responding which were learned in their first culture. Further, they are likely to be more upset at the hosts than is warranted by the rejection. If these ways of responding are unfamiliar to the hosts, misunderstanding is compounded. With pleasant interaction taking place over a period of time long enough to consolidate new categories, however, an isolated stressful event is not taken so seriously. Stress reduction, then, is one positive function of employing categories in thinking.

Encouraging short-term versus long-lasting change

The saliency of information was previously discussed as one basis of category formation. An implicit, if not explicit, goal of almost all sponsored sojourns is that people will develop more favorable attitudes toward the host country. The danger of such change is that it may last for only a short time. Sojourners may develop positive attitudes toward the host country during a sojourn but these may change when they return home. Friends at home may have unfavorable attitudes, and both common sense and the research literature (McGuire, 1969) suggest that returning sojourners will be influenced by the fellow countrymen with whom they interact daily.

Is there any guidance which can be given to program administrators who want to increase the probability of longer-lasting change? In answering this question, common sense and research evidence might lead to different conclusions. One approach is to emphasize the new experiences of sojourners and to provide for an easy transition period through the provision of housing, opportunities for pleasant interaction with others, and an orientation to daily life and work. The other approach is to remind sojourners of their own most salient basis for categorization, their nationality, and to encourage them to think about the relevance of their sojourn to life in their own country. Based on the analysis of Janis and Smith (1965, p. 203), such thinking would give people "the opportunity to resolve or adapt [themselves] to the conflict" between their experiences in the host country and the probable reactions of people in their home country. Evidence for this proposition comes from the work of Lesser and Peters (1957). After World War II, sojourners from Germany participated in programs, held in the United States, designed to increase their technical skills. Sojourners who kept their German citizenship salient in their thinking developed more long-lasting and positive attitudes *toward the United States* than sojourners who fit comfortably into American life and did not relate their experiences to work in Germany. Keeping nationality salient took the form of asking critical and difficult questions of program administrators concerning such topics as German-American relations and the development of postwar Germany. Put another way, when sojourners in the United States dealt with the difficult questions, they prepared themselves for their return to Germany. Colleagues in Germany were likely to pose the sorts of questions the sojourners had already learned to handle.

In my experience, this principle is not often applied. Another implicit, if not explicit, goal of sponsored sojourns is to develop favorable face-to-face relations among people who come into contact. This is a laudable objective. To implement it, administrators often smooth over difficulties, try to discourage controversial topics in conversations so that feelings are not hurt, and generally emphasize the positive while ignoring the negative. The danger is that long-lasting positive attitudes may be sacrificed even though the short-term goal of smooth interpersonal relations during the sojourn is achieved. It may be possible to combine the two desirable goals. In the early stages of a sojourn, administrators might do all they can to make transition easy. Eventually, participants will feel settled in their new environment and will be comfortable wtih each other. At this point, administrators can encourage sojourners to consider controversial issues and unpleasant possibilities. Orientation programs held during this stage might include treatments of how sojourners can deal with controversial topics in such a way that dangers to the development of interpersonal relations are minimized. If sojourners are subsequently willing and able to deal with controversy, especially the difficulties of relating their host country experiences to work in their own country, administrators can consider such behavior as one criterion of a successful program.

The indiscriminate use of some categories

Certain categories are so central to a person's thinking that they will be used again and again. Further, they are extremely resistant to change. Racial and ethnic categories are examples. These are sometimes so strong that any piece of information can be integrated into them. Allport (1954) gave examples from the categories held by anti-Semitic individuals. A person might say that Jewish people are concerned with money, always trying to get more and keeping it. When confronted with the fact that Jewish people contribute large amounts to charity, the same individual will respond that Jews spread their money around to gain more influence.

Sojourners risk an unsuccessful experience if they indiscriminately use categories of this type. In encouraging sojourners to change attitudes, the basis of the relevant categories must be found. In programs which bring members of various groups together for the development of interpersonal relations and prejudice reduction, Riordan (1978) advises administrators to begin working with people before the actual intergroup contact. In considering black-white interaction, for instance, he believes that white beliefs regarding the lesser competence of blacks are extremely strong and wide-spread. "This status inequality needs to be treated prior to interracial inter-action [p. 166]." No researcher or practitioner who has been involved in these programs will argue that change is easy (chapter 7).

A collection of categories for comparison

Recent research has suggested that people compare new and unfamiliar information to that already summarized by their collection of categories. They search through the categories until they find material which appears to be somewhat similar to the new information. They then make a de-cision on how to behave based on familiar responses associated with the established categories (Janis & Mann, 1977; E. Jones & Davis, 1965). Un-fortunately, people stop when a satisfactory match is made between the new information and the material in memory. They do not continue their search to determine the best possible alternative. Many times, a satisfactory rather than excellent match is all that is possible, given the pressures facing people every day. There is simply not enough time to do a complete search every time new information is received. In selecting advisers for overseas service, for example, an administrator may stop upon finding an indi-vidual with the minimal requirements. Too much time, effort, and money might be necessary to continue the search for a better candidate.

Searching for a satisfactory rather than the single best match is a com-mon method of thinking. It has been analyzed by Jones and Davis (1965) in their studies of how people make judgments about others, and by Janis and Mann (1977) in their analysis of how people make many types of decisions. The most influential work has been done by Herbert Simon (1957a & b) who has been concerned primarily with people's decision making about economic matters. He termed this type of thinking "satis-ficing." Simon's research on decision making was frequently mentioned in journalistic accounts after he was awarded the 1978 Nobel Prize in eco-nomics.

Another recent and important body of research has suggested that peo-ple summarize their categories in terms of a prototype (Rosch, 1977). In this use, a "prototype" means the most representative element in a cate-gory, the one which a person would indicate if asked to choose the "best example" from an array of related elements. Further, the prototype of many categories is an *image* which summarizes a person's thinking, or a *script* (Abelson, 1976) which briefly summarizes character, plot, and out-comes. The latter could also be called a short story. Examples of cate-gories summarized by an image include "physical attractiveness" or "comfortable home." People have an image of a handsome person or a nice place to live and can easily bring these to mind. When faced with new information, they compare people they meet or places in which they might live to those images.

Examples of categories summarized by a script include "proper welcome" and "good co-worker." People have strong opinions regarding what should happen when strangers meet, who should speak first, and what topics might be discussed. People can also summarize their feelings about what constitutes a desirable co-worker by giving plot details, i.e., showing up at a certain time; character descriptors, i.e., age, sex, and traits; and outcomes, i.e., high productivity.[1]

These two principles, the tendency to "satisfice" and to summarize categories through images and scripts, can affect the success of sojourns. People are accustomed to using familiar images and scripts in their own country. It is likely that they will continue to do so during their sojourn. Consider the case of housing: sojourners may look until they are satisfied with a dwelling which matches their image. In stopping their search, they may overlook more interesting housing which would both give insight into the host culture and provide more opportunities for interaction with host country members.

A common charge made of almost all sojourners is that they sometimes impose their own point of view. Knowledge of the principles presented here helps elucidate what actually happens during the alleged imposition. Sojourners judge new experiences in the host country based on their own images and scripts, and they do not go beyond a satisfactory match between the old and the new. They ignore the categories commonly held by host country members as well as the corresponding desirable images and scripts. Consequently, the match, which may merely have been satisfactory rather than excellent in the home country, is likely to be poor in the host country. Examples of imposition are pervasive even among very sophisticated people who have had a great deal of experience in other cultures. I have observed two cases very recently.

A businessman from the United States became upset when a co-worker from another country seemingly did not follow through on a task-related promise. The American became concerned during the month of June, upset in July, and wrote a firm letter in August suggesting that the co-worker might want to withdraw from the project. The co-worker wrote back that the American was imposing his own categories in expecting everyone to work during the summer months. In other countries, professionals in many occupations are expected and encouraged to take long summer vacations.

The second example concerns a disappointing and sometimes demoralizing fact about cross-cultural contact: some desirable sojourns are more readily available to people with money. Study in another country is the clearest example. Some students with large amounts of money are accustomed to ordering servants to attend to their needs. Demands, in a similar condescending tone, are made of low-level public officials, such as office clerks and secretaries. In the early stages of a sojourn, people from this type of background sometimes treat host-country advisers and their secretaries in a similar way. I have had some limited success in mollifying the angry feelings of Americans after their dealings with sojourners who behave in a demanding, condescending manner. The post-interaction discussions center around how different people form categories based on their everyday experiences, and how these categories are used to make decisions about one's behavior. An appeal to the neutral language of categories, with reminders that everyone constantly uses them, helps take the sting away from the negative interpersonal experience. Regrettably, these discussions are not completely effective. Some resentment remains and, consequently, hosts are on their guard when they come into contact with the *next* group of sojourners.

ATTRIBUTION

The uses of categorization are also relevant when the nature of attribution is studied. The analysis could continue as one more entry in a list which summarizes the uses of categories in people's thinking. Research on attribution has been so extensive and has led to so many fresh insights, however, that this important topic deserves a more extensive treatment (E. Jones et al., 1972).

Attribution refers to judgments made about the behavior of others as well as to judgments about one's own behavior. The basic assumption is that people actively seek out explanations for the behavior they observe. Assume that a sojourning businessman has been unable to persuade a host national to invest in a joint venture. The sojourner's judgments (attributions) about the host are likely to take one of two general forms. The first possibility is that a trait could be attributed to the host: (s)he is too conservative or not perceptive enough to see a good opportunity. The second possibility is to make an attribution to the situation. Here, the sojourner might conclude that governmental regulations prevent the host from investing, or that the host has received so many offers from familiar and long-term business associates that further ventures are unwise. Self-attributions also take one of the two forms. A trait attribution might be a realization that one is being too aggressive or too direct in dealings with the host. A situational attribution might be an awareness that one has insufficient access to key information in the host country.

Attribution is an important topic for study since sojourners constantly meet new people in the host country. Sojourners have to establish themselves and they must develop cordial relations with hosts to accomplish their objectives. As discussed previously, the hosts are likely to engage in behaviors which are unfamiliar and which carry different meanings from the sojourner's point of view. Stress develops, and people try to reduce it by seeking out explanations for their feelings. Consequently, sojourners are likely to make many attributions about the behavior of others, and they are also likely to analyze their own behavior to determine if they might be contributing to misunderstandings. A number of factors affect the quality, frequency, and type of attributions.

The vividness of information

Images or scripts which are especially vivid are extremely influential in determining attributions (Kahneman & Tversky, 1973; L. Ross, 1977; Taylor & Fiske, 1978). Vividness refers to sharp, clear images and scripts which command attention.[2] Further, people accept such vivid scripts from others as important input in learning about new situations, often ignoring other information which is packaged in a duller format. Consider this example: a foreign student wants to know whether or not to take a course from Professor X. The student looks into the ratings of teachers published by the campus newspaper and finds this analysis. "Professor X, according to ratings from 200 students, is highly regarded as a teacher and as a person. He carefully prepares relevant and interesting lectures and makes himself easily available for consultations with students." Then, the foreign student happens to get into a conversation with a friend. The latter says, "I took a course from Professor X last year. He was dull, scatterbrained, and never showed up for posted office hours. I'd never take a course from him." What will the foreign student decide? Readers of this example can undoubtedly visualize that many quite reasonable individuals would accept the friend's advice. But, when looked at carefully, people who accept the vivid, personalized script from someone else are ignoring much relevant information. They are ignoring the baseline ratings provided by the 200 students. Instead of considering information from 201 others, the 200 from the ratings plus the friend, the decision maker is using only the single piece of information. The attribution about the professor, then, is likely to be that he is a poor teacher.

Advisers who work with sojourners can use this knowledge by incorporating it into orientation programs. The advisers might recommend that sojourners should consciously seek out a great deal of information before making a decision and that they should not rely on the first piece of interesting input. Sojourners commonly interpret new experiences as vivid since they are not accustomed to the culture in which they are living temporarily. Much will be "different" or "distinct" which is not necessarily "important" or "relevant." Similarly, advisers can point out that sojourners are prone to mistakes if they make lasting generalizations from one or two early but colorful encounters with people from the host country. Sojourners are especially sensitive to interactions with host nationals and any tendency to form lasting impressions from early encounters should be fought.

The trait-situation distinction

When an individual observes another person behave in some way, there is a strong tendency to attribute the behavior to a trait. Situational factors are downplayed. When an individual engages in the same behavior, on the other hand, an attribution to situational factors is much more likely. Suppose an individual observes an immigrant seeking a high status job but failing in attempts to obtain it. The attribution about the immigrant is likely to be trait based: (s)he is underqualified or is not sophisticated enough to handle the job. If the same individual seeks but does not obtain the job, however, the attribution is likely to be situational. The individual might say that the employer already had a candidate in mind and went through the motions of an open search only to satisfy legal requirements. The tendency to underestimate situational factors when observing others is so pervasive that it has been called the "fundamental attribution error" (L. Ross, 1977).

Trait attributions are made because people's behavior is much more visible and salient than the situational factors which may have elicited that behavior. Tremendous amounts of time and effort would be necessary for an outsider to discern the situational pressures faced by another person. For example, suppose a sojourner decides to live in a neighborhood where other fellow countrymen reside. Hosts may make the trait attributions of "not interested in getting to know us." The sojourner, however, may be dealing with situational pressures such as demands from family members, regulations concerning how money can be spent, and directives from the employer demanding proximity to the workplace. The sojourner possesses such knowledge and thus can make situational attributions. There is a readily available language to describe people's traits, such as aggressiveness, dependence, and intelligence, but no widely accepted set of terms for situational descriptions. E. Jones (1979) suggests other reasons:

> The notion that situations can cause action is abstract and derivative, almost metaphoric in its implications. At best, situations capture and direct the energies provided by the organism. Situations are contextual shapers; they vary as more or less potent background conditions but they nevertheless remain part of the background. If we add to these primitive perceptual priorities the likely fact that socialization pressures capitalize

on the importance of taking [people at their word] or listening politely
to others and attending to the content of their remarks, the basis for an
omnipresent attributional bias is perhaps apparent [p. 114].

Combining concepts from research into the in-group/out-group bias
with the fundamental attribution error, Taylor and Jaggi (1974) studied
the self-perceptions of Hindis and their perceptions of the Muslim out-
group. When asked to comment on the same undesirable behavior, such as
a shopkeeper cheating a customer, Hindis attributed negative traits to
Muslims, such as dishonesty. When the behavior was desirable, however,
the attribution was situational: the Muslims must have been closely supervised. When commenting on in-group behavior, the pattern was reversed.
Desirable behavior was attributed to traits, and undesirable behavior was
attributed to situational pressures, such as requirements by others that
the shopkeeper engage in the dishonest practice. These findings can be
summarized in tabular form.

People's Perceptions

	desirable behavior	undesirable behavior
of own in-group	positive traits	pressures of situation
of out-group	pressures of situation	negative traits

Although Katz (1973a) did not use concepts from attribution research
in his perceptive analysis of school achievement among black college students, his findings can be discussed in those terms. Katz feels that a number of factors lead to poor school performance. There is social threat from
the powerful and prestigious white majority and the constant threat of
failure. Both of these factors lead to emotional responses which interfere
with schoolwork. Blacks also see a low probability of success since few of
their numbers seem to achieve the same standard of living as whites. Black
self-attributions are likely to include such situational factors, while white
attributions have traditionally involved negative traits like laziness and
lack of ability. The term "blaming the victim" is often used to describe
the white attribution (J. Jones, 1972): "these other people are responsible
for their troubles." Here, the fundamental attribution error is a mixed
blessing: blacks realize situational factors, but the trait attributions made
by whites displace blame away from the situation they have created. From
an objective point of view, the situational factors are, indeed, influential.
When blacks attribute school performance to situational factors, then,
they protect their self-esteem. Eventually, however, the attribution to
situation breaks down due to a constant barrage of abuse from the powerful majority group. People then begin to believe that they are inferior.

This phenomenon has been called "identification with the views of the aggressor," and it has been used as a partial explanation in analyses of Jewish concentration camp victims during World War II.

Changing the situation leads to changes in behavior. Katz (1973a) has shown that blacks are not threatened by comparisons with white intellectual performance when (1) the anxiety provoking face-to-face confrontation with whites is removed; (2) approval from valued and influential people is contingent upon good performance; and, (3) the standards provide important information against which one's own behavior can be compared. Given these conditions, the standards become goals which are worthy of achieving and blacks are able to meet them. In Katz's work, the blacks were from the Deep South where the only good schools had a whites-only policy. Consequently, information about white standards and possible approval from whites was desirable. Recent developments in the civil rights movement have emphasized that blacks should not be dependent on white approval. Rather, blacks should develop self-confidence, acquire a good education, and take valued positions in society so that future generations will be able to look to fellow blacks for approval and support. When these goals are achieved, black intellectual performance will not be affected by face-to-face competition with whites. Consequently, whites will not have a realistic basis for attributing negative traits to blacks.

The important point is that the situation can be kept so oppressive, as shown in the history of black-white relations, that positive attributions can never develop. The experience of Filipinos in the United States provides another example (Lott, 1976). During the early stages of their immigration, they were categorized as "nationals." This status allowed access to some rights, but the right to vote was not among them. The ambiguous status of "national," coupled with limited participation in American society, prevented Filipinos from assimilating in a manner similar to European immigrants. The attribution of "potential citizen" was discouraged by both laws and social norms. "The lack of citizenship reinforced the role of the [Filipino] as a temporary sojourner . . . eventually returning to the Philippines [Lott, 1976, p. 167]."

Increasing the probability of trait attributions

A number of factors increase people's feelings of confidence in the trait attributions they make after observing the behavior of others (Jones and Davis, 1965; Oskamp, 1970). If a person's actions are socially desirable, there is a *decrease* in the confidence placed in trait attributions. Most people behave in socially desirable ways most of the time: they are polite, courteous, and behave according to society's norms regarding good manners. When people behave in this way, one learns little new information about them. But when people break a socially desirable norm, attributions of rudeness or feistiness are likely. Triandis (1977a), drawing from the research of Kanouse and Hanson (1972), has concluded that negative information is much more influential than positive information. He proposes an interesting set of explanations for this fact:

> People learn through experience to avoid negative outcomes rather than seek positive outcomes, because they learn that the pursuit of highly positive outcomes is illusory. Happiness depends on a high proportion of non-negative outcomes rather than on a few highly positive outcomes. "Keeping out of trouble" is more valuable than "trying to make it big." Thus, any sign of "trouble" is very bad news. . . . negative attributes interfere with enjoyment of positive attributes, while positive attributes seldom reduce the experience of negative ones. For example, fine spices do little to alter the taste of rancid soup [p. 101].

Finally, another explanation based on a vicious circle is relevant. Consider the case of personnel directors. If they pay attention to negative traits, they overlook a candidate's positive aspects. However, after eliminating candidates on the basis of negative traits, they are less likely to receive complaints from department heads which stem from a candidate's faults. Personnel directors, like all people, are much more likely to receive negative feedback, such as complaints, than positive comments. To prevent unpleasant negative feedback, then, the personnel director gives special attention to negative traits.

Sojourners often experience negative evaluations over which they have little control. Socially desirable behaviors differ from culture to culture and different traits are considered negative. The example of in-group and out-group behavior has been used several times. If sojourners in Greece are asked personal questions early in an interview, a socially desirable behavior from a Greek's point of view, they may be offended. The Greek interviewer will sense this and is likely to form a negative trait attribution such as "unfriendly" or "uncooperative."

A second factor influencing trait attributions is the common effect of two behaviors. If the personnel director perceives that the candidate has a good education and steady employment, an attribution of "hard-working and reliable" is probable. Seemingly contradictory behaviors also lead to confidently held attributions. The candidate with a good education but unsteady employment may be labeled "smart but hard to get along with." Knowing what is and is not contradictory behavior, when judging the qualifications of sojourners, is difficult. I have observed American registrars evaluating transcripts from schools in Asia. Letters of recommendation for a candidate may be very favorable, but the transcript may show an academic average of 70 on a scale of 100. The attribution might be that the candidate is a poor student who is being purposefully discharged from the home university with a "kiss off" of good recommendation letters. In actuality, the 70 may be a very good academic average. Some schools grade very strictly, and the in-group joke is that "God gets 100, the professor a 90, the teaching assistant an 80, and the best student a 70." Evaluation of these transcripts is admittedly very difficult since grading procedures vary from country to country and for schools within countries.

Another example is the common complaint made by sojourners about American friendliness. Initial meetings between visitors and hosts are warm, but Americans do not follow through on their seeming friendliness. In later encounters, Americans often seem to forget that they have even met the sojourners. Attributions of "two-faced" and "insincere" are likely.

A third factor is the hedonic relevance of the other person's actions. If the behavior of others leads to rewards or punishments for an individual, attributions centering around the traits of "helpful" or "harmful" follow. The fourth factor, personalism, is closely related. If an individual perceives that the other person's actions were directed at him or her specifically, the corresponding trait attribution is even stronger. Sojourners sometimes perceive personalism when it is not meant by the host. Especially in the early stages of cross-cultural contact, a sojourner knows few hosts. The behavior of the hosts is likely to be so salient that non trait explanations are hard to consider. Further, the normal anxiety associated with adapting to another culture is likely to interfere slightly with clear thinking. In familiar settings, a person is able to examine calmly a number of reasons for behavior. On the other hand, a sojourner is more likely to see negative behavior directed at "me, personally!"

The example of the misunderstanding between the British official and the Indian sojourner was introduced in chapter 3. Because of differing interpretations placed upon certain language cues, misattributions of "hostile" and "unhelpful" were exchanged. Gumperz (1978) decried the tendency to minimize situational factors.

> . . . difficulties are not recognized as communication breakdowns. Judgments, rather, are made on the mistaken assumption that intent is understood. . . . Interethnic situations . . . are conducted within a context of mutual suspicion, or at least without the predisposition to assume cooperation on the part of the other [pp. 29–30].

The assumption that intent is understood, coupled with perceptions of uncooperativeness, leads anxious sojourners to feel that they are being singled out for discriminatory treatment.

Relation to existing stereotypes

As already discussed, behavior somewhat consistent with a stereotype is perceived as more supportive of an existing category than is warranted. Subsequent attributions are likely to be even stronger since two pieces of evidence are at hand: the old category, and the new, confirmatory piece of evidence. But what if the observed behavior clearly breaks a stereotype? For instance, what happens when whites observe blacks in high-status, well-paying professional positions? Combining ideas from a number of sources (Allport, 1954; Feldman & Hilterman, 1977; Taylor & Fiske, 1978), answers to this question are possible if key information about people and situations is known.

People with rigid, prejudiced attitudes are unlikely to be affected. They will be able to explain away the presence of black professionals with statements like: "They are put there for show." People with a moderate amount of openness in their categories, on the other hand, are likely to think about the blacks and to make favorable attributions. The blacks must be noticed and attended to, however. The one black in a symphony orchestra is unlikely to have much effect since (s)he is so hard to observe from a seat in the balcony. In addition, residential segregation still keeps blacks in areas where they are not seen by the white majority (Richmond, 1973). Even if blacks' occupational level, income, and quality of housing has increased, there can be no attribution based on these facts if whites do not perceive them.

Research done among blacks and whites coming into contact in work settings suggests that stereotypes can be challenged. Specifically, black workers who break a stereotype are rated more favorably than workers who previously had not been members of a well-formed category. As Feldman and Hilterman (1977) put it:

> A good deal of research is consistent with the idea that negatively stereotyped workers who perform well will be overevaluated relative to workers for whom no negative stereotype exists. Feldman (1972) and Feldman and Hilterman (1975) found that Black professional stimulus persons were rated more likely to possess characteristics such as intelligence, resourcefulness, etc., than were comparable Whites; this was explained by the contrast of the Black's attained position with that stereotypically expected of Black people, and the greater effort and ability thought necessary for a Black to attain professional status [p. 36].

In a study of factory workers, Feldman and Hilterman (1977) analyzed the perceptions influencing the type of ratings which lead to decisions regarding retention or firing of workers. Blacks from backgrounds described by the term "hard-core poverty," who were not performing well, were rated higher than poor-performing whites from similar backgrounds. The raters' attribution may have been that hard-core black poverty is worse than hard-core white poverty given the additional burdens of color prejudice. Consequently, blacks who achieve the same work level as whites, even though it is poor by factory standards, are demonstrating a good deal of progress in their work. As shown by the tremendous amount of journalistic commentary following the Bakke and Weber decisions by the United States Supreme Court,[3] different people have different opinions about these attributions. Some say that blacks are being given a realistic break; others feel that blacks are being patronized; still others feel that the attribution shows an anti-white bias.

Stereotype-breaking interaction between blacks and whites has also been analyzed by Yinger and Simpson (1973). They concluded that interactions with high-status out-group members have positive effects in universities, the military, and in public housing projects. Positive effects include modification of prejudiced attitudes and a broadening of stereotypes. There are dangers, however, that the effects will apply only to those people who are encountered in the face-to-face contact. People might say, in effect: "These out-group members I know are O.K., but they are not representative of the whole out-group." This has been called the Lena Horne-Harry Belefonte effect. Many white individuals are happy to interact in a cordial manner with these handsome non white entertainers. The more important goal, of course, is to increase interaction among more typical members of ethnic, racial, and national groups.

Effects of instability

People are more likely to make new attributions the more unstable they feel and the more instability they perceive in their current environment. Kelley (1967) presented a broad statement summarizing the effects of instability which can be applied to the more specific case of cross-cultural contact. Kelley's use of the term "susceptibility to influence" means a readiness to make new attributions.

> Person A will be more susceptible to influence the more variable his prior attribution. Attribution instability (and, hence, susceptibility to influence) will be high for a person who has (a) little social support, (b) prior information that is poor and ambiguous, (c) problems difficult beyond his capabilities, (d) views that have been disconfirmed because of their inappropriateness or nonveridicality, and (e) other experiences engendering low self-confidence [p. 200].

The factors listed in Kelley's statement are similar to those experienced by the typical sojourner. There is (a) *little social support* since friends and/or family almost always remain in the home country. Prior to the sojourn, it is difficult to obtain (b) *accurate information* about life in another culture, especially with respect to everyday interpersonal relations. The tendency to project from oneself, to believe that hosts are likely to behave pretty much like people in one's home country, is very strong. Further, my experience and that of Guthrie (1966) and Szanton (1966) suggests that even if sojourners are given accurate information about life in other countries prior to their departure, they are simply not ready to accept it. The idea of the "oneness of humanity" is a commonly held value for the broad-minded sojourner. While laudable for its inclusion of tolerance toward others, it does not permit an awareness and appreciation of very different, unfamiliar ways of accomplishing goals which people in other cultures use. On the other hand, "keep them at an arm's length" is a commonly held dictum for the narrow-minded. Such sojourners are not likely to pay much attention to recommendations regarding interpersonal interaction since they have no intention of spending time with hosts. For very different reasons, well-designed orientation programs are likely to be unappreciated by both types of sojourners.

On almost all sojourns, people are likely to (c) *encounter problems* which they are unable to solve by themselves. Even if their technical skills are unquestioned, the way they must use the skills is determined by the unfamiliar norms of the host culture. The form of the problem is often an inability to accomplish goals which were readily achieved, through familiar means, in one's home culture. As sojourners adapt to the other culture and attempt to solve their problems, they will inevitably find that (d) *preconceived views* have to be discarded because they are simply not true. There is a growing awareness for the broad-minded that they can appreciate very different ways of behaving and still retain the basic value of egalitarianism. In analyzing the experiences of Peace Corps volunteers (PCVs) in the Philippines, Szanton (1966) observed:

> After some while in the field, many PCVs did finally begin to accept emotionally the idea—and its extraordinary implications—that a people could be equally human, could be equally entitled to consideration, while at the same time they were significantly *different* in their values and behavior. Difference, in short, no longer implied inferiority. And to respect cultural differences meant first to understand them, which required one to take one's time, to empathize, to comprehend [p. 51].

For the narrow-minded, extended contact sometimes leads to increased knowledge about out-group members. A person learns that others *also* have occasional feelings of loneliness, are concerned with opportunities for their children, enjoy being complimented and not constantly disparaged, and worry about the ravages of inflation. Learning about commonly held concerns and emotions breaks down previously held beliefs that out-group members belong in a completely different category.

Finally, all sojourners will occasionally experience (e) *feelings of low self-confidence.* They can't get things done as quickly as they wish; over-tures meant to suggest friendship seem to be rebuffed; they are homesick for familiar food and their preferred brand of toothpaste that both whitens teeth and freshens breath. When too many of these feelings are expe-rienced at the same time, the fundamental attribution error breaks down. People begin to wonder if they are the causes of these misfortunes. A normally self-confident person will experience temporary periods of self-doubt.

When sojourners are in a state of instability, they are quick to make new attributions. Ideally, the attributions will show positive development and mature thought, as with the Peace Corps volunteers interviewed by Szanton (1966). Many administrators who deal with sponsored sojourns feel that orientation programs can help participants understand their feelings of instability as well as the normal tendency to make more attributions.

ORIENTATION PROGRAMS DEALING WITH ATTRIBUTION

The broad range of orientation programs meant to prepare sojourners for life and work in another culture has been reviewed by Brislin and Pedersen (1976). One approach deals specifically with the nature of attribution, and it uses many findings from the relevant research as starting points for the orientation of sojourners (Albert & Adamopoulos, 1976; Fiedler, Mitchell, & Triandis, 1971; Triandis, 1977a). Termed the "culture as-similator" approach, it has the goal of encouraging sojourners

1. to analyze situations involving face-to-face cross-cultural contact;
2. to make attributions about the feelings of the people involved;
3. to compare these attributions with those made by host nationals;
4. with the eventual goal being the development of "isomorphic attribu-tion," or the same interpretations of the face-to-face contact made by sojourners and hosts.

The culture assimilator is based on the presentation of short stories which frequently evoke vivid images. This is a good approach since people think in terms of images and scripts. Instead of listing the issues which sojourners might face, such as the establishment of cordial relations with hosts, the assimilator develops a number of stories around several important themes. For instance, a very common issue faced by foreign students studying in the United States is understanding the nature of constructive and sometimes vigorous criticism which is offered by professors and friends. Students from many countries are not accustomed to the fact that friends who take the same course can criticize each other in class and be very friendly outside of class. These students come from cultures (many in Asia, the Mideast, and the Pacific) in which the roles of critic and friend are quite distinct: friends don't criticize, at least in a setting where others can hear. Foreign students in the United States are sometimes deeply hurt when someone who is considered a friend criticizes their contributions in a classroom setting.

This idea could be communicated in a short essay like the one in the paragraph immediately above, or it could be communicated in a story such as the following from a culture assimilator. The story was originally written as one of over 100 incidents designed to prepare Americans to interact with Arabs (Foa and Chemers, 1967). The danger in presenting just one incident, however, is that readers will make attributions about the whole culture assimilator approach based on idiosyncratic reactions to this one item. Before doing so, readers are urged to study other items reprinted in the sources referenced previously.

> Haluk, an Arab exchange student, was working on a class project with several American students. At a meeting of the project staff, the Arab student was asked to give his suggestions concerning the way the project should be carried out. Immediately after he finished talking, Jim, one of the American associates, raised his hand and said in a clear voice that he disagreed with Haluk's proposals. Then he pointed out a number of specific difficulties that Haluk's approach would incur for the project as a whole and its staff. After the meeting, Haluk told Jim and another student on the project that he would not be able to go to the movies with them as they had planned because he had just remembered he had to get a book out of the library to prepare for a class the next day. When the two boys expressed disappointment and suggested that they could go the next evening, Haluk politely told them that he had already had another appointment for the next evening.

After reading the incident, the sojourner reads five alternative explanations based on attributions which could be made. On the basis of interviews with hosts, in this case a group of Arabs, one alternative provides the best explanation.

1. Haluk was certainly a more serious student than Jim.
2. Haluk was offended because Jim had disagreed with his ideas in front of others.

3. Jim really should have listened more carefully while Haluk was talking.
4. Jim always talked loud, but this shouting in the meeting had been unnecessary.
5. Jim should have gone to the library with Haluk.

The correct alternative is "2"; people who choose this alternative would read the following explanation and then proceed to another item.

> The hypothesis proposes that the differentiation between systems, in terms of status and affect, will be less strong in the Middle Eastern than in the American culture. In this story, Haluk is denied status by Jim in the work system. Haluk transfers this denial to the leisure system, in terms of affect, i.e., Haluk feels: "If Jim denies me status at work, this means he also denies me affect, so I must not give affect (go to the movies) to him." The correct explanation for the Middle Eastern culture which follows from the hypothesis is 2. The American, Jim, differentiates more than his Arab friend between work and leisure, so for him the relationship between denial of status in work and denial of affect in leisure is not as strong as for Haluk [pp. 50–51].

People who pick another alternative read other explanations which tell why their choice is wrong and are given additional information concerning the issues raised in the story. They are then asked to pick another alternative, and they do so until they choose the correct one.

One criticism of the culture assimilator approach has been addressed in recent research. Critics have argued that there is no *one* correct solution for many problems and that the assimilator may encourage oversimplified thinking about complex issues. Often, the most important problems are ambiguous for *host nationals,* and so sojourners seeking the one best solution are bound to be frustrated. The following example seems to communicate the point when used with American students about to study in another country. Assume that a student has an idea for a senior thesis or dissertation. (S)he describes the idea in a concise, well-written proposal which is about five pages in length. The proposal is presented to the professor who hopefully will agree to serve as principal adviser. How much time should pass before the student can ask the professor whether or not the proposal has been read? There are no clear norms in American academia which suggest a precise answer to the question. One person will wait a week, another two weeks, and still another will suggest one month. If a relatively simple problem has no clear answer, the "one best solution" is especially dangerous in considering complex problems such as working in bureaucracies or adapting modern technology.

Malpass and Salancik (1977) addressed the issue by investigating the difference between linear and branching formats in people's responses to culture assimilator items. The branching format was presented as part of the discussion of the Arab-American misunderstanding. People choose an alternative, and if it is correct they "branch off" to another item. In a linear format, people read all of the alternatives and make judgments about the acceptability of each. They then read explanations for all the alternatives, not just the one or ones they thought were satisfactory explanations. Malpass and Salancik (1977) provide a detailed set of arguments relating successful intercultural contact to the type of thinking encouraged by the linear format.

> Basic to the conceptualization of performance in a real intercultural interaction environment is the assumption that the person must generate alternative interpretations of the . . . situation and alternative courses of action, apply some decision strategy to choose among them, and act. A major underlying goal of training by culture assimilator is to develop in the trainee internalized judgmental processes and criteria [schemata: see Rosch, 1977] for use in generating behavioral or attributional alternatives and for choosing among them. Culture assimilators conceive of cross-cultural social interaction as a planning/choosing process and of the trainee in a new culture as a decision maker selecting alternative acts and obtaining feedback on their appropriateness [p. 77].

Using terms previously introduced, "schemata" refers to a well-organized set of categories which provide a framework for making attributions about people and situations, as well as corresponding judgments about the acceptability of various behaviors. The successful use of linear formats demands the presence of an internalized standard of comparison which is *not* part and parcel of the training materials. The standard is gradually developed by reading many incidents and study many alternatives. Slowly, sojourners learn what is acceptable and unacceptable in other cultures; what represents an imposed point of view; how previously unfamiliar behaviors are appropriate from the hosts' point of view. Comparing branching and linear formats, Malpass and Salancik (1977) found that people who had previously experienced the linear method made more accurate attributions on a new set of difficult items. Again, "accurate" refers to agreement with explanations given by host nationals.

The development of an internalized standard leading to accurate attributions, with its explicit connotation of "tolerance" and "cultural relativity," is not easy. There is some evidence (Fiedler et al., 1971) that sojourners who already had a cross-cultural experience benefited more from culture assimilator training than inexperienced colleagues. Assimilators probably help sojourners organize their previous, poorly understood experiences. The preparation of people for their first cross-cultural experience continues to be a difficult task. One promising approach is to orient sojourners after they have lived in another culture for two or three months. By that time, they will have had experiences which need explanations, and they will be motivated to work with materials such as the culture assimilator.

SUMMARY AND CONCLUSIONS

People think a great deal about their sojourn and do not act as passive pawns whose behavior can be predicted with near-mechanical precision. To understand their thinking, it is necessary to understand how they form categories which organize the millions of stimuli to which they are exposed. The very basic assumption is that people would go mad if they had to respond to every unique piece of information. Rather, they group individual elements into categories and respond to them. Stereotypes are categories which deal with generalizations about people. People form categories on the basis of:

1. conspicuous, easily seen differences;
2. overextensions of what is already familiar;
3. the functions categories can serve, such as keeping in-group members away from out-groups;
4. maximizing the positive view held of one's in-group;
5. projecting one's own feelings, for example, the common belief that people all over the world behave pretty much like people in one's own country;
6. the similarity of beliefs which people hold;
7. desirable and undesirable traits of people, which lead to categories encouraging "approach" and "avoidance";
8. the salience, or the immediate personal relevance of important information.

While the reasons for forming categories may seem dull and academic, the consequences are not. New, ambiguous information is perceived as more accurate than warranted if it agrees with an established category. A self-fulfilling prophecy is established: since the information agrees with a category, there is no reason to think carefully about the information. Consequently, there is no motivation to change the category. Further, the amount of information *increases* since the person draws from all the material in the established category when reacting to the new input. If recently arrived sojourners come into contact with hosts who have a well-formed category regarding visitors to their country, they will be treated according to the content of that old category. Sojourners themselves react to others on the basis of categories which were functional in their home country. Since these may be inappropriate given the nature of cultural differences, a more *intercultural* set of categories should be developed.

Two approaches are possible in encouraging this development. One is to think in terms of a metaphor from linguistics: etics and emics. Etics refers to aspects of a concept which are held by both hosts and sojourners. Emics refers to aspects which are specific to each culture. If sojourners keep in mind that most important concepts are likely to have emic and etic aspects, they can learn to expect such differences rather than be constantly surprised and upset by them.

The other approach is to encourage the development of isomorphic attributions, or the same explanations of behavior on the part of hosts and sojourners. The development of isomorphic attributions involves an internalized standard which incorporates tolerance, an avoidance of imposed points of view, and an appreciation of how different behaviors are functional in different cultures. One approach to orienting sojourners, called the "culture assimilator," is specifically concerned with how people make attributions and judgments of the acceptability of behavior. Sojourners read critical incidents involving face-to-face interaction between people from their own and host countries. They then choose among explanations, one of which is correct from the host's point of view. Recent research has focused on encouraging sojourners to:

1. not adopt a "one best solution" type of thinking to problems, since the most important issues may best be addressed by focusing on a number of alternative approaches.
2. go beyond the most vivid, salient, "eye-catching" information, since it is usually not the best input for decision making. Colorful experiences are especially influential in the attribution process. Sojourners are prone to rely on vivid input since they are especially attentive to new information which might be useful in their cross-cultural adjustment. Much information will be striking because of novelty, but there is no assurance that it is relevant or important.
3. realize that many decisions are made by "satisficing," that is, by matching new information to already-formed categories until a satisfactory rather than excellent solution is found. For important issues, sojourners should be encouraged to take their thinking beyond an easy match into analyses of more difficult issues. Cultural differences which have to be incorporated into collaborative efforts with host nationals are examples of difficult issues.

An administrator has to decide between smoothing over trouble spots for sojourners or encouraging them to deal with difficulties "head-on." The advantage of the former is that cordial relations will be established and the sojourners will have an enjoyable experience. The advantage of the latter is that transfer to the postsojourn experience may be greater. For instance, sojourners are often faced with a conflict between feelings about their own country and newly developed feelings about the host country. If they do not confront the conflict during the sojourn, they will be ill-prepared to deal with nationalistic countrymen who do not understand the newly developed attitudes.

Since sojourners are likely to meet many host-country people, they will make many new attributions. This tendency is strengthened if sojourners discover that prior information is not accurate and if they are frustrated in accomplishing their goals in familiar ways. A strong tendency in making attributions is to assign trait explanations in judging others but to account for one's own behavior by situational explanations. Two reasons for this difference are that people do not have much knowledge about situational pressures facing others, and there is a better developed set of terms for talking about other people's traits than about situational contingencies. For instance, in an interview conducted by Brislin and Holwill (1977), a Laotian verbalized the differences between an imposed trait explanation and a situational explanation based on knowledge and acceptance of societal norms.

I agree that Western observers complain about our indirect response to things. We consider it polite, Westerners consider it not frank but you have to bear in mind that among Laotians these are not problems. Being in that kind of society with these values, we have learned to understand the message that other people are sending without it being stated in words. It is not so much what you say but the way you say it that counts [p. 21].

By participating in a cross-cultural orientation program, sojourners can learn about situational pressures which affect behavior and can decrease their tendency to constantly think in terms of people's traits. Unfortunately, the ability to "discount" traits is rarely complete. Even with a detailed explanation of the situational factors which influence a behavior, observers still feel that a person's traits are partially responsible (E. Jones, 1979). Sojourners should realize this fact: they might think that hosts will forgive their blunders with the situational explanation, "the newcomers don't know our customs." This explanation may be taken into account at the beginning of a sojourn, but a residual trait attribution of "somewhat clumsy" or "slightly ill mannered" will remain. If sojourners understand the attribution process, host reactions are less likely to interfere with cross-cultural adjustment.

NOTES

1. Since many terms are being used, other examples may be helpful. Categories are often summarized by images and scripts. As noted several times, stereotypes are one type of category. Thus, stereotypes can be summarized. Images are literally "pictures in the head" of what a typical tourist, diplomat, or foreign student looks like. Scripts include details concerning what tourists typically do in other countries; what diplomats usually say; or how foreign students typically perform in classrooms.

2. The difference between "vivid" and "salient" should be noted. Vivid images command the attention of nearly everyone because of their novelty, color, speed at which they appear, amount of detail, unexpectedness, or status of the person who introduces the image. Saliency involves personal relevance. Consequently, a subtle image which goes unnoticed by most people may be salient to one person because of its immediate relation to the person's current concerns. Vivid images, because of their interesting nature, will often be salient.

3. The major issue in these decisions was whether race could be considered in selecting people for desirable programs which would determine career opportunities.

5

Membership and Reference Groups

One of the problems facing almost all sojourners is the necessity to establish cordial relations with people in the host country. Many sojourners travel alone and their basic needs for acceptance by and interaction with other people demand that they become members of various groups. Further, much information relevant to cross-cultural adjustment will come from other people, not from books or the mass media (Kim, 1978). The need to develop relations with others might seem diminished for sojourners traveling with their families. On the contrary, the problem is often compounded. One's spouse has to establish interpersonal relations since couples are rarely together throughout an entire day. If there are children, they will want to play with others their age. The normal stresses of cross-cultural adjustment often take their toll on couples who do not have friends outside their partnership. The two people in even the most successful marriages may attempt a catharsis by unloading their feelings on each other. The result may be an escalation of tensions which affects both cross-cultural adjustment and the quality of the marriage. In some cases, members of an extended family may move from one country to another. The larger, intact family group may be able to absorb the tensions of adjustment, but there is still a need to form new interpersonal ties. Information about job availability must be acquired; children have to be placed in schools; the new country's language may have to be learned.

The purpose of this chapter is to discuss the influence of reference and membership groups on cross-cultural adjustment. While certain problems may be eliminated if sojourners are able to establish membership in groups, other problems may be created. Frequently, sojourners who become part of host country groups find that ties to older groups are threatened. One of the clearest examples involves scientists from countries which do not have a high degree of technological development. If they sojourn in a highly industrialized society and become respected members of work groups, they may be hesitant to return to their home country. The well-known problem of "brain drain" is a constant threat. Membership in several groups can stimulate the development of creative ideas. Some sojourners are able to shift back and forth between home and host country groups in a way which has positive consequences. These include learning about one's own culture by contrasting it with the other, and expanding one's viewpoint by incorporating the concerns of other cultures.

MEMBERSHIP GROUPS

A strict, four-part definition is helpful in differentiating a "membership group" from a collection of casual acquaintances. A group (Homans, 1950) is a collection of individuals who have frequent face-to-face *interaction* with each other. They engage in *activities* of mutual interest or perceived importance. Members have well-developed feelings or *sentiments* toward the others, and they behave according to well-defined *norms* as to what is proper and improper. One consequence of sentiment and norms regarding propriety is that group members will come to each other's aid in times of trouble. In other words, group members "look after each other."

When the terms "membership group" or "group" are used, they will be based on this definition. Other collections of people might be referred to with a term such as "have some qualities of a membership group." For instance, sojourners may feel that they have established themselves in a group since the people involved spend so much time together in interesting activities. But if there is no assistance offered by the so-called group members when it is clearly called for, then the others must be termed "acquaintances" rather than group members.

According to Janis and Smith (1965), once groups are formed, a number of factors lead individuals to maintain their membership:

> The motivational factors that attach a person to his group can be classified under four headings: (a) affection, friendship, and other positive ties toward group leaders and fellow members; (b) desire for prestige and self-esteem or other psychological gains from being a member; (c) desire to escape from social isolation, or other unwelcome consequences that are avoided by being a member; and (d) restraints that act to keep the person within the group regardless of his desires in the matter. . . .
> Of these, the first two (involving positive or affectionate motives) probably contribute most heavily to the tendency to internalize group norms so that they are maintained even in the absence of external sanctions [p. 201].

Sojourners receive many benefits from group membership. People's needs for friendship are satisfied. They receive information about job possibilities, housing, schools, and the legal requirements of the new country. They receive guidance concerning what might be called "everyday survival." For instance, foreign students learn about good professors and heretofore unfamiliar grading procedures; businessmen learn about investment opportunities. The success of one group member is shared by all. Information about how the entire group is progressing can be more potent than information about an individual's efforts (Brewer, 1979). Groups can support a project and bring much more enthusiasm and effort than a collection of isolated individuals.

Disadvantages also exist. Groups can channel the undesirable qualities of individuals into hideous alleys. Many people obey orders unquestioningly and do not object to seeing disliked out-group members suffer. When those people are members of groups which turn the persecution of outsiders into norms, any expression of an individual's undesirable traits leads to support and approval. German oppression of the Jewish people, and white-American treatment of blacks, can be partly explained by the presence of group support.

Groups can set limits to the alternatives which its members consider when making important decisions. Group norms exist regarding what information is acceptable, how one goes about forming alternative courses of action, and what type of people should be consulted. An interesting example relevant to cross-cultural contact is the selection of people for the diplomatic service (Thayer, 1959). Historically, candidates were selected from the graduates of a few universities in the eastern United States. There may not have been a conscious discrimination against people from other parts of the country. The people doing the selecting were members of groups which included many alumni of the "acceptable schools." When a new candidate appeared, the categories of "good or bad schooling" were likely to be used. In addition, young Eastern establishment graduates had certain traits which fit the image of a successful candidate according to the group norm. They dressed in a "proper" way, had a certain patter, dropped desirable references in their conversation, and could bring up shared experiences with a colorful professor. Selectors and certain candidates were simply comfortable with one another. Legal requirements to open up opportunities for diplomatic service have thankfully reduced the narrowness which was developed and reinforced by the old system.

REFERENCE GROUPS

People often look to those they admire or envy for guidance about beliefs, attitudes, values, and behavior. The people may or may not be members of the same group. Whenever people seek such guidance from others, the term "reference group" is a useful shorthand descriptor. By Sarbin and Allen's (1968) definition:

> This term designates a group which a person values. It is often used to explain behavior oriented toward audiences not physically present. A reference group may be a membership or nonmembership group, a single other person, . . . a category of people, or even nonexistent groups or categories of people, for example the future generation, God, ancestors. . . . [t]he greater the compatability between the values of the individual and the perceived values of a new group, the greater the likelihood that the individual will accept the new group as a reference group [pp. 532–533].

Foreign graduate students in their first year of studies sometimes use the most successful Ph.D. candidates as a reference group. Immigrants look to host country people who have good jobs and steady incomes. Technical assistance advisers are interested in the hosts who will take over the maintenance of a project after the sojourners return home. University professors in technologically developing countries often look to recognized academics in the United States for guidance in their research projects (Kashoki, 1978). This causes problems if own-country needs are downplayed in the quest for other-country recognition (Kumar, 1979b).

MEMBERSHIP GROUPS AND ADJUSTMENT

The basic point that cross-cultural adjustment is dependent upon support and acceptance by others is well established (Taft 1977):

> . . . changes in a newcomer to a culture are less abrupt when he is able to fall back into a familiar and accepting group within the new society for his primary social relationships, his recreation, and catharsis for his frustrations and balm for his psychic wounds [p. 125].

The importance of group support will be examined through an analysis of four cases: Peace Corps volunteers in South America (Arnold, 1967; Benson, 1978); foreign students from Africa studying in the United States (F. Pruitt, 1978); immigrants from Korea settling in the United States (Kim, 1977, 1978), and from Eastern and Southern Europe settling in Australia (Zubrzycki, 1966); and refugee children from Vietnam staying in temporary camps established by the United States government (Harding & Looney, 1977).

Benson (1978) analyzed unpublished data on Peace Corps volunteers in Brazil (provided by the Center for Research and Education) to determine factors leading to successful and unsuccessful adjustment. He concluded that the development of close social relations with Brazilians had very positive consequences. While continuing familiar and valued activities practiced in the United States, adjusted volunteers participated in new activities indigenous to Brazil. They also participated in many social activities, forming friendships and spending large amounts of time with Brazilians. Adjusted volunteers visited the homes of Brazilians and shared food and drink with them.

The need for such contact can also be satisfied by interaction with fellow countrymen. Analyzing the experiences of other Peace Corps personnel in South America, Arnold (1967) noted that volunteers had adjustment problems, especially during the first six months. To alleviate the stresses associated with poor adjustment, all Peace Corps members in a certain area were brought together frequently to discuss any issues that they desired. The fact that change comes so slowly and the feelings emanating from adjustment problems were often voiced at the meetings. The groups also allowed the members to provide social support for each other. They could praise one member's project, try to lift another's spirits if (s)he was especially "down," or suggest means of implementing the goals of still another member. These group meetings were apparently quite effective. The number of premature returns—volunteers who returned to the United States before their two-year assignment was completed—was only 25 percent of the figure for nonparticipating volunteers assigned to other parts of South America.

Preventing adjustment problems

Group support can prevent tensions from having a debilitating effect on adjustment. Analyzing the experiences of Vietnamese children who had to be temporarily placed in California refugee camps, Harding and Looney (1977) found that lack of support groups, specifically family members and friends, had very negative consequences. Psychiatric and pediatric evaluations showed that children without group support were "significantly depressed" and suffered from somatic distress, "sleep disturbances, tantrums, violent anti-social behavior, and marked withdrawal . . . [pp. 408–409]." They also refused to study English. The children who were accompanied by family members, on the other hand, did not experience these symptoms and did not participate in antisocial behaviors. After placement in foster homes, children adjusted well if they were situated in the same city so that former friendships and contacts could be maintained.

Similarly, Zubrzycki (1966) concluded that immigrants to Australia from various parts of the "old country" strive to maintain group ties. When people from the same areas of Southern or Eastern Europe settle together in the host country, their sense of security is enhanced. People are comfortable associating with others who have the same background, dialect, sense of humor, and values attached to shared memories of the past. Apparently, the need for group support is so strong that immigrants unaccompanied by family members and friends quickly form new attachments. People become attached to families through various means. One is through the acceptance of the "godmother" or "godfather" role to another person's children. These relationships can become very strong and can be very significant in the functioning of the ethnic community. Another benefit to the group member is that countrymen who have been in the host country for a significant length of time are able to orient newcomers through such activities as translating between languages and interpreting the customs of the host society.

Types of people in the support group

A reasonable question to ask at this point focuses on the people who constitute one's support group. Is adjustment increased through interaction with host nationals or through interaction with fellow countrymen? There is no clear answer which will apply to all types of sojourns. My guess is that the same sojourner will benefit from interaction with hosts at some times and from interaction with fellow countrymen at other times. After extensive interaction with hosts, for instance, it is refreshing to discuss one's experiences with fellow nationals. Research has identified two influential factors; one is the sojourner's goal (Spaulding & Flack, 1976). Although the term "adjustment" includes the element of interpersonal relations with hosts, this may be an unimportant goal for some sojourners. If a foreign student wants only to obtain an advanced degree, *minimal* close or warm interaction with hosts is necessary. The needs for social contact and group membership can be satisfied in the company of fellow nationals who are studying in the same country. If the sojourner's goals include learning about the host country, on the other hand, then a wide social network is desirable.

The other variable is the amount of time spent in the host country. For short stays, extensive contact with fellow countrymen can interfere with the goal of a successful adaptation to the host country (F. Pruitt, 1978). With longer stays, on the other hand, a person can maintain membership in different groups comprised of either host nationals or fellow countrymen. In such cases, extensive interaction with fellow countrymen does not interfere with adjustment (Kim, 1977, 1978). Given time, sojourners undoubtedly learn how to interact with the two types of groups without interference, much like the average person learns to interact with different people at work, at church, at home, and as part of weekend interest groups.

In the case of sojourners, an influential factor is probably the societal norm regarding joint membership in groups comprised of people from different ethnic backgrounds. Recent developments in parts of the United States have led to support and approval for joint memberships. People often belong to different groups because of interest in their "cultural identity" or "roots."

Given the desire to expand one's membership groups, different sojourners find acceptance in very different places. Pruitt (1978) concluded that students from Africa who maintained their religious commitment while in the United States had a more successful cross-cultural adjustment. Three reasons for this effect are possible. A religious commitment provides similar beliefs and values which can be shared with host nationals. Second, hosts can be met at an organized church and visits to homes can follow. Finally, a religious commitment also provides a sense of confidence, belongingness, and identity which can be called upon in times of crisis. Many of the foreign students interviewed by Pruitt (1978) were fortunate to participate in churches whose norms included tolerance and acceptance of outsiders. There is no question that many church members go out of their way to be warm and helpful to sojourners. Some churches, on the other hand, have norms which demand exclusion of people not of a certain racial or ethnic background. Sojourners who experience such churches are likely to be so insulted and hurt that successful adjustment is threatened. A tremendous service that administrators of sponsored sojourns can provide is a list of churches and clubs which welcome people of various nationalities.

Another service is the guidance of sojourners into early social encounters which are cordial and pleasant. A number of factors lead to this recommendation. Since sojourners are unsure of themselves in the host culture, early encounters will be especially salient and will be perceived as important. Attributions are likely to be freely made. If the encounters are pleasant, then favorable attributions will follow. The other factor concerns the filling of time. Host country people have well-developed patterns which fill their day, such as time spent on the job, with friends, with family members, and in the development of various interests. Many sojourners, on the other hand, have traveled alone, have not yet established friendships, and do not know how to go about pursuing their interests in the host country. Put simply, they may spend too much time in lonely consideration of how miserable they are. Often, there are administrators in charge of the work-oriented part of a sojourn, such as a foreign student's schooling, but no one to suggest leisure time activities. If administrators ask themselves, "Do people have enjoyable things to do after work hours, and on weekends?", they will be making a good start toward providing for the social needs of sojourners. William McCormack (personal communication, 1979), who has had a great deal of experience administering sponsored programs for sojourners, puts the issue this way. "One of the most important factors in adjustment to another culture is an early, positive social experience."

Interacting with the dominant majority

Recommendations regarding the *amount* of interaction with host country members should be dependent upon sojourners' goals. If people desire assimilation or partial assimilation into the dominant culture, they must establish interpersonal relations with members of the dominant majority. "Partial assimilation" means active participation in some but not all host institutions. For instance, a recent immigrant might accept a job which is clearly part of the country's institutional structure, such as a business or governmental position. At the same time, (s)he might be an influential participant in community activities organized by fellow immigrants. No value judgment should be applied to the differing options of immigrant community maintenance vs. partial assimilation vs. complete assimilation into the mainstream of the dominant host society. Some people will prefer one option, some will prefer a second, and still others will have different preferences during various periods of their sojourn. Host country authorities, such as immigration officers or foreign student advisers, should respect the wishes of different sojourners and should provide support so that all options can be pursued.

Sojourners seeking partial or full assimilation must understand the concept "dominant majority." Pruitt (1978) found that African students made a better cross-cultural adjustment, including more progress toward assimilation, if they established relations with white rather than black Americans. Interaction with whites led to more knowledge about the United States, more opportunities or "open doors" for the pursuit of desired goals, and more information on the best ways to meet one's needs in the host society. Unfortunately, since whites have more social power than blacks in the United States, they have more to offer sojourners wishing to assimilate. Further, sojourners who lived with a well-established relative and who had contact with foreign student advisers made more progress toward assimilation.

CONFRONTATION BETWEEN OLD AND NEW REFERENCE GROUPS

People maintain many of their attitudes, values, and beliefs because of in-group support. Often, group membership is contingent upon holding certain attitudes, and people who continually deviate from accepted norms are excluded. One of the experiences common to almost all sojourners is the confrontation between feelings for their home and host country groups. During the early stages of a sojourn, people still cling to home country reference groups. These groups support a number of beliefs and attitudes. In developing new membership and reference groups in the host culture, however, those old beliefs may be in conflict with values held by host society members. The sojourner is confronted with the disparity and, somehow, has to come to grips with it. The confrontation has a number of consequences, including attitude change and strained relations with old friends and family members.

One possible consequence is a modification of existing attitudes and beliefs. In discussing the specific case of stereotypes, Ehrlich (1973) presents the general principle in these terms: "Changes in the established relations between ethnic groups will decrease the stability of stereotype assignments and modify their distinctiveness and their levels of diffusion and consensus [p. 38]." Even though most of the relevant research which led to the formulation of this principle has been concerned with actual groups of people coming into contact, it can be applied to the more specific case of sojourners. The assumption is that people do not completely abandon old group memberships upon beginning a sojourn. Rather, they bring that membership to a sojourn and are confronted with differences while establishing new reference and membership groups. For the specific case of sojourners, changes often occur among the people directly involved in cross-cultural contact, but there is no extension to others. Members of home-country groups remain behind, and they are not eager to change attitudes while helping to reintegrate the returning sojourner. Further, they are not especially interested in hearing about the cross-cultural experiences of the returnee, probably because they have no frame of reference to understand the enthusiastic reports of their friend. Not much is known about extending the benefits of a sojourn to people who remain in the home country (Shaw & McClain, 1979).

To deviate just slightly from the main presentation concerning the effects of confrontation, there is a long-term phenomenon which is unique to sojourners. After people return to their home country, they often form friendships with other people who have also had a cross-cultural experience. The countries in which the experiences took place may be very different: one person may have worked in Sweden, another in Kenya; or, one person may be an immigrant, and the other person a teacher in a desegregated school. It is challenging to ponder the reasons for friendship formation. There is no common interest in the same part of the world that can be shared, nor a common interest in the same social problem. The shared experience is probably the set of feelings stemming from the confrontation between old and new reference groups, and the feelings of satisfaction stemming from resolution of the tensions.

Some examples drawn from different types of sojourns may help develop an understanding regarding the types of confrontations which can occur. The problems stemming from generational differences among immigrants have frequently been analyzed (Leighton, 1945; Murillo-Rohde, 1976). Members of the first generation are likely to maintain old beliefs about such topics as child rearing, deference to parents, and proper leisure time activities. Children, who are in contact with host country peers at school, are exposed to different attitudes and beliefs. Newly learned behaviors are sometimes in direct contradiction to practices maintained in the home. For instance, teachers may welcome argumentation in school, but parents may demand unquestioning deference at home. If children accept the attitudes of host-country people, they begin to see their mother or father as "old-fashioned, ignorant, and . . . alien, . . . a source of shame and opprobrium . . . and . . . less important as a model, guide, and exemplar [Kern, 1966, p. 39]." While undoubtedly causing a great deal of conflict at home, the confrontation has some positive benefits for children who want to succeed in the host society. Children often assimilate much faster in the host society than their parents (D. Adler & Taft, 1966).

In addition to its influence on immigrant assimilation, the school can also be a place where prejudiced attitudes change. In studying the effects of black-white contact in desegregated schools, Stephan and Rosenfield (1978) found that attempts to develop new group ties led to favorable intergroup attitudes. Those adolescents who increased their informal interethnic contact, beyond that required in the classroom, developed positive feelings toward each other. Parental behavior could interfere with this development. Children did not change attitudes in a positive direction if parents insisted on an absence of out-group contact. In these cases, there was no way to break the cycle: parents prevent contact, new groups cannot form, therefore, no confrontaton can take place which might yield more favorable attitudes.

Perhaps some speculations might be offered here which are based on interviews I have conducted with children of extremely rigid, prejudiced parents. My impression is that, even if the children do not manifest favorable attitude change because of parental restrictions, there still may be an eventual long-term change. Some white children changed their attitudes toward blacks, partly because their parents gave consent for interethnic contact. Children whose parents refused to give consent probably *did interact* with their tolerant white peers. Consequently, all white children received some exposure to tolerant behavior. In addition, the natural tendency of American adolescents to partially break the childhood bonds which made them completely dependent on their parents, and to form support groups among their peers, means that tolerant behavior could have received further reinforcement. Tolerance may have become acceptable if only because the parents did not practice it and because some peer group members did. Sooner or later, the children not allowed contact will become independent of their parents and will be able to make their own decisions. For instance, they will come into contact with out-group members in their work. At that point, they will be confronted with old prejudices and new attitudes stemming from the close interaction. They may remember the behavior of their white peers who have long interacted with blacks and may take the lead from those friends.

These speculations find some support in the work of Pool (1965) who analyzed the experiences of adolescent sojourners from the United States. As part of a sponsored program, teenagers traveled to Europe without the company of their parents. Pool concluded that a beneficial effect of the so-journ was an "unshackling" from old attitudes, including those adopted from one's parents. After the freeing from old bonds, sojourners had the opportunity to see other cultures with a fresh perspective, not bound by rigid categories. Further, Deutsch and Merritt (1965) feel that the effect of external events such as pressures for increased intergroup contact are often greater for adolescents than adults.

> Often it takes the replacement of one generation by another to let the impact of external changes take its full effect. The greater openness of adolescents and young adults to new images and impressions—not only in the negative sense of being less burdened with old images and hardened psychic structures, but also in the positive sense of greater sensitivity and ability to learn—is thus a major resource for the long-run learning process of their societies [p. 183].

The greater openness of adolescents is one defense for the large amounts of money spent on sponsored sojourns by such organizations as the Experiment in International Living, American Field Service, and Youth for Understanding.

THE PROCESS OF REFERENCE GROUP CHANGE

The key element of a confrontation is that beliefs and values held by individuals and by members of their well-established groups are different from those of other people. In addition, the individuals wish to use the other people as a reference group or they wish to establish membership group ties. To understand confrontation, the way in which a person changes after interaction with members of the new group must be analyzed.

After investigating the intergroup perceptions held by Jewish people and by Palestinian Arabs in Israel, Hoffman (1977) hypothesized that intergroup perception, and eventually new group ties, start with a growing awareness of group differences. Subsequently, there is a move toward ambivalence, which can take a number of forms. One is seeing the positive and negative aspects of old and new reference groups; another is understanding why cultural differences are seen one way by in-group members and another way by out-group people. Finally, there is a synthesis, or the development of a unique set of feelings toward the old and new groups. In his research, Hoffman obtained the clearest results concerning this three-step framework in analyzing the mutual perceptions of religious and nonreligious Israelis. For instance, observant young Jews made a clear differentiation between values held by their religious peers and values held by Israelis concerned only with secular matters. However, they identified with both, finding attractive ideas in each reference group (see also Hermann, 1970, for a similar finding). Summarizing his analysis, Hoffman (1977) feels that the dual identification of religious Jews "could be interpreted as a sign of ambivalence, and beyond this of a strain toward integration. The religious may be experiencing greater conflict than their secular peers, but they are also the ones forging the new synthesis [p. 99]."

FACTORS INFLUENCING THE DEVELOPMENT OF NEW REFERENCE GROUPS

Several factors increase the probability that people will form new reference groups.

Ideology

The reasons for the dual reference group ties held by religious Jews may have included the perception that nonpracticing Israelis are putting a great deal of effort into the development of their country. The concept of a "homeland" may be an ideological goal, held by many people, which overcomes more petty differences. Such goals are called "superordinate" by Sherif (1958), and the search for and commitment to them are considered central to the reduction of intergroup tensions and to the development of new interpersonal relations. The sincere commitment to an ideology also leads to an easier cross-cultural adjustment. Commenting on the experiences of Jewish refugees, Sanua (1970) hypothesized that emigration to Israel has a tremendous amount of additional meaning beyond the simple movement from one country to another. Immigrants have a feeling of "coming home," as explained to them in the Bible, and this provides a strong sense of security. Further, the commitment to populating and developing a homeland encourages permanent residents of Israel to accept and provide support for immigrants. For instance, an elaborate educational program called the "Ulpan" system has been established which helps immigrants to learn the Hebrew language and to learn about life in Israel. All immigrants are expected to participate (Pincus, 1977).

During the period of extensive immigration to the United States in the nineteenth century, strong feelings about "the land of the free and the home of the brave" and "Give me your huddled masses . . ." undoubtedly helped overcome temporary difficulties. Cynical attitudes which came into fashion in the 1960s and 1970s have led to a less widespread acceptance of these views.

Mobility

Individuals who are able to move about in different environments are likely to encounter new ideas (Deutsch & Merritt, 1965; Guillotte, 1978). Sojourners are also likely to meet people who hold the different views, and interaction with them often leads to the sort of confrontation under discussion. Factors influencing mobility include:

1. the amount of education one has. Since people with large amounts of education have been exposed to many viewpoints, they will be more comfortable in the company of others who profess diverse views. A lack of education often keeps some people near home because of an uncomfortableness with the unfamiliar.
2. the amount of money for travel.
3. social status, leading to acceptance in a number of places.
4. freedom from commitments which force a person to remain in one place.
5. qualities which are desirable to hosts, such as physical attractiveness, a gregarious personality, and skills not easily found within a society.

For instance, people intelligent enough to earn an advanced degree in another country may possess unique, desirable skills which are central to the successful completion of a cross-cultural research project. Progress in cross-cultural studies is dependent upon understanding concepts from the point of view of people in the various cultures under investigation. Sojourners trained in research methodology may possess language skills which make possible in-depth interviews with fellow countrymen. Intimate ties with host-country researchers are likely to develop after collaboration on the same project. The recognition that sojourners receive for their work, however, may make it difficult for them to return to their home countries if rewards for research are not common there (Kashoki, 1978).

Mobility can have both positive and negative facets. An interesting and important fact which has emerged from research (Bochner, 1977) is that a person who is most successful at adjusting to a new culture is often not completely successful at readjusting to the old culture. Perhaps the explanation is that a person who adjusts readily is one who can accept new ideas, meet the talk intelligently with people from many countries, and be happy with the stimulation which (s)he finds every day. The same person may readjust poorly upon returning home since the new ideas conflict with tradition. The returnee finds no internationally minded people, discovers that old friends are bored upon hearing accounts of the sojourn, and experiences no stimulation in the country which is already so well known. This relation between adaptation to the new and nonadaptation to the old is undoubtedly related to individual differences in tolerant personality traits (chapter 3). Tolerant people can benefit from both the old and the new and do not necessarily experience debilitating feelings of impotence upon returning to their home culture. Still, my experience has been that there is always some discomfort stemming from thoughts about one's previous cross-cultural experience compared to life in the home country. In many cases, the discomfort becomes functional since energy is channeled to the support of other sojourners, as in cases where foreign exchange students are invited into a person's home.

Previous experiences of the sojourner: the comparison level

Some sojourners are better able than others at establishing group ties with hosts. Certain past experiences lead to the development of individual-level traits and attitudes which, in turn, lead to ease in meeting others. Technically, the combination of factors is called an *interaction* between individual variables (chapter 3) and the development of support groups.

Sojourners from Africa studying in the United States were more likely to feel lonely if they had grown up in extended families (F. Pruitt, 1978). Further, they were more likely to have difficulty adjusting to their new surroundings. The probable reason is that these students were accustomed to the company of many people. In extended families, there are always people available for informal interaction and help in times of difficulty. Sojourners accustomed to this level of interpersonal interaction were uncomfortable in the new environment since they knew few people. Similarly, females had greater difficulty in cross-cultural adjustment. The probable explanation is that, traditionally, females were confined to their homes and never had an opportunity to learn how to meet and interact with strangers.

A theoretical concept which may be helpful is the "comparison level"

(Thibaut & Kelley, 1959). People who have had a good deal of experience in a given society develop standards against which new information is compared. Standards are concerned with what is reasonable, correct, and comfortable. The African students from extended families had a standard concerning comfortable levels of interpersonal interaction. When they compared this to the level experienced in the United States, they became discontent. If sojourners are in a country long enough, its standards can be internalized such that the home culture is compared against them. In analyzing the experiences of academic sojourners returning to Brazil, Gama and Pedersen (1977) concluded that

> . . . the experience abroad seems to lead to the acquisition of expectation patterns and values compatible to the new system. In the United States, [sojourners] were exposed to different lifestyles and studied at a setting where many facilities are available. They returned to Brazil to work in universities which are academically, economically, and socially very different from the American ones. They were then confronted with a reality which was incompatible with their expectations and consequently experienced some problems readjusting [p. 56].

Attractiveness of the new environment

The lifestyle and university facilities valued by the Brazilian academics are examples of attractive features in the host country. As attractive aspects increase, sojourner satisfaction increases. Attractive aspects can include jobs for people previously unemployed in their own country; political freedom; greater opportunities for individual expression, away from the constraints of numbing bureaucracies; a less intense, fast-paced lifestyle; access to libraries and world-renowned scholars; and greater opportunities for achievement beyond the status ascribed at birth. For instance, Adler and Taft (1966) found that highly educated European immigrants intended to make Australia their permanent homes if they were able to find attractive employment which challenged their skills. Immigrants not able to find satisfactory employment were much less content.

The all-encompassing nature of the host culture

Different sojourners will have very different perceptions of how all-encompassing their new culture will be (Taft, 1977). For some, minimal interaction with host-country citizens is necessary. A team of technical specialists, for instance, may want to develop skills in computer science. They might live in another country for six months, take formal courses, satisfy social needs among themselves, and return to their home country. If the skills were learned, then the sojourn is perceived to be a success. At the other end of the continuum, some immigrants know that political factors completely prevent any hope of a return to their home country. The most realistic alternative for them is to adapt to their new culture. People's thoughts seem to be something like this: "We'll be here all our lives. There's no sense spending excess energy looking backward or dreaming about an unrealistic return." Kim (1977, 1978) feels that immigrants who cannot return home, and who have support groups in the host country, have a less stressful adjustment than other types of sojourners. For some people, adjustment involves high points and low points at different stages of a sojourn (Gullahorn & Gullahorn, 1963). Considering adjustment over a nine-year time frame, Kim (1977) found that Korean immigrants to the United States who had an adequate support group and no intentions of returning home, did not show a pattern of high and low points. They began their lives in the United States with moderately positive attitudes, and these increased over time.

Perception of acceptance in the host society

According to Taft (1977), one aspect of the adjustment process is an "identification" with the host country. Factors leading to identification include the development of new reference groups, a feeling of belonging, perceptions that sojourners are accepted by host-country citizens, and a sense of "shared fate" concerning current events in the host country. Feelings of acceptance were important in the adjustment of Peace Corps volunteers since the organization was dedicated to the goal of involvement on the community level. The adjustment of volunteers became easier as host-country people became accustomed to different Americans regularly coming into their villages. In the early years of the Peace Corps, hosts literally did not know what to do with Americans who came to their rural villages (Textor, 1966a). Hosts were surprised to meet Americans who were willing to live in the community rather than in a separate, more comfortable compound. The surprise was probably misinterpreted by some volunteers as rejection. Volunteers beginning their sojourns in later years, however, were not looked upon as unusual. They were more likely to be accepted in a shorter period of time and their adjustment was undoubtedly easier. Interestingly, hosts could become so accustomed to Americans that adjustment was hindered. If there were many volunteers in a certain country, no one person would be considered unique or special. A blasé attitude on the part of hosts was as damaging as total surprise. A point between the two extremes led to feelings of acceptance: volunteers were something different in the community, but not so unheard of as to demand the complete attention of hosts (R. Jones & Popper, 1972).

THE DEVELOPMENT OF DEVIANCE

People who participate in extensive cross-cultural interaction run the risk of becoming deviant in the eyes of their non sojourning peers. Returnees to the home culture sometimes do not readily fit back into their former groups. They have had experiences which are difficult to share and, ideally, have increased their level of tolerance and their ability to see many sides of complex issues. Returnees are often frustrated at the lack of interest in international affairs shown by their peers, and they are impatient with parochial views about world problems. Group members undoubtedly perceive the returnees' frustration, interpret it as rejection, and consequently keep their distance.

There are, however, advantages to deviance or marginality (Ehrlich, 1973). Marginal people are less concerned with group norms and are likely to break out of the restrictive behavior patterns demanded by ingroup members. Further, people who are willing to instigate change "are almost always variants in the system [Kluckholn & Strodtbeck, 1961, p. 45]." One conclusion from research on creative individuals is that they are somewhat marginal with respect to the mainstream society (Bruner, 1962). Moreover, they are willing to risk rejection in putting new ideas forward.

In my experience, returnees almost always feel that they are somewhat deviant from old in-groups. Reintegration into one's home society often takes a year or more (Kagitcibasi, 1978) One director of university-level study abroad programs, Dr. Harold Bradley (personal communication, 1979), interprets the returnees' experience in the following way:

> Returning students are very often upset for at least two reasons. One, none of their old friends wants to hear about their experiences in the other country. Two, returnees are uncomfortable and frustrated with the changes in *themselves.* They feel that their vistas have been opened, they know they think differently about the world than before their sojourn, but thy can't put their feelings into words.

Administrators can take advantage of the discomfort by organizing short workshops in which returning sojourners can meet others who have had similar experiences, share their adventures, and grope toward understanding the changes in themselves. Some evidence exists that returnees appreciate these efforts. Most teachers who incorporate material on cross-cultural interaction in their courses, for instance, are contacted after class by grateful students. These are people who, unknown to the teacher, have had a cross-cultural experience. The gratitude takes the form: "For the first time, I understand what happened to me because of the material and framework you presented in class."

THE CONSEQUENCES OF SHIFTING REFERENCE GROUPS: POSITIVE ASPECTS

Any discussion of the advantages and disadvantages stemming from the development of new reference groups begins with two major assumptions. First, sojourners do not always abandon their allegiance to one group and attach themselves permanently to another. Rather, they move back and forth in their thinking, using different groups as reference points at different times. Second, at any given time, sojourners will feel varying degrees of deviance, or marginality, from one or more of their reference groups. These emotions, however, can be channeled into constructive behavior.

Reaffirmation of one's first culture

A common-sense but incorrect belief about the effects of sojourns is that they interfere with people's patriotic attitudes toward their own country. The belief seems to be that favorable attitudes toward other societies cause a decline in commitment to one's home country. Hall (1980) feels that remnants of this belief contribute to the shifting of foreign service officials from country to country. In turn, citizens of other countries charge that officials are transferred just as they have learned enough to begin effective interaction concerning policy development.

Research has challenged this old belief. Sojourners often become more attached to their own country and to its values. Although the greatest number of studies have been concerned with citizens of the United States (Isaacs, 1961; Pool, 1958, 1965; H. Smith, 1955), the reaffirmation effect has also been found among Scandinavian and Indian sojourners (Kelman & Bailyn, 1962; Useem and Useem, 1955). One reason is that sojourners *learn* what they have always taken for granted. Much like the air we breathe, appreciation of something is difficult until it is no longer present.

In Gilbert and Sullivan's *The Mikado,* the lord high executioner had a "little list" of people who might be beheaded. One was

> The idiot who praises in enthusiastic tones
> Every century but this and every country but his own.

While the executioner did not say whether he was thinking about sojourners or stay-at-homes, he probably had the latter in mind. People who have lived in another country discover that many aspects of their home country are not as bad as once thought. For instance, Americans unhappy with their government take free elections for granted and do not have much understanding of them or the system which makes them possible. They quickly learn to appreciate free elections after living in a country run by a dictator who puts severe constraints on people's everyday behavior.

Pacific Islanders sometimes feel that their societies are backward because they do not have the modern conveniences they read about in magazines. They do not appreciate that their societies have a number of attractive features such as an absence of orphanages and old folks' homes. Elderly people who cannot take care of themselves and orphans are taken into homes by members of the extended family. When Pacific Islanders sojourn in the United States, they are surprised upon discovering the numbers of elderly people in nursing homes. For the first time, they become aware of a very desirable aspect of their home culture.

Expansion of one's home country reference group

While working in other countries, sojourners sometimes take a broader view of policy issues than others in their in-group (Bauer, Pool, & Dexter, 1963). While discussing foreign policy, American businessmen who had made at least five trips abroad took the view of their nation while discussing foreign policy, whereas nonsojourners accepted the narrower view of the specific industry in which they worked. Similarly, sojourning businessmen were looked upon by hosts as Americans, not as representatives of a particular corporation. Eventually, the businessmen accepted this role and discussed policy matters more like a Secretary of State than a representative of one firm. Using the example of tariff policy, Pool (1965) summarized the study:

> . . . the political effects of travel on tariff attitudes was to counteract the force of self-interest. It made a [person] see the trade issue in national terms, rather than in the parochial terms of [one's] own industry. . . . Foreign travel broadened the frame of reference in which the businessman considered the foreign-trade issue to be one which took account of world political and economic circumstances [p. 123].

The concepts of "reaffirmation of one's first culture" and "expansion of one's home country reference group" are related. If sojourners are expected to discuss policy matters in the role of an American rather than as a student, businessman, or technician, they are forced to do a great deal of thinking beyond what is already familiar to them. In their search for new information which will allow them to play the expanded role, they are bound to discover previously unknown but positive facts about their country. Further, the emotions put into explaining the position of one's country reinforce people's patriotic attitudes. Consequently, sojourners will develop strong feelings about the positive aspects of their country.

This discussion on playing the role of an American provides an opportunity to review briefly a technique for orienting sojourners to other cultures. Administrators who organize orientation programs often use role playing as a method (Brislin & Pedersen, 1976). Sojourners are asked to play the role of a host, or a broad-minded and tolerant person, or a technical assistance adviser who wants to incorporate the host's point of view. To do a good job in their role plays, sojourners have to learn a great deal about the other culture. Knowing a role play is expected, they might become motivated to read the previously untouched written materials provided by administrators. The emotions put into this orientation technique often encourage a commitment to the position which sojourners are role playing.

Working on behalf of reference groups

Once a person makes a commitment to a reference group in another country, (s)he often puts a great deal of effort into protecting the group's interests. Pruitt (1962, 1965; also Sawyer & Guetzkow, 1965) studied decision making among individuals in the United States Department of State and in other governmental agencies. There were frequent conflicts between the recommendations made by different departments regarding foreign policy. Members of the State Department invariably took the position that included more concessions to other countries. Pruitt (1962) interpreted these findings by pointing to two factors:

1. State Department officials have more expertise about other countries, including knowledge of how their leaders will react to various policy proposals.
2. They are committed to maintaining long-term relations with other countries, and they realize that one route to this goal is the incorporation of other people's viewpoints.

On a level less lofty than the development of foreign policy, returnees provide a good deal of help to their former hosts. Scholars on sabbatical in a given country often collaborate with hosts. Later, returnees may do the necessary paperwork so that their former co-workers will be given support on *their* sabbaticals (Brislin, 1979b). Foreign service officials usually have large numbers of commitments since they have served in several countries. Often, former hosts ask their support on behalf of sojourners about to live in the officer's home country. Officers are asked to house a sojourner temporarily, to interpret transcripts for a university registrar, or to intercede between the sojourner and a potential employer.

THE CONSEQUENCES OF SHIFTING REFERENCE GROUPS: NEGATIVE ASPECTS

At times, returning sojourners will wish that they hadn't participated in such a successful sojourn. Success is dependent upon establishing in-group relations, but group ties entail demands when *other* members need help. For people who have sojourned in a number of countries, demands on their time seem to increase exponentially with each assignment. Postsojourn demands on time are a negative consequence of shifting reference groups, albeit a mild one with which most returnees will cope gracefully. There are other consequences that are more troublesome.

Unwillingness to continue personal growth

After sojourners go through the discomfort associated with confronting and accepting a new group, they may experience further tension as they cope with the changes in themselves. As a result, they may make a point of avoiding situations which might lead to further discomfort, tension, and change. Consequently, people may not develop beyond the point reached during their sojourn. They may broaden themselves as a function of their cross-cultural experience, but go no further. A probable reason is that people may simply want to avoid the additional discomfort and change which would result from either a reorientation to their own culture or from efforts to integrate others into their new group.

In its milder manifestations, this phenomenon is sometimes experienced by former Peace Corps volunteers or Foreign Service Officers. They are sensitive to people in other cultures, are very polite and helpful to foreign visitors, but are ineffective in interactions with fellow countrymen who have never had a sojourn. Their increased tolerance for other points of view does not extend to home country peers. Their conversations are marked by moanings about current sponsored sojourns and proclamations concerning how good things were when they worked in another country.

When there are additional factors beyond commitment to a new reference group, manifestations of inhibited growth become more intense. An example is the relations among new and old immigrants who originally came from the same country. M. E. Smith (1978) did field work in a New England community where many members were either descendants of Portuguese immigrants or were newly arrived immigrants from Portugal. The descendants and the new immigrants did not interact in an effective and cordial manner. Three reasons were suggested. First, there was competition for scarce resources during a time of economic recession. The descendants considered themselves Americans who had paid their dues to society and who should not be shunted aside by newcomers. When new immigrants sought work, the descendants charged that jobs were being taken away from "real Americans." Second, there were greater expectations on the part of new immigrants, or a higher level of comparison. In the years since the first wave of immigrants had arrived in America, Portugal had modernized. The newer immigrants, better educated and more sophisticated, were accustomed to a higher standard of living than members of the first wave. The mass media also showed the many comforts and status symbols commonly owned by members of the American middle class. These may have been unavailable to older immigrants because of discrimination.

Third, opportunities were available to the new immigrants which allowed them to work toward the fulfillment of their expectations. Smith (1978) noted:

> As post-1960 ethnics, the New Portuguese were given access to resources not available in earlier years—special educational programs, housing and business loans, and the like. Such factors encouraged what Bennett (1975) has called "a coalition for advantage. . . . The base for corporateness . . . was minority aid funds, those federal, state, and foundation monies that encouraged entrepreneurial and managerial individuals to form organizations through which access to those funds (and jobs and power) could be gained [p. 72].

The older immigrants were much less likely to participate in the quest for governmental program support. Even if they wanted to compete for the available funds, and if they were eligible according to the Byzantine federal regulations, they simply were not prepared to do so. Older immigrants had adapted to the United States by downplaying their Portuguese heritage. The way to get ahead, government officials advised, was to be like Americans. They followed the advice and committed themselves to the United States. All of a sudden, they began to see newer immigrants getting ahead because they emphasized their Portuguese heritage, obtaining handsome grants in the process.

One of the lessons from this case study is that reference group affiliation, including ethnic heritage, is fluid. People use reference groups as tools to maximize their benefits. Even though an outsider may have predicted that the old Portuguese might embrace the new immigrants because of a shared background, the allocation of benefits in the United States deemed that other behavior would be more appropriate. Well-researched, effective, and easily adaptable interventions which might mollify negative attitudes in the New England town are not available. If they are to be developed, understanding the complexity of intergroup relations is essential (chapter 8). Research on the fluid nature of group affiliation has led to important insights. Research on the reintegration of people into old reference groups has also led to possible applications.

Reintegration into one's own culture

Earlier in this chapter, a few problems facing returnees were mentioned. Two are very common:

1. Sojourners are excited about sharing their experiences, but none of their old friends or family members want to hear about them. As one businessman put it, others would rather talk about Uncle Charlie's roses (Cleveland et al., 1960).
2. They realize they have changed but cannot explain how and why. Further, their friends sense a change and are likely to make trait attributions ("irritable," "mixed-up") rather than situational attributions based on the sojourner's recent experiences. Because of their disorientation and the reactions of others, returning sojourners are often rather unpleasant, feisty, and lacking in social graces.

Since 1972, I have been involved in designing and organizing workshops so that sojourners could come together, learn what frequently happens to returnees, and anticipate their own reactions (Brislin & Van Buren, 1974; Brislin & Pedersen, 1976). Programs were specifically designed for people from Asia and the Pacific who had been working or studying in the United States. The structure of the programs was formulated after interviewing sojourners about the issues that had to be faced in reorienting themselves to their home cultures. Although several themes emerged, by far the strongest was the reintegration of people into home country groups. This major theme was treated by developing six sessions within the workshop which focused on types of, and responses to, different groups.

The first session has been concerned with one's family members and friends. In most workshops, at least one sojourner who had been dating freely in the host country was about to enter into an arranged marriage upon arrival home. In making suggestions regarding how this person might adjust, other program participants project their own anxieties and consequently work through their own unique relations with parents and friends. Another common issue is that frequent interaction with old friends may not be possible since *they* may have accepted additional responsibilities which leave little time for social activities. Exploring the problem of different norms, one participant wrote to the program organizers after returning home.

One of the most difficult things to adjust to was living at home with my
family. . . . The forced independence being away from home became
something I grew accustomed to; living in a dorm or apartment; not
having to tell my whereabouts all the time, washing and cooking, travelling
alone. Things such as these which were considered of positive survival
value (independence) are not acceptable at one's home.

In the next session, relations with co-workers are discussed. The value of
a sojourn is not always recognized by a person's employer. Co-workers who
were previously subordinate to a sojourner may have been promoted, and
so the returnee is greeted by new superiors who may themselves be uncomfortable with the new work relationship. In those organizations where
sojourns *are* valued, the returnee may be exposed to professional jealousy.
Returnees are also faced with the problem of working in jobs which often
do not demand the level of specialized technical expertise which they developed during their sojourn (Gama & Pedersen, 1977).

The relation between short-term and long-term adjustment is discussed
in the third session. Returnees are encouraged not to confuse the two. For
instance, sojourners often adopt host country norms regarding everyday
etiquette. They may employ these behaviors in the home country, forgetting
momentarily that the norms may be different. Too often they conclude,
"I'm making too many mistakes and feel like a fish out of water." In the
workshops, people are encouraged to look upon such everyday mistakes
as normal and not to let them interfere with long-term goals. The latter
demand patience, planning, and a great deal of tact. Another returnee
wrote:

I want to put the "new math" into my school and follow it through all
four grades and see how it works. I am enthusiastic about this new way to
teach math. But before I can even plan any new curriculum, I must convince my principal and the staff of the school that this is a worthwhile
change. There is strong resistance, especially from older teachers. . . . I
believe it may take me two years before I can convince the staff to let me
try my new ideas.

In a separate session on attribution and nonverbal behavior, the basic
principles concerning how people make judgments about themselves and
others are discussed (chapter 4). Returnees are reminded that, since they
will be special and unique people back home, they will be the subject of
many conversations. Most returnees are modest people who wonder why
anyone would want to spend time talking about them, yet they have to
learn that home country members have many questions. "Have they
changed? Will they still like us? Will they try to change us?" One principle
derived from research on attribution is that people make judgments based

on very minimal and sometimes faulty information. For instance, many returnees will have adapted some gestures of the host country and will have modified home country gestures so that they are not as clear. Among sojourners from Japan, bows may not be as deep and a slight slouch may replace an erect posture. Fellow countrymen make strong attributions based on behaviors which seem trivial to sojourners. Countrymen will make a trait attribution: they've become disrespectful. The sojourners are more likely to make a situational attribution: I was in another country and simply learned some of their gestures. In my experience, this has been the most helpful session for returnees. Most have already done some thinking about family and friends, but information on the inevitability of attributions and the trait-situation distinction is very new to them.

In a session devoted to role playing, sojourners develop short skits and act out issues which they might have to face. People take different roles: one plays an employer, another a parent, and still another a friend who remembers "the good old days." Participants often develop humorous sketches. A common theme centers around sojourners who not only want to change their organization but also their entire society at the same time. They have to wait, however, because they can't fix a piece of equipment they learned how to use on their sojourn. Returnees seem to realize instinctively that a sense of humor helps readjustment to one's home culture.

The final session is concerned with maintaining cross-cultural relations. Each returnee is given names of previous sojourners who live in the same area within the home country. In addition, they are given the names of various organizations which are concerned with organizing sojourns for others. Returnees are also encouraged to inquire about the international divisions of their various professional organizations. These are surprisingly underused even though they provide much information about journal discounts, professional meetings, and fellow professionals who are visiting one's home country.

The basic principle behind the reorientation workshop is generalizable to any sort of cross-cultural preparation. When people know what might happen to them, and when they work through negative consequences in their minds, the actual events are far less debilitating. Since people learn about the relevant emotions during their self-examination, they are not completely surprised upon encountering the emotions outside the workshop. In designing the reorientation workshops, the application of this principle was borrowed from work with hospital patients (also reviewed by Janis and Mann, 1977). Some people facing surgery role-played how they might feel after their operation, how they would cope with financial difficulties, and so forth. Other patients did not participate in these role-playing experiences. Those who did participate felt less emotional stress after the operation, needed less pain-killing medication, and were released earlier than nonparticipating patients (Egbert, Battit, Welch, and Bartlett, 1964).

HOW MUCH PREPARATION?

Orientation programs can prepare sojourners for the experiences they are likely to face. But how much preparation is desirable? Can people be told so much that there is little spontaneity in their cross-cultural experiences, no confrontation based on their own actions in the other culture, and no learning from their own mistakes? There are no clear answers to these questions: different program administrators have different opinions. My own feelings are that sojourners are likely to encounter so many different types of people and have so many varied experiences that an orientation cannot possibly ruin very much spontaneity or novelty. Content of the orientation programs, then, should include as much information as sojourners are able to absorb, taking into account time, fatigue, and the dangers of information overload. Special attention should be given to aspects of a sojourn which can be especially stressful, such as the integration of people into groups discussed in this chapter. Again, orientation programs are no panacea: they will never completely prevent stress. But since they can *prepare* people for difficulties and tensions, they can increase the probability of benefits which stem from a sojourn.

SUMMARY AND CONCLUSIONS

A problem facing almost all sojourners is the need to establish cordial relations with other people. Membership groups are formed when sojourners (a) interact with hosts (b) in a variety of activities (c) according to clear and accepted norms. Further (d), a group is marked by shared affective ties and the assurance that members will look after each other in times of difficulty. Groups satisfy people's needs for friendship, and they also are the source of much information necessary for a successful cross-cultural adjustment. The disadvantage of groups include the strong tendency to pressure members into undesirable behaviors and to limit the number of alternatives which are considered "reasonable" in decision making. Limits are sometimes imposed on the sorts of people considered appropriate for group membership. For instance, in past years, only a small number of people were considered for the United States Foreign Service. The bases for consideration were certain factors which were shared with selection board members. The type of schooling people had received and their mannerisms were very important. Legal pressures to distribute desirable government positions more widely have decreased the pseudo-elitism created by the older, narrower focus.

Reference groups are defined as those people whom an individual admires. They provide guidance for the necessary behaviors which might lead to goals *held* by reference group members and *desired* by the individuals. Students desiring the prestigious sojourn provided by the Rhodes Scholars program, for instance, might consciously emulate the behavior of award winners to increase their chances of favorable consideration by selection boards. Reference groups can, but do not necessarily, involve actual membership. If an applicant receives the award, and develops close relations with other Rhodes Scholars, the reference group becomes a membership group.

Membership groups provide emotional support during the inevitable stresses and strains of cross-cultural adjustment, or "balm for psychic wounds [Taft, 1977, p. 125]." They can also prevent problems from occurring in the first place. Vietnamese children in refugee camps, for instance, had far fewer problems if they were accompanied by family members and if they were able to maintain close relations with old friends (Harding & Looney, 1977). The pressure to maintain group ties is so strong that immigrants sometimes develop substitutes such as the "godmother" or "godfather" roles when blood relatives have to remain in the home country.

Sojourners choose their membership and reference groups on the basis of their long-term goals. If they want to assimilate, they are best advised to form strong relations with host-country members. If they want to develop only their technical skills in the host country and have every intention of returning home, long-term adjustment is best assured by maintaining home-country ties. For sojourners who want to learn about the host culture, early positive social experiences are crucial. Program advisers can help adjustment by providing lists of organizations which welcome sojourners, and by arranging pleasant get-togethers with host-country people.

One of the potential benefits of a cross-cultural experience is the expansion of a person's tolerance for different points of view. Expansion often develops after a confrontation between the values held by members of a sojourner's old group and those held by members of host-country groups One of the clearest examples is generational differences among immigrants. Children learn new attitudes and behaviors in host-country schools, discover that these are crucial to assimilation, and view their parents as fossils for refusal to see the obvious. Schools should not be looked upon as villainous, however, since they can also be the place where a confrontation between prejudiced and unprejudiced attitudes takes place. One long-term effect of desegregated schooling may be the breakup of the system by which blacks are discriminated against in all parts of the society. Historically, white children never had the opportunity to interact with blacks since friendship formation was forbidden. Whites learned to view discrimination in the schools, workplace, and public facilities as perfectly acceptable and even proper. Contact in desegregated schools, and the possibility of group memberships cutting across racial boundaries, may yield the confrontation which "shakes up" the old system.

Several factors increase the probability that people will form new reference groups. Ideology is one; its influence can be seen in the development of Israel as a "homeland." Mobility refers to the qualities individuals have which allow them to move freely in the host society. Level of education, money, status, and a job which demands travel are examples. The previous experience of sojourners provides an internalized comparison level against which new experiences are evaluated. At times, experiences in the host culture can create a comparison level against which the home culture is judged. A common problem facing foreign students is that they become accustomed to extensive laboratories and libraries. They have trouble readjusting to a home country organization which does not have these features. For some sojourners, the development of new group ties is mandatory since they cannot return home for political reasons. In these cases, *some* stresses in adjustment are lessened because people are completely aware that there is no function in being homesick and that the best course of action is to work hard at adapting to the current situation. Adaptation to the new culture is made easier if sojourners feel that they are accepted by hosts.

The development of new reference groups admittedly leads to a certain amount of deviance. Yet deviance is often desirable since it can encourage creativity and a questioning of group-supported prejudicial values. Other positive aspects stemming from a shift in reference groups include the reaffirmation of one's first culture. Desirable aspects of a culture are sometimes not contemplated since they are so obvious. They become salient during a sojourn because of their absence in the host culture. One's home country reference group can also be expanded. In one study (Bauer et al., 1963), overseas businessmen took a much broader outlook in their discussions of tariff policy than the narrower position advocated by their corporations. Since they were asked to play "Secretary of State" by their hosts, they partially accepted this role in their negotiations. Another positive aspect is that, after a sojourn, returnees may work on behalf of their former hosts when the latter have an opportunity to travel.

Negative aspects of a sojourn include arrested development. Sojourners become broadened by their experiences, but sometimes they do not develop beyond a certain point. They spend too much of their time moaning about days gone by, not in activities which might help themselves or others. In more intense cases, the refusal to expand reference groups leads to conflict. Examples can be found in the relations among old and new immigrants from the same country. Perceptions of competition, and beliefs that one group is getting ahead by emphasizing its ethnicity while the other had been forced to deny it, cause problems which are hard to diagnose and to solve.

Another negative aspect is faced by almost all sojourners. Upon returning home, they have difficulties readjusting to their own culture. Old friends are uninterested in their experiences and sojourners sense a change in themselves and are uncomfortable about it. Many organizations have established reorientation seminars to help returnees fit themselves back into home country groups. In a program designed by Brislin and Van Buren (1974), participants discuss possible changes in their relations with family, friends, and colleagues; learn about the nature of attribution, since home country people will inevitably make many judgments about them; learn to differentiate short-term from long-term adjustments; role play scenes which depict issues they might have to face; and learn about opportunities to maintain cross-cultural contact.

Confrontation between reference groups and readjustment are two examples of the difficulties with which sojourners must cope. The range of difficulties can be better understood if the situations sojourners face are analyzed. The stresses which accompany a cross-cultural experience often stem from attempts to cope with situations which *seem* familiar but which are puzzling because of cultural differences on dimensions such as the importance of time constraints or the numbers of people who have roles in a situation. The frustrations stemming from an inability to cope with situations using familiar methods leads to the internalized feelings collectively called "culture shock." The analysis of situations, and its potential contributions to a greater understanding of cross-cultural contact, will be the focus of the next chapter.

6

The Analysis of Situations

INTRODUCTION

In addition to using their traits and skills to advantage, sojourners must also cope with pressures which are part of the culture in which they live. Collectively, these *external* pressures are called "situations" to differentiate them from the traits and skills which people *bring* to a sojourn. After situations are explained through an abstract definition and some specific examples, the need for a language to describe situations is discussed. A number of terms useful for the analysis of sojourns are suggested, such as the presence or absence of time constraints and the number of consequences for both the sojourner and others. The roles played by situations are also analyzed, especially their influence on determining favorable attributions and contributing to task productivity. One of the most frequently used terms in the analysis of sojourners' experiences is "culture shock," and it is best elucidated through the study of situations. The constant demand of coping with differences in climate, housing, transportation, food, and social norms leads to frustration and sometimes a sense of worthlessness. It is important to view this condition as a normal part of cross-cultural contact, not as an anomaly which signifies failure. Culture shock has positive aspects, including a motivational component which encourages people to learn about their feelings so that frustration is reduced.

A GENERAL EXPLANATION AND TWO EXAMPLES

In the most general sense, situations refer to combinations of factors external to individuals with which they must deal to accomplish their goals. Further, situations refer to aspects of the environment which, in combination with individual variables, determine people's behavior. Some specific examples are necessary to bring these abstract concepts down to earth.

Climate is a situational variable. It is external to the individual and must be dealt with in some way so that a sojourner's goals can be attained. Some climates in less technologically developed countries are so hot and muggy that long, sustained work is extremely taxing on one's energy. Individuals wanting to work on a certain task must cope with the situational variable of climate. They might decide to sleep during the day and work during the somewhat cooler nights. They might make arrangements to work at a museum where air conditioning is necessary for the preservation of art objects. Or, they might study the history of climatic factors in the country and choose the area which is the least uncomfortable.

The second part of the abstract explanation is that a combination of individual and situational factors determines people's behavior. Different people behave in different ways when faced with similar situations. Some individuals will have personality traits which include a high need for achievement and skills which include very efficient work habits. They will not be affected by climate and will get their work done regardless of their personal discomfort. Other people with less achievement need and fewer headstrong work habits may want to spend some of their time making themselves comfortable in the unpleasant climate. They may spend a good deal of their time coping with the climate rather than working on task-oriented activities. There should be no value judgment placed on different ways of dealing with the situational variable of climate. People desiring comfort are likely to meet a large number of hosts who might help them in their plight. The hosts might perceive certain similarities ("They're human, too!") and might develop long-term relations with sojourners. The high need-achievement person runs the risk of seeming so different from hosts that (s)he may not be able to develop cordial relations.

Another situational variable is the number of other people with whom an individual must interact. When policy decisions which take into account the needs of others have to be made, it is easier to deal with a small than a large number of people. This is a situational variable discussed by both Nicolson (1960) and Thayer (1959) in their analyses of diplomacy. In the early 1900s, there were a limited number of countries which sent representatives to international meetings. The diplomats became well acquainted with each other and work was made easier since they could predict each other's behavior. Norms developed so that clear, widely accepted procedures could be called upon to make work more efficient. Later in the century, however, more and more countries began sending representatives to meetings. The growth of science and technology added so much to the complexity of issues that specialists had to be integrated into a country's diplomatic corps. The sheer additional numbers meant that the old, widely accepted norms of the elite group became impossible to apply.

THE DIFFICULTY OF ANALYZING SITUATIONS

Situations are difficult to discuss because there is no widely accepted set of descriptive terms that might allow precise and insightful analyses. This lacuna contrasts with the well-developed set of descriptors for an individual's personality. It is useful to compare the difficulties of describing situations with the relative ease of discussing personalities. In developing assessment and diagnostic tests, psychologists summarize personality with a limited, manageable number of terms which have widely accepted definitions. For instance, personality, as defined by the California Psychological Inventory (Gough, 1964), can be summarized in terms of 18 variables, many of which were used in chapter 3. Terms such as sociability, social presence, tolerance, achievement via independence, self-acceptance, and flexibility are useful descriptors which clearly help the analysis of people's preparation for and reactions to their sojourns. Further, these personality terms are quite similar to the words laypeople use in discussing behavior. "Work hard by themselves" might be substituted for "achievement via independence," but the basic description of people is the same. The lack of a similar set of terms for situational analysis causes great difficulties when researchers and practitioners attempt to communicate their ideas about cross-cultural contact.

For instance, Simpson and Yinger (1973) are correct in their analysis of discriminatory behavior toward out-groups.

> Many studies show that individual behavior can be modified by changes in the situation, independently of personality structure. Or, to put this in terms that we believe are theoretically more adequate, a high proportion of persons have tendencies towards nondiscrimination that may be called out by strategic situational changes even though such tendencies normally are dormant [p. 146].

But what are these situational changes? How can they be described in an efficient way? This chapter will attempt to present an approach and to apply it to the analysis of sojourns.

At this point, readers, hopefully, will have some slight understanding of situations. The examples of climate and number of people have been given, and a comparison with the ease of describing personality has been attempted. Another explanatory method is to review some history of how analysts have come to realize the importance of situational factors. Certain research studies have been carried out in which situational effects seemed to take precedence over people's personality in determining behavior. These studies have become "classics" and they are well worth reviewing here. As has been the practice throughout this book, examples have been chosen based on their applicability to cross-cultural contact. Incidentally, the method I found most helpful in developing the subject matter for this chapter was to examine classic studies of cross-cultural contact in situational terms.

RESEARCH EXAMPLES: ANONYMOUS VERSUS FACE-TO-FACE REJECTION

An early study of cross-cultural contact which has long intrigued researchers was carried out by LaPiere (1934). At the time of that study, white Americans had strong prejudicial attitudes toward Orientals. LaPiere accompanied an Oriental couple on a long trip across the United States, stopping at 250 hotels and restaurants. They were refused service only once. Later, LaPiere wrote letters to each of the 250 establishments asking if they would accept the Chinese couple for either dinner or hotel reservations. Of the people who responded, 90 percent indicated that they would refuse to serve the Orientals. The two types of responses, letters and face-to-face interactions, seem to be contradictory. It would appear that prejudicial attitudes as reflected in answers to LaPiere's letter are not good predictors of people's discriminatory behavior. Similar results were found by Kutner, Wilkins, and Yarrow (1952). A black woman accompanied by two white friends was admitted without incident in 11 restaurants, but all of these institutions later refused to answer a letter requesting reservations for an interracial party of three. Six of the restaurants refused to make a reservation upon receiving a request made over the telephone.

In thinking about these studies, different researchers have suggested a number of factors which might account for the results (e.g., Campbell, 1963; J. Jones, 1972; Wrightsman, 1972). My preferred interpretation is based on the situational factors faced by the people who received the letters requesting reservations and by the people who engaged in face-to-face contact with the Chinese or black individuals. In responding to the letter, or in choosing not to bother with it, people were probably alone in their offices and could easily respond according to their prejudices. There were no counter pressures which might lead to a more tolerant response. But the people confronted by members of another ethnic group were in a different situation. It is much more difficult to refuse a person face-to-face than in a letter or even over the phone. Further, the Chinese couple was well dressed, had attractive luggage, and was in the company of a white (LaPiere). The black female was also attractively dressed and was accompanied by two whites. There are at least two situational variables: face-to-face relations, and status markers which the other people possess. LaPiere

(1934) commented on these two situational variables and added a third based on traits of the Chinese couple.

> Quality and condition of clothing, appearance of baggage (by which, it seems, hotel clerks are prone to base their quick evaluations), cleanliness and neatness were far more significant for person-to-person reaction in the situations I was studying than skin pigmentation. . . . A supercilious desk clerk in a hotel of noble aspirations could not refuse his master's hospitality to people who appeared to take their request as a perfectly normal and conventional thing . . . [p. 232].

The idea that qualities of other people constitute situational factors may seem odd. But the idea is consistent with the original explanation of situations. Other people are external to the individual and have to be considered if they have any bearing on the individual's goals. If the other people are confident, or powerful, or achievement-oriented, those factors have to be taken into account and, consequently, are part of the situations with which an individual must deal.

RESEARCH EXAMPLES: INDIVIDUATION VERSUS ANONYMITY

In some situations, the identities of all people involved are very clear. Consequently, people behave in socially desirable ways, or in ways consistent with their public image, so that their reputations are maintained. In other situations, people are anonymous. Since they do not have to worry about being identified by others, they may engage in socially undesirable behaviors for purposes of self-gratification. When people feel anonymous and are not subject to evaluation by others, they are said to be deindividuated (Zimbardo, 1970).

In research carried out by Zimbardo, people had the opportunity to deliver shocks to others. Although no pain was ever actually incurred, the research study was staged such that people believed that they could be aggressive toward others if they wished. When people were deindividuated, they were willing to administer more pain to others. Makers of deindividuation included ignoring people's names, darkness, and the use of hoods to cover people's faces. Another study, using information from anthropological field work collected and catalogued in the Human Relations Area Files system, yielded results which further documented the effects of deindividuation (R. Watson, 1973). Certain cultures are high on indexes of aggressive behavior, such as torture, mutilation of the enemy during war, and painful initiation ceremonies for adolescents. Members of aggressive societies were likely to deindividuate themselves before engaging in behavior that caused pain in others. They wore face paint or masks, both of which make recognition of individual identities very difficult. This finding caused me to reflect on the one initiation I had to experience during adolescence. I was blindfolded and so did not know which of my so-called friends was the source of this or that pain-inducing behavior. Other examples come to mind. Ku Klux Klan members wear robes and hoods while persecuting out-group members. Crime is more frequent at night since people are less likely to be identified. Triandis (1977a) speculates on the societal-level problems caused by deindividuation: "Industrialized society tends to create more and more settings in which people become deindividuated, and hence there is increasing aggression [p. 82]."

In milder forms, deindividuation occurs during sojourns. Since people are removed from their normal membership and reference groups, they are not under constant pressure to behave according to the norms of those groups. They are not completely deindividuated, since people in the host culture can observe them, but they are anonymous with respect to Aunt Minnie, Rev. Morgan, and other people back home. Pool (1965) feels that people's rudeness during a sojourn can be partly explained using these concepts.

> Good conduct, if not internalized, is often enforced by awareness of the ways in which important "others" will react. Travel is a way of escaping these censors. . . . By confining the scope of his sensitivity to censors at home, whom he has temporarily escaped, the tourist permits himself the indulgence of misconduct abroad. The man on a spree at a resort, the one who shouts at waiters and clerks, the woman who wears shorts into a cathedral, the traveler who talks disparagingly about the country he is visiting, might never at home so contravene the demands of etiquette [p. 120].

Deindividuation can have some positive effects. While on a sojourn, people might take risks and break out of familiar behavior patterns. For instance, they might struggle in the host country language or develop warm friendships with people who happen to have a different skin color. They might never behave in these ways at home because they would appear silly or because societal norms simply make the behaviors unacceptable.

KEY SITUATIONAL FACTORS

A number of situational variables are important in the analysis of these two research examples concerned with rejection and deindividuation. Summarizing the findings, these factors influenced the behavior of the people involved: whether or not there was face-to-face contact; status markers possessed by people; traits of other people with whom one had to interact; and degree of people's anonymity. Other situational variables will be considered in this section. The objective of such a presentation is to suggest factors which are at a desirable level of abstraction. Factors should not be so specific that they have little generalizability beyond a few concrete situations. "Recent exposure to tolerance on the Sesame Street television program," while perhaps an influential factor, is too specific a variable since the program is available in only a few parts of the world. "Recent exposure to tolerant attitudes in the mass media" is more useful for the analysis of situations. Different types of presentations aimed at large audiences, available in different parts of the world, could then be examined as the local manifestation of the general factor.

The situational variable, "encourages the evaluation of others," is too general and abstract to be of much help. Since people in almost all situations evaluate others on any of a score of dimensions, there is little gained by analyzing situations using such an abstract factor. Bringing the level of abstraction down to the more specific, "encourages people to evaluate others on the basis of competence/incompetence," leads to a more useful factor. It can be used in the analysis of many situations where people from different cultures interact, such as the school or workplace.

The collection of situational variables presented here is not complete. Rather, they are examples of variables which have been helpful in the analysis of diverse forms of intercultural contact. Hopefully, they will remind readers of other factors which can be used in the analysis of the intercultural contact situations with which they deal. The development of a complete list is an important task for research in the 1980s.

Structured versus unstructured

Some situations have clearly defined norms which all people accept. As long as people abide by the well-structured types of intergroup interaction allowed by the norms, there is no conflict, tension, or stress. Other situations are less structured since there are no guidelines regarding what behavior is acceptable or correct. Drawing on the work of Williams (1964), Richmond (1973) commented on intergroup relations in both the United States and Great Britain:

> . . . in stable, recurring intergroup situations well defined and mutually understood patterns of behavior become institutionalized. However, in unstructured situations, such as those frequently found in the northern states of the United States and in Britain, new patterns of either discriminatory or non-discriminatory behavior may emerge. They become the focal points for change in intergroup relations [p. 289].

The factor of structured vs. unstructured situations was very influential in determining the success of a Peace Corps volunteer's experience. In the first years of the Peace Corps program, volunteers not only had to work in various communities but also to structure their own jobs (Textor, 1966a). Hosts had no previous experience with the type of sojourner who participated in the program. There were no community roles which early volunteers might fill. After the first wave of volunteers established themselves is worthwhile jobs, later volunteers had an easier adjustment since they were able to fit into the then-existing structure.

Presence or absence of time constraints

People in some situations find that there are deadlines which force immediate action. Decisions concerning recommended behaviors often suffer because not all alternatives can be given adequate consideration. Since other situations have fewer time constraints, a more leisurely, careful examination of alternatives and their consequences can be undertaken. One of the benefits of a formal orientation program prior to a sojourn is that people are given time to prepare for the different experiences which they are likely to have. Rather than an immediate immersion into the unfamiliar, people can take the opportunity to learn about problems commonly faced by sojourners. Taft (1977), after reviewing a great deal of information on cross-cultural adjustment, concluded that the existence of a transitional stage was a major factor in lessening the difficulties sojourners face while coping with another culture. As examples, he pointed to both the formal training provided by the Peace Corps and the Uplan system in Israel which aids immigrant adjustment (see also Pincus, 1977). People should often delay decisions and somehow find the time for careful analysis. In discussing race relations, Yinger and Simpson (1973) point out that heated demonstrations concerning alleged racial discrimination can be intensified if time is not used wisely.

> . . . a group may "call on the cops," may throw down the gauntlet to discriminators when what is most needed is the careful analysis of causes, the skillful rallying of allies, and the creation of a more favourable environment for change [p. 103].

Overmanning versus undermanning

When there are a few people in a situation, each individual member of a group may be given a large number of tasks to perform. In contrast, people in situations with many other group members present may have only a few tasks assigned to them and, consequently, may not have enough to do. The first type of setting is called "undermanned" and the second type "over-manned" (Barker, 1968; Wicker, 1972). Interestingly, people in under-manned situations are often more satisfied. Since they have more to do, and since the successful completion of the group's task is dependent upon their efforts, they feel important. They feel that their work is valued and do not experience the sensation of being "lost in a crowd." Although there are undoubtedly exceptions based on individual personalities, people work-ing in cultures with only a few other sojourners present are often happier with their experience (R. Jones & Popper, 1972). This hypothesis is de-pendent upon the presence of another situational factor. There must be sufficient *structure* for sojourners such that they are not so unfamiliar as to be completely disconcerting to hosts. People in undermanned cultures are often given more attention, are asked to contribute to the host com-munity, and are more likely to be remembered since there is less "competi-tion" from other sojourners.

The concepts of overmanning and undermanning are frequently intro-duced to students who want to spend a year in another country, even if the exact terms are not used. American students, for instance, often want to study at such prestige institutions as the University of London or the Sorbonne. Advisers point out that high quality education is available in other schools within Britain and France where the students are likely to be given more attention by hosts since there are not so many Americans (Selltiz & Cook, 1962). Further, people in smaller communities often *make* their own entertainment rather than *buy* it; sojourners may be asked to participate in leisure time activities much more frequently than if they were living in big cities.

Presence or absence of a niche

Closely related to the concept of undermanning, a niche refers to a clear and valued role in the host society which a sojourner can readily fill. While occupying the niche, the sojourner becomes appreciated by hosts and gains satisfaction from doing work which is valued by others. Exam-ples have been suggested by analysts involved in many forms of cross-cultural contact. Ritterband (1969) pointed out that foreign students from Israel often have an easy adaptation if they choose to study in the eastern United States. They are able to find part-time work in Jewish com-munities as teachers of Hebrew or the Old Testament. Their work is ap-preciated by hosts, they form social relations with the parents of their students and, consequently, they develop a strong support group.

In studying the adjustment of Vietnam refugees housed in temporary camps, Harding and Looney (1977) found that some adolescents were able to find a niche. Those adolescents who were deeply involved in the care of younger or aged relatives felt that their work was important and useful. These feelings seemed to help alleviate boredom which otherwise might have led to antisocial behavior. Similarly, one of the general findings from research with Peace Corps volunteers is that the presence of a niche increased satisfaction with their sojourns (Ezekiel, 1968). Volunteers who were able to use their specialized training, and who found themselves in communities where hosts could take advantage of their skills, had a relatively easy cross-cultural adjustment. Further, they were judged as successful in their work assignment by superiors and outside evaluators. For example, volunteers with specialized training in the teaching of English as a second language were much more content than similarly trained colleagues assigned to communities which had no training program in this area.

Finally, my own experience with organized programs for cross-cultural researchers (Brislin, 1977, 1979b) shows the importance of keeping the "niche" principle in mind, even if I once did not. Participants took leaves of absence from their jobs in Asia, the Pacific, and the United States, came together in Hawaii for a four-month program, and then returned to their jobs. Those researchers who found or developed a small niche in the program, such that they were able to use highly technical skills, were satisfied with their sojourn. The skills might be the use of a certain test or an advanced statistical technique. My original prediction was that the researchers would be more satisfied if they were given opportunities to broaden themselves beyond the level which they brought to the program. While this prediction may have held true for a few participants, the opportunity to use already-developed skills seemed more important for the majority.

The niche principle is a sword with two edges. People can become so satisfied with their niche that they do not want to leave it. Ritterband (1969) points out that the Israeli students could become so accepted into an American Jewish community that they might not want to return home. Researchers might become so involved with a specific problem that they miss opportunities for a broader, more creative perspective.

Presence or absence of a model

In some situations, models are present who can demonstrate correct, acceptable behaviors. Sojourners often seek out a model, and sometimes the concept of learning from a model becomes institutionalized. Many multinational corporations stagger assignments so that newcomers overlap with the people they are replacing. The "old hands" can introduce newcomers to the unique aspects of life and work in the host culture. The belief exists that learning from fellow nationals who had to make a cross-cultural adjustment is a wiser method than learning directly from hosts. No solid evidence exists to confirm or to disconfirm this belief.

Models are influential in a wide variety of situations. In short-term, unclear, and transient episodes, one model can determine the action taken by many others. Analyzing the problem of discriminatory interracial behavior which takes place in public settings, Richmond (1973) noted that

> . . . in public places such as restaurants and hotels the manager or his representative frequently does not know whether or not he will act in a discriminatory way. Faced with an actual situation, he seeks clues from his white customers to indicate whether or not they will object to his serving Negro patrons. The first overt act by any white customer may be the most important influence on the manager's reactions. Direct intervention by a white customer on behalf of a Negro almost always brought service for the Negro concerned [p. 289].

Models are extremely important in situations which are much longer in duration and which have greater consequences for the people involved. The presence, absence, and suitability of models have frequently been analyzed by both social scientists and columnists who write for the popular press. Both types of analysts have used the term "role model" when referring to people whom a child might emulate. This term, once a piece of jargon found only in arcane journals, has become part of common parlance. One defense of affirmative action is that it puts more high-salaried, influential, and successful role models in public view so that children of various ethnic groups can see that hard work in school and acceptance of societal norms has a positive payoff. The absence of role models can destroy the link between schools and society. In analyzing the adaptation of Puerto Rican immigrants living in New York City, Murillo-Rohde (1976) concluded that the norms espoused by public schools concerning middle-class values are in sharp contrast to those experienced by children living in slums. Lacking role models among people from their own ethnic group, Puerto Rican children are not able to relate the process of education to later success. Instead, they are confused and alienated.

Presence or absence of ascribed power

A factor which frequently becomes very influential in cross-cultural contact is the reaction of a sojourner to power. Through absolutely no effort of their own, sojourners are often treated as if they had a great deal of power. This phenomenon occurs most often when sojourners from countries with a high gross national product live in a less technologically developed society. The examples presented here deal only with this relation between sojourners' background and technological level of the host country.

Sojourners are given a great deal of deference. They are seen as possessing tremendous expertise which can be applied to the solution of host-country problems. They are seen as wealthy people who might be able to help individual hosts. For instance, Kidder (1977) found that 60 percent of white sojourners in India believed that hosts used the terms "rich, wealthy, and money [p. 54]" in describing Westerners. It is important to keep in mind that the ascription of power is a situational variable. Sojourners are viewed in this way upon arrival in the host country regardless of whether or not they are considered powerful people in their own country.

Recent research has led to a great deal of insight into the effects of power on the powerholders. In general, findings indicate that Lord Acton had a great deal of insight when he posited that "power tends to corrupt and absolute power corrupts absolutely." Kipnis (1976) has developed the following sequence of events to describe the decline in humanitarian feelings on the part of powerholders. People in powerful positions come to enjoy themselves. After all, they are flattered by others, find that others agree with their opinions, and discover that their every recommendation is followed or at least listened to attentively. Since the use of power becomes enjoyable, people attempt to acquire more. Since others do not want to offend the powerful, no negative feedback or suggestions for improvement are ever put forth. In an environment where no disagreement is present, powerholders acquire an exaggerated view of themselves. One manifestation of the self-perception is that powerholders take credit for the accomplishments of others. The powerholders come to believe that others simply followed orders or accepted suggestions and so the *real credit* for the *ideas* should be taken by themselves. Consequently, they devalue the worth of the less powerful and avoid warm interpersonal contact with them. To complicate the situation even further, power ascription is not always necessary to cause these negative effects. The politeness of many hosts and norms which prevent inattention and face-to-face disagreement can be interpreted as power ascription by sojourners. Because they feel powerful, sojourners engage in negative behaviors such as derogating hosts.

These very common tendencies of powerholders can cause tremendous difficulties for relations among sojourners and hosts. Kidder (1977) also presented a sequence of events which she specifically applied to cross-cultural contact. Her data were gathered from sojourners who were carrying out various job assignments in India. She began her analysis with the fact that many sojourners from technologically developed countries live at a level far higher than hosts.

One argument [often heard] to justify the benefits and privileges West-erners enjoy is that they must be given some form of "compensation" for assuming such "hardship posts." Another line of reasoning states that in order to get qualified advisers, teachers, businessmen, or managers one must promise the salaries and fringe benefits commensurate with their qualifications; . . . such incentives are effective in recruiting qualified personnel, but [research suggests] that there may be some negative side effects too. If being a wealthy high-status foreigner contributes to the derogation of and alienation from one's hosts, then we might lessen both of these effects by diminishing the difference between the economic status and privileges of Western sojourners and their host nationals [pp. 58–59].

The latter principle of diminishing the economic distinction between so-journers and hosts has been adopted by the American Peace Corps and by volunteer agencies from a number of countries.

Relating the ascription of power to cross-cultural adjustment, Howard Schumann (1979, personal communication) summarized the problem in this way. "Sojourners have to deal with their feelings stemming from the frequent kow-towing of hosts."

Consequences for self or others

In some situations, sojourners do not have to deal very much with the consequences that their behavior might have on hosts or fellow country-men. In other situations, the consequences for others are very important. Ruben and Kealey (1979), for instance, hypothesized that different types of sojourners would be effective on task-oriented assignments depending on whether or not they could work alone or had to interact with others. When hosts are to be responsible for taking over a project after the sojourner returns home, cordial working relations have to be established. Sojourners have to take the needs of hosts into account. They must behave in a manner which reflects their partial responsibility for the work to be carried out eventually by their co-workers.

A person's concern for the consequences to others colors the content of questions asked during orientation programs. When people are to be ac-companied by their families, questions center on schools, housing, medical facilities, and diseases which might have long-term consequences for children. When sojourners are to travel by themselves, questions center more on the types of material covered in this book: adjustment, developing relations with co-workers, and support groups. Administrators of orienta-tion programs are often disappointed that the questions of the accom-panied sojourners are not more "deep." Just a moment's reflection, how-ever, will generate some empathy for those sojourners' point of view. If administrators can prepare an information packet on the needs of spouses and children, the orientation program can quickly proceed to other matters.

FAMILIARITY:. CONFRONTING CULTURAL DIFFERENCES

Another variable is whether or not the situations people face are familiar. If people deal with familiar situations, they know how to behave so that their goals might be attained. They know how to interact with others whom they might meet, what the probable response of the others will be, and even the type of events which might change the situation. When interacting in other cultures, however, many if not most situations are unfamiliar. Sojourners do not know what to expect from others and hosts often behave in ways which are unfamiliar. Further, the same behavior may be considered proper in one culture but bizarre or rude in another. Cultural differences can be considered situational variables since sojourners have to confront them directly so that they can achieve their goals. This approach to cultural differences has been taken by Mishler (1965) and others who have investigated the experiences of sojourners.

> The sojourn situation is inevitably a situation in which the individual is confronted with a culture different from his own, in terms of customs, values, standards, and expectations. Thus another set of factors that is likely to play a significant role in the nature of the interaction between host and visitor is the degree and nature of the cultural differences between the two societies. Here we are not dealing with the fact that the two societies *represent* different cultures and nationalities, but with the direct effect of these differences themselves, in other words, with the way in which these differences affect the course of the contact and interaction [p. 555].

A number of examples have already been given in various parts of this book. The difference between Greek and American views of the in-group and its consequences for the treatment of sojourners in Greece was covered in chapter 1. Differences between European and Masai concepts concerning the uses and care of cattle and the implications for rangeland development were covered in chapter 4. Other examples will be presented in this chapter. The investigation of cultural differences is sometimes called the "culture specific" aspect of a sojourn (Brislin & Pedersen, 1976). Most of the material in this book is "culture general" since it deals with the types of issues faced by all sojourners. The culture specific component involves the analysis of the society in which the sojourner will live and work. In many orientation programs, the culture general component provides the outline of concepts, and the culture specific component provides the examples. Obviously, no one book can cover all cultural differences which sojourners assigned to any part of the world might face. A few examples, however, can sensitize people to the necessity of seeking out culture specific examples in preparation for their sojourns.

Another point must be covered in any discussion of cultural differences. Examples have to be couched in generalities: Greeks have a certain definition of the in-group and Masai treat cattle in a certain way. Many people object on the basis that the examples are stereotypes. I do not know a reply to the complaint which will satisfy all critics. Surveys rarely exist which give numbers of hosts who behave according to the generality and numbers who can be considered exceptions. Sojourners do not have the time to interact with large numbers of hosts before discovering reasonable generalizations on their own. The best solution, in my view, is to recommend that sojourners study the generalizations but keep in mind that there will always be exceptions. As pointed out in chapters 3 and 4, the most effective sojourners have open minds which allow categories to be modified with experience. The generalities can provide a bare Christmas tree which allows a person to begin a sojourn with some limited knowledge about the host culture. Specific experiences then act as hatchets and ornaments which allow sojourners to trim and decorate the trees in unique ways. Two examples of cultural differences will be given concerning behavior in the United States, the U.S.S.R., the Philippines, and Arab countries. The two issues are negotiation style and norms regarding interpersonal behavior. Even though the specific examples may not be relevant to the experience of all sojourners, the issues certainly are.

Cultural differences: negotiation style

The manner in which people negotiate policy issues differs from country to country. Glenn, Witmeyer, and Stevenson (1977), based on an analysis of negotiations carried out in the Security Council of the United Nations, identified three styles. Their data were derived from discussions held in 1967 concerning the Arab-Israeli war. The three styles were:

1. factual-inductive, common in the United States. In their thinking, people move from pertinent facts to conclusions. People try to ascertain what the facts are, find similarities or points which can be discussed with the other party, and proceed to formulating conclusions such as a range of action alternatives.
2. axiomatic-deductive, common in the U.S.S.R. In their thinking, peo-

ple move from a general principle to particulars which can be easily deduced. The deductions should be easily understandable; clarity is one criterion of proof. Negotiators find it difficult to move to particulars unless there is agreement on general principles. One reason for continual difficulties in negotiations between the United States and the Soviet Union is that the general principles are so different: capitalism vs. communism, or decentralized vs. centralized governmental decision making. Further, the concept of "compromise" has a very negative connotation in the Russian language.

3. intuitive-affective, common in Arab countries. People express their positions through appeals and emotions. Facts seem to take second place to feelings. The style leads to intense public outbursts which have been given the label "sabre rattling" by non-Arabs. Yousef (1978) has also discussed Arab tendencies for linguistic exaggeration.

In addition to the distinctions among styles, there are the added dimensions of public vs. private discussions and the importance of close friendships between people from different cultures. Both of these dimensions were analyzed by Glenn et al. (1977) in their discussions of negotiations with representatives of Arab states.

> Rigid attitudes taken in public are often only one side of the total communication situation. They may often be accompanied by other, largely private, exchanges of views. The latter are often carried out through intermediaries. The softening of the overall position may be indicated by strong expressions of personal friendship and esteem towards the intermediary. This, of course, did take place in the shuttle diplomacy carried out by former Secretary of State Henry Kissinger [p. 64].

The concept of differing negotiation styles has applications to the experiences of many sojourners, not just those working on intergovernmental policy issues. People accustomed to one style find it difficult or at least confusing to cope with another. People who use the intuitive-affective style in a country where the factual-inductive style is more common are labeled "unpleasant hotheads" and "poor thinkers," and their opinions are not taken seriously. People who use the factual-inductive style where the axiomatic-deductive style is more common are puzzled by the high level of generality which is maintained during discussions. Abstractions seem to color the interpretation of specific facts. Americans in Europe, for instance, have a difficult time conversing about social problems since abstract political principles are the starting point and are present throughout the discussions. Sojourners about to live in Europe are well advised to do some reading on political parties.

Cultural differences: prescriptive versus proscriptive norms

If "the presence or absence of norms" was suggested as a situational factor, it would probably be of limited use because of its high level of abstraction. There are so many types of norms, and norms regulate behavior so frequently, that little is added by working with a highly abstract concept. Researchers who have studied the more specific concept of "norms concerning the amount and type of intercultural relations," however, have provided very useful insights.

In work carried out in a number of cultures, Triandis (1964; 1972) has identified different types of interracial behavior which seem to be regulated by different norms. These are etic, or general, principles which apply to many cultures. Knowledge of emic, or specific, manifestations is necessary for an understanding of how the norms apply in a given culture.

1. Intimate acceptance includes willingness to enter into a romantic relationship, to fall in love, and to marry. It also includes a willingness to have one's sons and daughters engage in these behaviors with members of another cultural group.
2. Friendship acceptance includes gossiping, sharing meals, willingness to do a favor, being on a first name basis, and spending free time together.
3. Positional acceptance includes a willingness to obey, ask an opinion, work on the same job, invite to a formal dinner, praise, and help elect to formal office.
4. Categorical rejection involves total exclusion from opportunities for intercultural contact in any situation.

Norms which regulate intercultural contact vary across the different classes of behaviors. In the United States, an individual might be allowed to work with a person from another culture (positional acceptance), but not to spend free time with the person (friendship acceptance).

Building on these findings, Ehrlich and Van Tubergen (1969) discovered that in thinking about possible intercultural relationships, people are more confident concerning what they will *not do*. Community norms which forbid certain behaviors, called proscriptive, are clearer in people's minds than norms which permit certain behaviors, called prescriptive. One reason is that proscriptive norms are very easy to communicate: people cannot marry someone from another group. Prescriptive norms undoubtedly involve subtle distinctions: an individual can be friendly with "those people," but not if grandparents are visiting or if a job working with a wealthy but intolerant employer is desired.

All societies have norms regulating intercultural contact, but the exact form concerning the who, when, and where of prescriptive norms varies from place to place. These are very hard for sojourners to learn. Foreign students meet Americans in classroom settings and find that relations are pleasant. The sojourners cannot understand why they are not included in after-class social gatherings. In some situations, the emic variant on the etic principle is the cause of cross-cultural misunderstanding. At a certain age in Filipino communities, the distinction between friendship acceptance and intimate acceptance becomes extremely small. If a man of marriageable age acts in a friendly manner toward a young woman of similar years, the attribution centers on romantic intentions. Many friendly sojourners have been caught: they thought they were being polite, but hosts thought otherwise.

COPING WITH UNFAMILIAR SITUATIONS: CULTURE SHOCK

Sojourners continually have to deal with situations which are unfamiliar to them. They are forced to change their behavior so that they may cope with cultural differences. They must struggle to discover what is meaningful and meaningless in a situation, keeping in mind that cues learned in their own culture may not be relevant. Many times, the only judgment they can make is that the new situation is ambiguous.

The constant coping with unfamiliar situations causes almost all sojourners to question their competence. The resulting self-doubt is the primary symptom of culture shock. Originally used by Oberg (1958) in his work with Foreign Service officers, culture shock is a shorthand descriptor which summarizes sojourners' reactions after they lose the security of familiarity. People know how to satisfy their everyday needs in their own culture, but they have to learn different methods during their sojourns. They have to find, or at least become accustomed to, new housing, food, jobs, and co-workers. They also have to keep themselves healthy despite an unfamiliar climate, water supply, and set of norms regarding personal cleanliness. While coping with these various demands, sojourners must feel like children. In fact, self-doubts are reinforced when they observe host-culture children behaving in a more effective manner. The inability to face situations in familiar ways and the continual need to grope for new behaviors which will more effectively meet one's needs lead to fatigue, discomfort, and frustration.

The concept of culture shock has most often been used when analyzing the experiences of people who live for significant periods of time in another country. Culture shock can also be experienced by individuals who have face-to-face contact with out-group members within their own country. While there may be *more* contributing factors when people participate in an overseas sojourn, out-group contact can also lead to fatigue, discomfort, and frustration. As an example, a brief look at the typical experiences of young schoolteachers, black or white, who enter a newly desegregated inner-city school may be instructive. The teachers have recently had the experience of at least four years of college where reading, writing, and oral performance were rewarded. Even if the teachers came from a lower-class background, they were in college long enough to use it as a reference point and to develop a new comparison level. Upon entering the desegregated school, they meet students who previously had not been expected to read or write. Oral communication is sometimes difficult because of dialectical differences. Homework assignments go undone. Students seem to reward each other for classroom disruption, certainly not for the sort of performance which leads to good grades. Teacher exhortations on the value of hard work fall on deaf ears. The teachers become fatigued from trying to communicate with students and, eventually, become frustrated because students seem to make no progress. Teachers feel rejected, a terribly deadening blow since the self-image of teachers includes the provision that they be able to communicate with students.

On the other hand, students are also likely to experience some culture shock. They have to interact with a teacher who seems quite different from those they have encountered in the past. They have a difficult time seeing the necessity of schoolwork since older acquaintances who *did* study and graduate cannot find jobs. The teacher's examples are unfamiliar since the students have not had the range of experiences which the examples might tap. Any positive expectations that were felt as a function of a new teacher and a new school are diminished in the wake of student frustration.

Symptoms of culture shock

No one sojourner will experience all symptoms of culture shock which have been reported (Brislin & Pedersen, 1976; Taft, 1977; Textor, 1966a), but almost all will experience some. There is an excessive preoccupation with personal cleanliness, manifested in worries about drinking water, food, and dirt in one's surroundings. People become irritable at very slight provocations. They overinterpret hosts' helpful suggestions as severe criticism, and they begin to feel that hosts are cheating them. Sojourners develop other negative feelings toward hosts, refusing to learn the local language and incorporating pejorative slang terms into their vocabularies. There is a sense of hopelessness with life in the host culture, and a strong desire to interact with members of one's own nationality. However, they may not interact if given the chance since they are uncomfortable with themselves and do not want fellow nationals to see them in such a state. Sojourners experience a decline in inventiveness, spontaneity, and flexibility, so much so that their work declines in quality. People feel lonely, find it difficult to communicate their feelings to others and, consequently, have a great deal of time to contemplate how unfortunate they are.

The mundane quality of culture shock

The word "mundane" can be used as an indicator of ordinary, everyday occurrences. In this sense, it should be used more frequently to explain the nature of culture shock. Since its inception as an explanatory device in Oberg's 1958 publication, culture shock has had an interesting history. When the Peace Corps first started training volunteers in the early 1960s, the concept was fresh and ready to be applied. Many thousands of sojourners were exposed to the concept and it became part of their language. It was introduced in a misleading way, however. Culture shock was treated as something only unsuccessful volunteers experienced. Any of the symptoms could be interpreted as an indicator of a poor cross-cultural adjustment. As a result, many volunteers took their feelings of culture shock personally and let the symptoms interfere with their work. Volunteers came to doubt their self-worth. While most people eventually coped with their feelings (Szanton, 1966), the time necessary to progress from frustration to coping took longer than necessary. If culture shock could have been introduced as a perfectly normal reaction which virtually all sojourners experience, then it would not have been taken so personally. Instead, some of the positive benefits of culture shock could have been explored. Interestingly, the term is now part of everyday language, frequently used by journalists who do not feel any necessity to define it.

The positive benefits of culture shock

The feelings which stem from culture shock can be looked upon as a prod. If accepted, the nudgings can lead to opportunities for new learning. Adler (1975) has proposed seven ways in which culture shock can contribute to individual growth.

1. Learning always involves some form of change. The different situations sojourners have to face can be looked upon as providing opportunities which demand new responses.
2. Culture shock can be analyzed as an individualized phenomenon. No two people are affected by the same situations or experience the same set of symptoms. Since most people enjoy feeling unique or special, culture shock can be a motivational force.
3. The feelings stemming from change can be provocative. People can be encouraged to examine themselves to determine why they have certain

symptoms. In everyday language, they can analyze why they feel the way they do.

4. The greatest amount of learning does not take place when individuals experience low levels of anxiety. At low levels, there is no reason for people to work on learning new materials or ideas. The frustration, anxiety, and personal pain stemming from culture shock can bring the level of anxiety to the optimal level. Then, people will be motivated to learn so that they will acquire new knowledge and skills which can be used to reduce the anxiety. The problem with this suggestion is, admittedly, that the anxiety level can be too high. People may be so upset that they are unable to focus on new learning possibilities.

5. One reason for culture shock is that people have to deal with others from very different backgrounds. Like the responses to culture shock, an individual's set of relationships with hosts is unique. In dealing with hosts, all of them previously unknown, the sojourner has many opportunities to learn since hosts are likely to provide extensive feedback. Further, a sojourner has a unique role as an outsider since (s)he is able to perceive ideas which are taken for granted by hosts.

6. New ideas lead to to experimentation with different behaviors. Sojourners can engage in trial and error attempts to best meet a situation, learning a great deal in the process. Sojourners experience the elation of success after discovering the most appropriate behavior.

7. The new ideas learned during experimentation are frequently based on comparisons and contrasts. Given the motivation provided by culture shock, sojourners can relate the new ideas to the functioning of various societies. As was discussed in chapter 5, the motivation to learn also encourages a confrontation with, and a greater understanding of, one's own culture.

The negative consequences of culture shock

In addition to the severe interference with new learning caused by high levels of anxiety, culture shock has other negative consequences. At times, professional intervention aimed at helping distressed sojourners will be required. Draguns (1977) has proposed four general types of symptoms which lead to an attribution of "abnormal" by those people who happen to observe a troubled individual. Tentatively, Draguns has suggested that these general patterns exist in all societies.

1. Affective experiences, also called "mood," which people express in behaviors at the low and high ends of a continuum. At the high end are people who are manic, excitable, and sometimes hysterical. At the low end are people who feel severely depressed.

2. Perceptual-cognitive appraisal, taking into account the absence of any obvious physiological defect. The range is from behaviors which are incomprehensible, idiosyncratic, and bizarre to those which are considered proper or desirable by members of a culture. Of course, the exact behaviors which are considered bizarre vs. desirable differ from culture to culture. The public behaviors of people who have adopted the norms of the so-called sexual revolution are literally incomprehensible to people from cultures in which all sexual behavior is conducted privately.

3. "Organismic expression, from tense, anxious, jittery, jumpy, and 'nervous' at the one end to related, composed, loosely yet appropriately controlled at the other [Draguns, 1977, p. 59]."

4. Social behavior, which is considered unreliable, unpredictable, dishonest, or extremely ill-mannered to their opposites of reliability, honesty, propriety, and decorum. Again, members of different cultures place similar behaviors at various points along the continuum.

One of the clearest examples of the importance of cultural background was seen among Hungarian immigrants in Detroit in the 1930's. The Hungarian peasant had a traditional right to "steal" wood from his lord's estate for fuel, and in their new cultural environment the immigrants transmuted this norm by deeming it permissible to steal coal from trucks standing on the railway [Bottoms, 1973, p. 445].

The advantage of the general framework proposed by Draguns is that sojourners can study it for help in interpreting their feelings. The possible universality of these symptoms can be used as an orientation device by program administrators. Any technique which takes away the feelings of a given sojourner that "I'm the only one!" is an aid to cross-cultural adjustment. More specific lists of problematic symptoms derived from investigations into various types of cross-cultural experiences are also useful.

In a review of the specific problems facing foreign students, Higginbotham (1979) suggested a number of concepts which are probably helpful in understanding the reactions of all sojourners who encounter highly stressful situations. The experiences of migrants have also been studied in enough detail (Sanua, 1970) to justify tentative conclusions. Until more research is done which might allow generalizations of the findings, however, "foreign students" or "migrants" will be used here rather than "sojourner."

Students and migrants are usually quite skillful at putting problems aside if they have clear goals to which they are deeply committed. Foreign students, for instance, are highly motivated to obtain a university degree. Their intensity often stems from a fear that home country reference group members will think ill of the returnees if they fail in their quest. During the sojourn, the desirable behaviors of making friends and the common problems of homesickness and financial planning take second place to schoolwork. Informed observers (Schwartz, 1975) are concerned that this headstrong orientation can eventually lead to psychosomatic symptoms.

When students *do* seek professional help and voice their complaints, the symptoms expressed are often somatic (Alexander, Workneh, Klein, & Miller, 1976). People complain of stomachaches, diarrhea, headaches, tiredness, problems with sleep, and pain which cannot be localized in one part of the body. Until very recently, physicians attempted to treat the sojourner's problem as if it were indeed somatic. Although there are surely cases in which this diagnosis continues, the increasing number of research studies which have replicated the "somatic symptom" effect among sojourners (Marsella, Kinzie, & Gordon, 1973; Sue & Sue, 1972) has led many physicians to look beyond verbal complaints. The difficulties in providing proper treatment are made more difficult since students rarely use facilities where mental health specialists work (Klein, Alexander, Tseng, Miller, Yeh, Chu, & Workneh, 1971; Pedersen, 1975). Rather, they seek help from general practitioners, teachers, educational counseling centers, or fellow countrymen. There is still a widespread view that any symptom which might involve one's mental health is a sign of weakness. Fellow nationals seem especially sensitive both to the frequency of severe culture shock reactions and to their friend's disinclination to admit psychological problems. Fellow nationals come to the aid of their friend, unasked, and tolerate eccentric behavior as well as their friend's frustration, irritability, and alienation (Clarke, 1975). The probable reasons are that sojourners identify with their own nationalities while in another country (Bochner & Perks, 1971), and they have insight into their friend's predicament since they are coping with similar situations themselves.

More intense psychological problems do not seem to differ between foreign students and hosts who attend the same university. The frequency of psychotic reactions and suicides are similar for both types of students (Alexander et al., 1976), suggesting that problems stem from the role of "student under pressure" rather than the role of "foreigner." Similarly, Taft (1977) is concerned that some analysts (DeVos & Hippler, 1969) have overstated the case for severe stress and mental breakdowns among migrants. These findings and opinions suggest that a broad view of culture shock or "transition shock" is useful (J. Bennett, 1977). Any person who is faced with unfamiliar situations is likely to experience transition shock. Examples are:

1. adolescents from rural backgrounds who go to college in a big city far away from home.

2. young couples accustomed to an active social life. Upon arrival of their first child they may have to spend much time at home.
3. senior citizens forced for medical reasons to move from their homes into an institution where they can receive care from nurses.

The advantage of taking the broad view is that research findings on these types of situational change can be studied for insights into the experiences of sojourners.

The treatment of severe problems

Even though they are more likely to use other means of coping, such as dependence upon their membership groups, sojourners occasionally seek the help of a professional therapist. Diagnosis has to precede treatment, but both aspects of psychological intervention are made more difficult because of cultural differences between the therapist and client. In commenting on a finding that island-born Puerto Ricans living in the United States have a higher rate of schizophrenia than the better-educated mainland Puerto Ricans, Sanua (1970) felt that the experience of being a migrant was not the major factor. Rather, he suggested that American psychiatrists may have difficulty communicating with the Spanish-speaking islanders, may become confused and, consequently, may use the catch-all diagnosis of "schizophrenia." Similarly, Higginbotham (1979) is concerned that diagnostic labels might cause the real problem to be missed. Using concepts similar to those introduced in chapter 4, Higginbotham feels that sojourners actively try to make sense out of new situations but inevitably will make a number of incorrect attributions.

> To maintain . . . a system of false beliefs about the environment may then earn the individual a psychiatric diagnosis of "paranoid." However, given the seemingly uncertain nature of the environment, it is predictable that the content of these beliefs would focus on personal danger. A social setting unsuccessfully negotiated creates a sense of helplessness; it leads to suspicion and fear of others and their actions. In short, it is more advantageous to analyze how this particular group of individuals came to learn a dysfunctional adaptation to their new environment, than to apply clinical labels like "paranoid" or "schizophrenic" to their actions [p. 55].

Assuming a diagnosis has been made, treatment can take a number of forms. There is now a specialized literature on the topic of treating sojourners when the client and therapist are from different cultures. Long reviews and books have provided many helpful insights (Draguns, 1977; Higginbotham, 1977, 1979; Kiev, 1973; Pedersen, Lonner, & Draguns,

1976; Sue & Sue, 1971). The topics given extensive treatment include:

1. Developing specific competencies among therapists concerning intervention into the problems of people from different cultural backgrounds.
2. Decision making regarding the focus of treatment offered to sojourners. Should it be in terms of the cultures to which sojourners will return, the host culture, some third culture (Useem & Useem, 1967) which takes into account the unique experiences of sojourners, or a little of all three approaches?
3. Integrating the helpful fellow national in treatment.
4. Utilizing various approaches to identify the client's difficulties, such as asking a third person to role play the "problem" in the company of the help seeker and therapist (Pedersen, 1977; 1980). Problem identification is especially difficult since the parties involved do not always share the same ideas about what is normal, appropriate, and reasonable.
5. Examining whether or not therapists should change their style. A major therapeutic school in the United States insists that a helper should be nonjudgmental and should encourage clients to examine their own behavior. The eventual goal is for clients to make their own decisions about which courses of action they should pursue in their everyday behaviors. Many sojourners, however. come from cultures in which helpers are expected to be much more direct. They want to be told what is wrong and they want recommendations concerning what to do.
6. Determining client expectancies concerning the outcomes of therapy. Unrealistic expectations can bring disappointment and an aggravation of problems.
7. Determining whether or not psychological tests, almost always developed within one culture, will be of any help when administered to sojourners.
8. Looking at the therapy situation as providing opportunities for new learning. Clients might also obtain insights into how they might transfer the learning to everyday situations after the therapy is terminated.

Given the existence of this specialized literature, and the impossibility of providing even a cursory review in anything less than a book-length volume, no further treatment will be attempted here. There is another reason for this decision. Draguns (1977) has pointed out that a fascination with the vivid and colorful aspects of severe symptomatology has led to gaps in our knowledge about cross-cultural contact.

For a variety of historical and other reasons some of which are obvious and others, obscure, research extant has been disproportionately concerned with adults exhibiting the most serious and/or dramatic distortions in cultures most different from our own. This tradition of exoticism has to be overcome, to give way to the study of the entire range of disturbance in cultures and subcultures at all degrees of similarity. Paradoxically, we know . . . a lot more about the cultural shaping of schizophrenia and psychotic depression than about that of anxiety neurosis and of transient maladjustment [p. 66].

Rather than review again the literature on severe symptomatology and appropriate treatments, I shall attempt to fill the gap which Draguns identifies: the transient, mundane stresses faced by virtually all sojourners.

THE ROLE OF SITUATIONS IN DETERMINING FAVORABLE ATTRIBUTIONS

The importance of situational variables in contributing to people's thinking was introduced in chapter 4. In making attributions about behavior, people employ both trait and situational factors. When judging the actions of other people, trait attributions are common. The situation contributes to the positiveness or negativeness of people's trait judgments. Findings were reviewed which supported the proposition that the stresses faced in intercultural encounters lead to negative trait attributions. Sojourners experiencing severe culture shock seem unwilling to examine the situational pressures which face them and seem disinclined to explain their own behavior and that of others in situational terms. Upon encountering disagreements with hosts, there is *not* a tendency to consider situational variables. Sojourners do not carefully consider cultural differences, pressures faced by hosts, or language conventions which might be misinterpreted. Instead, sojourners use trait judgments: the others are hostile, unfriendly, or cheats who look after their own. One goal of cross-cultural orientation programs is to encourage sojourners to consider situational factors before making negative judgments about hosts.

On the other hand, sojourners who have pleasant interactions are likely to conclude that the observed behaviors stem from a desirable set of traits. Sojourners conclude that hosts are kind, warm, and considerate. The extremely positive views of mainland China, described by the first wave of American journalists who visited in the mid-1970s, can be partially explained by the tendency to assign trait attributions. The journalists were treated well and they responded with the fundamental attribution error by concluding that traits were the determinative factors. There was surprisingly little inclination to consider that tours might be carefully staged, hosts hand-picked, and aspects of the Chinese culture painstakingly selected to communicate a favorable image. The tendency to perceive that favorable situations stem from desirable traits is sometimes purposefully downplayed. Some people are naturally cynical and always examine the motives of others. Experienced Foreign Service officers are expected to look into any Trojan Horse which seems to be offered with no strings attached. One motive for any person's actions, or any country's policies, is enlightened self-interest.

There are a number of situational factors which increase the probability of favorable trait attributions. As with most principles developed from research in the behavioral and social sciences reviewed throughout this book, applications can be attempted by both altruists and despots. My hope is that when potential "consumers" are knowledgeable, they will be able to make informed judgments about the opportunities offered by others.

The major factor encouraging favorable trait attributions is the availability of rewards for all people involved. Rewards are defined broadly as resources which people desire: love, status, information, money, goods, and services (Foa & Foa, 1974). This principle has been applied to the achievement of minority group students in school (Katz, 1973b). Students seem to estimate the probability of attaining a certain performance standard recommended by teachers. They also consider whether or not there will be any rewards should the standard be obtained. If they perceive that attainment of the standard and corresponding rewards are probable, they will do the necessary work. They will also conclude that teachers are reasonable people who are trying to help.

The absence of rewards leads to negative trait attributions. In analyzing race relations in the British school system, Verma (1977) indicated that many authorities feared an increase in student prejudice if curriculum materials on interracial tolerance were introduced. Earlier, Miller (1969) had completed a widely publicized study showing that curriculum materials could increase prejudicial attitudes. The reason seemed to be that broaching the topic of prejudice in the cautious manner typical of curriculum materials caused students to think about their attitudes. However, they were able to reject the weak arguments presented in the materials. Because they expanded some effort in studying and rejecting the materials, their original negative attitudes were reinforced. On the basis of Miller's results, school administrators were extremely reluctant to continue the funding of research which might lead to better materials. Instead, their judgment was that researchers who recommended the development and on-site evaluation of race-related teaching materials were dangerous. Fortunately, after a great deal of time and effort, Verma (1977) was able to overcome the fear of some administrators and to continue research.

Situational factors can be improved by giving attention to the self-interests of all parties. Since the spouses of Foreign Service officers want to keep occupied in host countries, they often seek employment. There is a problem, however, encountered by both Americans working abroad and representatives of other countries who serve in the United States. Host country visa regulations keep spouses out of the job market. Boredom, frustration, and resentment contribute to a negative evaluation of hosts. Joan Wilson (personal communication, 1979) of the United States Foreign Service Institute believes that the problem is being alleviated to some extent through intergovernmental negotiations. The Department of State, through its overseas missions, is negotiating with other governments for reciprocal agreements which will allow the spouses of employees to work in their country of assignment. For each country agreeing to the provisions, the spouses of embassy employees will be able to work in the United States if spouses of State Department employees are given similar permission when assigned to that country. Governmental representatives are familiar with this give-and-take negotiation style designed to protect the interests of both countries. Since clear benefits are available to the participating countries, positive judgments about the policy and policymakers should follow.

THE INFLUENCE OF SITUATIONS IN DETERMINING TASK PRODUCTIVITY

Situational variables can also be manipulated to increase the probability of successful task completion. Fiedler (1967) has argued that different types of people, when placed in leadership roles, are effective in different types of situations. Although Fiedler does not use the terms, the types of leaders for whom predictions are possible correspond to task-oriented and social relations-oriented people as discussed in chapter 2. Task-oriented people are concerned with group output and with successful completion of assignments. Social relations-oriented people are concerned with the feelings of others and the maintenance of cordial relations among group members. While most people exhibit behaviors typical of both types, one of the orientations is usually stronger. The situational variables Fiedler has analyzed are:

1. leader-member relations: whether or not the leader is liked and respected.
2. task structure: goals may or may not be clear, and means of attaining them may or may not be readily available.
3. position power: whether or not the leader can reward subordinates and be assured of backing by the organization.

Different situations can be placed on a dimension of favorableness to unfavorableness. If leader-member relations are good, the task structured, and position of power assured, the situation is said to be favorable. If the situation is marked by the opposite pole of all three variables, it is said to be unfavorable. Situations with a mix, high on one variable but low on another, are said to be intermediate.

Task leaders are more effective than social leaders when working in situations marked by the extremes of high and low favorableness. In highly favorable situations, there are few group-related problems: people like each other, tasks are clear, and the leader has power. Members can spend their time and energy on work under the guidance of a production-oriented person. In highly unfavorable situations, task leaders are apparently necessary if any work is to be accomplished. Perhaps there are so many problems that guidance from a task-oriented leader is the only input which might be effective. Task leaders do not necessarily welcome unfavorable situations. Rather, when faced with the challenge, they are more effective than social-oriented leaders. It should be noted, especially with groups composed of people from several cultures, that even the most accomplished task leaders will be ineffective when intragroup relations are extremely poor. This point will be examined shortly when the experiences of American businessmen working in Japan are discussed.

Social leaders are more effective in situations of moderate favorableness. One possible reason is that moderately unfavorable situations can be improved, and the social leader is more skillful at marshaling the efforts of group members and encouraging them to contribute. For instance, if leader-member relations are good but the task unstructured and power unclear, the social leader can encourage others to make suggestions regarding the task and an acceptable system of rewards and punishments. Since the leader is sincerely interested in others, group members are likely to respond.

Different tasks call for different types of leaders. In the planning stages of a technical assistance project, a social leader may be effective in encouraging hosts to provide input. Opinions about the appropriate level of technology, cultural imposition, and covert expectations which accompany foreign aid are important. But after hosts agree on an elaborate set of plans, a task-oriented person may be more successful in carrying them out. In applying Fiedler's (1962) work to problems of intergovernmental negotiation, Sawyer and Guetzkow (1965) proposed that creative suggestions are influenced by the amount of tension with which people must cope. Task leaders are more effective in tense situations and their behavior is marked by a formal elaboration of ideas and a general encouragement of more activity. In more relaxed groups, humorous and other types of unrelated comments increase creativity. "This suggests the possible importance, for promoting creative solutions, of tailoring the kind of interaction to the degree of tension inherent in the situation [Sawyer & Guetzkow, 1965, p. 486]." Skilled negotiators have many types of interpersonal management techniques in their repertoires and can call upon them as required.

Alternatively, a situation can be analyzed by an administrator and an appropriate negotiator assigned to it. Andrew Young first achieved prominence through this sort of assignment. During the Civil Rights Movement of the 1960s, he was very skillful in negotiations with extremely hostile, racist whites. Dr. Martin Luther King would assign Young to the most difficult and volatile interracial negotiations. Young's skills included the ability to encourage frank discussions of issues and to diffuse anger through talk instead of violent action. Possibly, these skills did not serve him as effectively in the role of Ambassador to the United Nations. There, diplomatic norms of softspokenness and careful phrasings of communications are enforced.

Other strategies are possible. Leaders might choose to correct a situational factor before proceeding to actual work on a task. In Japan, American sojourners have learned that a high value is placed on warm relations among business partners. Much time has to be spent on "getting to know one another" before substantive work can begin (Cathcart & Cathcart, 1976). Wise businessmen plan their sojourns to allow time for the development of interpersonal relations. Japan is not the only country where warm relations are necessary before work can begin. There are a few aspects of American behavior which have been the target of complaints in many parts of the world. The perceived rudeness of Americans in business dealings and their desire to start work immediately after meeting hosts have been mentioned often enough to warrant the status of informed generalities rather than stereotypes. Much situational stress can be reduced or avoided if sojourners develop genuinely warm relations with their hosts.

SUMMARY AND CONCLUSIONS

Situational influences are difficult to discuss since there is not a clear, widely accepted set of descriptive terms which might allow efficient communication of ideas. In broad terms, situations refer to combinations of factors, external to people, with which they must deal to accomplish their goals. In attempting to help readers grasp this very general definition, I felt that the use of several explanatory methods would be best. Everyday examples were given based on physical features of the environment in which people must work and the numbers of others present in a given situation. Research studies concerned with interracial interaction and aggression stemming from anonymity were analyzed. A preliminary listing of key situational factors was presented, together with their applicability for the understanding of cross-cultural contact. Finally, sojourners' experiences stemming from the confrontation of cultural differences were examined in situational terms. Given this introduction, the situational factors reviewed can now be pulled together in one place.

The result is still a partial list. An important goal for future research is to develop a complete set of descriptors.

1. Aspects of the environment, such as climate, which have effects on one's energy, and the terrain one must traverse in moving from one place to another. Anthropologists take into account the energy necessary to move from one mountainous village to another while planning their field work.

2. The number of people present. Common sense suggests that the more people in a situation, the less individual attention any one can receive.

3. Face-to-face vs. impersonal interaction with others.

4. Status markers possessed by others. It is easier to reject people who do not have status symbols valued by members of a given culture.

5. Demeanor of the other people. If others seem confident, an individual is likely to go along with their suggestions.

6. Feelings of individuation, or recognizability, versus anonymity. Anonymity can encourage antisocial acts, but it can also encourage new behaviors which a person might not attempt under the watchful eyes of acquaintances.

7. Structured vs. unstructured. In some situations, people know exactly what to do. In others, they have to provide a structure before they can even think of fulfilling their goals.

8. Time constraints. Effective cross-cultural adaptation takes time and wise administrators plan for a transition phase between arrival in a new country and the start of people's work there.

9. Overmanning vs. undermanning. Overmanning can lead to boredom because there is not enough for any one individual to do. In undermanned situations, people may be overworked but they also may feel needed and appreciated.

10. Presence or absence of a niche. If sojourners can find a clear and valued role in the host society, adjustment is facilitated. Successful niche filling, on the other hand, can contribute to brain drain if sojourners feel so appreciated that they hesitate to return home.

11. Presence or absence of a model. When there are people who can demonstrate appropriate behavior, a newcomer is likely to behave likewise.

12. Ascribed power. People with power are given deference, find no

disagreement with their opinions, and are flattered. Arrogance often
₂velops as a result. Sojourners are often treated as if they were powerful
₂ople even though they may be quite ordinary citizens in their home
ɔuntries.

13. Consequences for self vs. others. Some sojourners are to be accom-
anied by others, and/or are responsible for the work of hosts. They make
efforts to incorporate the needs of others.

14. Good vs. bad leader-member relations. If leaders are liked and
espected, their suggestions for task-related efforts are likely to be ac-
epted.

15. Familiarity vs. unfamiliarity. Sojourners have to cope with situa-
ions which are unfamiliar to them. They do not know how to behave in
an appropriate manner, are unable to interpret the reactions of hosts, and
do not know how to change situations for their benefit.

The necessity to deal constantly with unfamiliar situations causes stress.
Coping with different negotiation styles and proscriptive norms are examples. People know how to negotiate with others in their own culture and
know what behaviors are forbidden. Yet, as sojourners, they must relearn
these basic skills. The feelings of childishness stemming from an inability
to interact effectively and subsequent feelings of self-doubt are primary
symptoms of "culture shock." Now a term used frequently in everyday
conversations, culture shock refers to a loss of security caused by the
removal of familiar situations. Sojourners have to become accustomed to
new housing, food, norms of cleanliness, jobs, co-workers, hosts who
might become friends, and modes of transportation. The continual groping
for new behaviors which will meet these needs leads to fatigue, discomfort,
and frustration. Other symptoms include a decline in inventiveness and
spontaneity, a tendency to derogate hosts, and feelings of loneliness. Culture shock is best explained to sojourners as an inevitable part of their
experiences, not as something which strikes only unsuccessful people. In
fact, sojourners can benefit from culture shock since it can provide the
motivation for new learning.

To be sure, culture shock occasionally has severe consequences. Disagreement exists regarding the contributions of the sojourn experience to
severe neurotic or psychotic reactions. Foreign students, for instance, may
experience severe stress in the role of a "student under pressure" rather
than in the role of a "person from another culture." One finding which has
been frequently replicated is that sojourners often "translate" severe feelings of culture shock into somatic complaints. They complain of headaches, insomnia, and diarrhea. The open discussion of psychological symptoms is still seen as a sign of weakness by many people. Fellow
countrymen often come to the aid of the stressed sojourners, manifesting

tremendous tolerance for eccentric behaviors. The treatment of severe culture shock reactions has been the focus of a specialized literature (Higginbotham, 1979; Pedersen, Lonner & Draguns, 1976). Two key issues are: (1) increasing communication, understanding and overlap in expectations between the client and therapist; and (2) deciding whether treatment should focus on host culture adjustment, the society to which sojourners will return, some "third culture" of people who share the experience of adjusting to another culture, or some combination of the three possibilities.

One goal of cross-cultural orientation programs is to encourage sojourners to make more situational attributions. When faced with culture shock, there is a tendency to make negative trait attributions about the behavior of hosts. In reality, since stress is most often a product of coping with unfamiliar situations, negative trait attributions are maladjustive and may destroy potentially helpful interpersonal relations. The probability of *positive* attributions can be increased if there are resources available which are valued by all parties. Foreign Service officers, for instance, are accustomed to incorporating the self-interests of all nations in their negotiations.

Situations can sometimes be manipulated before a person actually goes about completing task assignments. This point is especially important in cross-cultural interaction. A very common complaint about American businessmen is that they start work before developing warm and cordial relations with hosts. Wise administrators allow extra time for Americans to do little but interact with hosts in the early months of their sojourns. Much stress will never occur if good sojourner-host relations have been developed.

Now that both groups (chapter 5) and situations (chapter 6) have been introduced, actual cases of intergroup interaction can be more profitably studied. Interaction among group members takes place in various situations, such as the workplace, school, or neighborhood. Using concepts from research on groups *and* situations may yield generalizable findings which can be used to structure new programs designed to encourage intergroup contact and understanding. This interaction of group and situational factors is the focus of the next chapter.

7
Groups in Situations: Managing Cross-Cultural Contact

INTRODUCTION

While many people might prefer to interact only with in-group members and to exclude outsiders, they no longer have the complete freedom to make such a decision. Legal requirements force people to interact with out-group members in schools, on their jobs, or in their neighborhoods. Examples can be found all over the world:

- Blacks and whites in the United States (Stephan & Rosenfield, 1978);
- Jews and Arabs along the West Bank of the Jordan River (Amir et al., 1980);
- Catholics and Protestants in Northern Ireland (Doob & Foltz, 1973);
- White descendants of European immigrants and native aboriginal people in Australia (O'Brien & Plooij, 1976);
- Sojourners from Africa and Muslim citizens in Pakistan (Zaidi, 1975);
- Members of the Kipsigis and Gusii tribes in the southwestern highlands of Kenya (LeVine, 1965).

One of the most extensive and helpful set of research findings has been developed out of work in these "contact situations." Researchers and administrators have cooperated in documenting how the probability of favorable outcomes resulting from contact might be increased: positive attitude change, communication of various points of view, cordial interpersonal interaction, and helping relationships which cut across in-group/out-group distinctions. Many of these findings have centered on changing the situation in which group members are to interact.

The focus of this chapter is to suggest guidelines for administrators who, for legal, political, moral, or economic reasons, have decided to encourage intergroup contact. An assumption is that many administrators are charged

171

with the responsibility for improving intergroup relations in addition to their other goals, such as educating children in school or meeting production quotas in industry. Further, many administrators are not trained or have no experience in intergroup relations. A treatment of the lessons learned from research into a wide variety of contact situations may be helpful.

Besides simply bringing people together through ordinary bureaucratic means such as recruitment and selection, can administrators really do anything to decrease stress and to increase tolerance and understanding? Should administrators be aware of factors centering around groups and situations which might make their work more difficult? Are there *various* types of individual changes which might be examined, above and beyond favorable feelings toward out-group members? The answer to all these questions is "yes," and the evidence necessary for a defense of this position provides most of the chapter's content.

The organization of the chapter is focused on four topics: (1) a few caveats about the possible negative effects of intergroup contact; (2) the issues or "givens" which administrators face when beginning organized efforts to increase intergroup contact; (3) the situational factors administrators can manipulate in attempting to increase the probability of favorable outcomes; and (4) the various types of changes, or positive benefits, which might occur as a function of increased intergroup contact.

SOME CAVEATS

Intergroup contact is by no means a panacea to problems of prejudice and discrimination. Sometimes well-meaning people exhort: "Let's bring members of different groups together so that they will learn to understand one another and become friends." I sincerely wish the world was this simple and that group members would automatically benefit from simply encouraging intergroup interaction. However, contact per se often intensifies intergroup hostilities (Allport, 1954; Amir, 1969; Gudykunst, 1977; Riordan, 1978). The attitudes of many people concerning out-groups are so strong that contact can actually reinforce prejudice and discrimination. Hostile people are able to interpret any behavior in negative terms: friendly behavior on the part of out-group members is "apple polishing," and creative contributions are seen as coached by radical-liberal members of the dominant majority group. Riordan (1978) cautions that "certain personal and interpersonal attributions infuse contact situations, . . . providing behavioral expectations which cannot be wished away [p. 165]." In some cases, members of the minority group have been the targets of discrimination for so long that they internalize a negative view of themselves (Hare, 1977). Gudykunst (1977) concludes that to achieve the goal of "amity, contact is not enough, especially if protracted contact serves only to accumulate a series of assaults on the self esteem [p. 6]" of minority group members.

One of the conclusions of the material reviewed in chapter 4 is that there is good news and bad news about people's thinking. The good news: people are active in thinking about their world and in attempting to develop an understanding of it; the bad news: the thinking is often not very good. Rather, it is marked by overgeneralization, integration of inadequate information into already existing categories, and misinterpretation of information with which people disagree. Another caveat, then, is that, given a chance to misinterpret information and ideas which are part of a contact situation, people will find it. This point was touched upon in chapter 6 when Verma's (1977) interpretation of Miller's (1969) curriculum materials project was discussed. Arguments in the materials were weak, prejudiced people could easily deal with them, and the "success experience" of rejecting the materials reinforced the original prejudices.

The conclusion from the review of these two caveats also provides an introduction to the discussion of what administrators *can* realistically do when attempting to increase the positive benefits of contact. As Amir and Garti (1977) also conclude: "Clearly, the outcome of ethnic contact depends upon conditions prevailing at the time of the contact, and conditions of both a situational and personal nature [p. 58]." The conditions which exist at the time of intergroup contact and the personal inclinations of group members are called the background factors or "givens" in the following treatment. Many situational factors are subject to a certain amount of control by administrators, and these will be reviewed in a later section.

THE BACKGROUND FACTORS OR GIVENS WHICH FACE THE ADMINISTRATOR

In attempting to increase intergroup contact and its positive outcomes, administrators are faced with a number of factors over which they have little control. The people who might participate in the arranged contact situation have long-established attitudes; societal norms regarding the propriety of contact already exist; and recent events which receive wide publicity can heighten tensions. Even though administrators cannot control these external factors, they can be aware of resulting threats to intergroup harmony. They also may be able to select among the situational aspects they *can* manipulate to best meet these preconditions.

In a general way, a number of givens have already been described in chapters 2 through 5. Many of these can have major effects in contact situations:

1. the historical myths with which people are familiar;
2. the language people speak;
3. childhood experiences, especially discipline received from parents;
4. people's traits, attitudes, and skills;
5. the tendency to stereotype, and the "benefits" obtained from doing so;
6. people's well-established categories, and their thought processes while using them;
7. the tendency to be affected by recent, vivid events;
8. the attributional bias of explaining behavior in terms of traits instead of considering the situational pressures faced by others;
9. membership groups, and the strength of reference group ties.

A number of factors, however, have proven so important in the analysis and interpretation of contact experiences that they deserve separate treatment here. These factors are also influential in determining how much generalization from one situation to another is warranted. Administrators might study the preconditions in one contact situation, list the givens of a new situation, and compare the two for degree of similarity. They can then, decide whether or not conclusions from research in the first situation are applicable to the new work.

Extremity of initial attitudes

A number of researchers have analyzed the extremity of attitudes people hold *prior* to contact (Baty & Dold, 1977; S. Cook & Selltiz, 1955). Based on work carried out in Israel, as well as an interpretation of other research, Amir et al. (1980) concluded:

> It appears that intergroup contact reduces negative attitudes held towards the members of another ethnic group among those subjects whose initial attitudes were moderately negative and not among those whose initial attitudes were extremely unfavorable. [Contact can also increase favorability among people who already have slightly positive attitudes.] Thus, Taylor (in Cook, 1957) reported that white tenants with initial positive attitudes towards Blacks became more positive when Blacks moved into their neighborhood, while for tenants with initial negative attitudes, such enforced contact with Blacks intensified the previous attitude [p. 4].

A pictorial representation may help communicate this important point. People's attitudes can be summarized by means of a continuum:

1	2	3	4	5	6	7	8	9	10	11
very unfavorable		somewhat unfavorable			neutral		somewhat favorable			very favorable

Tremendous difficulties are encountered when trying to change people from point "1" to a point further along the continuum. It is much easier to change people from point "7" or "8" to a more favorable position of "9" or "10." Assume a research article reports on positive attitude change after an innovative situational manipulation is introduced. In studying the report, it is important to determine what sorts of participants are changing such that the *summary* result is one of positive attitude shift. If people are changing from "7" to "9," it would be unwise to conclude that the same manipulation might be effective with participants who have an initial attitude at points "1" or "2." Unfortunately, research reports frequently do not give information on initial attitudes, only that people changed in a positive direction.

The issue of initial attitudes plagues interpretation of research when participants *volunteer* to increase their intergroup contact. Can results be generalized to the experiences of people who are *forced* to increase contact? The answer is often "no." Baty and Dold (1977) analyzed the experiences of American college students who chose to participate in a home-stay program for academic credit. The basic core of people's experience was integration into families whose members belonged to different cultures. Positive changes as a result of the experience were documented: greater self-confidence and a greater sense of accomplishment than were felt before the home-stay experience. Before administrators at other schools consider establishing a similar program, they should be aware that the students were self-selected. As Baty and Dold carefully point out, participating students differed in a number of ways from the general college population. They were more nonauthoritarian, held politically liberal beliefs, were more concerned with intellectual development than the average student, and were self-consciously dissatisfied with their life in college. The latter set of feelings undoubtedly included unhappiness with the typical college routine of courses and grades and, perhaps, confusion about their role in college and their ambitions for life after formal schooling. A program which is effective with students manifesting these characteristics may not be applicable to all college students.

Conditions at the time of contact

Unforeseen circumstances summarized by the term "current events" can influence attempts to improve intergroup relations. Recent colorful events which receive media attention often intensify attitudes: the latest Ku Klux Klan cross burning; IRA bombings in Northern Ireland; charges of unfair elections in African countries attempting to shift away from white majority rule. In studying Jewish-Arab contact along the West Bank, Amir et al. (1980) pointed to the influence of publicity. The government of Israel, as a consequence of the quest for a permanent peace treaty, wanted to show that Arabs and Israelis could interact without untoward incidents in the same factory or in the same settlement. This governmental attitude may have contributed to the limited tolerance which Amir and his colleagues found among Israelis who worked in the same industrial plant as Arabs.

In attempting to desegregate schools in the United States, parental opposition to any current plan involving busing heightens tension among children. To deal with this issue, reasons for the opposition should be understood. Parents reject busing for reasons other than a desire to keep their children away from outgroup members. Some parents are committed to the idea of a neighborhood school where they might have contact with teachers and where children might participate in after-school activities. Other parents wonder if the money needed to support a fleet of buses, a gasoline supply, and the salaries of drivers might be better spent on educational materials. Some parents are upset to find their children tired after the additional daytime hours spent riding on a bus. Others are disturbed with the amount of time, energy, and money spent in revolving-door courtrooms where advocates on one side or the other constantly appeal the rulings of judges so that no "final" decision ever seems to be accepted. Since these parents are to be involved in the enforcement of any eventual decision, their opinions should be considered during early negotiations. No positive function is served by dismissing their views as "racist."

The number of preconceptions

If members of different groups hold strong prejudicial stereotypes about each other, contact carries no guarantee that attitudes will become more positive (Gudykunst, 1977; Selltiz, Christ, Havel, & Cook, 1963). The greater the number of prejudicial stereotypes, the greater the difficulties facing administrators who attempt to encourage intergroup interaction. The number of preconceptions seems to vary across different types of cross-cultural contact. When people are from different racial groups within the same country, stereotypes abound. People think they know a great deal about race because of exposure to "ideas" in school, the mass media, and conversations with friends and family members. When people are from different countries, preconceptions may be fewer (Selltiz et al., 1963). In general, there is not as much conventional wisdom spread by the mass media or through conversations among people within their community.

Exceptions, of course, are countries which have some control over people's everyday lives: Arab oil-producing nations and the United States, or Egypt and Israel. When coming into face-to-face contact, people from different nations may have few misconceptions simply because they know very little about each other.

History of dominance-subordinate relationships

As much as they would like to wish away the past, administrators cannot dismiss the history of interracial relations within a country. Any contact situation they establish will be affected by the levels of trust versus suspicion and hostility versus cooperation which have been created in the past. In analyzing interracial relations in the United States, Rich and Ogawa (1976) pointed to class and economic variables:

> . . . communication between White and non-White in the United States . . . is characterized by strain and tension resulting from the dominant-submissive societal and interpersonal relationship historically imposed on the non-White by the structure of White America. . . . The dimensions of class and economic stratification and the multi-ethnic composition of the White and non-White populations of the United States further complicate the possibilities for interracial communication [pp. 28, 31].

Realizing these facts, Riordan (1978) has recommended that the problems of economic stratification somehow be treated prior to expectations that contact will be beneficial. Admittedly, this is an extremely difficult recommendation to implement and progress will not be made overnight. The thinking behind this policy recommendation, however, is similar to the defense of various affirmative action programs aimed at recruitment of minorities, hiring, scholarships for advanced education, and loans for the development of entrepreneurial activities. For shorter-term assaults on the problem, behavioral scientists have recommended that members of different ethnic groups possess equal status in arranged contact situations (Allport, 1954). Equal status here refers to similar availability of desired resources and the absence of structures such that one group has more power than the other. The difficulty arises when people move out of the arranged situation and return to the "real world" (Doob, 1975; Riordan, 1978). More will be said about equal-status contact when factors under the control of the administrator are discussed.

Preparedness for contact

In some cases, well-meaning administrators may recommend change, group members may be willing to participate, but the people involved may simply not be prepared. There *are* differences in communication styles, norms regarding proper behavior, and readiness for the acceptance of innovative ideas. Many have been reviewed in different parts of this book. People who have every intention of expressing tolerant behavior become confused when confronted with cultural differences. Whether they blame themselves or others, they are unlikely to seek out similar situations which also might cause feelings of uncomfortableness. "Well-mannered indifference" (Yousef, 1978, p. 51) may be the result.

Some sort of preparation prior to cross-cultural contact is almost always wise (Brislin & Pedersen, 1976). What constitutes the preparation, of course, differs from one type of contact to another. For people trying to establish a livelihood in another country, key information on economic concerns is desirable prior to any face-to-face contact with hosts. K. David (1970) has concluded that migrants who are forced to move from one country to another adapt more easily if they are given accurate information regarding what to expect in their new lives. Hosts who volunteer to sponsor immigrants can be given information on such customs as gift giving, the beliefs regarding guest-host relations which immigrants bring to the situation, and the normal symptoms of culture shock which should not be overinterpreted. Teachers about to work in a newly desegregated school can receive information about reasons for previous hostilities, the manner in which parents and children are likely to express their feelings, political pressures facing the school system, and possible guidelines for defusing classroom disruptions. Apprentice technicians in Third World countries, about to interact with high-status development assistance specialists, can also benefit from preparation. They can be introduced to the equipment for which they will eventually have responsibility and their probable feelings as they change from their previous level of technological sophistication, as well as the manner in which they will receive training from the overseas specialist. Before being thrown to the lions, people are entitled to as much preparation as possible.

The climate supporting cross-cultural contact

Although difficult to pin down, there is a concept which might be called the climate which supports or discourages intergroup interaction. Climate cannot be discussed as precisely as the conditions concurrent with contact reviewed earlier. Further, current conditions can contribute to climate, which is also influenced by norms, laws, the encouragement of respected leaders, and people's impressions based on recent events. In the United States, for instance, the climate surrounding black-white relations has improved since the 1950s. Laws have been passed, leaders favoring integration have been elected to public office, money has been made available to provide opportunities for minority groups, and schools are willing to wrestle with the tremendously difficult problems of incorporating the background experiences of minority-group students while coping with tighter budgets. To be sure, the applicability of these generalizations differs from area to area within the United States, and more work has to be done virtually everywhere. Further, the remaining problems are more difficult to solve: voting rights can be legislated and enforced, but economic equality cannot. There is a greater willingness to address problems of interracial relations, however, than there was twenty years ago.

The climate surrounding other forms of cross-cultural contact is not as favorable. Technical assistance is not the unquestioned prize it once was (Bochner, 1979; Glaser, 1979). Leaders in various countries are wondering what strings are attached to foreign assistance, what dangers might be caused by innovative technology, and what the long-term presence of overseas advisers might entail. More and more, leaders of less technologically developed countries are unshackling themselves from their old role of passive recipients. They are assuming the dominant position in negotiations concerning the acceptance or rejection of foreign aid. There has also been a shift over time in the climate surrounding foreign students on American campuses. Historically, foreign exchange programs were viewed as enriching a campus. Currently, foreign students are seen as a resource to help balance operating budgets. Recruiters travel to other countries and sign up students, sometimes receiving a bonus if they exceed an agreed-upon number. Promises which stretch the truth about a college's programs, the falsification of transcripts, and the illegal use of visas have been reported (Lockyear, 1979). The isolated lawbreaking activities of a few foreign students receive wide coverage in the media, leaving the impression that illegal behavior is typical.

FACTORS UNDER THE CONTROL OF ADMINISTRATORS

Administrators of arranged contact programs have a certain amount of control over timing, choice of participants, settings, and tasks. Taking the givens with which they are faced into account, they can increase the probability of favorable outcomes if they choose carefully among available courses of action. A helpful set of research findings has been developed around people's attempts to increase intergroup interaction. The lessons learned provide excellent guidelines which should be considered prior to the establishment of new contact programs. Not all variables are under the control of administrators in every situation. The purpose of reviewing previous studies and summarizing results around key concepts is to provide a checklist for possible applicability.

Equal-status contact

The most frequent recommendation is that administrators do everything possible to ensure that people have equal status in the contact situation (Allport, 1954; Amir, 1969; Riordan, 1978; Yinger & Simpson, 1973). Equal status insures that one group will not have greater accessibility to resources, will not be more powerful than the other, and will not constitute a threat to members of the other group. Ideally, equal-status contact encourages people to learn from others, unencumbered by feelings that the others are not worthy of attention.

Equal status is a good beginning point for analysis, but it is by no means a panacea. Riordan (1978) is unhappy with the emphasis placed on equal-status contact and worries that the principle may be overused. He makes a distinction between the arranged contact situation and the rest of the everyday world in which people interact. For instance, blacks have less status than whites in most arenas within American society. In an arranged situation such as a desegregated school or factory, administrators may strive and even achieve equal status for members of all ethnic groups. But the effect of prejudice and discrimination outside the school or factory may negate these well-intentioned efforts. Riordan feels that administrators must somehow address the unequal status which participants *bring* to the new situation. One approach (Riordan, 1978) is to encourage interaction between whites of moderate status and blacks of very high status.

> In situations such as this the low status expectations that Whites hold of Blacks may be influenced prior to or concomitant with cross-racial interaction by the high status role of Blacks. Generally, studies of this nature have shown favorable results in reducing *White* prejudice. . . . Equal-status interaction may be produced, therefore, when the minority has higher status than the majority on some characteristic which will offset the negative effects of race and thus balance the overall status of both groups [p. 173].

The obvious action recommendation is not without its critics. J. Katz (1977) feels that asking high-status blacks to participate in arranged contact is a form of exploitation. The argument is that blacks are victims, and it is not their duty to provide experiences which cater to prejudiced whites.

Another criticism of the equal-status concept is its amorphousness. Status is such a general concept, with different meanings to different people, that administrators might never know when it has been achieved. Since other factors are more precise, communicable, and applicable in different situations, they may have more usefulness.

Stereotype-breaking contact

An example of a more precise concept, often a concomitant of attempts to achieve equal status, is stereotype-breaking contact. If out-group members are believed to possess negative qualities, such as laziness and hostility, contact which allows the manifestation of nonstereotypical behavior is likely to make an impact. Yinger and Simpson (1973) reviewed a number of studies which analyzed interactions between white college students and black professors. Apparently, observing minority group members in high-status roles made preconceptions untenable and led to the formation of more positive attitudes. Yinger and Simpson (1973) carried out other studies in the military services.

> A somewhat unusual kind of stereotype-breaking contact was experienced by many soldiers in the U.S. Army in Europe during the winter and spring of 1945. In March and April, 1945, several Negro rifle platoons were attached to White companies. Two months later, the Information and Education Division of the Army Service Forces conducted a survey to discover the responses of White officers and men to this change [p. 121].

Responses indicated that over 80 percent of white officers and enlisted men felt that blacks performed very well in combat, and over 75 percent had more favorable attitudes toward blacks. The strong possibility exists, however, that these feelings did not generalize beyond people's Army experiences. Upon returning home after the war, there was little evidence of any generalization of these new attitudes to life in American communities.

Reference group support

The presence of tolerance in one situation and its disappointing absence in another is partly due to the existence or lack of reference group support. Whites may have learned tolerant attitudes in the Army while observing competent blacks carry out war related tasks. When they return to communities where discrimination is practiced, however, they are unlikely to challenge the norms of people whose friendship they value. In a study carried out in a desegregated housing project, Deutsch and Collins (1951) found that some white women did not object to interacting with blacks. They simply did not want to lose the friendship of other white women who were actively opposed to interracial interaction. Stephan and Rosenfield

(1978) found that white children who might have formed friendships with black and Chicano age peers did not because of parental disapproval.

The advice to administrators is easier to give than it is to implement: to increase tolerance among targeted individuals, work with members of their support groups. Sometimes implementation is not impossible. Principals of desegregated schools can organize informative sessions to which parents are invited. Participants in an integrated housing project might be encouraged to form new membership groups so that they can reinforce each other for newly developed tolerant attitudes. If these possibilities are not workable, administrators can certainly encourage participants to work through the future difficulties they will face after leaving the contact situation. By role-playing potential problems, such as the reactions of intolerant friends, people will be less affected once the problems actually occur (chapter 5).

The choice of facilitators

Administrators can avoid many problems if they carefully choose people who will be effective facilitators. These are the people who will introduce participants to the contact situation, present key information, answer questions, demonstrate tolerance, solve problems, and model an even temperament during times of stress. The criteria presented in chapter 3 for the prediction of successful sojourners may be helpful in selecting facilitators. Although Gerard and Miller (1973) found generally disappointing results after analyzing a massive school desegregation program in a California community, they did find "pockets" of interracial tolerance. They attributed these selective results to good facilitators: there *are* teachers who communicate tolerance, who are able to encourage positive interpersonal behaviors, who bring out the best in students, and who are imitated by students because they are respected. Similarly, Leighton (1945) analyzed the experiences of white civil servants who administered internment camps for Japanese-Americans during World War II. Although there were tremendous problems, Leighton concluded that they could have been worse at one camp. The administrator there, however, was a tolerant individual who did not make decisions based on overly facile, negative stereotypes. His ability to see many sides of an issue, including the Japanese-American point of view, led to the containment of potentially stressful problems.

Pleasant and comfortable intergroup contact

Facilitators should strive to ensure that people will enjoy contact and that they will not feel threatened in the presence of out-group members. Obviously, this is not always possible but potentially stressful situations can sometimes be modified and improved. Unpleasant contact causes people to make negative attributions about out-group members, and threat causes people to defend their original, prejudiced attitudes. Interestingly, positive contact does not necessarily have positive consequences. Rather, it avoids the negative consequences of name calling and defensiveness. If administrators depend only on positive contact, predicting that positive experiences will transfer to favorable feelings about the people involved, they are ignoring what Sherif (1966) calls "hedonistic associationism." People are skillful at taking pleasure out of a situation and maintaining old attitudes at the same time.

Sometimes, a good deal can be learned from arranged contact situations which were not particularly successful. Trubowitz (1969) organized field trips for schoolchildren which were interesting and informative. Since he was interested in determining whether or not the effects of the pleasant experience could be documented, different participants had different amounts and types of interracial contact. Children (a) did or did not have a field trip with members of the other group, and (b) did or did not have a subsequent discussion with the others. The experiences can be summarized in pictorial form.

Joint Field Trip

		yes	no
Joint	yes	field trip and discussion	discussion, but no field trip
Discussion	no	field trip, but no discussion	no field trip, no discussion

Children expressed little favorable attitude change toward the out-group members. Participants in the joint field trip and discussion expressed feelings which were similar to their peers who did not have an interracial experience. Simply putting members of different racial groups together and providing them with pleasant experiences and discussions were not enough to "shake up" old, well-established attitudes. Apparently, pleasant experiences are a necessary but not sufficient condition for increased tolerance. Other factors have to be added to the situation, and one of the most important is the quest for goals which demand the efforts of both in-group and out-group members.

Superordinate goals

Group members may desire a certain outcome which cannot be attained without the help of out-group members. When members of the other group are also willing to pool efforts so that the same outcome might be attained, the groups are said to be working toward superordinate goals (Sherif, 1958). The principle has been applied to many types of intergroup relations, and it rivals equal status as the most frequently discussed recommendation for the reduction of intergroup tensions (Gudykunst, 1977; Milburn, 1977; Richmond, 1973; Sherif, 1966). For instance, Sawyer and Guetzkow (1965) discussed superordinate goals in diplomatic negotiations:

> Probably the factor most promotive of the mutual satisfaction of both parties to a negotiation is the extent to which their goals are, or can be made to be, in agreement. As Thucydides observed in ancient Greece, "identity of interests is the surest of bonds, whether between states or individuals" [p. 469].

In integrated classrooms, Blaney, Stephan, Rosenfield, Aronson, & Sikes (1977) have introduced teaching methods which demand the cooperation of children from different ethnic groups. Children are divided into teams which cut across racial affiliations. Since each child is given only some of the information necessary to solve a problem, (s)he must interact with the others. The common desire to solve the problem and please the teacher reduces intergroup tension and encourages cross-race friendship formations.

Scientific ventures involving participants from many countries often involve superordinate goals. Glaser (1979), for instance, has pointed out that geographers experience less tension than other professionals while participating in a sojourn. One of the reasons is that the very basic orientation of the field demands a worldwide information base to which scholars in all parts of the world can and must contribute. Other common goals have been space exploration, the International Geophysical Year, and the International Year of the Quiet Sun (Rabinowitch, 1964). The complex administrative structures necessary for the exchange-of-scholars programs involve the common goals of assuring a successful experience for participants. For each sojourner, a number of other people have to be involved in the advertising of opportunities and selection of participants, the provision of visas, travel arrangements, and support services in the host country. When sojourners become frustrated at the seemingly endless amount of red tape, they can lighten their load somewhat by counting all the people who are directly or indirectly responsible for their cross-cultural experience.

I have also had some personal experience with superordinate goals and am convinced of their importance. Between 1975 and 1978, I administered three programs for cross-cultural researchers (one of the programs was described in Brislin, 1977). Participants came together for four months at the East-West Center in Honolulu, Hawaii, taking leaves of absence from their jobs in the United States, Asia, Australia, and Pacific Island nations. The most successful aspects of the program, I believe, centered around commonly shared and valued goals. For instance, one group of participants critiqued draft chapters for the *Handbook of Cross-Cultural Psychology* (Triandis et al., 1980) knowing that they would later interact with chapter authors on a face-to-face basis. The common goal of participation in the *Handbook* rallied people together and helped to overcome the day-to-day tensions inherent in a sojourn. Common goals also united people despite differences in both cultural background and disciplinary orientation (psychology, sociology, anthropology, political science). Given this personal experience, which agrees with recommendations in the research literature, I have consciously designed new programs so that they incorporate superordinate goals.

The joint effort required for the attainment of superordinate goals contrasts markedly with competitive behavior in which the success of one group means failure for the other. In this type of situation, tensions spiral and attributions about out-group members become negative. The tensions cause people to either avoid contact or to engage in hostile intergroup relations. In both cases, there are no opportunities for a relaxed exchange of information which might challenge preconceptions people have about out-groups. If the goal of cross-cultural contact is to improve favorable feelings among people, competition should be avoided.

Acquaintance potential

Contact is more likely to have positive benefits if people from different groups have many opportunities to interact with others. In some situations, people are able to meet out-group members with little effort. When contact with significant numbers of out-group members is almost certain, the situation is said to have a large acquaintance potential. Like the variable of pleasant contact, a high acquaintance potential probably does not ensure positive benefits. However, it encourages the challenging of preconceptions and establishes a framework for intergroup relations to which other factors can be added.

Sheer numbers do not guarantee interaction. In analyzing contact among foreign students and hosts in the United States, Selltiz and Cook (1962) found that sojourners living in small communities had greater opportunities for intergroup action. Students were more likely to be treated as unique, special people and were not "lost in the shuffle" of a bigger city. Often, the pace of life is slower in small communities, allowing time for hosts to seek out sojourners and to involve them in the local social life. Further, people in smaller communities are more likely to be active in clubs and churches. Foreign students might be invited to their organizations to give a speech or to participate in question-and-answer sessions about their country. In larger cities, frankly, the foreign students would be overlooked in favor of a "name" journalist or political figure.

Professional societies have changed in recent years to increase opportunities for face-to-face exchange among members with similar interests. Complaints about large national organizations, with their conventions involving 10,000 to 20,000 participants, are frequent. The American Psychological Association and the American Anthropological Association, for instance, have held national meetings with this level of attendance. People grumble that "There are so many people that I can't meet anybody!" To counter this legitimate complaint, organizers of large national conventions have adopted a number of innovations. They have scheduled social hours for people interested in a specific topic, designated areas of the convention site for interest groups, and encouraged novel presentations involving more exchange among speakers and audience members. Another innovation is the development of much smaller societies with 500 to 1,000 members. People are much more likely to meet others with similar interests in these societies than in large national organizations. There are a number of these whose concern is cross-cultural research and its applications: e.g., the Society for Intercultural Education, Training, and Research; the International Association for Cross-Cultural Psychology; the International Society for Educational, Cultural, and Scientific Interchanges. I have met far more colleagues from other countries in these smaller societies than in the larger organizations to which I belong.

Some basic structural features in one's neighborhood can also increase acquaintance potential. In studying the reason for and consequences of contact in an integrated housing project, Deutsch and Collins (1951) found that women often met in a laundry room which had facilities for use by residents of several buildings. Playground areas were also shared. Young children would meet age peers from other ethnic groups on the playground and would introduce the new friends to their parents. When collecting their children to bring them home, parents would have an opportunity to chat. Administrators of contact situations can often arrange physical features to ensure opportunities for contact. The advantages of shared rest rooms in office buildings, coffee pots, and cafeteria lines should not be overlooked. People in organizations frequently make the observation, "I meet more people from outside my unit near the coffeepot than any other place."

Intimate personal contact

Once an acquaintance potential is established, a further goal should be the provisions of opportunities for intimate contact (Amir, 1969; Amir et al., 1980; Ashmore, 1970; Gudykunst, 1977; Yinger & Simpson, 1973). Intimate contact, in contrast to more casual interaction, involves the sharing of personal feelings, concerns, and goals for the future. Intimacy breaks down the barriers between an individual and the amorphous bunch of others called "them." Attraction due to similarity can develop. People learn that out-group members are also concerned with inflation, opportunities for their children, crime rates, the decline of inner-city neighborhoods, and the tight job market. With intimate contact, people have the opportunity to formulate some variation on this basic thought: "I always thought they were different, something from another world. Now, I've learned that they are much like us in many ways." For instance, this sort of thinking developed among residents of an integrated housing project (Deutsch & Collins, 1951). Put another way, intimate contact allows the development of a more differentiated view of out-groups. With casual interaction, there is little opportunity for old attitudes and opinions to be challenged.

Ashmore (1970) has developed a set of hypotheses concerned with the outcomes of intimate contact. He suggests that attraction toward out-group members met during contact experiences does not always extend to the entire out-group. If administrators can emphasize that the participants in the contact situation are representative of their entire ethnic or national group, transfer to the "rest of the world" is possible. Regrettably, there is always the possibility that favorable feelings will be confined to a limited number of people. Another factor is the range of contact situations. If interaction takes place in neighborhoods, workplaces, churches, and clubs, prejudiced people are less likely to confine favorable change to one setting. Commonly heard feelings about the suitability of out-group members as workers but not as neighbors will not be as strongly held.

Ashmore (1970) also suggests that friendship formation forces a challenge to people's motives.

> Intergroup friendship causes a redeployment of motivation with respect to the intergroup attitude. The prejudiced person wants to hang onto his prejudice; but becoming friendly with a member of an out-group makes him more amenable to information that favors tolerance [p. 320].

The confrontation between one's old attitudes and new friendships, I believe, is one of the experiences shared by virtually all people who engage in a sojourn or in extensive intergroup contact within their own country. The intense experience of having old views challenged, not by the arguments of others but by their actions, is very uncomfortable. Coupled with a growing awareness of the basic decency of out-group members, all of whom were previously viewed as bogeymen, the intergroup interaction becomes a major event in people's lives. The common experience provides a basis for friendship among people who have *not* sojourned in the same country and who have *not* worked in similar jobs. Rather, the basis for understanding is a person's empathy for the feelings of others who have experienced a confrontation between the old and the new.

Overlapping group ties

As a consequence of opportunities for intimate contact, people can form friendships and, ultimately, strong group ties which cut across ethnic and racial affiliations. "Group ties" is being used in a strict sense: people care about one another and help group members in times of trouble. LeVine (1965) has written extensively about the benefits accruing from overlapping group ties. In his arguments, he included observations from his field work carried out with the Kipsigis and Gusii of Kenya. There is more internal peace among the Kipsigis than the Gusii, and the reasons include crosscutting ties which bind people together in face-to-face, intimate relationships.

> The military regiments, age groups, and clans were territorially dispersed, so that they cross-cut the territorial units and made unified military action by one village against another virtually impossible. Family residence patterns gave rise to even more cross-cutting ties. Kipsigis men tended to set up their own homesteads after about a year of patrilocal residence. Since the entire society was a peaceful unit, and since land was plentiful, it was possible for sons to move anywhere in the tribal territory, and most often they moved far away from their fathers and brothers [p. 58].

Further, puberty rites were organized so that all eligible adolescents in a territory participated. Friendships which lasted a lifetime developed after adolescents had the shared experience of the ceremonies. Adolescents were also allowed to wander all about the territory in their play activities. Again, friendship ties would be developed in many areas as the adolescents roamed from place to place. As a consequence of all these factors, people were motivated to avoid intense conflict because they would have to fight against friends. The dehumanization of the enemy, a common tactic to motivate soldiers, would be a less effective technique.

The example provided by LeVine may seem exotic but the basic point he makes is not. The principle of overlapping group ties has been applied to work in international organizations such as the United Nations (Alger, 1965). For instance, some officials sent by a given nation are asked to assume nonnational roles in the administration of these organizations. To do their jobs effectively, they must develop close ties with people from other countries, learn their points of view, and avoid the tendency to simply maintain their own country as a reference point. In general, sojourners develop strong feelings toward the country in which they spend a significant amount of time. There is

> a sense of personal involvement in its fate. . . . This increased understanding and involvement are not likely to overcome real conflicts of interests that exist between the nations. They are likely, however, to create a greater openness in individuals' attitudes toward the other nation [Kelman, 1965b, p. 573].

Sojourners frequently work in behalf of the host country. They lobby their governments for favorable consideration, support hosts when they come to the sojourner's home country, and do volunteer work for organizations which sponsor opportunities for potential sojourners. When people develop overlapping ties with individuals who previously were out-group members, it is much more comfortable to help them than to be hostile toward them.

Increased self-esteem

When participants in a contact situation feel that they are respected, have a contribution to make, and can put ideas forward without fear of ridicule, their self-esteem is bound to increase. A number of studies have shown that when self-esteem increases, people become more tolerant of out-groups. Stephan and Rosenfield (1978) measured self-esteem in schoolchildren about to enter a desegregated school. Students agreed or disagreed with statements such as these: "I would say that I am happy," and "I wish that I were different from the way I am." Interracial attitudes were measured by perceptions of out-groups on a number of dimensions: friendly-unfriendly, trustworthy-untrustworthy, selfish-unselfish, attractive-unattractive, and similar to me-dissimilar to me. When children's self-esteem increased in the integrated school, racial attitudes became more favorable.

Summer camps have frequently been used as the setting where arranged interracial contact takes place and is analyzed. One reason is that children can be disassociated temporarily from their normal reference group and can participate in a new experience in the company of tolerant counselors. Campbell and Yarrow (1958) attempted to establish an equal-status contact summer camp in which black and white adolescents participated. Keeping in mind Riordan's (1978) reservation that a short-term experience cannot compensate for the discrimination faced during a lifetime, the camp seemed to have limited but positive benefits. Campbell and Yarrow (1958) found that "necessary beginnings of change have occurred, particularly changes reflecting an enhancement of the Negro girls' self-concept [p. 126]." In another analysis, Yarrow, Campbell, and Yarrow (1958) reported that white children chose equal numbers of black and white children at the end of camp in contrast to their strong in-group preference at the beginning. Although speculative, one possible reason is that whites perceive self-confidence in blacks, make favorable attributions, and consequently approach blacks and engage in friendly behavior.

The importance of children's self-esteem was frequently addressed in the mass media during the 1970s. Teachers were advised to respect children, listen to their points of view, and to answer their questions in a nonpatronizing manner (Raspberry, 1979). Blacks who recall their "roots" express gratitude to their parents and grandparents who insisted that children keep their heads high and never internalize feelings of worthlessness even though they were victimized by discrimination (Murray, 1978). The basic message of Rev. Jesse Jackson of Operation PUSH is that children must see themselves as "jewels" who can learn skills and advance in society. Dr. Kenneth Clark (1979) pointed to the critical role that schools play in the upward mobility of minority group members. Teachers should set high standards and help students attain them. Self-confidence will come from the pride of accomplishment.

Self-esteem is not a unidimensional concept. It varies across the different situations in which people spend a great deal of their time. Hare (1977) has shown that black schoolchildren maintain "specific self-esteems" in the school, at home, and among their peers. They can have positive feelings about themselves in one setting but negative feelings in another. This differentiation is a mixed blessing. A good aspect is that hostile treatment in one setting can be mollified by success in another. Supportive parents can provide some balance to offset discriminatory treatment in school, and good teachers can have an impact even if the child comes from a troubled home. The bad aspect is that energies may be channeled away from prosocial behaviors. If children can find support from neither parents nor teachers, they may attach themselves to a peer group whose norms include disruption and cynicism concerning the value of hard work.

The channeling of conflict

The major insight suggested by Hare's (1977) work is that conflict in one setting can sometimes be balanced by intervention in another. The more general point is that, as much as we might wish otherwise, conflict is inevitable and administrators must be prepared to deal with it. Self-interests of two or more people often collide. In such cases, arrangements which might allow pleasant and equal-status contact, with or without superordinate goals, may be dismissed as naive.

In these situations, administrators sometimes can channel conflict away from hostility and violence. Simpson and Yinger (1973) feel that "the aim of policy should not be the elimination of conflict, but its redirection into constructive channels [p. 148]." For instance, open meetings between parents and school administrators, and even public demonstrations against busing, are preferable to the destruction of property and the harassment of schoolchildren. Nonviolent "sit-ins" leading to jail sentences may be preferable to internalized feelings of impotence and bitterness among the targets of discrimination. The bone-numbing boredom generated by speeches in the United Nations is preferable to armed conflict. The hostilities sojourners often express, possibly due to anxieties about an uncertain future, are better channeled into orientation programs than into angry encounters with hosts.

Earlier in the chapter, the point was made that contact does not guarantee improved intergroup relations. Since people are sometimes not prepared, contact can intensify initial attitudes. Expanding this point to intergovernmental negotiations, Rummel (1979) feels that the relation between cooperation and conflict must be recognized.

> Pushing nations to cooperate beyond their goals, power, or will can disrupt the framework of their relations and produce conflict. You do not produce harmony by bringing together nations not ready for contact; you produce conflict. Idealists the world over have yet to learn this basic fact of social man . . . it is better to have some conflict now than more severe conflict later. . . . It is not to be feared but managed. The proper cultivation of conflict can ease nations through trying transition periods and promote eventually a harmony that might otherwise be only that of the dead and vanquished [pp. 291–292].

In many cases, then, the goals of an arranged contact program cannot be the total reduction of prejudice or conflict. Rather, the goal should be a decrease in tensions or a channeling of conflict away from hostile, destructive behavior. When violence begins, previously established communication networks break down. Contact then occurs in a tense and sometimes vicious atmosphere which is not conducive to the search for policies acceptable to all parties.

Institutional support

Although administrators in charge of a contact situation may put forth their best efforts, they must have the support of their institutions before success is possible. The participants in contact situations are sensitive to tokenism. They know when the heads of institutions are simply going through the motions of encouraging intergroup contact and when there is a valid commitment. In analyzing school desegregation, Stephen and Rosenfield (1978) concluded that institutional support is one reason for favorable change. School principals, district superintendents, and other community leaders were committed to the desegregation program and wanted to make it work. They were undoubtedly able to communicate their feelings to the participating students without the necessity of constant speechmaking.

Along the West Bank of the Jordan River, Amir et al. (1980) found slight shifts in favorable feelings among Israelis toward Arabs when members of both groups worked in the same factory. One suggested reason was that the Israeli government wanted to show that people of the two countries could live and work together. Consequently, government officials spoke in favor of intergroup relations and lent legitimacy to those areas along the West Bank where contact opportunities were being organized. In the community Amir and his colleagues studied, "The Israel military government provides the West Bank Arabs with health services, professional and agricultural training, and [employment] with the Israeli work force [p. 9]."

Another form of institutional support is the provision of enough time to establish a workable program. One complaint about dvelopmental assistance is that donor nations pull out before a funded project has a fair chance to become established. A great deal of time is necessary for advisers to train hosts and to encourage developments in the local bureaucracy which will ensure successful continuation of a project after advisers return to their home countries (Goodenough, 1964). One reason for the premature removal of support is that new projects always seem more exciting and glamorous. Bright promises and opportunities for newly appointed administrators to "make their mark" accompany new proposals. These seem much more exciting than the field reports from ongoing projects which indicate modest progress, inevitable trouble spots, and the need for continual small but steady steps toward eventual success. When today's glamour project is funded, it becomes the duller and overly familiar old shoe in future years. Good administrators undoubtedly realize the tendency to give more attention to the new project and are able to balance the necessity of developing new plans with the need to maintain old commitments.

Another form of support is institutional backing when controversial programs come under fire. Whenever an administrator begins a contact program, inevitably, there will be criticism from one faction or another. One complaint will be that programs are moving too slowly, and another will be that the programs fan ill-feelings which are better addressed by natural changes over time. When administrators face flak, they must be confident that their supervisors will either back them or at least remain silent. Once plans are formulated, after long and careful deliberations among administrators and their supervisors, there must be assurances that adequate time and effort will be devoted to the program. Administrators' morale and effectiveness can be irreparably damaged when they receive no support in times of tension and strife.

THE CHANGES WHICH MAY FOLLOW INTERGROUP CONTACT

Although favorable attitude change and increased tolerance have been most frequently mentioned as the possible result of intergroup contact, other benefits are attainable. They range over behaviors, cognitions, emotions, and types of attitudes.

Behavior change

One of the active research areas in the behavioral sciences concerns the relation between attitudes and behavior. The basic conclusion is that favorable attitudes *by no means* guarantee positive behaviors (Wicker, 1969). There are so many factors which affect behavior, in addition to people's feelings or evaluations, that a direct link between attitudes and behavior is a poor model of a more complex reality. Several factors have already been noted. In the study of LaPierre (1934), negative attitudes toward Chinese were not predictive of discriminatory behavior. The difficulty of refusing confident out-group members during a face-to-face encounter proved more influential than people's attitudes. Many other factors interfere with a direct relation between attitudes and behavior (see also Bagozzi & Burnkrant, 1979; McGuire, 1975):

1. knowledge. A person may want to interact with out-group members but may not know how to approach them and may not know what to talk about once contact is made.
2. social pressure. Favorable attitudes toward out-group contact may be balanced by an awareness of in-group disapproval (Pettigrew, 1958).
3. recent experiences. Well-meaning people may have had a clumsy encounter with out-group members. To avoid additional discomfort, they simply stick to their own group.

If administrators want to encourage behavior change, they must focus directly on behavior. In Spector's (1969) work with members of the

United States Army stationed in Korea, he recommended that sojourners engage in specific behaviors: spending free time with Koreans, eating local food, and learning some of the local language. At the same time, he gave information on how the recommended actions can be carried out. Rosenberg (in Brislin & Pedersen, 1976) has a similar approach in his work with the United States Navy. He recommends that sailors on leave stay out of tourist traps and engage, instead, in activities which may lead to intercultural learning. But he realizes that exhortations are not enough. Detailed information is given regarding how the sojourners' behavioral goals can be achieved.

Increases and decreases in anxiety

Anxiety can interfere with new learning, but reality often demands that people *should* have some trepidation about intercultural relations. Contact can be tense, uncomfortable, and unpleasant, and orientation programs should stress these important points. A number of studies (O'Brien & Plooij, 1976; Randolph et al., 1977; Weldon, Carlston, Rissman, Slobodin, & Triandis, 1975) have shown that anxiety about intercultural interaction increases after orientation programs and that *untrained* sojourners are preferred by hosts. The hosts' reactions are probably due to discomfort in the company of tense people. If this was an isolated finding, attempts to explain it away would be justifiably suspect. But since it has been demonstrated in three independent studies, the finding of increased anxiety following training seems solid. The best explanation is that increased anxiety reflects an awareness of intercultural communication difficulties. Over time, the anxiety may motivate sojourners to become more aware of cultural differences and more sensitive to hosts' points of view. Ideally, the anxiety decreases over time and the trained sojourners are preferred because of their host-culture sophistication.

As discussed in chapter 6, too much anxiety can interfere with learning. One reason for people's anxiety is the threat of comparison with others who are perceived as superior. Katz (1973a) has pointed out that one benefit of well-administered integrated schooling is a reduction in anxiety among minority group members. If they interact on a day-to-day basis with members of the dominant majority, in a supportive setting containing characteristics described in this chapter, familiarity will breed nonchalance.

Nondevelopment of prejudice

Long-term, sustained attention to favorable conditions surrounding intergroup contact may prevent prejudicial attitudes from ever developing. In analyzing school desegregation, Entwisle and Webster (1974) interviewed white and black children who had attended school together ever since their kindergarten years. The children did not have to face the tensions associated with change since desegregation was the policy when they started school. The researchers found that neither black nor white children developed attitudes and expectations on the basis of skin color. Commenting on the study, Riordan (1978) concluded:

> This study suggests that a school context of long-term integration is likely to eliminate the *initial development* of invidious comparisons based upon race. As previously noted, however, integration per se may worsen intergroup relations when hostilities and stereotypes have been learned prior to contact (which is the more typical case) [p. 169].

The long-term effort necessary for improved intergroup relations is often hard to maintain. When programs are federally funded, for instance, budgeting is on a year-to-year basis. Questions about goals and progress toward goals are hard to answer at the end of funding periods if visible change takes at least five years. The temptation to promise a "quick fix" has to be balanced against the realization that changes in interracial and intercultural attitudes do not occur overnight.

Assertive versus reactive attitudes

Traditionally, researchers have focused on reactive attitudes among minority group members. Since the starting point of investigations has been the views of the dominant majority groups, researchers have most often analyzed the minority group's reactions to these views. Decrying this approach, Hare (1977) has pointed to a number of inevitable problems.

> For too long researchers have assumed that lower class and/or minority people are simply acceptors and reflectors of negative dominant messages, and possess little or no capacity to mediate between what others think of them and they think of themselves. This bias has, until recently, precluded the social scientist's ability to adequately assess anything that is culturally different beyond labelling it deviant, disorganized, or pathological [p. 47].

An alternative is research which investigates assertive attitudes and self-pride among minority group members. As an example, Gurin and Epps (1975) have shown that black students do not necessarily blame themselves for all problems they encounter; they can focus on the benefits whites gain from holding prejudicial attitudes and develop positive feelings about themselves. Most of the references to attitude change in this chapter have dealt with increased tolerance, and this focus has implicitly included minority tolerance toward the dominant group. An equally important focus is minority attitudes toward their ability to share power and influence with the majority.

Increased knowledge

Although attitudes may not change, intergroup contact can lead to clearer perceptions of people's opinions, reasons for behavior, and future plans. This sort of mutual understanding can be increased if participants are asked to take the point of view of the out-group. Further, they could be asked to state the out-group position until its members agree that understanding has been demonstrated (Stagner, 1977). Realizing the difficulties associated with changing attitudes as reviewed throughout this chapter, Tajfel (1973) feels that large-scale contact programs should deal with information about beliefs and views concerning in-group and out-group behavior. He feels that even if the motives for intergroup prejudice and discrimination were better understood, they could not be addressed in any large-scale effort to change attitudes. Programs dealing with information have at least a chance of success. The problem addressed by Tajfel is genuine. Hopefully, future research will suggest methods which allow both motives and information to be addressed in the same large-scale program.

As a possible outcome of intergroup contact, increased knowledge has a unique difficulty. It is mentioned too frequently when no other positive benefit comes to mind. After diplomatic negotiations, governmental representatives who can claim no policy developments report that "there was a frank exchange of views." Knowledge alone, then, has achieved the unfortunate status of a cliché. While I feel that increased knowledge is a laudable outcome, administrators should realize its negative connotations when writing their progress reports. They might focus on the more complex aspects of people's thinking reviewed in chapter 4, or might emphasize the types of knowledge which are necessary for people to use favorable attitudes during intergroup contact opportunities.

SUMMARY AND CONCLUSIONS

Even though people might prefer to interact only with members of their in-group, legal developments have made the fulfillment of this wish impossible. Regulations governing open housing, desegregated schools, and affirmative action mean that people from different ethnic groups will frequently come into contact. The assimilation of refugees from Indochina, the breakdown of apartheid governments, and settlements along the West Bank of the Jordan River are recent political developments which have increased intergroup contact in various parts of the world.

There has been a great deal of research on how intergroup contact might be managed to increase the probability of positive outcomes. The findings can be organized according to a set of caveats for administrators planning to become involved in managing intergroup contact; the givens with which they must deal; the situational factors which can be manipulated; and the types of changes which may occur.

Contact itself does not guarantee favorable results. Some people are so rigid in their prejudices that any out-group behavior can be interpreted as supporting their initial attitudes. Minority group members who continually are the targets of discrimination sometimes internalize negative views of themselves. Administrators must realize these possibilities as well as some background factors which participants bring to the contact situation. Prior to any newly established opportunities for intergroup interaction, people may have had sufficient contact to form a set of attitudes. Moderately positive or negative attitudes are easier to change than those at the extremes of a continuum. Very negative attitudes are resistant to change because they are usually well developed and are protected by defense mechanisms. The same can be said for extremely positive attitudes. In addition, very positive attitudes simply cannot change any more as a function of contact. When people reach a ceiling, they can go no higher. Volunteers who participate in intergroup contact are usually not representative of people who might be forced to participate. Administrators should not indiscriminately apply methods which were effective with volunteers.

Other givens include the conditions at the time of contact and the history of dominant-subordinate relations among the groups. If recent events have led to an increase in tensions, the administrator's work is made more difficult since people will be less open to new alternatives and approaches. The history of dominance by one group over another often means that new contact opportunities begin in an atmosphere of distrust. Policies which reduce the dominance, such as affirmative action and greater attention to the quality of schools, are admittedly long-range but probably are the only realistic attacks on the problem. At times, people are simply not ready for contact. Orientation programs organized by tolerant, nonthreatening, and knowledgeable individuals should precede contact which is likely to involve tensions and strife.

Even though inevitable problems face administrators, intergroup contact sometimes results in positive benefits. Reasons for success are that a number of factors are built into the contact situation. *Equal-status* interaction means that one group does not have more power than another. This factor is sometimes achievable within the contact situation, but the rest of the world must also be taken into account. Members of the dominant majority might interact with high-status minority group members. This approach might compensate for the low status of minority groups outside the contact setting. *Stereotype-breaking* contact is related. If people have preconceived but false ideas about an out-group, administrators can arrange contact to include the out-group members' normal, everyday demonstrations of competence.

Another aspect of the real world is *reference group support.* Even though attitudes may change during arranged contact, there may be no transfer since old friends and neighbors disapprove of the newly developed tolerance. If administrators encourage people to form new support groups, there may be less inclination to abandon tolerance when faced with counter-pressures. Some administrators are better than others at encouraging the development of group support. More generally, the *choice of facilitators* is an important factor. Certain people are tolerant, open-minded, and are accepted as models by others. For instance, studies of integrated schools have shown that some teachers are much better than others at encouraging favorable relations among black, white, and Chicano children. Some are better than others at encouraging the development of *self-esteem* among participants. When self-esteem increases, intergroup attitudes become more favorable since people no longer feel threatened by the tensions associated with integroup contact.

Contact should be as *pleasant and comfortable* as possible. This factor may not insure favorable outcomes, but it may decrease the probability of negative ones and allow the addition of other factors. One of the most important is *superordinate goals* which are valued by members of all groups and which demand joint effort. While working toward attainment of the goals, petty differences and tensions seem to diminish in importance. Another factor is *acquaintance potential,* or the opportunity to meet out-group members without great effort. Foreign students in small communities, for instance, often have more opportunities for interaction with hosts than students in big cities. In small communities the students are perceived as special and are asked to participate in the local life. Contact should be *intimate and personal,* allowing similar beliefs and interests to form a basis for attraction. Intimacy also allows the development of attitudes which differentiate people from the preconceived mass called "them." It also allows the development of *overlapping group ties* which cut across ethnic and racial barriers.

At times, tensions will be so strong that the only realistic goal of contact should be the *channeling of conflict* rather than its elimination. Administrators can encourage the airing of disagreements through verbiage at public meetings rather than through rocks thrown on the streets. Whatever approach to managing intergroup contact is taken, administrators must be confident of *institutional support.* Negotiations between administrators and their superiors should involve careful consideration of all options, disagreements, and potential consequences. Once a decision is made, however, administrators must be confident that their superiors will be supportive when the flak appears. Good programs have been ruined through the premature removal of funding and institutional backing.

The potential benefits of contact include favorable attitude change, tolerance, and a more open-minded orientation toward out-groups. While important, other benefits are also possible. People might engage in favorable behaviors toward out-group members. Behavior does not necessarily follow from attitudes since some people do not know how to engage in desirable behaviors or they may be recovering from a clumsy attempt at interaction. Both increases and decreases in anxiety can be beneficial. Increases can motivate people to learn about the real difficulties in cross-cultural interaction; decreases can remove the debilitating bonds which limit effective behaviors.

Long-term attention to favorable conditions can eliminate the development of prejudice. Children who have always attended integrated schools never learn to form attributions about others which are based on race alone. People can also learn to be more assertive in their attitudes. Minority group members, for instance, can develop attitudes about their abilities, not about the majority point of view toward those same abilities. While increased knowledge is a laudable outcome, it has achieved the status of a cliché. Too often, people point to "a frank exchange of views" when there is no other development to report.

Once the situation for intergroup contact is made favorable, people can pursue other goals. On long-term sojourns, for instance, most people have tasks they want to complete successfully. The ways in which sojourners have pursued task completion will be the subject of the next chapter.

8
Sojourners' Task Assignments

With few exceptions, people have tasks they want to complete during their sojourn. Foreign students are strongly committed to attaining a college degree; technical assistance advisers want to introduce innovative methods of production; and overseas businessmen want to expand output or distribution in the host country. In attempting to achieve their goals, sojourners are frequently faced with a predictable set of issues, and these will be reviewed in this chapter. The issues can be grouped according to three very broad organizing principles:

1. problems faced by virtually all sojourners regardless of their home country and the country to which they are assigned;
2. the unique problems faced by sojourners from less technologically developed societies who live in highly industrialized countries;
3. the unique problems faced by sojourners from highly industrialized countries who live in less technologically developed societies.

As always, material reviewed in other chapters relates to the present discussion. Sojourners expected to complete a task have certain attitudes and traits (chapter 3), process information using idiosyncratic methods (chapter 4), and must establish support groups in the host country (chapter 5). They also must deal with unfamiliar situations (chapter 6) and must interact with out-group members in these situations (chapter 7). The suggestions presented in this chapter presuppose that well-meaning administrators have acted in good faith while choosing people, that sojourners have become comfortable in the host society, and that the tensions associated with culture shock have not been debilitating. Given these preconditions, sojourners ought to be ready to begin their work. While doing so, they are likely to encounter a number of barriers which must be overcome.

PROBLEMS FACED BY ALL SOJOURNERS

Regardless of their country of origin, all sojourners face a number of predictable problems while pursuing task-oriented goals. There are variations
on these themes, of course, depending upon the type of cross-cultural
experience and the host country. The concepts presented here can be
considered "etics" to which the "emic" coloring of specific experiences
must be added.

The standards for success

A good example of emic-etic usefulness is the judgment of a sojourner's
accomplishments. All people want to be judged as successful, but there are
differing standards from country to country for assigning this label to
people. Foreign students in the United States, for instance, are judged
regularly since they receive grades at least twice a year. They are also
expected to write original essays and, occasionally, to disagree with professors. American students studying in some overseas countries, on the
other hand, do not receive regular grades. Instead, they take one series of
exams at the end of their studies. They are ill-advised to argue controversial positions while taking the exams. If students perform well according
to the local standard, they are given the label of "success." Clearly, the
same student might be successful in one place but not in the other.

A similar problem has contributed to the consistently poor prediction
of performance in the Peace Corps (J. Harris, 1973, 1977). In the first
few years of the organization's existence, volunteers participated in a
rigorous selection and training procedure during which administrators could
request the premature termination of an individual. Prior to their overseas
assignment, volunteers were interviewed and were given various psychological tests by American administrators as well as consultants representing
various behavioral and social sciences. A summary prediction was then
made regarding whether or not a given volunteer would be successful. In
following up a group of volunteers assigned to the Philippines, Guthrie
and Zektick (1967) found absolutely no relation between the American
prediction and judgments by Filipino supervisors and community leaders.
One reason was that the Americans and the Filipinos had different standards in mind when they were asked to rate "success" or "effectiveness."
Americans may have been impressed by clear goals, emotional maturity,
and a seemingly serious outlook on the future. Filipino supervisors may
have been more impressed with gregariousness, ability to get along with
others, and the *lack* of a desire to recommend change. There is a strong
Filipino value of *pakikisama,* or the ability to maintain smooth interper-

sonal relations. Its centrality and importance is bound to be reflected in supervisory ratings made by Filipinos. Partly because of its poor record in predicting success, the complex assessment procedure was abandoned by the Peace Corps in about 1970 (Harris, 1977).

The issue of differing standards exists in other domains. A common problem in the Peace Corps was that some volunteers had to cope with differing standards of physical beauty. Young men and women who were not considered especially attractive in their own country found that they were valued in the host society. They sometimes had difficulty coping with attention from members of the opposite sex since they had no previous experience. Some volunteers who had long worried about their attractiveness entered prematurely into marriage, grateful that someone was interested. The additional pressures of adjusting to the new roles of "socially desirable person" and "marriage partner" adversely affected the work of some volunteers.

The obvious way to improve the *prediction* of good performance, as well as performance itself, is to study host society criteria of success. There are scattered efforts of this type: more work on this issue would return handsome benefits. For instance, Van Zandt (1970) had discussed the criteria by which Japanese businessmen evaluate a sojourner who works in their companies. Their ability to work within a group decision-making process called the *ringi* system, the avoidance of power plays, the importance placed on friendship, understanding various uses of the word "no," and the importance placed on organizational goals other than profit are all critical aspects of success in Japanese businesses.

Criteria for choosing sojourners

Once the issue of differing standards for success is understood, the closely related problem of selection criteria can be addressed. The general point is that, once criteria for a successful sojourn are specified, various selection devices can be used which have been shown to predict these criteria. At the same time, other criteria and selection devices have to be discarded since limits on time, money, and effort necessitate choices among various alternatives. A good study of criteria specification and measurement was carried out with the cooperation of the Peace Corps in Ghana (Ezekiel, 1968). It should be noted that, even though large-scale testing and prediction did not prove successful in the Peace Corps, smaller-scale research such as Ezekiel's was supported. Administrators and researchers collaborated in the hopes of discovering better selection devices appropriate for the special demands of work in another culture.

Ezekiel was interested in predicting successful job performance as judged by supervisors, visiting social scientists who conducted extensive interviews, and peers. A number of important relationships between job performance and other activities were found. In interpreting the findings, however, one must keep in mind that other criteria are not under consideration. No information is presented on acceptance by hosts, transfer of skills to hosts, learning about another culture, or learning about one's own behavior. This comment is by no means meant as a criticism. It is simply a caveat that the criteria under consideration relate to job performance and that administrators interested in other criteria must search elsewhere.

Volunteers rated as successful job performers, largely in their teaching assignments, had a number of other characteristics. They supplemented their teaching roles with other work, possibly so that they would not become bored in the rural village to which they were assigned. They were skillful at adapting teaching methods after experiencing communication difficulties with students. They invested time in deliberate programs of self-improvement, endeavored to encourage self-respect among students, and viewed their overseas work as an opportunity for personal participation in the shaping of major events. While these factors associated with good job performance correspond to socially desirable behaviors, other factors should force administrators to wonder about well-roundedness and balance. Volunteers rated high on job performance centered most of their lives on the school compound, were bothered by feelings of loneliness, and felt that the teaching tasks assigned them were not challenging enough. It seems to me, then, that the total picture reflects a "grind." This vernacular term refers to a very hard-working person, somewhat headstrong, who performs tasks successfully but sometimes misses other opportunities not directly associated with work. While the person's dedication to work is unquestioned, (s)he sometimes irritates hosts in the rush to get things done and to improve the local system. Hosts sometimes become jealous, fearing that their positions will be threatened if the sojourner's dedication and energy become a standard for comparison.

Grinds seem to go in and out of style. They were valued in the early 1960s when Ezekiel gathered information from the Peace Corps volunteers and their supervisors, but they faded into a less appreciated background as the self-fulfillment movement of the late 1960s and early 1970s came into being. In the later 1970s, there was a resurgence of prominence since their skills were valued in a tight job market. The important point for the present discussion is that job performance is only one criterion of a successful sojourn. If administrators are interested in its prediction, the work of Ezekiel can be profitably studied. If they are interested in other criteria, they would make mistakes if selection techniques were chosen based on Ezekiel's work. The general point is that administrators should always consider the criteria for "success" when studying the work of others. Unfortunately, criteria are often not specified as clearly as they might be.

Relevant prior experience

If aspects of people's home country work are also part of their assignment during a sojourn, job performance is better and tensions are less. Glaser (1979) has speculated that people who have had experiences in non-office work settings within their country may perform better on a sojourn. Professionals in forestry, fisheries, and agriculture are accustomed to working out-of-doors, traveling to remote places, adjusting to less-than-desirable accommodations, and working with counterparts who have not always achieved high levels of formal education. While on a sojourn, they are faced with these same requirements and may work more successfully because of their previously acquired skills and attitudes. In an interesting but highly technical and difficult-to-read analysis, Berry (1976) has suggested that people from some traditional, rural communities may have fewer problems than others when adjusting to life in large cities. People from societies where the major subsistence activities are hunting and gathering develop specific skills to be successful in their work. They must be independent since hunting is done alone or in small groups, and they must be analytical to perceive extremely subtle signs of nearby game. These skills may be useful when seeking work after migration to urban areas since many jobs demand independent judgment and analytical skills. Since there are not always well-established social services to ease transition, independent people may be able to survive in the new society without assistance from others. A highly speculative possibility is that analytical people may be able to find the *one* small aspect of a complex bureaucracy which can be tapped to solve some specific problem.

On the other hand, people from farming communities learn to be more dependent on each other. They often cooperate in the labor-intensive activities of planting and harvesting. They also cooperate in storing food as preparation for the nongrowing season, an inadequate crop sometime in the future, and the possibility of famine. Agriculture encourages the establishment of permanent settlements which, in turn, requires joint defenses against predators. When moving to urban areas, these people may not be as well prepared to accept factory jobs. They may, however, be better prepared to accept the crowded conditions typical of urban neighborhoods. They may also be better able to develop group support systems to cope with the changes in their lives.

Hosts' expectations based on previous sojourners

When hosts have had experience with other sojourners, they develop categories into which new visitors are placed. Even though a given sojourner may be quite different from his or her predecessors, the already established categories color the reception, treatment, and opportunities offered by hosts. The important point for sojourners is that they will be assigned stereotypes which must be overcome if work is to proceed satisfactorily. For instance, Americans in general are seen as somewhat brusque and overly eager to begin "productive" work. Technical assistance advisers are considered to be uncaring, rigid, and interested only in spreading the influence of the donor country. Peace Corps workers are seen as energetic but naive, unseasoned, and insensitive to the status of host country citizens. Cross-cultural researchers are pereceived as interested only in doing studies to increase their own publication list, and not in making a contribution useful to the host country. Foreign students are often given the label of "ungrateful." They use a university's counseling facilities, involve advisers' time and energy in their problems, but rarely come back with thanks when the advice proves useful. Missionaries are perceived as interested only in acquiring converts and as unconcerned with treading on a society's traditional norms.

The end result of previous experiences is that new interactions begin on a defensive or even hostile note. A fact which sojourners should keep in mind is that much behavior is role-based. When hosts are rude, they may not be directing their feelings at a specific person. Rather, they are directing their feelings at a concept which happens to be exemplified by a given sojourner. Some types of cross-cultural contact are explicitly role-based. Diplomats who are the target of vicious verbal assaults (Glenn et al., 1977) realize they are participating in mini-dramas and that no one involved feels the least amount of personal animosity. Another fact to remember is that the development of new relationships takes a long time. Since all diplomats have been misled by colleagues from other countries, they develop new relations carefully.

> . . . trust between diplomats builds up slowly, even when they come from nations that are basically friendly. Each must learn the other's "code"— learn to distinguish between the occasions when he is speaking officially, as a representative of his government, and the occasions when he is speaking informally. Each must spend a period of time testing the credibility of what the other has said informally. If a trusting relationship finally develops, it must be guarded carefully, because it can be destroyed by telling a few lies in an informal manner. Once destroyed, it is hard to rebuild. To the extent that a nation wishes to keep credible channels open, it must scrupulously refrain from using them to transmit lies [D. Pruitt, 1965, pp. 406–407].

Further, all sojourners can learn the host society's norms which mark the development of warm interpersonal relationships. These might be the frequent use of "thank you," keeping hosts informed regarding the outcomes of joint decisions, gift giving, offering aid to friends and relatives, adapting one's work so that a contribution to the host society is more likely, and actively participating in host society ceremonies when asked to do so.

A very general point, to which there will inevitably be some exceptions, is that work and social relations are more closely interrelated in Asia, South America, Africa, and Australia than they are in the United States. Work simply cannot begin in some societies until collaborators know each other and are comfortable in each other's presence. This point is increasingly being applied when administrators select people for sojourns (Glaser, 1979). I know of a recent case in which a well-established researcher from the United States contacted people in South America to discuss possible collaborative work. The researcher was subjected to a rigorous screening in which many people known to the South Americans were asked to write letters of recommendation. The referees were asked to comment on the researcher's ability to get along with others, commitment to true collaboration, and ability to cooperate and not offend hosts. It seems to me that this sort of screening would have been insulting and, hence, unthinkable ten years ago. The researcher, however, realized the importance of the process, argued that it should be utilized more frequently, and patiently waited for the outcome.

Status markers

Sojourners should also realize that certain status markers are possessed by those who perform important tasks in the host society. If large numbers of relevant markers are possessed, sojourners will have greater ease in completing their tasks. Obvious examples are one's age and sex. In some countries, males with gray hair have an easier time in completing their tasks than fellow sojourners not blessed with these situation-specific desiderata. Other markers are the schools attended, the famous professors with whom one studied, family background, and patrons. People sometimes invest tremendous amounts of time and money obtaining these markers. I knew a foreign student, working with a very well-known professor, who spent an extra three years of graduate study in obtaining the Ph.D. degree. The professor was incredibly slow in reading dissertation proposals, approving data collection plans, and giving feedback on draft chapters. I asked, "Why don't you change dissertation advisers?" He answered that the professor was highly respected back home. His signature on a student's dissertation guaranteed both a good job and continuing access to career opportunities.

At times, the same markers will lead to high status in one society but low status in another. In some places, the concept of a "college student" is highly respected and people occupying this role are treated well. In other countries, the concept is not accorded much status and role occupants are not given any special respect. Foreign students in the United States, for instance, are sometimes upset when discussions of their current activities are greeted by yawns from hosts.

Since status is a quality assigned to people by others, it is bound to change. The status of the technical assistance adviser, for instance, has decreased as the Third World countries become more nationalistic and sensitive to the obligations foreign aid might entail. Well-published researchers are no longer automatically welcomed, as already discussed. The Peace Corps has had a recent history of complete exclusion from certain countries, and it no longer has the aura of something innovative and exciting. Businessmen find that the once respected "American know-how" is no longer unquestioned given the greater productivity and smaller inflation rates of other countries.

Sensitivity to power

An interesting factor which has been identified as important in task performance, but which has not received much extended discussion, is sensitivity to power. Ezekiel (1968) found that Peace Corps workers rated high in task performance had an interest in and concern for power relations. Implications of this intriguing result, however, were not suggested. The general factor has also been mentioned as important in the work of diplomats (Sawyer & Guetzkow, 1965), people involved in school and neighborhood integration (Williams, 1964), technical assistance advisers (Kidder, 1977), and overseas businessmen (Cleveland, Mangone, & Adams, 1960).

Looking at the range of commentary provided by these scholars, the basic assumption seems to be that important work is accomplished within a complex system. The efforts and egos of many people are involved when projects are planned, implemented, and given sustained attention over a period of years. In some countries, the system is called a bureaucracy, and there is little point in bemoaning its existence. Some sort of bureaucracy is always present to review new proposals, comment on their merits, offer or withhold support, choose the specific people who will be involved, and offer rewards for either accomplishment or carefully planned sabotage.

An interest, concern, and sensitivity regarding power does not refer to a mad control over others reminiscent of a deranged monarch. Rather, it refers to an understanding of how complex tasks are accomplished in a specific society. Assume a sojourner has a large-scale project which (s)he would like to introduce into the host society. The project could be a business venture, a new curriculum for a school, the introduction of machines to increase output over that produced by manual labor, a treaty involving international cooperation, or funded programs to encourage the support of foreign students. Questions such as these are important:

1. Who are the authority figures whose judgment can help, hinder, or kill the project?
2. How are they best approached: directly, with the help of an intermediary, through written or oral introductions?
3. Some people are better at developing projects than in winning acceptance for them. Are there people on the project staff who are well-suited to interact with the authority figures? Will similarities in background or personality lead to a greater probability of acceptance?
4. Are there times of the day, month, or year when there are so many preoccupations with other matters that little attention can be given to the new project?
5. What sorts of situational variables might surround the presentation of the proposal: ceremonies, meals in lavish settings, privacy, or publicity?
6. Identifiable factors keep people in power. Are there any factors being threatened by the project? Does the project help the authority figures in any way?
7. Who can be hurt by the project? Can anything be done to neutralize these dangers?
8. If one route to a goal is blocked, another can sometimes be taken. The project staff may be able to avoid one power figure by courting people in other parts of the bureaucracy. But might the staff risk winning the battle but losing the war? Long-term resentment might be developed which will eventually threaten the project.
9. Envy, jealousy, and hostility often exist among authority figures. Can a project be threatened if it is caught in the middle of a traditional feud between two power holders or factions?
10. Has support been established at various layers of the bureaucracy, not just the top? Power figures can sometimes order implementation but cannot actually launch a project due to their lack of time or technical skills. Many projects have failed because of inattention to the center of a bureaucracy (Heclo, 1977).
11. Assuming approval, how often do authority figures want progress reports? Do they want to be consulted? People are always complimented when their advice is asked.
12. How much credit do authority figures want when the project yields successful results? Or would they prefer to remain anonymous?

These questions by no means cover all aspects of power relations among people. They do, however, give some indication of what is meant by "sensitivity to power" in the accomplishment of a sojourner's goals. Participation in power relations, however, can itself threaten a project's success. As discussed in chapter 5, activity associated with power becomes fascinating. People become arrogant, develop exaggerated feelings of self-importance, and take credit for work done by others. Eventually, their behavior can cause strife among the members of a project's staff.

The acquisition of information

A person cannot even contemplate a project without extensive information related to its planning, implementation, and administration. When working in other cultures, however, people often encounter difficulties in both identifying and finding key facts. Information is often culture specific:

1. What are the established ways by which decisions are made?
2. What historical precedents might be called upon when supporting or rejecting a new project proposal?
3. What legal requirements have to be fulfilled?
4. Given the norms of a society, which might be affected by the introduction of a new project?
5. How long will members of the bureaucracy likely take in making decisions?

Obtaining this information is often difficult, especially in countries where access to key documents is carefully controlled. Recent developments in the analyses of sojourn experiences have included the gathering of information which is much more specific than what was available in the past. Materials for foreign student advisers, for instance, are not concerned with just any sojourner but with those from specific countries (e.g., Althen, 1979). Businessmen have been given detailed guidance concerning negotiations in specific countries (Van Zandt, 1970), as have cross-cultural researchers (McCormack, 1976) and technical assistance advisers (Amuzegar, 1966). Hopefully, this trend will be continued. An extremely useful contribution would be the development of a library retrieval system for specific information on any given country. The system might be modeled after two which have been of great benefit for some types of sojourns but less helpful for others. These are the Human Relations Area Files (HRAF) and the Educational Resource Information Center (ERIC), both of which are available in many large libraries.

Managing cooperative effort

The advantages of cross-cultural collaboration on important tasks have been mentioned in different parts of this chapter. The greater experience and expertise of people from one country can be put to use during a sojourn. Outsiders may be able to bring a fresh perspective to host country problems. Sojourners may be able to transfer their skills so that hosts can carry out future work with more self-assurance. A number of studies have been concerned with how the positive benefits stemming from cross-cultural collaboration can be increased (Brislin, 1979; Ruben & Kealey, 1979). One study, which dealt with the work of cross-cultural researchers, resulted in advice which may be generalizable to the work of other sojourners (Brislin, 1979). Interviews were conducted with 52 experienced researchers to determine their opinions about improved collaborative efforts and potential benefits. The responses could be summarized around six themes. Three have already been discussed: the building of a knowledge base about cross-cultural relations, which is the concern of this entire book; the careful selection of individuals; and recommendations regarding interpersonal behaviors (respect, tolerance, patience) which lead to positive feelings among collaborators. The three other themes were the specification of plans and objectives, integrating one's work into the structures/roles within the host country, and greater attention to the role of leaders.

The most frequently suggested piece of advice was a variation on this theme: specify plans and objectives so that everyone involved understands what has to be done and who has to do it. One respondent was quite specific:

> Have a crystal clear plan in mind concerning (1) what you want to do and (2) what you think your host and/or collaborator wants to do. Likewise, encourage your host/collaborator to ask the same questions. . . . Perhaps be somewhat businesslike, after formal amenities and mutual reassurances . . . and enumerate specific criteria about *what* is to get done (or attempted) *why, who* will do what, and what will be done with the resultant [plans and information]. If these rather cold and calculating criteria cannot be satisfactorily met, then I am afraid my advice would be: stay home, or consider a more attractive, less troublesome alternative [from Brislin, 1979, p. 230].

Further, respondents advised that the meaning of "collaboration" should be spelled out since different people may have different definitions. This analytical approach to specifying plans early can undoubtedly be a cultural imposition in some projects since this type of analysis is not universal. This disadvantage, however, is outweighed by possible advantages or reduced misunderstanding and tensions. While preparing a report on "Advisory principles for ethical considerations in the conduct of cross–cultural research," Tapp, Kelman, Wrightsman, Triandis, and Coelho (1974) solicited advice from researchers in a number of countries. The same sort of "need for advanced specification" was made clear in the following recommendations.

- Explore and arrange fully the nature of the collaborative relationship before activating the project and making major, irreversible decisions.
- Establish a pattern of regular, frequent, and open communication throughout the course of the [work] in order to resolve grievances, verify perceptions, and review expectations [pp. 246–247].

Finally, negotiations should take place concerning the sharing of credit for possible accomplishments. Again considering the case of researchers, Jacob and Jacob (1979) report that they have wrestled with this issue but have found no satisfactory solution. Often, major accomplishments are associated with the name of one or possibly two people, even though a large team may have been involved. Even though collaborators may make every effort to share credit, the public may learn of the work only by its association with the name of the senior or most colorful person. In some countries, the public will learn about the project through the team member who is best suited to appear on TV talk shows.

Respondents also felt that sojourners would have a greater chance of success if they could integrate their plans into organizations, role relations, and mutual obligation networks within the country where work is to take place. Governments now have screening committees whose members review proposals and make recommendations concerning whether or not the sojourner should be granted a visa. To work within such a bureaucracy, people might attach themselves to organizations which have a long history and a good reputation within the country. Examples are the overseas study programs sponsored by American universities since many maintain offices in various countries. Administrators there know how to go about obtaining clearances, cutting red tape, introducing sojourners to potential collaborators, and warning about potential roadblocks. Undoubtedly, there would be a careful review by such an office since its administrators will not want to jeopardize their position by sponsoring a poor piece of research.

Finally, respondents speculated about the behavior of leaders but did not suggest hard-and-fast rules. One Asian respondent felt that successful projects must have a person to whom others defer. He felt that many hosts would be more comfortable since deference to respected leaders is familiar to them. If this observation is accurate, then "collaboration among equals," often suggested by sojourners working in Asia, is an unwise idea. Another respondent suggested that a sojourner can enter a collaboration with the hopes of a jointly-produced design and administrative plan, but this goal will not always be achieved. He recommended having a "hidden agenda," a carefully prepared plan designed *prior to* meetings with potential collaborators. This plan could then be presented to the group if talks bog down. If this seems manipulative, it should be remembered that (a) the plan is presented only if the group cannot produce a collaborative design; and (b) the "hidden agenda" is subject to action by the group.

In large-scale projects, one respondent wondered whether leaders must behave more like entrepreneurs than like representatives of their professions. He warned that one-half to two-thirds of a sojourner's time can be spent on administrative matters if a leadership role is undertaken. Several respondents were concerned that leadership roles have usually been assumed by people from the West. This creates possible biases in the planning and implementation of the work. This problem is difficult to overcome, given the fact that funding sources, materials, and previously experienced personnel are more commonly available in the West. Because of these problems, rather than despite them, respondents indicated that research is needed on how to create balance in the distribution of leadership roles.

Job enlargement

Some intriguing comments by sojourners suggest that the research area known as "job enlargement" may be a worthwhile source of ideas. Michael Hamnett (1979, personal communication) served as a Peace Corps volunteer on the Pacific Island of Kapingamaringi. Although his main task assignment was teaching, he and some colleagues established a business which allowed hosts to sell their handicrafts. Benefits to the volunteers included satisfaction from doing valuable work, the reinforcement received from enthusiastic host participants, and the alleviation of boredom. Some sojourners do not have enough to do after completing daily work on their major task assignment. Some have difficulties filling free time since there is not the variety of activities to which they are accustomed. Extra work can satisfy the same needs as a serious hobby. Ezekiel (1968) also mentioned that the volunteers rated highest in task productivity were those who took on extra work not directly related to their job descriptions.

Job enlargement involves adding new tasks and responsibilities to a current set of workers' assignments. Possible advantages (Hackman & Oldham, 1976; White & Mitchell, 1979) include greater commitment to the profession, satisfaction, and productivity. There are two possible reasons for the benefits of job enlargement. One is in the intrinsic aspects of the job itself. There is greater task variety, identification with the newer tasks, greater feelings of job significance, greater autonomy, and more feedback. The final advantage stems from the fact that since jobholders are doing more, there are more tasks on which they obtain feedback regarding how well or how poorly they are doing. The second reason for the benefits

(White & Mitchell, 1979) is the reaction of co-workers. Seeing the job-holders perform the new task, co-workers may communicate respect, which is rewarding to the jobholders. Research on job enlargement also indicates that the beneficial effects may occur especially for individuals who have a high need for achievement and who feel the need for growth in their chosen profession.

Other types of cross-cultural experiences have been investigated to determine if job enlargement will increase productivity and satisfaction. Brislin (1980) has analyzed the role of the simultaneous interpreter and Mestenhauser (1974) has examined the potential contributions of foreign students.

Interpreters attached to permanent multinational organizations may become more familiar with policies and procedures than people holding other jobs. For instance, interpreters will know more than (a) elected representatives, in the case of political organizations such as the United Nations or European Parliament, or (b) sojourners on temporary assignment, in the case of businesses or embassies. The interpreters might become the basis of an "institutional memory," passing on information about day-to-day activities, elements of protocol, and historical precedents to new sojourners. Another possibility is that interpreters could be consulted by others during the *preparation* of a speech or written document. The interpreters could suggest wording which would be satisfactory in the source language and would lead to a readily understandable version in the target language. Many translation problems could be alleviated if a phrase could be substituted in the original language which has the same meaning as material in the first draft but which is easier to translate. For instance, the phrase "gossip about" is hard to translate into the Chamorro language since a speaker has to designate a female or male gossip, and the extra meaning may not be appropriate. However, "talk about someone else's business" does have a readily available equivalent in Chamorro (Brislin, 1976a). Since the two English phrases convey the same meaning in many situations, the second would be chosen because it leads to a better translation. Interpreters would be excellent advisers concerning the wording of material which must be conveyed in more than one language.

There are other possibilities, admittedly more speculative, which might be incorporated into a job-expanded set of work expectations. One is that interpreters be given explicit permission to stop a conference if they feel that a misunderstanding is causing difficulty. Such misunderstandings could be based on the sorts of intercultural communication problems reviewed throughout this book, or on mistranslations which cause an inappropriate reaction from the other party. Reactions to the mistakes or misunderstandings may cause problems to spiral. At present, interpreters rarely feel that they have the responsibility or authority to stop a meeting even if they are confident that an identifiable problem is causing misunderstandings. Communication problems might be lessened if interpreters were invited to prepare orientation materials for new sojourners. *Users* of an interpreter's services might receive instructions in desirable behaviors which are likely to increase the accuracy of the translation as well as intercultural communication in general. These behaviors include language usage, timing, gestures, avoidance of colloquialisms, and proper use of relevant equipment.

The varied activities of acting as institutional memory, consulting while speeches are prepared, interrupting conferences, and orienting newcomers increase the visibility of the profession. During a recent conference devoted to simultaneous interpretation itself, participants voiced their feelings that the profession does not command as much respect as it should (Gerver & Sinaiko, 1978). Interpreters are treated as if they were parrots without an original contribution to make. They are used for short periods of time but are not considered worthy of much attention after a conference's working hours. Job enlargement may help increase the status of the profession.

Mestenhauser (1974) feels that the resources foreign students bring to host universities are underused. They have language competencies, firsthand knowledge of other countries, and experiences in adjusting to a changing world which are rarely tapped. Potential contributions include the development of new courses which focus on countries and issues not previously given attention in a college's curriculum. A less administratively complex possibility involves inviting foreign students to participate in existing courses. They could provide information which complements current course materials. American students might be asked to interview sojourners and to keep careful records of their interactions. Dr. Felipe Korzeny (1979, personal communication) has used this approach and reports a good deal of success. The ethical issues of exploiting foreign students should always be kept in mind. Sojourners should feel comfortable if they choose not to participate. In my experience, however, many will be flattered and will enjoy the attention and the additional opportunities to meet hosts. Another contribution could be input to hosts' term papers or independent research projects. Finally, participation outside the classroom is possible. Foreign student advisers on some campuses have established informal language exchange programs. Sojourners are asked to participate in conversations with a host who is trying to learn another language. In exchange, sojourners participate in conversations to increase their English language skills. In communities where many languages are spoken, sojourners may volunteer to act as interpreters at hospitals, legal service agencies, and schools.

There are many advantages which sojourners gain from participating in these activities (Mestenhauser and Barsig, 1978):

- The organized program can help create a better atmosphere for foreign students by involving larger numbers of people (students, staff, and faculty) in their lives.
- Significant numbers of Americans are educated about countries, values, and international developments.
- Sojourners will make a positive contribution on a voluntary basis. Social service is intrinsically satisfying.
- Foreign students gain a new perspective through interaction with host students and faculty. The nature of world independence is introduced through firsthand experiences.
- New skills in effective communication and teaching will be developed by foreign students. These are leadership skills which are transferable to future careers.
- Students from other countries will develop equitable and cooperative relationships with hosts in place of simply "receiving" an education [pp. 7–8].

Job enlargement can also be viewed as an opportunity to use the valuable skills which people bring to a sojourn. Administrators should always start with the assumption that people want to do a good job and want their efforts respected. If administrators provide opportunities so that sojourners can use their varied skills, many difficulties common to cross-cultural adjustment will diminish in importance.

THE MOVE FROM LESS TO MORE INDUSTRIALIZED SOCIETIES

A number of unique problems are frequently faced by sojourners who previously have not had a great deal of experience in technologically developed societies. Most often, they are placed in the role of a "learner" or a person not yet able to make an original contribution. There is often a loss of status since the sojourners may have been highly respected in their home countries. Since the hosts are accustomed to receiving sojourners, any one individual is not treated as unique or as deserving of special attention. Even when special organizations are established to aid sojourners, their facilities are underused (Pedersen, 1975). One reason involves pride: sojourners are sensitive about their loss of status and want to prove that they can solve their own problems. Some of the problems are faced by all sojourners and have been discussed throughout this chapter. The unique difficulties facing people from less technologically developed countries center around the relative attractiveness of the home and host societies.

The industrialized nation as a new reference group

Many analysts have agreed that the norms of industrialized nations often become attractive to sojourners (Gama & Pedersen, 1977; Inkeles & Smith, 1974; Kashoki, 1978). Problems arise when sojourners bring the new reference point back to their home country. Kashoki (1978) argues that Africans who study abroad look to more developed countries for approval. An appropriate task for returnees would be to take over jobs previously held by expatriates. They could then "set the record straight," correcting mistakes which were based on impositions by and inappropriate borrowings from colonial powers. On their sojourns, however, people were rewarded for thinking in terms of certain ideas which were fashionable at the time. The necessary task of cleaning up old problems is not viewed as exciting or as something which will be appreciated by the new reference group. Further, the value placed on the sojourn itself contributes to an attitude that Western norms are superior to African traditions and potentials.

Brain drain

When dissatisfaction with opportunities in one's home country become intense, people may leave to seek employment in an industrialized country. "Brain drain" is a term which refers to the voluntary movement of well-trained individuals who leave their home country in the pursuit of more attractive work elsewhere. The term is more frequently used when sojourners study or work temporarily in another society, become attached to it, and decide to stay. Glaser (1974) has done the most extensive research on this topic. His findings should be useful in designing sponsored programs to increase the probability that sojourners will return to their home countries.

Behaviors which might cause the attribution of "brain drain" are often more complex when examined carefully. Work abroad, in addition to formal education, is considered by some sojourners to be part of their training for a career. What seems to be a case of emigration can actually be a long but carefully planned sojourn for educational purposes. The people involved may have every intention of returning to their home countries. Certain factors increase the probability of an eventual return:

1. integration into the home community. Relevant factors can be a family, a job to which a person can return, and continued correspondence with

one's relatives, friends, and professional colleagues during the sojourn.
2. having a scholarship or grant from the home country. In some cases governments require sojourners to return as a condition of the grant.
3. contact maintained by governments. Although Glaser (1974) mentions that it rarely occurs, when representatives of a country's government keep in contact with sojourners, there is less likelihood of emigration.
4. personal involvement in the home country. Once people do return, any plans for an eventual emigration become overwhelmed by developments at home. These include marriage, children, and advancement on the job.

Other factors increase the probability that sojourners will remain in the host country:

1. uncertainty about the future. If governments frequently change and specific educated citizens are favored one day but condemned the next, sojourners may feel insecure about returning home.
2. membership in minority groups within the home country. If people feel that they are the targets of discrimination and perceive greater tolerance elsewhere, they are less likely to feel an attachment to their home country.
3. opportunities in the host country. These include the probabilities of obtaining a permanent visa and finding permanent employment. In tight job markets the brain drain problem may not be as intense. Since positions in the host country cannot be found, people are forced to consider the option of returning home.
4. much more association with hosts than fellow nationals. This represents one of the "can't win" issues which administrators face. They can encourage interaction with hosts to increase cross-cultural learning. In doing so, however, they may be contributing to the probability of brain drain.
5. marriage between sojourners and hosts. In addition, the children of these marriages may become acculturated to the host culture, as might the children who accompany adults from the first days of the sojourn. People may stay because of better perceived opportunities for their children.

Many administrators with whom I have spoken refuse to become involved in brain drain cases. The implicit, if not explicit, purpose of sponsored programs is to provide opportunities which can later be put to use in people's home countries. Administrators realize that if too many people from a certain country choose to brain drain, opportunities for others will become unavailable. Administrators do work in behalf of refugees who cannot return for political reasons, but these are not brain drain cases since they lack the element of voluntary emigration. Administrative work with emigrants takes incredible time and effort which should be saved for special cases. Legal requirements have to be met, permanent jobs must be found, and provisions for the family must be given attention. These tasks can interfere with an administrator's major job of assisting sojourners in their adjustment, opportunities for learning, and return. The tasks can also interfere with job satisfaction. I know a person who left a job involving face-to-face contact with sojourners because so much work with emigrants was demanded. He reports, "I entered the field to help sojourners with their work and to provide opportunities which might lead to enhanced cross-cultural experiences. I got tired of being a visa lawyer."

The problem of irrelevant training

Complaints are frequently made about the education or training which sojourners receive. The major theme is irrelevance: the knowledge sojourners acquire is not usable in the home country. Students learn about complex equipment, a limited set of research ideas on which senior professors are currently working, and the problems facing highly industrialized nations. This knowledge is not applicable in the home country where the equipment is not available, opportunities for basic research are limited, and the problems are different or at least take different forms.

In analyzing the work of technical assistance advisers, Heisey (1977) makes similar arguments.

> For too long the industrialized nations aided the so-called underdeveloped nations in an exploiting or at best a patronizing manner. From a communicative point of view it was monological—one directional with little regard for the perceived needs and priorities of the recipients. Americans went abroad with their material, their technical assistance, and their experts to train the nationals according to the research development problems as Americans saw them and as they thought [the problems] should be seen. Such an inadequate conceptualization of the communicative dimensions of the relationships has resulted in much harm and damage both from the standpoint of international relations but more importantly from the standpoint of the best interests of the developing countries [p. 64].

Heisey claims that the International Seminar in Physics at the University of Uppsala, Sweden, has developed a better model. All training is geared to the situations sojourners will face after returning to their homes. Participants are firmly attached to institutions, decreasing the probability of brain drain. They are encouraged to analyze the needs of their own countries and to develop individualized study programs which will best meet those needs. They learn to combine their interests with those of others instead of "doing their own thing." This approach provides a better preparation for their eventual return since professionals rarely have the option of doing individual research based solely on their own interests.

Some of these methods can be incorporated into any university curriculum. Students can be encouraged to do term papers, theses, and dissertations on issues relevant to their home countries. Special courses might be established with content based on potential relevance to less industrialized countries. In many cases, these changes would not demand the expenditure of additional funds. Many university professors have had overseas experience but have never been asked to incorporate it into their courses. They may benefit from job enlargement. Instead of reading the same sorts of term papers year after year, professors themselves can increase their knowledge by encouraging sojourners to write about home country issues.

THE MOVE FROM MORE TO LESS INDUSTRIALIZED SOCIETIES

Sojourners who move from more to less technologically developed societies are often assigned jobs as advisers, teachers, or consultants. The major additional burdens faced by these people center around the definition of their roles, the uncertain consequences of their work, and their collaborative efforts with counterparts.

The definition of roles

There are many types of contributions sojourners can make, and it is always difficult to decide on the type of work which should be emphasized (Goulet, 1979). Sojourners can act as a stimulant, encouraging hosts to move in certain directions. They can study the local situation and then present alternatives for actions, pointing out the advantages and disadvantages of each. In a related role, they can act as educators by encouraging hosts to consider various options which may have been overlooked. More active roles are also possible. Sojourners can work to ensure that technical assistance aid is directed at appropriate targets rather than into the pockets of an already wealthy elite. They can act as critics, although this role carries obvious risks. Or, they can do the work necessary to develop a model project in the hopes that their hosts will eventually take over its maintenance and, perhaps, develop similar projects in other parts of the country. No hard and fast guidelines can be given regarding where and when one type of role is more appropriate than another. The frustration associated with this uncertainty undoubtedly has an impact on sojourners' morale.

Uncertainty of consequences

In addition to the difficulties inherent in choosing a role, sojourners cannot always predict what the consequences of their work will be. If they work hard and attract a number of hosts, so much dependence may be created that projects might not be continued after the sojourners return home. Visitors rarely understand a culture well enough to visualize possible negative effects of their work, or the "latent disconsequences" (Merton, 1957). For instance, a group of Peace Corps workers was assigned to university-level teaching jobs in an Asian country (Guskin, 1966). Upon observing that host colleagues engaged in little research, they encouraged younger professors to collaborate on a number of projects. Some efforts were successful, and jointly published articles in reputable journals were proudly circulated around the university. Senior professors, however, became jealous since they were no longer the center of attention. The careers of the younger academics may have been damaged by the sojourners' well-intentioned efforts. I have worried about a similar problem. Participants in programs at the East-West Center (described earlier) have a chance to spend a good deal of time learning about current research ideas and methodological innovations. Upon their return home, however, will they be a threat to colleagues who have not had similar opportunities?

Criticism, or its absence, also has its consequences. The current norm is that sojourning advisers should tread lightly. Hosts have received so much advice and criticism in the past that they are sensitive and resentful. More and more, hosts have the option of expelling advisers from one country and accepting those from another. Based on a study of the actual decisions technical assistance advisers have to make, Glaser (1979) commented on this problem:

> The now prevailing eagerness to please the host is not without drawbacks: some of the less tractable experts [who were interviewed] pointed to urgent reforms in the governments and societies of developing countries, and curbing their criticisms meant that technical assistance would become a means of strengthening rather than revolutionizing established orders [p. 224].

Although the amount of published literature on the advisory, teaching, and expert roles is large (e.g., bibliographies in Kumar, 1979a), there are few conclusions which might provide guidance for sojourners. Important contributions could be made by people willing to synthesize the literature and to suggest guidelines which seem useful in specified situations. Possible approaches might be: (a) to study the apparent reasons for successful and unsuccessful projects, and (b) to do a content analysis of the opinions held by various practitioners, academics, and hosts. Even if the guidance appropriate to various situations cannot be formulated, the advantages, disadvantages, and possible latent consequences of different options could be presented. Given this information, better decisions can be made.

Working with counterparts

The work of Ruben and Kealey (1979) on the importance of working with counterparts was reviewed in chapter 3. Their basic point is that the most effective advisers need more than technical skills. Sojourners also must be able to communicate their knowledge to hosts so that projects can continue after they return home. Selection criteria for advisers should include the ability to transfer knowledge.

There is at least one difficulty in applying this important finding. Advisers often have difficulty finding the appropriate hosts who will eventually be responsible for the maintenance of projects. Often, the assigned counterpart is promoted into an administrative role after the sojourner leaves the country (Kashoki, 1978). The adviser's time, then, is not well spent since the new administrator may be far removed from day-to-day maintenance of the project. Realizing this problem, advisers should keep two points in mind. First, they might spend time with a number of hosts who are the subordinates of the assigned counterpart. One of these people may actually run the project in future years. Second, they might attempt to increase the counterpart's skills in transferring knowledge. The adviser's eventual contribution, then, might flow from work with one host who later instructs another.

Counterparts sometimes occupy their roles for undesirable reasons. At times, they see work with advisers as a vehicle for obtaining grants for further study in another country (Glaser, 1979). Marginally competent counterparts are sometimes assigned to advisers so that they will be removed from the host country's bureaucratic system. If less-than-competent people can be sent away for a time, more work can be accomplished. All advisers face the risk of being assigned incompetent counterparts if hosts wish to kill a project. Since the norms in many countries demand face-to-face politeness, observing the quality of assigned counterparts is one way advisers can discern the true feelings about a project.

Greater anonymity

To accomplish tasks, sojourners must often invest great effort but let other people take credit for accomplishments. Successful diplomats in the

United Nations, for instance, often prepare materials for others, develop new ideas, and quietly use their skills to guide proposals through the necessary channels. When publicity begins to surround the work, however, credit may be taken by someone else (Alger, 1965). Often, diplomats from industrialized countries work anonymously in behalf of colleagues from newly-independent nations. The complexity of international negotiations demands that the more experienced diplomats offer support to newcomers. Both parties gain from the exchange. The work of the less experienced diplomats is made more sophisticated, and the diplomats from industrialized nations gain goodwill which may later be reflected in supportive votes.

Other types of sojourners work more effectively when their efforts are not as widely recognized as they might be. Szanton (1966) found that Peace Corps workers in the Philippines were completely unsuccessful when they attempted to introduce innovative teaching methods. They were met with resistance by people who would be threatened by the change as well as by the friends of those people. The volunteers were much more successful when they worked quietly with a few respected Filipino teachers who incorporated the suggestions for improvement. The Filipino teachers could then introduce the methods and be assured of greater attention due to their status as insiders.

In both the diplomat and Peace Corps cases, the work is accomplished with little credit going to the innovator. A few people will know of the contributions which were made, and there may eventually be rewards in the form of promotions or good job ratings. For people who enjoy having their contributions recognized by large numbers of people, however, sojourns may provide few opportunities for self-promotion.

Greater range of expertise expected

Sojourners working in less developed countries are often called upon to give advice beyond their formal training. Overseas businessmen are asked to interpret the policies of their countries (Bauer, Pool, & Dexter, 1963), not just those of their companies. Foreign students are often asked to talk about the policies of their countries' governments. This experience occurs so frequently among Americans studying abroad that orientation programs should routinely prepare students for the give-and-take of political dialogue.

Researchers are asked to comment on many possible applications which their discipline can offer. Guthrie (1979, personal communication) has done a number of large-scale studies in the Philippines. His discipline is psychology, and he reports that hosts ask about its potential contributions to many problems. Conversations such as the following often take place.

Question: "You're a psychologist. That's the study of human behavior?" Answer: "Yes." Question: "I'm a nutritionist. The government provides free dietary supplements which would reduce malnutrition, but people won't incorporate the new food into their diets. What can be done to persuade people to change their eating habits?" Or: Question: "If you've studied human behavior, you can help me out. People in the city are crowded into small apartments. There are more spacious homes available near the city limits which would cost people no more, but nobody will move. How can the overpopulation of the central city be reduced?"

Answers which are variants of "that's not my speciality" clearly provide no help. The overly frequent use of this response has undoubtedly contributed to the less-than-enthusiastic reception given to visiting researchers. Sojourners must be prepared to entertain questions which tax the limits of their knowledge. They should also be prepared to modify their original plans when faced with problems identified as significant by hosts. Further, they must be prepared to do this work without extensive reference aids. Only rarely will libraries exist which match the facilities to which advisers are accustomed in their own country.

The acceptance of sojourners' recommendations

Even though sojourners are asked for advice, it will not always be followed. There seems to be a contradiction in the sojourner's role which inevitably causes difficulties. On the one hand, hosts enjoy having high-status advisers who appear interested in local problems and who might apply their expertise. Even granting the points made in previous sections concerning sojourners' status loss in recent years, there is still a residual element of respect. This fact should cause hosts to give recommendations a great deal of attention. On the other hand, two counterforces exist. One is the slight self-insult hosts feel when they must import advice rather than solve problems on their own. Secondly, since sojourners can never know local conditions as well as hosts, recommendations can always be rejected. Comments like "interesting but impractical" or "could be workable elsewhere but not here" are frequently made. Even in very carefully done research and well-written reports, sojourners almost assuredly will make a few points which ignore important facts about the host culture. Applying the principles presented in chapter 4, these points will become especially salient to hosts, may overwhelm the good aspects, and cause rejection of the total report.

There are a few recommendations which might improve the probability of a report's acceptance. After extensive discussions with officials in Asia who might use recommendations, Kleinjans (1979, personal communication) reported that several pieces of advice were frequently offered. One was concerned with the practice of interviewing hosts and summarizing their atitudes and opinions. When reports are based solely on interviews, sojourners may not learn anything beyond what hosts already know. Another piece of advice concerned reading and studying the same sorts of materials which hosts must digest in their everyday work. Since no one can study all available information, sojourners will make a contribution by calling attention to key details. Further, sojourners may be able to bring a fresh perspective to the information. Another possibility, common-sensical but often ignored, is to have many hosts read drafts of the report before final submission. Brislin and Holwill (1977) tried to document the rich and helpful additions which hosts can make after reading the reports prepared by sojourners. They found that hosts can correct and update information, make applications to local conditions, point out impositions of a sojourner's preconceived point of view, and indicate ways in which the report might benefit the society.

SUMMARY AND CONCLUSIONS

People almost always have tasks they wish to accomplish during their sojourns. These include the attainment of college degrees, negotiation of agreements, or establishment of technical assistance projects. There are a number of issues with which all people must deal as well as several which vary according to sojourners' backgrounds. Different problems are faced by people who move from more to less technologically developed societies compared to people who move in the opposite direction.

General problems include understanding a country's standards for the label of "success." American students accustomed to good grades based on frequent examination have to adjust to a different system in Europe, involving far less formal testing. Hosts sometimes have very different criteria in mind than those of sojourners. Prediction of overseas performance in the Peace Corps has been disappointing, and one reason is that the criteria differ from society to society. Where American administrators might *predict* success based on enthusiasm and ability to plan ahead, hosts might *judge* success on the basis of the personal relationships people establish. Once criteria are established, administrators should be careful not to over-generalize beyond a given situation. Ezekiel (1968) carried out a study of Peace Corps workers in Ghana, and the criteria for rated success were clearly task-oriented. His important findings will have limited applicability to situations where other criteria are considered.

Prior experience is sometimes relevant to the demands of a new situation. Professionals in forestry and fisheries who are accustomed to "roughing it" in their own country may work effectively on sojourns where the same situational demand exists. Hosts often have expectations based on work with previous visitors. Categories are often formed, such as the naive Peace Corps worker, influence-peddling technical assistance expert, or ungrateful foreign student. As reviewed in chapter 4, new experiences are modified slightly to fit the preexisting stereotype. Successful sojourners probably learn that much host behavior is role based. If hosts seem rude, visitors should not always internalize blame. The hosts are often reacting to a concept, built up through previous experiences, which the newly arrived sojourner happens to represent. Another result of prior negative experiences is that hosts often go through elaborate screening procedures before accepting new sojourners.

Status markers have an effect on sojourners' work plans. Acceptance is based on a match-up: do people have qualities considered desirable in the host society? Qualities can be based on age, sex, educational background, occupation, and names of patrons. As with many aspects of the cross-cultural experience, severe reactions occur when people find that markers considered desirable in one culture are demeaned in another. Given a certain amount of status, sojourners have a chance of accomplishing tasks. Since important work almost always takes place within a bureaucracy, people must have a sensitivity to power relations. This quality should not have a negative connotation. This sensitivity refers to an understanding of how things are done, who the important people are whose support is necessary, what must be done to work effectively with those people, and why they might support or condemn a proposal. A related quality is the ability to obtain information on the historical precedents and legal requirements which must be taken into account.

Collaborative effort is necessary to insure successful completion of sojourners' goals. Empirical studies of cross-cultural collaboration have been carried out *among* researchers, and findings may have wider applicability. Experienced researchers advised that plans should be carefully specified. Sojourners and hosts should know what is expected, who will carry out certain tasks, why work will take place at a given time, and who will receive credit for accomplishments. Although this procedure may appear to be a cultural imposition, its disadvantages are outweighed by the advantages stemming from a clear understanding of mutual expectations. The leadership role in collaborative efforts needs further analysis. A social scientist from Asia has suggested that some people are comfortable with high-status leaders to whom deference is freely given. If this is true, then the frequently heard recommendation for "collaboration among equals" may be unwise. Leaders may have to behave more like entrepreneurs than as representatives of their professions. If they are not prepared for this possibility, leaders can become very disappointed with their contributions to a project.

Job enlargement may be of benefit to sojourners. Outcomes include greater professional commitment, productivity, and a more satisfying use of potentially empty hours. Benefits may accrue, however, only to sojourners with a high need for achievement and a need for professional growth. Intrinsic reasons for positive outcomes include greater task variety, identification with new tasks, and greater autonomy. Extrinsic reasons include greater respect from co-workers. Examples of job enlargement possibilities can be found in the work of language interpreters and foreign students. Interpreters might act as consultants *before* a presentation is given to suggest phrases which are easily translatable. Foreign students might act as guest lecturers, providing hosts with firsthand knowledge about other countries.

Unique problems are faced by sojourners moving from less to more technologically developed societies. They are most often placed in the position of "learners" and frequently experience a loss in status. When they adopt the host country as a reference group, their later work in the home country may be perceived as less interesting or important. If they decide to seek permanent employment in the host country, they become participants in the brain drain process. Refugees and brain drainers have different relationships to their home countries. The former are forced from their homes for political reasons; the latter are highly educated people who voluntarily choose to emigrate. Factors which discourage brain drain include integration into the home community, continuing contact with one's government, and requirements to return as a condition of the sponsored sojourn. Factors encouraging emigration include uncertainty about the future, greater opportunities in the host country, and the acculturation of one's children into the host community.

While attempting to improve their professional skills, sojourners sometimes receive training which is irrelevant to home country conditions. Students learn about equipment which is unavailable, problems which do not exist, and research ideas which are not of high priority. Heisey (1977) argues that a program at the University of Uppsala, Sweden, provides a better model. Participants engage in projects which are relevant to home country needs and which use the level of technology to which they will return. Many of the ideas developed at Uppsala could be incorporated into any curriculum. Foreign students, for instance, could be encouraged to write term papers and theses on problems of their countries.

Sojourners moving from more to less developed countries are often assigned the role of expert, adviser, or teacher. They have difficulties, however, in choosing among various approaches to their role. They can act as a stimulator, analyst, educator, conscience, or critic. In choosing among approaches, they are rarely able to visualize all outcomes. If they act as "doers," they may create dependence. If they encourage others to work on projects which are eventually successful, they may cause jealousy among hosts who are involved. If they criticize, they may be asked to leave since hosts can now pick and choose among advisers. The frustration resulting from uncertainty about roles and consequences undoubtedly contributes to low morale. Important research could be done on how advisers have successfully and unsuccessfully tackled this problem.

Work with host counterparts is a necessity. One difficulty is that the host assigned to a project is often promoted into an administrative position. Advisers are wise to consider working with a number of counterparts at different levels of the host bureaucracy. One of them may eventually assume responsibility for the project. Counterparts sometimes become involved for the wrong reasons. They may seek work with sojourners as a grant-getting opportunity, or they may be assigned by colleagues who perceive absence as a virtue. The quality of assigned counterparts is one way sojourners have to judge host interest in a project.

In carrying out their work, advisers often have to let others take credit for accomplishments. If their efforts become publicized, sojourners may be perceived as threatening to the status quo. Further, they may be asked to consult on issues about which they do not have specialized knowledge. If they do not offer to help after receiving requests for advice, sojourners risk damaging their relations with hosts. To compound the problem, the advice may not be accepted. Hosts enjoy the presence of high-status visitors who might be able to help. On the other hand, hosts can always dismiss advice with the charge that sojourners are not completely knowledgeable about the local situation. Recommendations have a greater chance of being accepted if hosts criticize early drafts of a sojourner's report.

The accomplishment of tasks is always difficult, but the probability of success can be increased if sojourners work in effective organizations. The qualities of a good organization will be the focus of the next chapter.

9
Organizations

Many benefits which might stem from an intense cross-cultural experience
have been discussed in previous chapters. Individuals may become more
complex in their thinking about international problems and may change
toward less ethnocentric points of view. Strong feelings based on in-group/
out-group distinctions may diminish as people develop overlapping ties
which cut across cultural barriers. Expertise regarding desired technological
development can be transferred while sojourning specialists work with
host country counterparts. None of these benefits can occur, however,
without effective organizations which encourage programs for sojourners
and provide logistical support. The qualities of support services, and the
assistance which well-administered organizations can provide to sojourners,
are the major topics of this chapter.

Like situations, organizations are difficult to discuss since there is no
widely accepted set of terms which are understood by social scientists,
members of the organizations under scrutiny, interested lay people, and
administrators in fledgling institutions who might learn from others. To
provide an introduction to organizational variables, a series of examples
will be reviewed involving problems which a more effective organization
may have been able to prevent. Given some understanding of what organizations can do, a number of policy issues will be considered. The basic
question to be asked is: "What are the rules, regulations, and policies of
a given organization which might help or hinder sojourners to attain their
goals?" Even though such a treatment may give the impression that organizations will be assuming the role of villain, no such result is intended.
Since organizations never exist in a vacuum, they must cope with a number
of external pressures and inevitable difficulties, especially when the added
dimensions due to their international activities are considered. Another
section of the chapter reviews the problems faced by virtually all organizations which encourage cross-cultural experiences for its members
and for interested outsiders whose activities might be sponsored. The final
section reviews a number of positive and negative outcomes which can
result from an effective international organization.

CASE STUDIES OF ORGANIZATIONAL DIFFICULTIES

An appreciation of the kinds of difficulties organizations cause or alleviate can be gained through a review of some actual problematic situations. Three will be described: choice of administrators, logistical support, and coping with red tape.

Organizations have policies for selecting administrators. In international organizations, the criteria should include previous cross-cultural experiences and intercultural sensitivity, but often they do not. So many organizations are dependent upon lobbying for external funds that one's "contacts" and ability to attract money become desiderata. In the early days of the Peace Corps, extensive negotiations with the United States Congress were necessary to secure funding. Textor (1966) points out that administrators were selected who were effective in these negotiations, but their skills in that arena bore no relation to working with people about to have an intense cross-cultural experience. In reviewing early Peace Corps work in Somalia, Mahoney (1966) was blunt in his assessment of a poorly-selected administrator:

> The (volunteers) were unfortunate . . . in one of the Representatives whom Washington had sent out to lead them, a man totally lacking in previous transcultural experience—in Somalia or anywhere. This official, doubtless with good intentions, tried to live up to the absolute letter of Peace Corps regulations, but in doing so, his very inflexibility and lack of human sensitivity succeeded instead in violating the underlying spirit of the Peace Corps idea. He promptly proceeded to threaten the PCV's sense of maturity and responsibility. Instead of relying to some extent on the Volunteer's own judgment, he treated them like children. He laid down a series of strict rules and regulations regarding conduct . . . [pp. 129–130].

As volunteers began to flow back into Washington with their tales of inappropriate administration, the person in question was eventually replaced. The issue of administrative flexibility in interpreting a central office's regulations will be discussed later in this chapter.

The second example deals with the effects of inadequate planning and coordination. Organizations must, of course, provide effective logistical support. This is especially true in the case of sojourners who arrive in a new country unfamiliar with sources of housing, food, and companionship. A tremendous difficulty facing some people is that they cannot take money out of their country. On a sponsored sojourn, then, they are completely dependent upon the host country organization. The people must have money to be claimed upon arrival so that they can obtain their first day's meals and lodging. I have observed organizations, however, in which administrative foul-ups caused the money to be unavailable. Sojourners had to borrow from sympathetic hosts, a terribly embarrassing ordeal. The actual goals of the programs, whether they be advanced study, introduction to innovative technology, or the collaborative design of development projects, had to be set aside. Even after the money became available, the sojourners were so upset that they were unable to concentrate on their work.

The final example focuses on coping with red tape. To fulfill their goals, sojourners must often complete reams of forms and wade through seemingly endless rules and regulations. Organizations which sponsor sojourners should have divisions which inform people about host country procedures which must be followed. As an example, consider the obstacles which a sojourning behavioral scientist must overcome to carry out a host-government-sponsored research project. Assume the work is to be carried out in the United States, and that approximately 100 people are to be interviewed. Permission must be obtained from all people who are to become part of the study. A committee of peers must review the project proposal and be assured that participants are in no danger and will suffer no harm. If the participants are themselves associated with an organization, such as school children or institutionalized populations, permission must be obtained from officials in that organization. Research assistants familiar with the language and norms of the participants must be hired, and arrangements must be made to pay them. Computer facilities to analyze the resulting data might be obtained. These steps, all of them understandable precautions, are not additional burdens set aside for sojourners: host country researchers must also face them. In my experience, however, it is absolutely impossible for visitors to meet these bureaucratic demands without organizational support (Brislin, 1979b). Knowledgeable insiders must, as part of their job assignments, be responsible for helping sojourners cope with red tape. If this function is not institutionalized, sojourners become frustrated and ultimately dissatisfied with their cross-cultural experience. The function of helping sojourners with complex goals takes various forms for various types of cross-cultural experience. A foreign student advisers' office is present on many university campuses; counterparts are often expected to help technical assistance advisers adapt projects to local conditions (Glaser, 1979); and social service workers are often assigned responsibility for helping with the adjustment of immigrants.

ORGANIZATIONAL FACTORS WHICH HELP OR HINDER SOJOURNERS

Organizations have rules, regulations, and well-established policies which affect what its members can and cannot do. Some members occasionally attempt to circumvent the policies, but they cannot continuously challenge the organization and (a) retain employment, (b) work with any degree of effectiveness, or (c) retain their mental health. These myriad policies often have unforeseen consequences for sojourners who become involved with the organization. Administrators do not sit at conference tables and ask, "What regulations can we develop which will complicate the lives of sojourners?" Rather, the policies develop so that the organizations can cope with problems which sojourners themselves often recognize. The basic difficulty, however, is that most policies are not reminiscent of Solomon's decisions[1] which seem to have pleased everyone. Most policies allow certain goals to be achieved at the expense of others. Foreign students cannot play a role in university administration *and* have unlimited time to study for their degrees. Peace Corps workers cannot earn large salaries and live at a level similar to hosts. Diplomats cannot become recognized experts on one country and gain broad experience by serving in various posts on two-year assignments. Immigrants who enroll in host-country language courses cannot spend all their time in programs encouraging native language maintenance. Researchers concerned with cross-cultural studies cannot be as productive as colleagues who work in the familiar confines of their own country (Jacob & Jacob, 1979), given the added complexities of organizing the efforts of people in diverse parts of the world.

A number of factors have been identified by various analysts as important in a certain organization. The treatment which has most explicitly analyzed organizational factors was prepared by Tendler (1975). Her major concern was the work of technical assistance advisers, and she also integrated observations about foreign service officers. I have attempted to collect those organizational factors which should help in analyzing various types of cross-cultural experience.

Regulations

Money. A number of strict rules, which have legal sanctions if violated, are concerned with people's ability to acquire and to use money in ways they prefer. In many countries, sojourners are not allowed to earn money by working in the local economy. The purpose is to protect jobs for citizens and to decrease the flow of currency outside the country. In addition, some countries (e.g., Ethiopia: Pruitt, 1978) prevent funds from being sent to sojourners living elsewhere, again to stop the export of money. Obviously, sojourners not receiving grants from the host country are in a bind. They can't work and they can't receive money from home. So how do they cope? A frequent method is to accept employment while realizing the risk of visa difficulties. In large cities, there seems to be an underground in which sojourners share information regarding job possibilities. In the United States, high turnover jobs such as restaurant workers and taxi drivers are favored. People come and go so frequently in these jobs that it is hard to trace any one person.

When citizens from highly industrialized countries are assigned to less technologically developed societies, the jobs are frequently viewed as hardships. Tendler (1975) and Kidder (1977) have analyzed the case of sojourners from the United States working in Latin America and India. The sending organization offers inducements to aid in recruiting new employees, and these often include the provision of American goods at a nearby military Post Exchange (PX). When sojourners obtain goods from the PX, they cannot be exchanged for cash in the host society, a policy probably designed to prevent contributions to the local black market. Further, a direct cash inducement cannot be substituted for PX privileges. This regulation means that sojourners who want to live at the level of hosts are stymied. They are forced to buy American goods at the PX, inevitably causing a difference between themselves and hosts. Organization officials would argue that so many sojourners are accustomed to the American goods that recruitment would be hindered without assurances that amenities will be provided. They would also argue that once a PX is established, sojourners must buy there so that it does not become an economic liability. As well as creating a distance between sojourners and hosts, the policies probably contribute to social distance among types of sojourners living in the same area. Peace Corps workers who did not have PX privileges were unable to live at the level maintained by technical assistance advisers from other government agencies. This differential in access to amenities undoubtedly created discomfort since one group could not entertain at the level of the other. To avoid the discomfort, people from the two groups kept to themselves.

Housing. The arguments for subsidized housing are similar to those for PX privileges. Recruitment of capable employees would be difficult without added incentives. Although funds are sometimes provided to sojourners who can then live where they wish, a frequent alternative is low-cost housing in a separate community within the host country. Schools, hospitals, churches, and recreational facilities are also sometimes present. While undoubtedly easier to administer than a system allowing housing in various places, the in-country community discourages interaction between hosts and sojourners. Further, since sojourners are in close proximity, they can support each other while attempting to cope with life in an unfamiliar place. Coping may become a superordinate goal around which sojourners, who have little else in common, rally and unite. They may form a strong in-group which excludes outsiders—in this case, the hosts.

I have observed the housing problem at a major American university. Officials at the University observed the difficulties foreign students had in finding accommodations. Dormitories were impossible since some students brought families. Sojourners were forced, then, to spend tremendous amounts of time and energy finding their own housing through newspaper advertisements and real estate agents. Unfamiliarity with procedures and occasional prejudice, however, often led to accommodations which they could not afford. To ease these difficulties, the university guaranteed the owner of an apartment building that it would always be filled. The owner was then able to offer quite reasonable rates. This policy meant that all foreign students were asked to live in this building or else the university would lose money. The inevitable happened: students complained that they were assigned to a ghetto in which they had little opportunity for interaction with hosts. Problems like this are more intense, it seems to me, in organizations which encourage cross-cultural exchanges. The policy seems to contradict the program's explicit goals of providing opportunities for cross-cultural learning. Further, there is no memory of "life before the policy." The students who had to cope with the open housing market, and who undoubtedly welcomed the sponsored apartment building, have finished their degree work and have returned to their homes. Only the present is visible to the new set of students who cannot understand the severe problems which the policy successfully overcame.

Funding. Many organizations receive funding on a year-to-year basis. Examples are the Agency for International Development, the National Association for Foreign Student Affairs, the Peace Corps, and the Foreign Service Institute of the State Department. This simple fact has a number of important implications. The defense of an organization's budget must be done yearly, and this means that much staff time is spent in report writing, justifications for funding requests, and face-to-face interactions with funders. If the latter choose to exercise their oversight functions, they may request quarterly reports. On long-term projects, such as the introduction of complex technology or an educational curriculum, it is very hard to divide the project into yearly segments and totally absurd to attempt explanations in terms of three-month units. In my experience, the time, energy, and occasional creative fancy necessary for these reports leaves people so exhausted that the substantive work of a sojourn is affected. Yet, the value of the reports cannot be denied. There is such a physical distance between the sojourner and funding source that administrators must have reports to know what is being done. Further, justification must be constantly available for projects using government funding as well as private sector support based on voluntary contributions. An entire organization can be discredited if an elected official or investigative reporter discovers just one project which cannot be adequately described and defended by administrators.

Another implication is that pressures are exerted within the organization to spend all appropriated funds within the year (Downs, 1966; Fisher, 1970). Failure to spend money may be interpreted by funders as a sign that the organization does not need as much money *next year*. Consequently, there is a rush to spend leftover funds toward the end of any budget period. In the ensuing haste, expenditures are frequently not well thought out and silly projects receive support. Worse, the recipients sometimes interpret the funds as a long-term commitment and request additional support for future project expansion.

Many people make a living designing projects funded by others. The flow of money is (a) from the government or private sector into a funding agency such as the Ford Foundation or the International Communication Agency, (b) and then to individuals or groups who develop proposals approved by the agencies. Since there are many more proposals than available funds, however, people have to spend tremendous amounts of time writing careful, well-documented, and elaborate proposals. The danger is that people can spend too much time writing proposals for *next* year's funding and give inadequate attention to the projects approved for *this* year. Further, proposal writing has become a highly specialized skill with details shared among cognoscenti but unknown to outsiders. People heretofore outside grant-receiving channels must spend a great deal of time learning how to be competitive in the funding arena. The necessary skills may not be part of a person's previous training. Since funding is scarce, for instance, public relations skills are required if people are to attract the attention of grant-giving agencies.

Time Demands. In addition to report writing, organizations put demands on employees' time which interfere with substantive work. One duty is entertaining visitors, mentioned as problematic by Ilić, Jha, Sawe, and Sokirin (1973) and by Casino (1979). Sojourners who become well established in the host country must spend so much time explaining their work to visitors that they cannot give sufficient attention to the project itself. Penalties are added for successful projects since they will attract the greatest attention and the most interest. The problem is compounded in those societies which have strong norms concerning the importance of hospitality. Hosts and interculturally sensitive sojourners feel uncomfortable if visitors are not entertained lavishly. Casino (1979) has suggested that organizations which send visitors could cooperate so that representatives come at one time rather than trickle in over a long period. This policy would have the added advantage of encouraging interaction among people from the different sending organizations.

Another time demand is the requirement of some organizations that sojourners must return home periodically over the course of their assignment (K. Wilson, 1979, personal communication). Two reasons are given for the policy. Home leave can provide rest and relaxation, and it allows opportunities for face-to-face progress reports. The difficulty, however, is that the host country project may suffer. The development of many successful projects is based on the informal networks which a sojourner establishes. Examples are the relation with counterparts discussed in chapter 3, and the informal helping networks which were introduced in chapter 5. To be sure, wise sojourners have the eventual goal of insuring the project's long-term success after their assignments are completed, but the steps necessary for accomplishment cannot occur overnight. Wise sojourners also know that they must work in harmony with norms not present in their home country. A reasonable generalization is that informal networks are extremely important in Latin America, Asia, and the Pacific. They are as important to task accomplishment as formal agreements and integration into respected organizations. The delicate interpersonal relationships which make initial progress possible inevitably cease when a sojourner temporarily leaves the host country. One experienced adviser with whom I spoke said, "The project goes to hell during the home leave. When I return, I have to patch up problems created in my absence *and* see that normal progress is made during my post-return phase."

A Transition Period. One policy which organizations might consider is the establishment of transition periods between the start of sojourners' assignments and the commencement of substantive effort. This transition could take the form of a long training period, as has been traditionally required of Peace Corps volunteers. It could also take the form of an overlap with experienced sojourners who are about to return home. Immigrants who move to a country are sometimes given special attention by social service agencies until they obtain housing and jobs. Introduction to a new society is institutionalized in Israel through the Ulpan system (Pincus, 1977) in which immigrants learn Hebrew as well as critical information about functioning in Israeli society. Foreign students often come to university campuses a few weeks before classes begin to learn about differences between their previous school experiences and host country demands. The basic assumption of any such transition period (reviewed in Brislin &

Pedersen, 1976, pp. 104–105) is that sojourners can be introduced to the sorts of problems and prospects which are discussed throughout this book. If they are introduced to potential difficulties during the transition period, sojourners will be less negatively affected when the problems are actually encountered. There are always disadvantages with such a policy. Time, money, and effort spent on transition experiences are unavailable for other uses. Personnel in charge of the programs may encourage too much dependence among new sojourners. In my experience, however, the advantages far outweigh the disadvantages.

Rewards offered by organizations

Employees should be rewarded if their efforts contribute to the attainment of an organization's goals. Rewards can take the form of promotions, salary increases, recognition, and the feeling that one's work is appreciated. Organizations which do not reward people appropriately risk employee dissatisfaction and high turnover. More specifically, after an extensive review of the relationships among rewards, performance, and turnover, Vroom (1969) offered the following summary statement:

> . . . we have identified four classes of variables which, on the basis of existing evidence, appear to determine the attitude of a person toward his role in an organization and the probability that he will leave it, permanently or temporarily. The four variables are (1) the amounts of particular classes of outcomes, such as pay, status, acceptance, and influence, attained by the person as a consequence of his occupancy of that role, (2) the strength of the person's desire or aversion for outcomes in these classes, (3) the amounts of these outcomes believed by the person to be received by comparable others, and (4) the amounts of these outcomes which the person expected to receive or has received at earlier points in time [p. 208].

While Vroom's general statement may be helpful as a starting point, it will not lead to a thorough understanding of any one organization. Additional information is needed concerning which goals are valued by an organization and which are rewarded. While the two sets of goals will ideally be the same, there often are differences. Disparities are infrequently described in an organization's published reports and are rarely discussed openly. Rather, newly hired employees learn about reality by observing who is rewarded and for what apparent reasons.

For example, the case of the technical assistance adviser has already been mentioned. The organization's expressed goals include the development of effective projects. However, since the organization receives year-to-year funding, it may reward those employees who are able to spend money within the budget cycle so that none will remain uncommitted. The example of small organizations whose continuance is based on the preparation of grant proposals is similar. These organizations may espouse the goal of first-rate projects, but rewards may accrue to those employees able to bring in money. After writing a successful proposal, people are sometimes assigned to preparing another while someone else does the substantive work which has been promised. After six months of observing whose work is most appreciated, the person who obtains the money or who manages the project, the ambitious employee learns which activities lead to the greatest rewards.

The major point, then, is that employees study the reward history of their organizations and make decisions about which aspects of the jobs to emphasize. Employees in international organizations devoted to providing opportunities for sojourners often learn that the interests which led them to their profession are not those which are rewarded. A large number of organizations have been established to provide intercultural experiences for adolescents and young adults, such as year-long exchange programs for high school students. People might enter the organization to work with students and to arrange activities which lead to increased cross-cultural learning. Actual job success, however, may be dependent upon finding volunteers willing to house the students or the ability to orient the surrogate parents. I have observed professionals in such organizations spend hours on the telephone trying to enlist host families. The skills they developed are reminiscent of telephone salespeople who make a pitch for unseen desert land in Nevada.

There are many other examples of difficulties in reward allocation. Researchers sometimes shun cross-cultural studies because they take much longer to complete than work carried out in their own country (Dinges, 1977; Jacob & Jacob, 1979). If the institutions which employ the researchers give rewards for a steady stream of published output, rather than for one complex study which might take five years to complete, cross-cultural specialists are at a distinct disadvantage. Many Peace Corps workers had to balance their desire to make visible progress on their projects against the need to develop warm and cordial relationships with hosts. The American supervisors looked for the former, while the hosts often preferred the latter (Guthrie & Zektick, 1967). Diplomats learn that of the many skills which might be rewarded, the ability to write informative dispatches to the country's capital is a major factor in promotion. Since hundreds of dispatches are received, the person able to write with flair may be better remembered by superiors. Most diplomats have to struggle with the content of their reports. Should they communicate all important problems, or should they echo what is politically fashionable at the time (Thayer, 1959)? Foreign students might become involved as guest lecturers in a variety of college courses (Mestenhauser and Barsig, 1978), but they may decide that attainment of their degrees will be delayed. Organizations can improve if their administrators ask:

1. What is being rewarded?
2. Does the present reward dispensation system interfere with the attainment of important goals?
3. What other activities should be given increased status through greater reward allocation?

Status to support services

Good candidates for further attention in such an exercise are the people who provide support services for sojourners. For every group of foreign students from the People's Republic of China who attract national media attention, there is a group of employees who make arrangements for housing, visas, relevant coursework, orientation to everyday life in the United States, and aid with individual problems. In my experience, these people are not given sufficient recognition and, consequently, there is a high turnover. Tremendous amounts of an organization's resources, then, must be devoted to recruiting and training replacements. Certain large categories of employees are underrewarded. In general, employees who are skillful at dealing with human relations problems receive less recognition than colleagues who work on tasks which have visible outcomes. For instance, Kelman (1965b) relates a common problem faced by any sojourners who attempt to offer help in another country.

> . . . there are strong forces in the direction of hostility toward the donor country that are inherent in the very nature of the aid situation. The fact that nationals from the donor country have come to his country to give aid is concrete evidence, from the recipient's point of view, of his own inferior status. . . . The very fact that he finds himself in this situation with its negative implications for the evaluation of his country and himself may generate hostility. This hostility is most naturally directed at the one who, by giving, underlines the recipient's authority. In this situation, therefore, meeting the conditions for attitude change will depend on the extent to which status-enhancing features are built into the project itself as well as into extra-project relationships [pp. 570–571].

To put Kelman's good advice into practice, rewards must be given to employees able to incorporate the status-enhancing features. Too often, these are ignored as visible medical facilities, highways, schools, and dams are constructed.

Rewards do not always have to be monetary. Even if administrators wanted to be more generous, budgetary constraints often place strict limits on the use of monetary incentives. Other types of rewards are valued by employees. For instance, recognition can take the form of short notes upon the successful completion of a task, invitations to lunch, and inclusion on the guest list when visiting dignitaries are entertained. The key concept is that members of an organization should feel that they are making an important contribution, that their work is valued, and that their efforts are recognized. The best administrators realize this fact and use all possible rewards which are available to them.

Participative decision making

Another type of reward is the compliment administrators give when they seek the advice of employees before organizational policy is formulated. The term applied to the practice of seeking and using employee input is "participative decision making" or PDM. Applying the general principle that employees should feel valued, the use of their advice in decision making recognizes both their expertise and ability to contribute. In international and cross-cultural organizations, employees at moderate and low levels of an organization often have the greatest amount of direct contact with certain categories of clients. Foreign student advisers have more contact with sojourners than university administrators; teachers in desegregated schools have more knowledge of student problems than their principals; embassy staff members have far more face-to-face interaction with different types of sojourners than the ambassador. Administrators who do not seek out the advice of experienced employees are foolish.

Another benefit of PDM is greater acceptance of the organizational policy which is finally formulated. The histories of many organizations are littered with policies which failed because employees did not put decisions into effect (Heclo, 1977). I remember my first encounter with this issue, which also provided my introduction to several major organizational variables. During the activism which followed the civil rights movement of the 1960s, Admiral Elmo Zumwalt was the Chief of Naval Operations. He was very persistent in advocating the types of cross-cultural orientation programs, designed to increase interracial and intercultural sensitivity, advocated throughout this book. I was a consultant at the time preparing a review of human relations training programs (part of which was incorporated by Brislin & Pedersen, 1976), and I observed very little effort among Naval personnel in carrying out Zumwalt's directives. I asked a colleague who had observed bureaucracies for many years: "When the highest ranking administrator gives a directive, why isn't there activity to put it into practice?" My colleague observed, "The bureaucracy can wait Zumwalt out. It knows that he will be in his post for two to four years at the most. Members of the bureaucracy have tenure and will be there forever."

Possibly, there would have been more progress in establishing cross-cultural programs if the opinions of key personnel had been sought. In addition to providing the fruits of their experiences, they might have become identified with the final decision. One of the most frequently cited principles on the relation between individuals and organizations relates to PDM (Coch & French, 1948). It states that employees who participate in policymaking view the final decisions as their own and, consequently, are more likely to carry them out. Another possible benefit (E. Bennett, 1955) is that a given employee sees respected colleagues who also accept the decision and so the strong factor of group identification is added. Employees at a similar organizational level frequently have stronger positive feelings toward each other than toward their administrators.

Unfortunately, like all complex organizational innovations, participative decision making is no panacea. Vroom (1969) summarized a number of studies, most of which were conducted in the United States. No special attention was given to international organizations or to the sojourners who are either employed or are served by them. His conclusions can be examined, however, as they apply to the sorts of organizations under consideration here.

> . . . It appears that differences between the quality of autocratic and group decisions are dependent on a large number of variables including (1) the extent to which the manager and those reporting to him have information relevant to judging the organizational consequences of different courses of action, (2) the extent to which their interests are consistent with organizational objectives, and (3) the skill of the manager in leading the group discussion. There is some evidence that interaction among individuals is dysfunctional during the creative phase of problem solving, in which alternative solutions are being generated, but may be functional during the evaluative phase, in which solutions are screened and chosen [p. 233].

The difficulties in putting these principles into practice were analyzed by Tendler (1975). The two types of sojourners she studied were technical assistance advisers and foreign service officers, but her insights are generalizable to any type of sojourn in which there is a physical distance between workers and administrators. Tendler's basic conclusion was that sojourners working in other countries should be able to participate in decision making since they have day-to-day contact with resources, options, and problems. The large number of variables specific to a given location means that general principles formulated by an organization must be modified—emics to complement etics, in the language of chapter 4. Vroom

(1969) discussed the "skill of the manager," but even the most conscientious administrator will have difficulty encouraging PDM when employees are geographically scattered. Further, the sojourning employee would, of course, like to be consistent with organizational objectives, but they are too far away from the center of decision making to be up-to-date. Given the year-to-year funding policy already reviewed, objectives may change as administrators search for proposals which catch the attention of money-givers. Another difficulty is that sojourning employees are frequently so overwhelmed with cultural differences and coping with their own adjustment problems that PDM is an additional burden. They would like to be told what to do so that there will be some stability in their lives, but administrators are too far removed to give good advice.

Finally, there is no "PDM button" which can simply be pushed.[2] Many employees have been accustomed to taking orders for so long that there is an additional adjustment necessary when their input to policy is sought. The foreign student advisers, teachers, and embassy workers mentioned earlier should eventually be able to make contributions, but the jump from people's everyday insights to policymaking is not easy. There has to be a transition period during which employees become accustomed to thinking for themselves, putting their thoughts into communicable form, seeking out assurances that their opinions will truly be valued, and discovering innovative ways by which decisions can be put into practice.

Goal setting

The work of sojourners will be colored by the goals which they either set for themselves through PDM or which are established by superiors. Goals can be general or specific, realistic or unrealistic, ideological or practical, short term vs. long term, and so forth. They can be designed to create an in-group identity or to foster cooperation among groups with a history of hostility. They can marshal the efforts of people toward the solution of a problem or can provide a distraction which muddies important issues.

Several analysts have commented on goal setting as it relates to the behavior of people who work in multicultural organizations. In diplomatic negotiations, one of the hardest tasks is to cut through vastly different ideologies and to delineate issues on which action is possible (Glenn et al., 1977; Thayer, 1959). Diplomats from some countries become familiar with methods designed to identify topics on which substantive negotiations are possible, but they also must learn that the methods are not universally accepted. Glenn and his colleagues (1977) point out that cultural differences regarding the value placed on a general ideology must somehow be addressed. Diplomats from certain countries strongly prefer agreement of general principles before attention is given to specifics, while others insist on dealing with specific principles since there is little hope of agreement on ideological points.

> Non-English speaking delegates at international conferences are often surprised by the insistence of the representatives of countries such as the United States and Britain to have a drafting committee appointed at an early stage of a conference: How is it possible to draft a binding contract, they wonder, before having at least agreed on the principles which the draft ought to reflect? For the delegates of the English-speaking nations, drafting together is the most expeditious way to delimit a possible area of agreement: in international negotiations, drafting together is the equivalent of working together, and working together is a typical manner in which pragmatically oriented societies achieve agreement [pp. 54–55].

Goal setting is important when underrepresented ethnic groups attempt to organize and to influence policy. A number of observers have concluded that goal setting has a major influence on the success of these movements (L. French, 1978; D. Katz, 1965; Pearson, 1977). Cloud-chasing behavior has to be discouraged (Katz, 1965):

> To be an effective organizational leader the individual has to acquire skills in building and maintaining a structure and in increasing its effectiveness and productivity. All this requires a heavy task orientation and an assessment of objective and social realities. The leader who spends his time in flying flags, getting embroiled in symbolic fights, is often left behind in the competition for higher positions [p. 370].

In my experience, some bilingual education programs in the United States have not received support because of misplaced goals. Arguments in favor of bilingual education include children's comfortableness in schools when they discover that their language is used and appreciated; greater reading readiness in one's native language; and the possibility of a gradual rather than abrupt transition to a language, such as English, which offers a multitude of learning opportunities. These goals could have been emphasized in the planning and implementation of educational programs. Instead, bilingual education was seen as a way to increase the visibility of underrepresented ethnic groups. Demands for educational programs were treated as forums for gaining publicity, encouraging a feeling of identity among previously uninterested ethnic group members, and collecting a piece of the "good life" which leaders saw among members of the white middle class. While understandable, the political goals interfered with educational objectives. The officials in charge of administering funds had to justify their monetary commitments and had to choose among many competing proposals. Other groups such as the aged, handicapped, and hard-core unemployed were desirous of the same educational program money. While it would be naive to suggest these other groups had no political goals, their leaders used political clout as a means to an end. Ethnic groups saw bilingual education as the means to a political end point.

While giving their attention to political objectives, the leaders proposing bilingual education did not spend sufficient time generating competitive proposals. Reasonable questions on the costs of preparing and distributing bilingual materials, on the relative advantages of separate English-as-a-second language classes, and plans for long-term evaluation could not be answered satisfactorily. Leaders of organizations who did not use educational objectives as the means to a political identity fared better in the funding process.

Funding has been mentioned a number of times in this chapter and readers may charge that a dead horse is being flayed. Yet, so many organizations which sponsor opportunities for sojourners are dependent upon external funding that the topic can hardly be overemphasized. Funding and goal setting are related. My observation is that, over the last ten years, the increased demand for a shrinking money pool has forced funding agencies to set priorities. Guidelines are now published which say that a certain agency will entertain proposals for only certain types of programs. Organizations which want the funds are forced to set their own goals and to match them with possible funding sources. At times, organizations decide on a certain goal after reviewing the sorts of programs which funders are willing to support. The important point is that, even if an organization would prefer to have broad goals, perhaps believing that more people will be attracted, they are forced to be more specific because of funding.

Overadministration and responsibility versus authority

If unchecked, the administrative branch of an organization tends to become overmanned. Too many people become available for the amount of actual work which must be done. Consequently, "busy work" is created so that people have something to do with their time. These observations are variations on Parkinson's (1957) law. If the Peter principle is added (Peter & Hull, 1969), then the people filling the high-level and overmanned positions may not be the best qualified. Since they demonstrated competence or even brilliance in lower-level jobs, they were obvious candidates for promotion. But if the new jobs do not tap the same skills as the old ones, people may be prompted into jobs for which they are unsuited.

Again, the quest for funding is a factor and it contributes to the overmanning of bureaucracies. The end result is that a large number of administrators attempt to oversee a relatively small number of people who actually work on cross-cultural projects. The development seems to follow a pattern. Organizations establish a number of central offices to increase the competitive potential for grants. Some administrators are put in charge of publicity and public relations; others specialize in lobbying the agency officials in charge of releasing money; still others maintain impeccable accounts so that "the books" can be examined at any time. Once established, these separate offices become protective of their territorial imperative and strongly resent any encroachments by people who try to cut through red tape. These administrative offices may have been established to fill clear needs, yet the end result is a confusing bureaucracy in which decisions are delayed, paperwork generated, opportunities lost, efforts duplicated, and ambitions frustrated.

Administrators begin to make more and more demands. Both the advantages and disadvantages of participation in policy development were reviewed, but at times the disadvantages become so frustrating that decision making becomes centralized. But is efficiency increased? The answer is often "no," as in the example of project accountability. More and more administrators are assigned the task of reviewing the efforts of project workers so that programs can be monitored and reports eventually written. Yet, since the project workers must supply the input for the progress reports, everybody's time is claimed. Since different administrators have different preferences about format, multiple reports summarizing the same information have to be prepared.

When complaints about overadministration become too numerous and too loud, an external management consultant team is frequently contracted. Not surprisingly, a frequent recommendation is to eliminate a number of administrative layers within the bureaucracy. I have been told that certain organizational problems are so frequent that training programs for management consultants invariably include them as targets for investigation. One is the number of bureaucratic layers. A second is the number of memos which must be written to keep members of the layers informed, and a third is the tendency of administrators to control projects rather than to help them.

The large number of administrators makes the functions of authority and responsibility vague, a problem which I recently encountered. I was asked to consult on a program designed to train technical assistance workers. The participants were citizens of less industrialized countries who were to receive training in the United States before returning to their own countries. The program was funded by a very large agency within the United States government. Participants encountered a severe problem: the money promised for their living expenses was not available at the beginning of the program. While the program directors, whose salaries were provided by the grant, wanted to talk about the basic incompetence of the agency's personnel, the consultants urged that the structure of the organization be examined. The basic premises of the examination were: (1) people in the agency had no conscious desire to frustrate the participants; (2) incompetents are not recruited and hired; (3) that situations and organizational factors encourage certain types of behavior that can be mislabeled as traits; and (4) charges aimed at individual personalities will rarely be very productive, even if they are accurate. After discussions, the diagnosis centered on the responsibility-authority problem. No one in the agency had a clear responsibility for participants in the program. Was it the section concerned with training? Was it the unit devoted to the areas of the world from which participants came? Was it the office concerned with the types of projects which participants might eventually establish? Even if an individual decided to assume responsibility, (s)he had no authority to issue the money. That duty had to be carried out by the fiscal office, and administrators there could only do so after obtaining several sets of signatures. What happened to the participants? Given the immediacy of their needs, no direct attack on the responsibility-authority issue was possible since it would demand the long-term cooperation of many offices. One of the project directors simply contacted the agency and personally went around from office to office until the checks were issued. He made it clear that the only way to get rid of his presence would be to "sign off" the necessary paperwork. In doing so, he took the risk that resentment might be translated into ill-treatment during the next grant-giving cycle.

FACTORS WHICH MUST BE FACED BY ORGANIZATIONS

A number of organizational factors which affect the experiences of sojourners were reviewed in the previous section. To provide a greater understanding and more balance, however, the pressures facing organizations and the constant problems with which they must deal should also be reviewed. Frequently, policies and new offices are established in response to factors over which organizations have little direct control. Since the organization's survival is sometimes at stake, sincere and well-meaning administrators are forced to take action which they feel is appropriate. A number of factors seem especially pertinent in the case of international organizations. Even if the sojourners' adjustment, productivity, and job satisfaction are not increased by knowledge of these factors, at least they will understand why certain organizational decisions have to be made.

The field-home office distinction

A factor which is so prevalent that it provides the basis of in-group humor relates to the bifurcation between the home office and the units within various host countries (Robinson and Snyder, 1965). Sojourners view people in the central office as a bunch of ethnocentric do-nothings who are completely unaware of the realities facing host country citizens. The field workers also charge that, if central office personnel would stop going to cocktail parties long enough to initiate some substantive work of their own, they might have something better to do than request more reports. As would be expected, people in the central office also have opinions. They feel that sojourners identify too much with hosts and have no idea of the work necessary to acquire and defend funding for international projects. If they would stop whining long enough to read the home office's carefully prepared guidelines, sojourners would have fewer difficulties. Everybody wants special attention. All field workers seem to feel that unless their special requests are granted, the world will stop spinning. Why don't they try to empathize with the home office person who has to deal with 30 "special" requests from all over the world?

In international organizations, these charges become a third inevitability along with death and taxes. The specific gripes, based on the type of cross-cultural experience, are variations on a few general themes. People in various countries who screen students for study abroad complain that they never have up-to-date criteria for intelligent recruitment and selection. Researchers worry that their graduate students are "going native" and can no longer maintain an objective viewpoint while investigating theoretical ideas. Businessmen in branch offices argue that organizational policies which exclude the recruitment of host-country executives cut down on marketing possibilities (Heenan & Perlmutter, 1979). Technical assistance advisers charge that the central office purchases too much complex equipment which cannot be adequately maintained in the host country.

The differing perceptions of field and home office employees will never completely disappear given their reference groups, day-to-day pressures, and physical distance from each other. One mollifying factor is the organizational policy requiring people, over a period of years, to accept both types of assignments. The Peace Corps became more efficient as some of its best volunteers completed their initial assignments, became area directors, and eventually accepted positions in the central office. Another policy which limited the total number of years a person could be employed by the organization, however, may have prevented the development of highly sophisticated personnel. The Foreign Service Institute in Washington, D.C., is reportedly enforcing regulations that employees accept overseas assignments once every seven years. One explicit reason is that a person's empathy for the needs of various organizational units becomes unbalanced if too much time is spent in one place.

"Localitis" and provincialism

One unifying thread behind the field-home office distinction is the tendency to become involved in one's immediate environment. This has been called "localitis" by Macomber (1975) who was concerned with the dangers it posed for the work of diplomats. When sojourners cannot separate their feelings for hosts from the demands of their work, their interpretation and reporting of local events may be colored.[3] When "localitis" becomes so strong as to affect policy, institutions which profess international goals become provincial.

A common form of provincialism stems from an organization's location. The community in which an international organization is situated may have more influence than it should. Yet a number of factors force international goals to be reconciled with local problems. Some employees are chosen because they live nearby, and those who move to the area must learn enough about local conditions to find good housing. Children are sent to schools and adults participate in community service activities. The community's tax laws must be obeyed and its power figures courted. To contract outside consultants for short-term services, it is much easier to phone someone nearby than to write letters and wait for the international mails to bring replies. The costs of bringing in outside consultants compounds the tendency to use "locals."

The result of local pressures is that organizational goals become straitjacketed. If the organization which selects students for overseas scholarships is located in a certain city, then applicants in that city receive more attention. Diplomats tend to use a limited set of newspapers to gain information about a country's events. Businessmen learn about management practices in one city and recommend that their organizations establish certain policies throughout the country. But because of a unique history of labor-management relations, or the important urban-rural differences present in many less technologically developed countries, the lessons learned in the one city may be ungeneralizable.

Two ways to limit parochialism are training programs and (yes, more!) policies. I have found that people who are committed to international goals at least tolerate analyses of parochialism and accept warnings that it might be affecting their work. Policies can be established which encourage or require the utilization of resources outside one area. The selection committees referred to earlier, for instance, can be expected to document that candidates from all parts of a given country were considered. Organizations can also encourage broader vistas by better selection of committee members. Wise policymakers often attempt to establish organizational support by asking elected politicians to serve. Since their jobs are partially dependent upon serving a local constituency, however, politicians often have a narrow view of their committee work. They seem to feel that their job is to support people from only a certain number of communities, and they behave in exactly this manner. When the selection committee is dominated by politicians, provincialism is assured. Even if a team of outside consultants participate in the selection, they may bow to local pressures. The consultants may feel that if they press for a broader policy, there will be another outsider-local squabble to fuel the constant charge of "intervention" mentioned several times throughout this book.

I should admit that I have advocated policies which very reasonable critics could call provincial. I have served as adviser to an organization whose goals are to study and support cross-cultural interaction. Its membership includes researchers, practitioners, and educators in various parts of the world. Dues alone cannot support a central office which disseminates information about sojourn possibilities, career opportunities, and research findings. I have advocated that the headquarters should be in Washington, D.C., since most of the potential funding agencies have offices in that city. Propinquity has a number of advantages. Representatives of a funding agency can be invited to the organization's meetings at little cost; face-to-face relationships can be established; progress can be reported on the phone; and off-the-record comments exchanged. Since organizations dedicated to providing opportunities for sojourners are located in the same city, information can be shared and mutual-help networks established. The intangible qualities called "morale" and "group identity," both of which result from working with others who have similar interests, become possibilities. To be sure, the policy has drawbacks. Members in other parts of the world feel left out and complain that their unique concerns are forgotten.

Absence of a constituency

The pressures leading to provincialism force the sojourner to combine local and cross-cultural perspectives. Many times, the problems are intensified since there is no clear, organized constituency to provide counterpressures. Tendler (1975) uses the example of technical assistance advisers who argue that too much complex equipment is sent to less industrialized societies. Host country personnel have not been properly trained, and the additional equipment necessary for maintenance is not available. Investments in smaller-scale, labor-intensive projects would create more jobs and would have a greater chance of long-term success. The receiving countries, however, have no organization which allows them to lobby the sending country's agency in charge of technical assistance. The pressure group which *does* have power is comprised of manufacturers within the sending country. The manufacturers, of course, are very happy to have their complex equipment purchased and sent overseas.

In general, international programs dealing with sojourners have little support to provide muscle for their recommendations. For this reason, they are easy targets for gadflies wishing to vent aggression or to grab headlines. A critic lashes out at the Agency for International Development, Foreign Service Institute, or the World Bank. What consequences does the critic risk? Virtually none, since few people care about the day-to-day work of these agencies. In the case of the Peace Corps, the critic faces greater risks since there is an idealism attached to the organization and an alumni group whose members could complain. But consider the differences between international organizations and the Social Security System, the Veterans Administration, or, God forbid, the National Rifle Association. A critic risks tremendous backlash since these groups are supported by powerful lobbies which have considerable influence over voters. The relative lack of organized pressure within the international arena has an interesting consequence. Some elected officials, notably American presidents, enjoy international relations since they can act without constant worries about political difficulties. Exceptions are beginning to appear, as with the relation between the American Jewish community and policies concerning Israel, and the American consumer movement and policies toward oil-producing nations.

Working with contradictions

If organizations are to work toward worthwhile goals, they sometimes must do so with the realization that other institutions may put roadblocks on the path to progress. The integration of schools is an example. Progress has been made in opening school doors to minority group students and in providing easier access to a good education. To be sure, not all problems have been solved, but minority group students have more opportunities for a good education than they did twenty years ago. Few critics would argue that schools should not be an arena for the social advancement of people who have been the targets of intense prejudice. A problem arises, however, when educated students cannot achieve their goals because of discrimination in other parts of society, such as the labor market or a city's unwritten system of neighborhood "regulations" (Blau & Duncan, 1967; Richmond, 1973). Schools, then, may be encouraging people to dress themselves up when there is no place to go. The "revolution of rising expectations" is more than a catch phrase. Minority group members learn to expect more out of life but are frustrated if their goals are blocked.

Education should prepare minority group members for this possible eventuality. Coursework on how to use the admittedly complex, expensive, slow-moving, and frustrating legal system has been incorporated into some schools. If people know how to use a society's institutions, there is less likelihood that bureaucracy can be used against a group.

The problem of working with contradictions exists in less publicized organizations devoted to improving cross-cultural relations. Many organizations which sponsor programs involving face-to-face contact are dependent upon volunteers. These include people who host students from other countries; the wives of Foreign Service officers who orient new families assigned to a given country; and the parents of children who are to attend newly integrated schools. A problem arises when the volunteers become interested in their work and seek permanent employment. The Experiment in International Living (Brattleboro, Vermont), for instance, sponsors programs which allow thousands of adolescents to travel abroad and to live with host families. Each group of about twenty students is accompanied by an adult volunteer who makes final arrangements for housing, travel, and expenses. The *Experiment* is totally dependent upon these volunteers who receive only a token remuneration. Parents could not afford to have their children participate if salaries for all program personnel had to be paid. A given volunteer might work hard, enjoy making a major contribution, and become interested in pursuing career opportunities. There are few permanent jobs, however, since the person desirous of a salaried position has to compete with others who are volunteering their time. Obviously, an organization will be unwilling to pay competitive salaries when people are willing to work for little or no money.

In general, organizations which encourage cross-cultural interaction risk frustrating those young adults who become involved. There are not enough jobs with an international orientation to absorb Peace Corps alumni, graduates of a university's School of Foreign Service, and leaders of exchange programs for adolescents. Some of those affected take a domestic job and volunteer their time in international organizations, and this is a reasonable use of their talents and energy. But note the circular process which is created: these volunteers make the hiring of permanent staff members unnecessary. A major change in social norms within the United States, brewing over approximately the last ten years, may have an impact on this process. The majority of volunteers under discussion are females. If women continue to become more career oriented, they may demand monetary rewards for their work in addition to intrinsic feelings of satisfaction and the pleasures of interacting with other interested individuals. While interviewing people about the issues covered in this chapter, I found that they were beginning to incorporate the volunteerism issue into their fore-

casts. Some were in charge of coordinating the work of volunteers in programs similar to those sponsored by the Experiment in International Living. They predicted that the organization will have to cope with major
changes, perhaps increasing its fees so that only the very wealthy can participate, should present-day volunteers demand salaries.

Dealing with employee burn-out

The sorts of problems which have been reviewed in this chapter, while perhaps understandable and even inevitable, have effects on employees' morale
and motivation to continue working. A common difficulty seen in many
types of cross-cultural experiences is the sheer number of demands which
are made on people day after day. Technical assistance advisers have to
write report after report which prevents them from giving adequate attention to their work with hosts. They also have to accept the criticism of publicity seekers desirous of an easy target. Foreign student advisers spend
tremendous amounts of time sharing the problems of sojourners but rarely
are thanked if good advice proves helpful. Bilingual education teachers become tired of the constant struggle to find or to prepare adequate
teaching materials. Staff members involved with youth exchange programs
would like to work with the participants, but they must spend all their time
recruiting host parents and/or finding adequate housing. After placement,
since the staff member is asked to intervene only when the volunteers have
problems, (s)he sees only the negative side of the program. Volunteers
can also drop out with no warning since there is no penalty which an organization can impose.

Officials at the Foreign Service Institute or the World Bank might like
to prepare families for adjustment problems which will be faced in a given
country, but so little time is allowed that a sophisticated treatment is impossible. Consequently, they must base orientations on a few superficial
concepts which are used again and again for different families. The entire
procedure, then, becomes boring for the staff people. Even if a sufficient
amount of time is alloted to orientation, there can still be morale problems. The participants in orientation programs are often very hostile, perhaps displacing the anxieties stemming from their upcoming sojourn. The
targets of their attacks are the staff members who are simply trying to do
the best they can, given the constraints they face.

When pressures mount, the phenomenon called "burn-out" often appears. Maslach (1978) presents a concise description. When applied to
cross-cultural interaction, "clients" refer to the people participating in face-
to-face contact, and "staff people" refer to employees who arrange opportunities for contact.

Burn-out involves a loss of concern for the people with whom one is working. It is characterized by an emotional exhaustion in which the staff person no longer has any positive feelings, sympathy, or respect for clients. A cynical and dehumanized perception of clients develops, in which they are labeled in derogatory ways. As a result of this dehumanizing process, clients are viewed as somehow deserving of their problems and are often blamed for their own victimization (Ryan, 1971). Consequently, there appears to be a deterioration in quality of care of service that they receive. The staff person who burns out is unable to deal successfully with the chronic emotional stress of the job, and this failure to cope can be manifested in a number of ways, including low morale, impaired performance, absenteeism, and high turnover. A common response to burn-out is to get out, by changing jobs, moving into administrative work, or even leaving the profession entirely [p. 113].

Maslach suggests a number of innovations which may reduce burn-out. In general, they are examples of input into the sorts of orientation programs suggested a number of times throughout this book. All suggestions assume that organizations will establish policies encouraging longer orientation programs.

The necessity for problem identification and problem solving in cross-cultural interaction could be introduced. Rather than presenting themselves as the source of all wisdom, staff members could communicate general points to sojourners but, at the same time, emphasize that many issues must be faced after the formal orientation when quick assistance is not available. If clients become more self-reliant, staff members will not be asked to participate in an overwhelming number of problems. More attention could be given to the difficulties of cross-cultural interaction so that all participants will have clearer and more accurate expectations (Higginbotham, 1977). Staff members could also specify what they can and cannot do, given their human frailties and other pressures on their time. This recommendation goes against the tendency for people to keep difficulties to themselves as if they were a big, dark secret. Probable reasons include the fear of perceived weakness if staff members have to admit that a problem is difficult, and the narcissistic tendency to believe that one's problems are so complex as to be uncommunicable to others. In addition to creating and encouraging unrealistic expectations, staff members insult clients when they withhold information. They are saying, in effect, "You are not intelligent enough to understand these pressures or sensitive enough to empathize with our problems." The assumption behind the present recommendation is that staff members and sojourners will be better able to develop workable solutions to problems if all pertinent information is shared.

Orientation programs can also encourage staff members and sojourners to keep in mind the advantages of positive feedback and open communication channels as well as the dangers of hostile, angry encounters.

> Staff need to know explicitly from clients when things have gone well, as well as when they have not. An occasional word of praise, a smile, or a pat on the back can be enough to take most staff people through many hours of stressful interactions, ambiguous outcomes, and frustrating red tape [Maslach, 1978, p. 122].

A client may win an argument by being a "squeaky wheel," but the target of an angry monologue may become demoralized and, ultimately, less effective. Organizational policy can contribute to morale maintenance by requiring that information about positive outcomes be widely circulated. I have observed organizations in which communication between administrators and their staff occurred only when there was a negative event for which blame had to be assigned. Opportunities to communicate were viewed with dread, not as opportunities for joint examination of problems and prospects.

The mushiness of success versus the visibility of failure

In any type of cross-cultural program, so many factors are involved that the reasons for success are hard to determine. Theoretically, the same is true for failure: exact reasons are difficult to diagnose. With failures, however, the principles concerning the salience of vivid events, reviewed in chapter 4, must be added to any analysis. Since failures are so visible, there is a strong tendency for people to assign blame. These general concepts might be better understood if a few specific examples are considered.

Assume that foreign students from a certain country enroll at an American university as part of a program funded by a state legislature. They become involved in campus life, make friends with hosts, give guest presentations in various classes, and write theses relevant to concerns in their home country. By all accounts, this is a successful program. But why? The administrator in charge of organizing the program may have been especially skillful. The foreign student advisers may have been helpful. Hosts in student government activities may have been sensitive to the problems facing strangers in a new country. Or, the foreign students may have been such capable people to begin with that any program bringing them to the United States would have appeared successful. No one reason or set of reasons can be readily identified. A formal evaluation by an outside researcher might be helpful, but it is important to note that there will be little motivation to use funds on an evaluative study. Things are going smoothly; there are other uses of people's time besides working with an evaluator; and since people "know" the program is successful, there is little perceived need for an outsider to repeat the message.

Assume, on the other hand, that the program runs into difficulties. Some of the students supply newspapers with articles about American imperialism, and a few even travel to the state capitol and lobby legislators. The flak raised by taxpayers who wonder why their money is being spent on unscrubbed revolutionaries causes the program to be labeled a failure. And someone is going to get the blame: the administrator, advisers, or some untenured assistant professor. Since the program is in jeopardy because of precarious funding, staff members will be tolerant if legislators ask evaluators to become involved.

The general point of greater attention to negative than positive outcomes has important implications for the work of technical assistance advisers (Tendler, 1975). A reasonable policy in many cases would be direct assistance for projects which hosts perceive as important. The result might be smaller-scale, labor-intensive projects which the country can "absorb." The trouble with this policy, from the sending country's point of view, is that accountability is lost. Little control over the money's use remains with the donor. If the hosts use the money unwisely or participate in graft, the sender cannot answer inquiries about failures. Officials in charge of the sending agency's budget conclude their investigation with the attribution of "incompetence" and appropriate less money in future years. The accountability problem is decreased when large pieces of complex equipment are given to the host country. The sending agency can, then, point to the equipment as an indication of success. If hosts cannot use it properly, the agency is surely not to blame, especially in this era of limited intervention in the development of Third World resources.

To make the problem more complex, many receiving countries are happy to receive the equipment. They can point to it as a glamorous symbol of progress, and it is much more exciting for visitors to tour a modern factory with large, humming machines than a small building occupied by wage earners. L. Smith (1977) has studied the use of language learning laboratories in Asia:

> Generally, language laboratories are a dream for those schools and colleges which don't have them and a nightmare for those who do. School administrators seem to believe that a language laboratory will solve all their English teaching problems—perhaps because they are so expensive to install. (There is a tendency to believe that we always get value for money.) Usually there is no budget provision for maintenance, replacement, or to buy tapes and other laboratory material. Only after the lab is installed do the administrators and teachers realize what havoc the lack of adequate electricity, the ever-present dust, and the constant humidity wreaks on the language lab. Except in Japan, where lab facilities, although

not always used wisely, are excellent, language laboratories have created
more problems than they have solved [p. 97].

The demand for accountability in anticipation of possible failure leads to
conservative, low-risk, noninnovative proposals. The problem is compounded since many funders, such as legislators, have not necessarily had
any cross-cultural experience. The correct advice to program advisers is to
make the program understandable through nontechnical language and
anecdotes which funders can understand. At times, however, the need to
make proposals acceptable forces significant changes which can affect usefulness in the host country. These factors undoubtedly drive some creative
people from programs involving cross-cultural contact, leaving behind
those willing and able to accept the constraints.

The uncertainty of any policy

There is one big secret shared by practitioners who have had long experience in organizations dedicated to cross-cultural concerns. No one really
knows any general principles which can be automatically applied, with a
reasonable chance of success, in the planning and implementation of large-
scale programs. I like to think that the principles reviewed throughout this
book are well grounded. Putting them into practice, however, cannot be
done according to cookbook-like rules. The principles are helpful starting
points for one's thinking, but they must be combined with a knowledge of
situational factors specific to a given location. No sources will ever exist
in which all these factors are analyzed.

The absence of widely applicable principles forces practitioners to be
inventive when solving problems. In applying their newly formulated ideas,
however, people can never be sure that they are acting wisely. Organizational policy has to be put into practice, but exact methods are unknown.
For instance, foreign student advisers should certainly apply the general
principles of respect and sensitivity toward those from other cultures. Difficulties arise since advisers have to interact with students from so many
countries. In the course of a morning, an adviser at any large university
may interact with people from Japan, Israel, Iran, Germany, Sweden,
Egypt, and Nigeria. Since it is absolutely impossible to know about rules
for displaying sensitivity and respect in each culture, advisers will always
make errors and will always wonder if they could have been more helpful.
Advisers have told me that the necessity to "switch" frames of reference
while interacting with students from different countries is physically tiring
and, sometimes, emotionally exhausting.

The researcher must also be inventive when applying general principles
of scholarly, scientific investigation in a specific culture. A good example

can be found in research which assesses people's intellectual skills (Irvine & Carroll, 1980). When working among the Tiv in Central Africa, Price-Williams (1961) was interested in testing the presence of cognitive skills identified by Piaget. Since the Tiv were unfamiliar with the types of beads in the standard Piagetian task, Price-Williams substituted a local species of nut which children had frequently seen. Children's performance was much better with nuts than beads, even though all materials were of the same size and could be manipulated with the same amount of ease. In deciding to substitute, Price-Williams was applying the general principle that children must be accustomed to the materials so that discomfort upon seeing a completely unfamiliar task does not affect performance. For other cultures, different substitutions would have to be made. Researchers must learn a great deal about a society before they can adapt previously standardized procedures for the valid and fair assessment of people's abilities. There will always be some uncertainty whether or not another change might have led to a more valid assessment.

School principals implementing a statewide policy of school desegregation may want to bring teachers and parents together to determine if some superordinate goals can be identified. The hope would be that work toward these goals would reduce tension. While planning to apply this general concept, however, the principals have to keep local conditions in mind. There will be specific people whose support must be obtained so that teachers and parents will attend meetings. In some cases, the attendance of students is crucial, while in others, it will just add confusion. Timing is critical: if meetings are scheduled too soon after a controversial event, people will focus only on that. Even the place of meetings is important. Some sites are associated with so many bitter memories that they should be avoided. The specific goals are certainly crucial. Mistakes have been made because officials have imposed their concerns without allowing input from those who would be affected by the choice of goals. Again, there will always be some uncertainty regarding the choices made in these decision areas.

Whose values to choose?

In cross-cultural situations, organizational policy decisions frequently have to be made which favor the values of one interest group over another. The three examples introduced in the last section involve value-oriented decisions. A foreign student adviser might try to counsel in a style familiar to the sojourner. Or, since the student will inevitably interact with many people who use only host country styles, the adviser may decide that behaving in a familiar manner may create false expectations and provide poor preparation for the future. In making changes in standardized procedures, the researcher may obtain better performance among a culture's members but may lose comparability with other sets of data gathered according to widely accepted methods. If peers in a discipline can be called the "organization," the researcher always risks disapproval since there are no approved ways of modifying standard methods. Principals in desegregated schools, or in some systems the district superintendent, have to decide whether curricula should include material about each cultural group in the school. Emphasis on a local dialect such as black English may create self-pride, but it may also lead to nonvalued skills when students attempt to enter the labor market. Considering the case of Mexican-Americans, Pearson (1977) recommends that attention be given to middle-class skills.

> Otherwise, as Lopez (1973) points out, 'romantic notions' of cultural pluralism may lead some people to see the severely depressed economies of historically isolated Mexican-American villages . . . as 'alternative life styles.' Once such a perspective is taken then middle class Anglo skills may also be ignored on the grounds that they are not suitable for culturally different children [p. 93].

I do not know of any more difficult aspect of cross-cultural relations than to be faced with value-laden decisions of this kind. Very recently, I was asked for advice on programs for refugees from Southeast Asia. The official in charge said, "We find that good refugees are not good immigrants. They are not troublemakers, but they are hesitant to learn skills useful in the United States. They feel that they will return home in the near future. We have no problems with a second group, those who want to be immigrants. How can we work with the first group?" The easy answer would be to present members of the first group with various options, accompanied by suggested advantages and disadvantages of each, and let them decide. While sometimes a good policy, the lack of formal education and exposure to Western society among the refugees causes tremendous difficulties in their ability to make informed decisions. Officials in the sponsoring organization, after obtaining as much information from as many different types of sources as they can, have to predict whether or not the refugees will ever be able to return to Southeast Asia. Obviously, crystal-ball gazing of this sort will not always be right. If the political situation will likely prevent return, the organization's staff must persuade the refugees to prepare for this strong possibility. This type of persuasion is often distasteful to people involved in cross-cultural contact since they prefer to incorporate sojourners' desires, values, and points of view in any decision-making activities.

Political pressures

The importance of political sensitivity was introduced in chapter 8 as an essential factor in task accomplishment. Many analysts feel that sensitivity must be institutionalized since organizational survival is sometimes based on political decisions. Even in countries where democracy is the preferred form of government, parties in power sometimes make a point of withholding support from organizations identified as sympathetic with rivals. The Peace Corps, for instance, was closely identified with the Democratic Party since its first director was President John Kennedy's brother-in-law. Support diminished later when a Republican became president.

Other analysts have been very frank in encouraging organizations to monitor political developments.

> I've been doing some work with community organizations in Venezuela and have been impressed with how many people, even at the lower income levels, are more interested in preserving the strength of their political party or other petty source of personal power than in increasing the services available to the community. They would subvert any influence for change, especially from an outsider [Gomez, 1978, p. 52].

> . . . even though the government of Thailand has often been advised that decentralization and community involvement would produce better results from its social services programs, it rejects this approach based on its perception of the political risks inherent in strengthening local organizations [Stifel, 1978, p. 52].

> [The technical assistance adviser] must work within an institutional structure which may not share his objectives of raising the levels of life for the common people, particularly when this involves land reform. If we are going to be helpful to the manager in this situation, we must come to grips with the political questions in our training programs [Ickis, 1978 p. 55].

In my experience, political issues are most often discussed in face-to-face encounters among experienced practitioners. Current and helpful information is rarely available in the published literature, perhaps because people realize that the written word may make them persona non grata in other countries. Administrators planning the type of training program advocated by Ickis must be resourceful in finding knowledgeable people willing to share their insights.

Constant reorganization

A combination of factors leads to a strange phenomenon in international organizations. Administrators frequently order reorganization of offices and projects with the hope that goals will be better met. The reorganization is a response to uncertainty. No one knows when or why a project will succeed, when an outsider will use the organization as a target, when a group of clients will behave so as to attract negative publicity, how volunteers are best recruited and mobilized, or when funding sources will dry up. The resulting frustration causes people to be desirous of action, and reorganization is something that administrators can always do. The basic optimism in many people's outlook also contributes to this tendency. "We should be better prepared for eventualities if we can make the proper changes." The rationale is much like putting another $300 into one's beloved 1968 Mustang: "This one last repair should make purchase of a new car unnecessary."

Possibly, administrators create an excuse which can be used as the answer to an outsider's probing questions. They can compliment the questioner's insight and explain that a current reorganization has been undertaken to better deal with the issues, and that a more complete answer will be available next year. Finally, structural changes are sometimes made to deal with problems which have been created by specific individuals. Since it is so painful and difficult to deal with individual personalities, however, structural changes are made which affect everyone but do not center attention on any one person.

While interviewing people during 1978 and 1979, I observed attempts at major changes in many cross-cultural organizations. These included the Agency for International Development, the International Communication Agency, the East-West Center, an organization devoted to sponsoring sojourns for adolescents, several foreign student advisers' offices, and the Peace Corps central office. At times, the changes were based on significant shifts in goals which, however uncomfortable, justified reorganization. In other cases, the modifications reflected the preferences of limited-term but high-level administrators who had only a short time to "make their mark" (Heclo, 1977). But just as frequently, the changes were only cosmetic: who reports to whom at the initial stages of a project; modifications in a project's name, even though the content remains the same; a new form for predicting expenditures; or procedures for entertaining visitors. For each change, meetings have to be held and memos must be written. Staff members justifiably complain that they spend too much time in reorganization efforts and have little left over for substantive work. The only way to limit the constant tendency to reorganize, I believe, is to write and talk about it. If the tendency becomes public knowledge, administrators might catch themselves when tempted to make changes for the sake of doing *something*.

BENEFITS STEMMING FROM SUCCESSFUL ORGANIZATIONS

If problems can be overcome or at least neutralized, a number of benefits can result from the establishment or maintenance of effective organizations. Benefits refer to those outcomes which permanent organizations can encourage far more effectively than either individuals working in isolation or ad hoc groups working for short periods of time.

The nonpublicity effect

The disadvantages of constant publicity are seen most clearly in the work of diplomats. In permanent organizations such as the United Nations or the European Parliament, long-term analyses of problems can proceed. This is undoubtedly a necessity when dealing with complex issues which involve a number of countries. The trouble with short-term conferences is that they invite the glare of publicity. Newspeople print information of the day-to-day deliberations and they sometimes force a person to defend a position, originally presented as very tentative, since the media made it public. Pride, and feelings that one does not want to be seen as weak or wavering, force hardening of positions and, thus, less chance of a negotiated solution acceptable to parties from many nations. Worse, the newspeople may report on the sorts of cross-cultural misunderstanding which have been discussed throughout this book. Undoubtedly, these will be harder to resolve once they have been made public. Coverage of much longer conferences which take place at permanent organizations is frankly duller. Consequently, after an initial flurry of coverage at its opening sessions, newspeople are likely to give the organization much less attention at a long than a short conference.

Reduction in tension

Countries which have conflicting positions on important issues can benefit from the presence of sponsored cross-cultural contact programs. The development of workable policies for encouraging and supporting sojourners, as in programs for students and scholars in various countries, necessitates some kind of organization. By belonging to such organizations, countries commit themselves to a reduction in tension on *at least* the exchange-of-persons issue. Some people in the organization have to deal with visas; others with medical clearances; and still others with the transfer of funds from one country to another. To complete their work successfully, the bureaucrats have to maintain neutral if not tolerant attitudes toward counterparts in other countries. Since the majority of people on academic sojourns return to the home country with favorable reports on their cross-cultural experience (Abrams, 1978; Klineberg & Hull, 1979), a favorable atmosphere is either developed or reinforced. Kelman (1965b) speculates further about the presence of a bureaucracy concerned with sojourners:

> Needless to say, these more positive interactions will not cause the basic conflict between the two nations to vanish and will not persuade them to abandon the pursuit of incompatible goals. They can, however, contribute to the creation of an atmosphere in which these basic conflicts can be negotiated more effectively and political settlements can be achieved. . . . Moreover, the establishment of cooperative relationships in some domains may help to counteract tendencies toward complete polarization of the conflicting nations and thus make it easier to find ways of "fractionating" the conflict between them [p. 574].

Exchange of persons programs sometimes precede other types of intergovernmental contact. Some of the very early programs involving any sort of contact between the United States and the People's Republic of China dealt with short-term exchanges of athletes and scholars. Although analysts disagree about its long-term success, Henry Kissinger has said that his shuttle diplomacy was made possible partially because of an exchange program. In the early 1950s, young politicians from various countries came to Harvard where they studied international affairs. Kissinger was closely involved, and by the time he was Secretary of State, many of the participants had become extremely influential in their home countries.

The long-term analysis of complex problems

Organizations can provide a forum so that people can analyze complex problems and develop possible solutions. International issues have become so complex, due to increased nationalism, decreased colonial influence, the worldwide impact of inflation, the rise of power based on energy, and the relative impotence of the once so-called superpowers that quick analyses are either naive, unworkable, or both. Individuals working alone have a terribly difficult time obtaining the information necessary to address international problems or to secure a hearing for suggested solutions. Even if the suggestions are reasonable and might lead to an amelioration of some problem, people affected might object since they had no input into the work. Effective organizations can assure that (a) information is made available, (b) opportunities are provided for widespread participation at very early stages of an analysis, (c) support is provided during the inevitable low points of a complex project, and (d) conclusions resulting from the analysis receive adequate dissemination.

An organization's influence on the use of research findings has been analyzed by E. Glaser and Taylor (1973). While not specifically concerned with international problems, I believe that one of their findings has a great deal of significance. People who *might use* the results of an analysis are much more likely to do so if they participate in some way. Participation can take the form of questioning, criticizing, suggesting, or informing, especially at the early stages before concepts and methods become hardened. Analyses were better with participation since more accurate information was made available concerning stumbling blocks and resistance to potential changes. Further, people appreciated the fact that their opinions were requested and that solutions were not being imposed by cavalier outsiders.

Some specific examples of complex solutions to international problems, suggested by various analysts, may be worth mentioning. One of the most critical needs, of course, is for better diplomatic negotiations concerning the reduction of armed conflict among nations. A number of scholars have suggested such imaginative solutions as the following (Katz, 1965; Wright, Evans, & Deutsch, 1962).

1. Extensions of the United Nations which might take the form of regional entities rather than individual countries, and a forum in which members of multinational, nongovernmental corporations could cooperate. Possibly, if countries with regions worked together for common goals such as favorable trade policies, hostilities would be seen as counterproductive.

2. A reduction in conflict through unilateral moves in areas not currently contributing to international tensions. Most frequently associated with the work of Osgood (1962), the technique is based on actions which are not crippling to the country making the first move; which invite reciprocity; which can be publicized internationally; but which are not dependent upon another country's actions. Although terribly difficult to identify with assurance, some scholars argue that the Osgood approach was known to the Kennedy administration and was used in the development of treaties banning atmospheric testing (Katz, 1965, p. 388).

3. Economic policies, for instance, tax incentives to companies which change from manufacturing weapons, as part of international arms control treaties, to the production of goods aimed at nonmilitary markets.

4. "International military forces. The problem of national security is now met by national military forces and generally by alliances between nations for the cooperative use of their armies and weapons. This cooperative arrangement could be extended by setting up a new international institution to which nations would contribute their armaments and armed forces. Countries would maintain their identities in every other respect, but would

turn to this international force for protection against attack [Katz, 1965, p. 387]."

Some of these suggestions may sound unworkable, some might be improved through further study, and some will stimulate further thinking in quite different organizations. The simple point argued here is that organizations, even admitting to all the difficulties already reviewed, must exist for the effective development of these ideas. On a level slightly less lofty than diplomatic negotiations, certain aspects of any person's sojourn can be improved only through organizational policies acceptable to sending and receiving countries. Klineberg and Hull (1979) explain that sojourners who come to a country

> . . . hoping to earn money abroad are frequently frustrated by local regulations forbidding remunerative employment. Some succeed working in a clandestine manner (what the French call "le travail au noir") without working papers which . . . they find it impossible to obtain. This problem can only be solved, in our judgment, through some sort of international agreement which will take into consideration the special needs of [sojourners], but as far as we know there have been no steps taken so far in this direction [p. 37].

As Klineberg and Hull recognize, it is much easier to identify the problem than to do much about it. The issue of work for sojourners is complex since it involves a country's level of unemployment, the power of unions, the bureaucracy which issues work permits, and a host of other difficulties. Individuals concerned with the welfare of sojourners must be willing to deal with this complexity and with all factions which have a stake in the issues.

Solutions will not come quickly since the views of so many interest groups must be heard. Even if agreements are reached, enforcement is difficult, as seen in the economic policies formulated by the European Parliament. Continuing effort is always needed to follow up on agreements, again demanding an organizational base for concerned individuals. Another example is international adoptions. A social worker in charge of adoptions in Hawaii has told me that effective organizations in both the sending and receiving countries are necessary. While many parents in the United States might want to adopt immediately and complain about delays, the social worker insists that it is necessary for the long-range welfare of child and family. Quick adoptions risk glossing over legal steps which ensure that adoptions cannot later be challenged by natural parents. Effective organizations are needed in both countries to do the necessary paperwork for legal clearances, approval of families, and the sharing of this information. Although it is heartbreaking to read of orphans among refugees, it is also heartbreaking for parents to fight court battles five years after adoption.

Managing conflict over long periods

While individuals or small groups working in isolation might usefully participate in efforts to resolve problems, limits on time and energy place restrictions on their potential contributions. The advantage of an organization is that constant vigilance is possible. Adjustments can be made, sometimes before a problem becomes so intense that conflict results. In analyzing the much maligned United Nations, Alger (1965) points out the benefits of constant attention.

> In handling problems, the United Nations not only offers decision making bodies, such as the Assembly and councils, but builds an intergovernmental society around a problem. When a problem arises, such as . . . the financing of peace-keeping operations, this society is continually active on the problem, whether more formal bodies are in session or not. It facilitates continual adjustments in national policies, tending to substitute a host of small adjustments for extraordinary confrontations that require adjustments of great magnitude. Thus, relations are conducted more through a host of capillaries and less through a few main arteries. When a problem eventually reaches the public arena in the Assembly or one of the councils, the outcome will be importantly shaped by the nature of the intergovernmental society that has developed around the issue [p. 546].

The slow, plodding, often dull work necessary for these contributions does not capture the public fancy. A lack of excitement, in the United Nations and other multinational organizations, is mistakenly seen as a symptom of ineptness.

Meetings held at permanent organizations, in contrast to shorter-term conferences with a scheduled termination date, have another major advantage. Diplomats can discuss and debate without reaching an agreement (Rusk, 1955; Sawyer & Guetzkow, 1965). Realizing that the organization will still be operating tomorrow, diplomats do not feel pressured to reach possibly unsuitable compromises. The risk of shorter conferences is that participants might adopt a deadline orientation. They may accept a resolution during the final hours with which they are not entirely satisfied. The unsuitability of the resolution may eventually cause more problems than it solves.

Conflict management occurs in many organizations. The substitution of a less intense form of conflict for another was reviewed in chapter 8, where problems resulting from school integration were analyzed. Other examples can be reviewed here since the substitution is most effective when organizations support the efforts of individuals. The shift of aggressive confrontation from a dangerous to a safer target frequently occurs in foreign student advisers' offices. Sojourners who experience frustration in adjusting to a new examination system, different norms for interacting with professors, and competition for grades in an unfamiliar language might direct their aggressive feelings at hosts. Since hosts are not aware of the sojourners' frustrations, however, they are unlikely to forgive the outbursts. Foreign student advisers, on the other hand, are familiar with sojourners' problems and, ideally, will not take attacks personally. Advisers know that hostilities are better channeled toward them rather than toward unsuspecting hosts. Although not one of the pleasant aspects of their work, advisers should realize that they will often be used as targets, even though they have made great efforts to help sojourners with their adjustment problems. Experienced administrators realize this fact and do not become upset with every complaint that sojourners make about advisers. This entire process must be made part of the knowledge base shared by all organization members. I have observed administrators without much international experience look very foolish when overinterpreting the gripes of sojourners. If administrative support is not present, employees are likely to burn out much faster.

Improved patterns of communication

Another organizational factor relates to the amount of interaction with staff members from many different countries (Heenan & Perlmutter, 1979). This variable is central to the study of diplomatic communication carried out by Alger (1965). Diplomats were interviewed after they had served both in embassies, located in the capital city of a given country, and in the United Nations. In the first type of assignment, people were expected to deal with hosts but not necessarily representatives from other countries which also had embassies in the capital cities. In the United Nations, on the other hand, diplomats had day-to-day contact with representatives from many countries.

Alger found that diplomats perceived a very different atmosphere at the United Nations which was largely based on improved communication patterns among representatives. The diplomats from given nations felt there was: (1) more contact with representatives from a variety of countries, with greater oral communication being especially noticeable. Presumably, individuals can receive more appropriate information on specific issues during the give-and-take of discussions, in contrast to the one-way routing of formal speeches and memoranda; (2) less emphasis on diplomatic rank, meaning that people feel comfortable while communicating with others who have much more experience, expertise, or status. Representatives also felt that contact was less formal, with a deemphasis on protocol. Note that no conclusions about complete absence of protocol were made; there was simply less in the United Nations than in embassies. Representatives of some countries are comfortable with certain norms governing interaction, and these should be respected; (3) more contact with unfriendly countries. In preparing to vote on issues involving little or no international tension, representatives of unfriendly countries must interact with each other. During the ensuing discussion, a variety of issues not directly related to the current vote are undoubtedly raised; (4) more information is available which is less likely to be restricted to specific channels. If information is shared only by certain representatives, factions may be encouraged since different people will have different perceptions of reality. The widespread availability of information also provides opportunities for upward mobility to representatives from low-status countries.

As people work on the same problems, the development of workable solutions becomes a superordinate goal. Less important issues, such as rank, protocol, and status, are set aside. Information is widely shared since more people will have the background necessary to make contributions. Representatives begin to identify with the success of the multinational organization in addition to the advances made in their own countries. As more and more organizations move toward greater internationalism in staffing, goals, and number of offices in different countries, these advantages will, hopefully, accompany the changes.

SUMMARY

The positive outcomes of a sojourn are not possible unless organizations sponsor programs and provide logistical support. Although individuals occasionally travel to other countries and work on their own, the majority of sojourners are employed or sponsored by established organizations. Certain aspects which are inherent to international organizations, as well as predictable external pressures which must be faced, should be analyzed to develop a more complete understanding of cross-cultural contact.

Organizations have to deal with a number of factors over which they do not have complete control. These factors force the development of policies which affect the day-to-day work of individual members. An issue so pervasive that it provides in-group/out-group identity is the distinction between the field and home office. Some people become identified with the problems of the central office, and others with the difficulties in a specific country. One group cannot understand the insensitivity demonstrated by the other. When people become overly involved with problems in the immediate environment, "localitis" and provincialism frequently develop. These outcomes interfere with the international goals espoused by the organization. People close to an organization, whether in the field or near the home office, sometimes become a vocal, powerful constituency which must be satisfied. One problem with technical assistance, for instance, is that manufacturers near an organization's home office are more likely to apply pressure than are citizens in the receiving country. The former are accustomed to participating in pressure groups, while the latter are not. Consequently, aid programs develop which may be more beneficial to the senders than the receivers.

Organizations must cope with a predictable set of personnel problems. Because of a successful sojourn, people may want to make a career in an international organization. Unfortunately, there are not enough jobs for former Peace Corps members, graduates of a university's foreign service department, or host country volunteers who orient newly arrived sojourners. Contradictions become common: volunteers might seek permanent employment, but they have to compete against volunteers. Those people who do find jobs sometimes wonder if they made a wise decision. Any helping profession has its trials and tribulations, but the dimension of cultural differences can lead to additional problems. The frustrations sojourners feel while adjusting to another culture, for instance, are frequently displaced on people trying to help. Combined with the tendency for sojourners to rarely thank those who assist them, staff members run the risk of becoming burned out. Recommendations for reducing burn-out include better orientation programs in which sojourners would learn the advantages of positive feedback.

In any type of complex program, failure is more noticeable than success. There is less perceived need to account for positive outcomes than to assign blame for negative results. Policies are developed to protect against the possibility that an organization will be blamed for failures. Consequently, risky projects do not compete as well for funding. Applying these observations to the work of technical assistance advisers, glamorous symbols of progress, such as complex machinery, are funded since they are relatively easy to build in the sending country and to deliver overseas. If the machinery is not wisely used by the receivers, the senders can point to current limitations on intervention in other countries. To compound the problem, many politicians in receiving countries enjoy having the equipment since they can point to it as a product of their incumbency. Unfortunately, looking at large machinery humming away is more exciting than viewing large numbers of workers earning money in small-scale industries.

Uncertainty pervades all but the most routine decisions. Even though small-scale industry was implicitly recommended in the previous paragraph, it would be very hard to find scientifically acceptable evidence that this is a good policy for widespread adoption. Terribly difficult decisions have to be made by educators concerning the best use of resources for minority group students; by social workers working with refugees who have un-realistic plans to return home; and by advisers regarding placement of foreign students in classes where their language capabilities may prove a handicap. Few guidelines exist which can be automatically applied. General principles have to be integrated with the specifics of each situation. No set of organizational policies will be without mistakes. One tendency is to develop more and more policies, especially concerning reorganization of offices and changes in employee job descriptions. Too often, such activity is busy work which interferes with organizational effectiveness.

Policies often have unforeseen consequences: regulations covering the use of money have important implications. Since foreign students who need tuition money cannot work in the host country, they must risk visa diffi-culties and accept employment where they are not likely to be identified. If the university tries to help with a major money expenditure by providing low-cost housing, students may charge that they are forced to live in a ghetto. To recruit technical assistance advisers, governments offer salary increments and provide housing/shopping privileges, but these inducements create a distinction between sojourners and hosts. Since funds for projects are appropriated on a year-to-year basis, money may be unwisely spent during the final months of any fiscal year. There are more potential projects than funds for their development. Organizations must set very specific goals and match these to the priorities established by funding sources. The skills necessary to write successful proposals have become so specialized that present day "outsiders" have a difficult time becoming part of an aid-giving agency's clientele. Reports have to be written which justify the expenditure of funds. If there is a universal complaint among any organization's mem-bers, it centers around the time necessary to keep funders informed. "There is not time left over to actually do the work promised in the agreement."

Other time demands include entertaining visitors. The problem is in-tensified for people who do the best work. If a foreign student adviser's office, technical assistance project, or bilingual education program is suc-cessful, it will attract a greater number of visitors. Participative decision making (PDM) has advantages, but employers and employees must realize that it is a slow procedure. Further, while sojourners are still coping with a new culture, PDM may be an additional burden rather than an aid. Even though it also demands a time commitment by organizations, the provision of a transition period for sojourners is universally recommend as a wise policy.

The skills necessary to secure funding and write interesting reports leads to problems of reward allocation. Who shall be promoted and given recognition: the person who prepares the proposal or the one who carries out the work? While the same people are involved, ideally, the competition for funds often leads to specialization. The specific functions then become the prerogatives of different offices, contributing to a clumsy bureaucracy. The competition for scarce tenured positions encourages university researchers to avoid cross-cultural studies. When cultural dimensions are added to a study, the time necessary for completion is much longer than a study carried out in one country. People who provide support services to sojourners are frequently underrewarded. For every headline-grabbing group of students from the People's Republic of China, there are unseen people who worked on visas, housing, and language courses. Wise administrators ask these questions: (a) What is being rewarded? (b) Does the present reward dispensation system interfere with the attainment of important goals? (c) What other activities should be given increased status through greater reward allocation?

Even with all the problems organizations have and sometimes encourage, they still provide the only arena in which complex international problems can be addressed. Satia (1978) discussed innovations in agriculture:

> Over the past few years we've become aware that by using appropriate technologies such as fertilizer, even small farms can be quite productive. Yet to implement these changes in farm practice there first has to be an organization which is able to reach out to the farmer and gain his commitment to a new behavior. Thus, the technical, resource, and organizational concerns are highly interrelated [p. 58].

In addition to making certain projects possible, work carried out in permanent organizations has advantages over similar efforts carried out in short-term conferences. Work in organizations may attract an initial flurry of publicity, but drabness soon encourages the media to search elsewhere for material. Policy development does not become impeded by premature reporting of discussions. Even if workable solutions are suggested by individuals working in isolation, there may not be means of dissemination and implementation which organizations can provide. Decisions which affect people's lives, such as guidelines allowing sojourners to work, must be monitored and enforced which, again, can only be done through organizations.

Organizations can also encourage a reduction in tension among nations. By encouraging exchange-of-persons programs, a bureaucracy develops to support the work of sojourners. Tolerant, or at least neutral, attitudes toward counterparts in other countries become functional in providing visas, medical clearances, and transfer of funds. Since most sojourners return with favorable reports on their cross-cultural experience, goodwill is either developed or reinforced. Permanent organizations such as the United Nations can make small adjustments in policies to decrease the probability of major confrontations. Representatives do not feel pressured to reach agreements, as they might at a shorter conference. Resolutions accepted only because of an upcoming deadline may cause more problems than they solve.

Generalizing from the work of Alger (1965), experience in an organization which draws staff from many countries has positive effects on individual employees. Alger contrasted assignments to the United Nations with embassy positions in a nation's capital city. In the multinational organization, people felt that more oral communication occurred with representatives from different countries. More information was available and it was not channeled along limited routes. There was more contact with unfriendly countries. Since problem solving became a superordinate goal, values were placed on ability to contribute rather than on diplomatic rank.

These advantages are possible only if an organization has norms which encourage respect for people's contributions regardless of their home country. Respect for individual status is an important predictor of adjustment to, and long-term satisfaction with, life in another culture. The nature of adjustment and satisfaction is the focus of the next chapter.

NOTES

1. Then said the king, The one saith, This is my son that liveth and thy son is the dead: and the other saith, Nay; but thy son is the dead, and my son is the living.

    And the king said, Bring me a sword. And they brought a sword before the king.

    And the king said, Divide the living child in two, and give half to the one, and half to the other.

    Then spake the woman whose the living child was unto the king, for her bowels yearned upon her son, and she said, O my lord, give her the living child, and in no wise slay it. But the other said, Let it be neither mine nor thine, but divide it.

    Then the king answered and said, Give her the living child, and in no wise slay it: she *is* the mother thereof.

    And all Israel heard of the judgment which the king had judged; and they feared the king: for they saw that the wisdom of God was in him, to do judgment [1 Kings 3:23–28].

    2. Participative decision making may not be effective in countries where large numbers of employees prefer being deferent to authority figures (Harris & Moran, 1979). Research on social change (Inkeles & Smith, 1974), however, suggests that PDM may eventually be accepted by people who come into contact with institutions patterned after those in highly industrialized societies.

    3. Given this perceived problem, the United States Department of State has a policy demanding that its Foreign Service Officers relocate every two years.

10

The Processes of Adjustment

INTRODUCTION

Adjustment to another culture is dependent upon people's traits and skills, the groups they join, the tasks they want to accomplish, and the organizations in which they work. Consequently, a discussion of adjustment has been delayed until these other topic areas were reviewed. Although a longer explanation of adjustment will be introduced later in the chapter, a shorter and convenient definition includes the core elements of people's satisfaction, perceived acceptance by hosts, and ability to function during everyday activities without severe stress.

The differences between short- and long-term adjustment will be covered in this chapter. A major distinction, in addition to the obvious variable of time, can be found in the perceptions of hosts. During short-term sojourns, hosts frequently do not expect culturally appropriate behavior in all situations; mistakes are forgiven as long as the sojourner seems sincerely interested in learning about the culture. Over a longer time period, on the other hand, hosts expect greater sophistication and may react negatively if sojourners have not learned appropriate behaviors. While long-term adjustment is facilitated for some people by accepting the melting pot ideal of a monistic culture, other people adjust more readily in pluralistic societies. Advantages of cultural pluralism will be considered, as will the concept of individual pluralism since sojourners frequently develop attitudes which incorporate the points of view held by people in other cultures. If correlates of adjustment can be found, there should be principles which program directors can use to increase sojourner satisfaction. This topic has, indeed, received attention, and the resulting recommendations will be reviewed. Finally, the long-term, beneficial effects which can stem from sojourns will be considered. This may be a fitting end to the chapter since one prediction about the future of cross-cultural contact is easy to make. As more and more worthwhile programs compete for less and less available money, administrators who request support for sponsored sojourns must be able to tell funders what the benefits will be. If explanations are poor, then competing programs organized by better prepared administrators will be funded. Another prediction, made in chapter 1, is that the future will see more and more cross-cultural contact. Yet, until interested professionals organize their proposals and explain what they have to offer to businesses, technical assistance agencies, and universities, the benefits of cross-cultural contact will continue to be "hit-or-miss." Programs which could increase the probability of positive outcomes will not be supported since customers do not have a clear idea of the return on their investment.

PROCESSES IN SHORT-TERM ADJUSTMENT

Clear examples of short-term programs are summer-abroad opportunities for adolescents. Yet, all sojourns have aspects of short-term programs at certain points no matter what their length. Put another way, sojourners planning to stay in another culture for several years have short-term adjustment problems which must be faced. These must be understood by people who organize programs and who make efforts to maximize benefits.

The term "process" refers to the "why" and "how" of people's behavior rather than to the "what." When sojourners are asked about the problems they had or about experiences which were particularly memorable, their descriptions provide an account of *what* happened. Attempts to understand process focus on *why* people behaved as they did and *how* their actions solved problems and led to favorable outcomes. The distinction is important. Too often, sojourners think of adjustment as overcoming problems with housing, food, language difficulties, and working conditions. In their analysis of multinational corporations, for instance, Heenan and Perl-mutter (1979) found that these mundane gripes took attention away from other aspects of cross-cultural contact. While not downgrading their importance, or the need to prepare people regarding *what* problems will be faced, the processes of adjustment should receive equal attention. Further, since almost all sojourners eventually solve the sorts of everyday problems mentioned above (Klineberg & Hull, 1979), the important factors which differentiate one type of sojourner from another are *how* the problems were solved and *why* a certain approach was chosen.

The three analyses of short-term adjustment which I have found most useful proceed from very different starting points. Pool (1965) analyzed the experiences of adolescents from the United States who visited Europe as part of a sponsored summer program. While the findings have the most obvious direct generalizability to other programs for adolescents, I believe that some of the results have more widespread applicability. Seelye and Wasilewski (1979) approached the topic of adjustment by examining different ways in which sojourners cope with difficult problems. They proceeded by examining various types of sojourns, as well as strategies to deal with major changes within any one culture, in an attempt to formulate generalizations about coping. Klein (1977) also based her conclusions on a literature review and gave special attention to the terms most frequently used to describe adjustment. People's motives for desiring or participating in a sojourn are major components in most treatments of short-term adjustment. Klein (1977) identifies three motives and corresponding adjustment patterns based on task accomplishment, social orientation, and desire to be an ambassador for one's own country. A fourth process, withdrawal, occurs when any of these goals is thwarted. Although not all people fit into one of the ideal categorizations, the patterns occur often enough to justify their use in understanding sojourner adjustment.

Instrumental adaptation

People who use instrumental adaptation have clear goals concerning tasks to be accomplished. Social contact with hosts and fellow nationals takes second place to goal fulfillment, and the interactions which do take place are with professional colleagues. The major tensions which arise are due to difficulties in accomplishing goals. Any change sojourners make in their typical ways of behaving are designed to serve their needs or, more specifically, to be instrumental in task accomplishment. Foreign students adapt to new grading policies, technical assistance advisers become politically sensitive, and businessmen learn to participate in decision making according to host country norms. Problems such as loneliness and frustration are sometimes addressed by devoting even more time to one's work.

Some sojourners engage in instrumental activities which may not appear task related at first glance. Pool (1965) concluded that some adolescents use short-term sojourns as an escape from a home country grind of dedication to schoolwork and steady progress toward a prestigious career. During their travels, they feel free, relaxed, and less anxious. After the sojourn, they return to their goal-oriented lives, perhaps enriched and refreshed. Other adolescents use the sojourn as a chance to test themselves and as an opportunity to make a transition between the self-perceived ease of adolescence and the challenges of adulthood. They are not always relaxed during the sojourn since they feel pressured to prove themselves by constantly overcoming new challenges. After the sojourn, they would, ideally, return home with increased feelings of self-confidence. Still other sojourners look upon the experience as enhancing their status. Again, this is task oriented since they see the status increase as helping them to achieve long-range goals. After interviewing adolescents who had traveled to Europe, Pool (1965) indulged in a bit of speculation which is disturbing if true.

> They dream of enhancing themselves by becoming part of the great life of Europe or by enjoying the good life of the American in Europe. . . .
> It is from this group that a disproportionate share of our professional

international communicators will tend to come, whether for the State Department or for other public or private agencies [p. 126].

The instrumental motives of escape, self-conscious testing, and status enhancement are not found only among adolescents. Many adults accept overseas assignments as a respite from problems, fully realizing that the difficulties will still be present upon their return. In my work with cross-cultural researchers, I discovered that some scholars accept sojourn opportunities to escape dull routines in their home universities. The dullness is still there after the experience, but the internalized excitement from new skills, broadened vistas, and a wider circle of colleagues from other countries helps them to cope. In the case of foreign students, many report that they enjoy being tested. Their competent responses to challenges undoubtedly contribute to the startling result that over 90 percent feel their experiences were valuable and a good use of their time (Abrams, 1978). Peace Corps workers who possessed a strong task orientation made a point of creating additional work for themselves (Ezekiel, 1968). Diplomats enjoyed the additional work demanded in United Nations assignments compared to the responsibilities required of embassy positions (Alger, 1965). The importance of status enhancement (Morris, 1960) should never be underestimated. Kelman and Ezekiel (1970) concluded that communication specialists were most satisfied with a sojourn if hosts accorded them and/or their country a reasonable degree of status and respect.

Social orientation

Some sojourners place task-related goals behind a desire to involve themselves in the host culture. They want to meet people, learn the local language, participate in community activities, and develop close relationships with hosts. Activities which seem task related, such as an interest in dance, art, or philosophy, may be used, primarily, to gain entry into social relationships. Adjustment problems stem from failure to interact effectively with, and perceived rebuffs by, hosts. If many host country friends are made, sojourners may have difficulties readjusting after their return home. For instance, sojourners who develop close relationships with hosts will begin to share the same sort of activities. Upon their return home, they may not be able to find people who share the newly developed concerns.

Many people are able to combine their desires to complete specific tasks and to develop close relationships with hosts. My impressions from talking with sojourners and reading large-scale surveys (e.g., Klineberg & Hull, 1979) is that there are more "combiners" than single-minded people. However, all surveys may have a bias. People with a task orientation, or who combine motives, can be interviewed in fairly predictable places since they have work sites at which they can be contacted. Strongly motivated socializers, on the other hand, may literally be interacting with hosts at some unknown spot during the time a survey takes place. In addition, the strong socializers may not be as interested in taking part in a survey with its businesslike aspects of scheduling an appointment, completing all parts of the questionnaire, and so forth.

For combiners, the satisfaction of one motive is frequently made possible by use of the other. Sojourners often develop cordial relations with a co-worker and then meet and interact with other members of the host's social network. Sensitive hosts, realizing the difficulties sojourners have meeting others, often create opportunities for social interaction outside the work setting. Success in one's work sometimes makes people into public figures, such that they are in demand at social functions. Conversely, the success of one's work is often dependent upon cordial social relationships. Finding out what has to be done, which important leaders must be wooed, and when work can be started are often discovered with the help of friends in the host community. Work and social relations are also more closely linked in some countries than in others, and sojourners should recognize this fact. People who have worked in Pacific Island cultures, for instance, often say that if hosts do not like a certain sojourner, that person can accomplish little or nothing. Materials are never available, requests for support go unheeded, and introductions to key decision makers are never made. The development of cordial relations is dependent upon participation in social activities, not just congeniality in the work setting.

Ambassador for one's country

Some people resist informal interaction with hosts and make only the minimal adjustments necessary to complete certain tasks. They are very concerned with their status and enjoy playing the role of cultural ambassadors. They are willing to exchange information with hosts about features of their respective countries, but there is rarely a sharing of personal experiences and insights which could lead to real friendships. They are much more willing to talk about positive than negative aspects of their countries. Most social ties are with fellow nationals who happen to be living in the same area. These sojourners will travel for an hour across town to interact with a fellow national rather than chat with a cordial host who happens to live next door. These sorts of behaviors have been noted among residents of technologically developed countries who feel that the major mission of their sojourns is to spread wisdom developed in the West. When the sojourners happen to be from the United States, Great Britain, or Australia, the motives are cynically called the "White Man's Burden."

When there are large numbers of sojourners from a specific country, additional patterns of interaction occur. It must be noted, however, that these patterns are much more likely to occur among people from some countries than others. The eldest person among the sojourners is often looked to for advice and is considered an arbitrator for culture-based disagreements. If a person begins to adopt a dress style which peers consider immodest, the elder might be asked to communicate disapproval. Or, when a person begins to date outside the cultural group, intervention might be requested. In a university community, the elder would likely be a professor on a sponsored leave such as that provided by the Fulbright program. While it might be predicted that the professor would resent the additional role and that the time demands would interfere with the accomplishment of other goals, I have not observed this to be the case. When sojourners form a close-knit group, they reinforce each other's maintenance of first-culture norms, share letters and news from home, and support each other's adjustment difficulties. These people may have few problems returning home since they have kept abreast of developments and have not involved themselves in host country activities. At the risk of overgeneralizing, I should indicate the home countries of sojourners who often (certainly not always) behave according to these patterns. The patterns seem to be common among sojourners from countries whose norms include a strong sense of tradition, a value placed on group rather than individual achievement, and deference to elders. People from Korea, Japan, Hong Kong, and parts of India value these norms, while sojourners from the United States, Australia, and many European countries do not. At times, an individual sojourner will realize the tendency for fellow nationals to group together and will make a point of avoiding it. One sojourner from Hong Kong told me: "I wanted to learn about the United States. If I was to live in a neighborhood with many other Chinese-speaking people, I would never get out of it. I definitely decided to become involved with Americans through my choice of living arrangements, social activities, and even clubs that I joined."

Withdrawal

Both Pool (1965) and Klein (1977) have identified withdrawal as a reaction to either (a) failed attempts at social involvement with hosts, or (b) an inability to establish relations due to basic shyness (Zimbardo, 1977). In my experience, withdrawal can also describe the reaction of people who cannot accomplish their task-oriented goals. With respect to the latter group, it is important to keep in mind that, in some countries, family members manifest extreme pride when someone receives the honor of an overseas assignment or study opportunity. When an individual fails, (s)he perceives that dishonor will be brought to the family. As part of withdrawal, sojourners seek out contact with fellow nationals even though they originally may not have had much interaction with them. Or, they may spend large amounts of time with impersonal aspects of a culture, such as its tourist attractions. A common reaction following withdrawal is that negative aspects of a country are intensified in people's minds. Although the number of people who develop negative attitudes may be small (Abrams, 1978; Klineberg & Hull, 1979), they can be extremely visible after their return. Since their complaints are so loud and public, they can be overinterpreted by those people who helped arrange the sojourn in the first place (chapter 4).

To deal with the threat of burn-out, these helpers should keep in mind that most sojourners cope with the difficulties they face and make responses which satisfy themselves and produce a sense of accomplishment. Coping, of course, has to occur no matter what the length of a sojourn. To gain further insight into short-term sojourns, and to provide an introduction to long-term adjustment, coping mechanisms will be considered.

Coping

The major assumption behind any discussion of cross-cultural adjustment is that difficulties which demand coping responses are normal and expected. While the view may once have existed that only poorly adjusted people have problems, it is no longer perceived as representative of reality. With the assumption of normalcy as a starting point, Seelye and Wasilewski (1979) identified five types of coping processes or strategies. Interestingly, after interviewing 200 sojourners, they found that 75 percent used three or more strategies to meet different demands at different times. Coping is not a one-strategy-for-each-person phenomenon. Rather, people have a repertoire of strategies from which they are able to draw.

The basic difficulty is that sojourners are faced with problems for which they have no familiar response. If they use the strategy of *nonacceptance* (also called *avoidance*), sojourners simply behave as they would in their own country. They refuse to spend extra time and effort learning host norms. The second process is *substitution*. Sojourners learn the response judged most appropriate by hosts and behave accordingly. *Addition,* on the other hand, refers to a more selective use of one's knowledge. Sojourners make a judgment regarding appropriateness of behavior in different situations, and then behave either as they would at home or according to host country norms. For instance, they might behave one way with fellow nationals and another way with hosts. If sojourners choose to use the strategy known as *synthesis,* they combine and integrate elements from different response patterns. Examples are easiest to see in material aspects of culture such as clothing or food. A person might combine elements of dress from two cultures and wear a sari along with a colorful American blouse (Seelye & Wasilewski, 1979). Finally, *resynthesis* (also called *creation/innovation*) refers to an original integration of ideas not found in either culture. This strategy demands a nonethnocentric attitude since no one culture can be looked upon as having *the* standard of excellence. Further, resynthesis involves risk since the sojourner never knows if the response will be effective. By definition, the person stands alone. If other people could be easily consulted regarding appropriateness, the response is not original.

Seelye and Wasilewski made a point of emphasizing that the five strategies do not form a hierarchy. One is not considered better than another. Sojourners should draw on different strategies at different times, and the use of one which seems sophisticated may be wrong in a specific situation. At times, the nonacceptance strategy will be best. Businessmen who work in countries where kickbacks and bribes are an acceptable part of negotiations may refuse to participate, realizing that the company's long-range interests are best served by noninvolvement. In more commonplace situations, sojourners should refuse to pay for services not rendered, exactly the response they would make in their own country. According to the norms in some places, hosts are expected to take advantage of sojourners *and* lose respect for them when there is no retaliation. Sojourners are foolish if they search for some kind of creative resynthesis in the presence of landlords demanding triple what they would charge their fellow countrymen.

The processes can be best understood as people use them during different types of sojourns. Suppose an American businesswoman is in charge of negotiations between her company and one owned by Japanese entrepreneurs. She wants to introduce an innovative marketing scheme and has to make it acceptable to both her countrymen and the Japanese hosts. She encounters difficulties persuading people that her ideas are worthwhile. If she copes through nonacceptance, she simply tries to persuade the Japanese in the same manner she uses with her countrymen. If she substitutes, she learns negotiation styles familiar to the Japanese and also uses them with her countrymen. Or, she might cope through addition and use one style with the Japanese, the other with Americans. If she synthesizes, she combines elements of the two styles and uses them with both groups. For instance, Japanese prefer to discuss matters prior to a well-attended meeting. Disagreements are aired in private and incorporated into the proposal prior to approval by the entire group. Since there is no public disagreement, there is no loss of face. Americans, on the other hand, are familiar with the give-and-take of discussions held in a public forum. The businesswoman might combine these approaches, perhaps feeling that some Americans have been in Japan long enough to have adopted the host country style, and that some Japanese have seen certain advantages in public discussions.

In a resynthesis, the businesswoman might design an entirely new approach to the problem. For instance, she may decide that people are *not* hesitant about accepting her marketing policy and that roadblocks are due to past frustrations concerning decisions on other people's pet projects. Americans consider Japanese slow and unresponsive; Japanese consider Americans insensitive and overly eager to implement ill-considered proposals. The businesswoman, then, may introduce programs which appeal to members of the two groups in different ways but which have the goal of increasing communication. Arrangements could be made for people to visit each other's companies. Face-to-face relations could be established, which are very important to the Japanese. In addition, flow charts of typical Japanese and American decision-making processes could be prepared, which Americans familiar with this pictorial approach will appreciate. There is a risk involved since the businesswoman cannot be sure that the program will be effective.

While various strategies should not be given labels of "good" or "bad" without extensive knowledge of individuals, situations, tasks, and organizations, some are possible only with extensive knowledge of another culture. Much of the relevant knowledge can be obtained only if sojourners spend a great deal of time living in another country. Additional problems must be faced as sojourners become more sophisticated and feel more "at home" in the host society.

Adjustment over time: the W-shaped hypothesis

After examining the adjustment processes of sojourners over time, Gullahorn and Gullahorn (1963) proposed that the ups and downs of people's self-reported satisfaction follow a predictable pattern. Pictorially, the adjustment resembles a W-shaped curve:

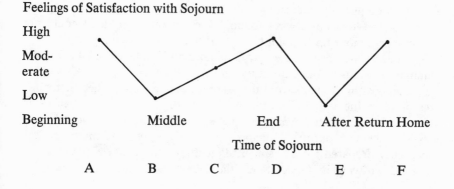

The W-shaped curve has been frequently cited as a good way of examining adjustment. It is one of the few concepts shared by virtually all professionals involved in cross-cultural programs, rivaling only "culture shock" as a well-known starting point for analyzing sojourners' experiences. Other researchers have given clever names to areas of the curve which summarize typical adjustment patterns. Trifonovitch (1977a) calls point A the "honeymoon stage" during which excitement and enthusiasm with new experiences leads to tremendous feelings of satisfaction. Point B is when "hostility" begins since sojourners become frustrated with an inability to solve problems in familiar ways. They begin to lash out at hosts and, in general, make nuisances of themselves. At point C, "humor" becomes evident as sojourners begin to adjust. They can laugh at the mistakes they used to make and can accept new challenges with more lightheartedness. When they reach point D, they feel "at home," comfortable, and able to meet day-to-day problems with efficiency. Part of the upswing in mood may be due to their excitement about returning home. At point E, however, "reverse culture shock" is experienced. People feel confused and alienated; they should fit into the home culture but do not. Friends have married or moved away; reorganization has taken place at work; one's neighborhood has had a facelift; and not everyone wants to listen to new ideas learned during the sojourn. Again, there may be a period during which people lash out at fellow countrymen who just happen to be nearby. The returnees learn to cope with these problems, however, and at point F have made a "readjustment."

The W-shaped curve is a compelling depiction of people's experience, the sort of vivid image reviewed in chapter 4 which remains in people's minds. Given the complexity of sojourners' experiences, the curve provides a port in a massive storm. Unfortunately, it may not be very accurate. Klineberg and Hull (1979) analyzed the long-term experiences of foreign students and sojourning professors, and they could find no evidence for a W-shaped curve. Reported experiences varied greatly, marked much more by individual differences than by a set of responses generalizable to many people. An especially interesting result was that the downswing from point A to point B was not always found, which means that there could not possibly be a move up to point C. Half of the picture is eliminated.

It is interesting to speculate why Gullahorn and Gullahorn (1963) could summarize results through the curve and Klineberg and Hull (1979) could not. One possibility stems from the time of data collection. The first study was done in the late 1950s, the second in the late 1970s. Changes in sojourner preparation have taken place. As previously mentioned, professionals *know about* the W-shaped curve. Quite possibly, sojourners are now better prepared for adjustment difficulties and do not experience the severe downswing in mood. Since the 1950s, hosts have become more accustomed to sojourners. They may not react to sojourner mistakes so intensely and may even make minor modifications to accommodate them. Further, as more sojourners travel abroad, there are more countrymen to consult during difficult periods and more professional resources, such as foreign student advisers' offices.

A more technical analysis of why the W-shaped curve may or may not exist must deal with individual differences. Possibly, people's responses *do* follow the curve, but they occur at such different times that they cannot be captured during a research study. This general point needs a specific example for clarification. Assume a group of foreign students arrives in the host country on October 1. When should the first interview take place? For some sojourners, a downswing may begin on October 5, for others on the 15th, and for still others on November 1. If the researcher interviews on only one date, some important results will be missed. The researcher might interview a number of times to assure that important experiences for each sojourner are documented, but limitations on time, resources, and sojourner patience make implementation of this option difficult.

Many cross-cultural trainers have used the W-shaped curve by presenting it to experienced sojourners and asking them to comment. Many sojourners say it is a good tool and helps them to understand their experiences. They can label points A–F with their own terms and can note the key experiences which led to ups and downs in satisfaction. This fact is difficult to reconcile with the Klineberg-Hull results which were based on an attempt to find the curve after unstructured interviews. There is one obvious difference: in the first example, sojourners look at the curve and recall experiences. In the second, sojourners recall experiences and the researcher determines how they can best be summarized. Perhaps the reminder of the curve guides thinking more than it should; or perhaps the uniqueness of individual reports cannot possibly be summarized, after the fact, by any sort of oversimplified graph.

At the present time, the W-shaped curve has an uncertain existence. Enough has been learned, however, by simply asking if the curve is real. Future research should focus on when, where, and why the curve may be real, for which sojourners, given what types of preparation. More specifically, future research will undoubtedly focus on adjustment's relation with other variables such as (a) individual traits and skills, (b) range of situations which must be faced, (c) amount of change demanded in different countries, (d) presence or absence of support groups during the early stages of a sojourn, (e) length and adequacy of training programs, and (f) amount of time spent in the host country. During long sojourns, people often have additional choices to make since they can use the various coping strategies already reviewed. Some strategies involve responses which would be used in the home country, some which are familiar to hosts, and some are creative combinations. As they become more skillful, they begin to cope with the demands necessary for long-term adjustment.

PROCESSES IN LONG-TERM ADJUSTMENT

Since different types of sojourners have different goals and spend varying lengths of time in another culture, one explanation of adjustment is not likely to fit all. The same segment of time will likewise not be "long-term" for all people, although many experienced observers (e.g., Brein & David, 1971) feel that sojourns of two or three years have qualities which distinguish them from shorter visits. Given that amount of time, people must cope with enough everyday problems to force some kind of significant adjustment above and beyond their familiar ways of behaving in their own culture. Individual differences, of course, are important. One person, on a three-month sojourn, might be asked by hosts to participate in many activities, while another might remain an outsider after two or three years.

Still, even acknowledging the nature and blessings of individual differences, broad but helpful statements can be made which help in understanding long-term adjustment. One approach is to look at the type of sojourners who are motivated to make a complete adjustment, and then to examine those aspects of their lives which distinguish them from other types of sojourners. Immigrants who accept a melting pot ideal are motivated to make a complete adjustment if they choose to accept the host culture while not retaining ties with their first culture. Their jobs, food, language, friends, leisure time activities, and (over a period of time) kinship ties are all found in the host society. If they are successful, they not only adjust completely but are totally assimilated (Berry, 1977) into the host society. Although there is a tendency for specialists in cross-cultural studies to decry this type of assimilation, no absolute value judgments should be imposed. Immigrants who decide to assimilate should receive the same respect as immigrants who choose to retain aspects of their first culture. Returning to individual differences, the adjustment and mental well-being of some people is undoubtedly facilitated by assimilation rather than half-hearted attempts at cultural pluralism. On the other hand, cultural integration (Berry, 1977), in which members of the dominant majority within any society accept and encourage pluralism, leads to better adjustment among other people. Both assimilation and pluralism can become molds into which some people are unwisely forced.

A complete adjustment is marked by four developments which involve peoples' beliefs, attitudes, values, and behaviors: cultural adjustment, identification, cultural competence, and role enculturation (Taft, 1977).

Each has a subjective component, referring to people's self-perception about their lives; and an objective component, referring to easily seen behaviors and to hosts' perceptions.

Cultural adjustment

The subjective component of cultural adjustment involves sojourners' feelings of comfort in the host society. Further, it includes a feeling that one is "at home" in the society and is not a total outsider. Cultural adjustment also refers to smooth integration of personality with culture. If an individual has an achievement motive, ideally, there are opportunities in the host culture which allow satisfaction of the need. If the person is affiliative, then, ideally, there are opportunities to meet, interact with, and help others. This aspect is frequently a source of difficulty, especially for women. They might want to secure employment or engage in social service activities, but a society's norms may dictate that acceptable roles for women are limited to caring for children and cooking for husbands.

Objective indicators refer to judgments by hosts that the individual is aware of appropriate behaviors, is able to maintain cordial relations with people, and, in general, knows how "to behave like one of us." Other indications are that the individual has acquired a means of livelihood in the host culture and is a member of groups which can assist in times of need. These indicators bring to mind many of the ideas considered in chapters 5 and 8: cultural adjustment is dependent upon establishing group ties and successfully completing one's task-related goals.

Identification

Subjective feelings of identification include acceptance of new reference groups in the host culture. Importantly, people have the feeling that they belong in the new society. I remember discussions with a friend about his decision to relinquish citizenship in the United States and emigrate to Israel. Although he was not deeply religious, he was very concerned about the future of Jewish people. He had visited Israel for long periods and had led adolescents on the sorts of short-term sojourns discussed previously. He was aware of the problems stemming from rampaging inflation, unemployment, overcrowded cities, difficulties in finding adequate housing, and volatile relations with neighboring countries. He said, "I realize my decision does not make much sense in terms of a tote board of plusses and minuses. All I can say is that when I'm there, I feel as if I belong." There is also a feeling that a person's own fate is linked with the host culture and that the individual and hosts have shared concerns. The success of hosts becomes important to the sojourners. Objective indicators include the granting of citizenship, which is a very time consuming and difficult procedure in some countries. Other objective indicators are specific to certain countries. In democracies, people who are observed voting and who are chosen by peers to fill leadership positions are said to be closely identified with the host society. In some places, housing is so expensive and difficult to buy that, once a person purchases a home, observers conclude that (s)he wants to become part of the host society. Sending one's children to schools typical of the host society rather than to one patterned after those in one's home country is another indication. Finally, sojourners can become integrated into group activities in which there is a clear common fate for all members. Examples are negotiations for a union in one's workplace, or the upgrading of one's neighborhood through group action.

In the case of immigrants, Taft (1977) found that indications of cultural adjustment and identification were closely associated. People who demonstrated cultural adjustment felt identified with the host society, and vice versa. Other types of sojourners, who have a clear date in mind for their return home, can undoubtedly demonstrate cultural adjustment without identification. They can feel comfortable and at home without concluding that the host country is where they belong.

Cultural competence

People's own feelings of competence are based on positive attitudes and self-confidence. Favorable attitudes regarding language learning and increasing one's knowledge base are critical. Many adjustment problems stem from ignorance of basic facts which can be easily learned by people willing to make the effort: where to find housing, how to enroll children in school, and the best ways to meet others. Attitudes and language learning are strongly related. Sojourners with favorable attitudes toward a certain culture learn its language faster than people with unfavorable attitudes (Lambert, 1974). Once people are confident of their language ability and cultural knowledge, they can meet their everyday needs through interaction with hosts in a variety of situations.

Hosts are quick to form conclusions concerning the insider-outsider status of sojourners based on language abilities and shared knowledge. The principle that people in a culture develop an identity by sharing a set of ideas about history, discussed in chapter 2, was also noted by Taft (1977). Americans living abroad are especially prone to negative judgments since, in general, they are charged with knowing little about the history of other countries. Hosts also make judgments based on sojourners' ability to satisfy their needs in a variety of situations without calling special attention to themselves. Once hosts cease behaving in special ways toward obvious outsiders and, instead, react in the same way as they do toward countrymen, one objective test of sojourner adjustment has been passed. An anthropologist once told me, "I knew I had learned the language well enough to do a complex study when members of the culture *stopped* telling me how well I spoke the local dialect."

Competence has received a great deal of attention as a central concept in understanding various types of cross-cultural experiences (Dinges & Duffy, 1979; Smith, 1966). A good general definition has been suggested by Lee (1979).

> Social competence is . . . proposed as a dynamic process that draws on the individual's cognitive, linguistic, and social capabilities. It is the translation of these capabilities into functionally appropriate interpersonal strategies for use in particular situational and/or sociocultural contexts. It implies adaptive as well as assertive action with regard to the environment. It is knowing how to use one's existent knowledge. Social competence is, therefore, the ability to draw on one's capabilities and social knowledge and combine them for *lines of action* or strategies in functionally appropriate ways. Hence, the more lines of action or strategies the individual possesses, the more choices he or she has in dealing with the environment. This in turn gives the individual greater flexibility in responding. As the individual develops, the integration and coordination of these strategies will result in increasingly complex strategies [p. 795].

Key aspects of competence are the number of strategies a person possesses, their complexity, and the number of situations in which they can be used. Cultural competence is a factor in adjustment demanded of all long-term sojourners. People must be able to meet their everyday needs and to achieve their goals if they are to have a meaningful sojourn. This is true whether people plan to return home or remain in the host country as immigrants. Sojourners and hosts might have quite different views of the competence dimension and, like characters in a play by Luigi Pirandello, all be correct. Foreign students might feel competent if they can survive the host university's system of hurdles and attain a degree. They may have no ambitions to interact in the local community and to develop interpersonal skills which are valued by hosts. While the sojourners may be pleased with the accomplishments, outsiders might wonder if the students are being too narrow. Many selection boards I have observed, for instance, would rather give scholarships to applicants with several goals, not just degree attainment. Technical assistance advisers might feel competent if they successfully introduce innovative equipment. Hosts, on the other hand, might object if there was not enough attention given to transferring maintenance skills so that the project could continue after the advisers return home.

Contradictory judgments, then, are often based on differing perceptions of the number of skills a person should have and the number of situations in which they are to be used. More and more, organizations are addressing the problem by carefully specifying what is expected of the various people who participate in cross-cultural contact. Family members who host adolescent sojourners are given carefully prepared lists outlining the responsibilities of all parties. Less technologically developed countries continue to request Peace Corps volunteers but frequently specify the technical skills volunteers should possess and the projects which should be developed. Graduate students in sponsored programs at the East-West Center enter into negotiations specifying what they can expect from Center involvement and what they can contribute. Tapp et al. (1974) have explicitly recommended such specification for members of cross-cultural research teams. Generalizing from recent work done within organizations not specifically concerned with cross-cultural contact but which encourage interaction among people from very different backgrounds (Mirvis and Seashore, 1979), a prediction about future guidelines can be made. The agreements participants reach will not only specify expectations but will also detail the problems which may arise and methods of coping with them. As more and more people document typical problems faced during cross-cultural contact, these forecasts will become more sophisticated.

Role acculturation

For convenience in discussing the complex factor of role acculturation, adjustment into a culturally monistic society will first be considered. Subsequently, differences between monism and cultural pluralism will be noted.

Subjective indicators of role acculturation center around people's attitudes toward the host culture and the self-perceived appropriateness of their behavior. There is an increasing sense of convergence between one's own attitudes and values and those held by a large number of hosts. People feel that they are behaving in appropriate ways, consistent with beliefs about their own personalities, by accepting role models valued by hosts. Put another way, people do not feel as if they are behaving in a certain manner only because they are being forced or because the actions contribute to a temporarily convenient adjustment. For instance, in cultures where individualism and achievement are valued, sojourners are said to be role acculturated when they internalize beliefs about the importance of these traits. If the societal norms reject pluralism, people begin to accept monistic attitudes, believing that it is good to have a unified country without the distraction of multiple factions drawing energy away from a common good. Objective indicators include actual role behaviors easily observable by hosts. These can include markers such as dress, food habits, and exclusive use of the local language. Slightly less obvious cues might be gestures typical of hosts or use of slang terms. Full assimilation is demonstrated by a "blending" into society such that hosts unfamiliar with an individual's history do not think of the person as having lived anywhere else. If hosts make comments such as the following, full role acculturation is suggested: "Is he a recent immigrant? I never would have known! I suppose he does have an accent, but I never really noticed until you pointed it out."

Pluralism is such an important topic that it will be covered in a later section within this chapter. For the present discussion, a few relationships between pluralism and role acculturation will be mentioned. In those societies where pluralism is tolerated or encouraged, there are additions to and modifications of the list of indicators. People begin to feel that *some* of their attitudes and values converge with those commonly held by members of the dominant majority group. These might include attitudes concerning how people are ideally advanced from one position to another within a corporation, or the type of neighborhood in which a person prefers to live. At the same time, a different set of attitudes and values may be comfortably expressed in settings strongly influenced by minority group members, such as the interest groups a person joins or the religious beliefs a person possesses. Even within these general areas, there can be mixes. If a person is accustomed to collective action toward group-defined goals, rather than individualistic achievement, modifications might be made in the workplace to accommodate this type of preference. Objective indicators such as dress, food, and language use follow from these choices. People dress appropriately and use certain language conventions during their hours at work and when expressing their religious beliefs. While the external manifestations of attitudes and beliefs may be very different in the two settings, there is no inconsistency in a pluralistic society and no pressure to change.

With the exception, again, of certain immigrants whose adjustment will be facilitated by accepting monism, most sojourners will not experience a complete role acculturation. Rather, they will adopt certain roles consistent with their goals but will not necessarily change old behavior patterns or even bring newly developed role behaviors back to their home countries. At times, to be sure, the role acculturation has to be quite sophisticated. Technical advisers have to be sensitive to the part they are playing in the web of host community interpersonal relationships. They must understand how their role *could* interfere with the power base possessed by certain influential hosts and how project sabotage could be the response to mistakes. Foreign graduate students must adopt roles which increase the chances of success within their academic discipline. Certain professors have more influence and can offer more assistance than others. If a student accepts the role of assistant to a key professor, many adjustment problems are automatically solved. If a student becomes associated with an untenured professor who may be asked to leave the campus next year, additional problems are created. Other professors to be avoided publish students' work as their own, give inadequate and delayed feedback to student proposals, and are so negatively judged by colleagues that their assistants become tainted by association. The cues needed to detect dangerous professors are often so subtle that *host* country students miss them.

In making these complex judgments, sojourners risk difficulties when they return home. Although more documentation would ideally be available, a number of observers have commented that sojourners who make the most successful adjustment may have a "reverse culture shock" when they return home (Bochner, 1973; Brislin & Pedersen, 1976). Sojourners may have adopted new roles successfully which are not welcome in their own country. Tendler (1975) pointed out that, because of the unique aspects of every field situation and the distance between an overseas assignment and the home office, technical assistance advisers have to make major decisions which are often beyond those required in their job descriptions. Yet, to accomplish the goals of complex projects, hosts often ask difficult questions and expect precise answers. If they are successful, advisers undoubtedly enjoy the increased status which decision makers command. Upon returning to an assignment in the home office, however, they may find that another decision maker is about as welcome as a plague. A similar disappointment may await diplomats on United Nations assignments who become accustomed to greater amounts of information, less protocol, and more contact with experienced colleagues. Foreign students who accept the role of independent and creative thinker, valued in many technologically developed countries, may find that their newly developed skills are not rewarded in their home country (Kashioki, 1978). These problems are eased in societies which value pluralism and in organizations which can harness the diverse talents of their members.

ADJUSTMENT IN PLURALISTIC SOCIETIES

Although inadequate evidence exists to be certain, the use of many coping styles and several long-term adjustment strategies may be easier, less stressful, and more effective in pluralistic societies. In contrast to a monistic society, where a single set of norms is enforced, pluralistic societies encourage or at least tolerate heterogeneity with respect to the values and customs of different groups. Instead of a homogeneous society marked by a single set of acceptable beliefs about the country's history, religious practices, desired skin color, ethnic heritage, and the type of people who can make valued contributions, members of a pluralistic society see worth in variation. Different sets of religious beliefs are tolerated, skin color is not a criterion of mobility, many different ideas can be freely expressed, and a wide range of behaviors are seen as appropriate in meeting everyday needs of food, shelter, clothing, and interpersonal relations. Any one sojourner, then, will likely experience an easier adjustment to a pluralistic than to a monistic society. There is more likely to be a match between what the sojourner brings and what some segment of the society values, and more tolerance for any set of strategies and styles which (s)he chooses to use.

Berry (1977) has suggested that pluralistic societies can be identified by the presence of three markers. If answers to the following questions can be answered "yes," pluralism is indicated.

1. Is there retention of people's ethnic identity with visible cues such as dress, language, clubs, and even special schools?
2. Do people in the various ethnic groups, and members of any dominant majority group, have positive attitudes toward each other and engage in frequent interaction?
3. Do members of the various groups have a choice about the answers to questions one and two? In other words, are people allowed a choice, or does a dominant majority group or governing body impose its will?

There are eight patterns of affirmative and positive answers to the questions, and Berry gives labels to the types of societies indicated by each pattern. For instance, an absence of identity retention, together with positive relations and free choice, marks assimilation into a melting pot. If only the choice indicator is changed from "yes" to "no," then a forced "pressure cooker" type of assimilation is present. The type of society marked by three "yes" answers is called "integration" by Berry (1977).

> In this decision pattern both ethnic retention and positive intergroup relations are valued by the ethnic group(s). The free and regular association of culturally-distinct groups is motivated by some mutual (national) set of goals, which is sufficient to maintain positive relations. Because the choice is free, the individual is not obliged to retain his own ethnicity, but could theoretically move from one group to another. Switzerland is an obvious example of this pattern [p. 20].

Integration is probably a goal which will never be completely achieved. There are inherent conflicts in any attempt to meet all three criteria. If ethnic group members maintain their identity through clubs, schools, or neighborhoods, there may be exclusion of people not sharing the same real or imagined heritage. Which aspects of society can be sources of ethnic identity, and which should be open to all people? In Hawaii, Japanese-Americans have traditionally held many positions of responsibility in the

Department of Education. The percentage of jobs they hold in the educational system is far beyond the percentage of Japanese-Americans in Hawaii. Education may be a source of ethnic pride, and it undoubtedly was a means of obtaining upward social mobility, but children from Samoa and the Philippines are prevented from seeing members of their own groups in prestigious positions.

Several other aspects of Berry's typology bring up interesting problems. If free choice is encouraged, then those people who hold monistic attitudes must be respected. From what evidence exists, sizeable numbers of people prefer a single set of values and behaviors. Despite the tremendous exposure to ideas about black ethnic identity during the 1960s and 1970s, Lampe (1979) found that 9 percent of a sample of black college students in the United States agreed with this statement: "The ultimate goal of the country regarding ethnic groups is to have all citizens share the common culture of our English founders and developers." Nine percent may not seem like a large number until another figure is calculated: the number agreeing with the question is almost one out of ten people. Elections have been decided on the basis of much smaller numbers. Even if this figure is dismissed as a manifestation of black humor (and other evidence presented by Lampe suggests that the figure is real), other results are worthy of examination. Twenty-four percent of black students felt that the primary purpose of their college's ethnic studies program should be to "inform the minority groups about the majority group and prepare them to fit in and compete successfully [p. 181]."

The importance of choice can also be seen in the work of Pruitt (1978) on sojourners from Africa living and studying in the United States. Adjustment was better predicted by assimilation into the mainstream, dominant-white society than by identification with black Americans. Although assimilation is not defined in the exact terms suggested by Berry, the issue of choice is still quite important. Sojourners from Africa who participated in the following types of activities with white Americans reported less stressful adjustment and more satisfaction with their cross-cultural experience. Collectively, the following activities constitute Pruitt's index of assimilation: (a) spending leisure time with people, (b) feeling free to share thoughts, (c) willingness to marry, (d) liking American culture, with special affinity toward values and ways of life, (e) liking American food, and (f) having contact with American families.

The choice in favor of assimilation was probably due to the sojourners' goals. Most wanted to attain a degree at an American university, and they perceived knowledge of "white culture" as more relevant. Even though people concerned about the progress of minority groups might feel that other goals are equally worthwhile, pluralism demands that the single-minded pursuit of a university degree be respected.

The value placed on positive or tolerant intergroup relations is sometimes difficult to reconcile with free choice. If people are free to choose in a pluralistic society, does this mean that they should be able to discriminate against out-group members? If government officials make laws requiring that people be nondiscriminatory in their behavior, is this a form of paternalism? Evidence from research provides no answers since the issues involved are ethical. Many behavioral scientists (Clark, 1979; Williams, 1964) have argued for policies which place human dignity ahead of political pressures. By no means should the policies be quickly formulated. As discussed in chapter 7, input from the people affected by decisions improves outcomes. Wisdom is added, roadblocks are foreseen, and people's energies are harnessed through participation. Still, once the long and hard work of devising policies has been completed, enforcement must be forthright. A major conclusion from years of experience and accumulated research is that integration is not as destructive and difficult as critics would have us believe. Progress *has* been made in the United States over the last 30 years, as it has in other parts of the world (e.g., Rhodesia, the Middle East). In any one arena, administrators can make it clear that intergroup tolerance is the basis of policy. In schools, teachers can be told that the principal's ratings of job performance will include contributions toward tolerant relations. At a slightly higher administrative level, district superintendents can examine the progress made by school principals. In industries, foremen can be given monetary incentives based on their ability to integrate workgroups. In making decisions about promoting division managers, company presidents can use contributions toward tolerance as one criterion. Summarizing observations about the armed forces and various industries in the United States and Great Britain, for instance, Richmond (1973) concluded: ". . . studies have shown that a clear and forceful managerial policy against discrimination is effective in achieving satisfactory work relations between whites and Negroes [p. 295]."

The value placed on positive relations affects people's ability to make important contributions. Earlier, a tentative generalization was made concerning the relative ease of adjustment into pluralistic societies. One piece of evidence in support of the generalization, admittedly more metaphoric than direct in its application, deals with the readjustment of sojourners into home country organizations. Myer (1979) found that people who had studied in the United States encountered a variety of reactions after returning to their jobs or accepting new positions. Some were able to use knowledge gained during their sojourns and some were not. The factors which differentiated people centered on organization acceptance. Put simply, some returnees found that they were encouraged to use their education and some encountered resistance. Further, some felt that employees expected people to find innovative solutions to problems and that co-workers were eager to consider new ideas. These factors are reminiscent of pluralism: acceptance of diverse ideas, appreciation of different types of experiences, and value placed on ability to contribute rather than on superficial status markers obtained at birth.

EFFECTS OF A SOJOURN, AND RESEARCH DIFFICULTIES

The ability to contribute to organizations in one's country represents a benefit which may accrue to sojourners. While others have been mentioned in various chapters, it is useful to discuss the potential benefits in one place. Another important topic, however, is the difficulty of documenting a sojourn's effects. Research on outcomes has been weak because of methodological difficulties which are nearly impossible to solve. The ideal research design would require a program director to interest 100 people in a sojourn and then to randomly select 50 people for the actual experience. Later, the people who had the sojourn would be compared to those who did not. Various measures could be used to assess changes in attitudes, values, skills, and behaviors. Because of random selection, the only difference between people is the experience, so causal inferences from sojourn to effects can be made. The objection to this method, of course, is ethical. No past or foreseeable program will be able to interest large numbers of people and then randomly select a smaller number. Even if random selection *might be* the fairest method, there will always be pressures to select on some other basis. Examples are availability of money, past records of individual achievement, kinship relation to past sojourners sponsored by a certain program, or the presence of traits discussed in chapter 3. Anytime a researcher presents evidence on program effects, then, someone will always be able to ask this question. "How can you say that it is the sojourn experience which led to the effects? Perhaps the people were competent to start with and they matured and/or learned during the program just as they would if they spent the time in their own country." This question cannot be answered to anyone's complete satisfaction.

In attempting to formulate better answers and to improve research designs, approximations to the ideal have been made. The single best study of sojourn effects was reported by Kagitcibasi (1978). He studied young students from Turkey who spent a school year in the United States sponsored by the American Field Service exchange program. All 88 students chosen for the program were given questionnaires and asked about their experiences. Measures were taken before and after the sojourn, as well as two years after the participants returned to Turkey. Sojourners were compared with students who did not participate in the program and who remained in Turkey. These comparison students were of similar age, previous education, family background, sex distribution, and socioeconomic status. They were questioned at approximately the same times as the sojourners.

This is a strong design given the realities of doing research in real situations rather than in contrived laboratory settings (see Cook and Campbell, 1976, for an excellent discussion of field research). By comparing sojourners before and after their experiences, suggestions about changes can be made. By comparing these results with measures taken from the other group, changes stemming from the cross-cultural experience can be contrasted to changes due to maturity or simply to the passage of time. Note, however, that there are other possible explanations, albeit complex. Assume there are changes in a positive direction. It is possible that some concerned parents encouraged their children to participate, and that these parents *would have* provided stimulating experiences even if their children had not been chosen. Note that there was no control, when developing the comparison group, for parental concern. Other problems in forming comparison groups have been discussed by Brislin (1976b).

Does all this sound rather dull? It may, yet if programs for sojourners are to see increased support in the future, I believe that questions like those presented above must receive greater attention. People who might lend support will want to know, "What are the advantages? Why should I support programs for sojourners rather than other worthy causes?" Collaborations between researchers and administrators, and an appreciation of each others' perspectives, are necessary to answer these questions.

Despite the difficulties, I believe that Kagitcibasi's (1978) results are worth examining. His findings are based on two types of comparisons: (a) between pre- and postsojourn measures for the program participants, and (b) between measures gathered from sojourners and people in the comparison group. When analyses of types (a) and (b) lead to the same results, additional support is lent to conclusions about a sojourn's effects. Only those findings supported by both types of analysis will be presented here. Since these *findings* from one type of sojourn agree with *informed speculations* about general outcomes (Adler, 1977; Hall, 1976; Shaw & McClain, 1979), my suggestion is that the following results form a core set of effects which stem from successful sojourns.

World-mindedness

The clearest finding was that sojourners became more world-minded in their thinking. This means that they became more accepting and tolerant of people from other cultures, and more aware that solutions to important problems demand contributions which transcend national borders. The concept is best explained by examining several of the items with which respondents agreed or disagreed. The response indicative of world-mindedness is given in parentheses (scale from Sampson & Smith, 1957; reprinted in Shaw & Wright, 1967).[1]

- Immigrants should not be permitted to come into our country if they compete with our own workers. (disagree)
- Our country is probably no better than many others. (agree)
- Our country should not participate in any international organization which requires that we give up any of our national rights or freedom of action. (disagree)
- We should teach our children to uphold the welfare of all people everywhere even though it may be against the best interest of our own country. (agree)

Decline in authoritarianism

Although not evident a year after their return, sojourners reported fewer authoritarian tendencies two years after their experience. Such delayed effects have been found by other researchers (J. Watson & Lippitt, 1955), perhaps indicating that sojourners have to reflect upon their experiences over a period of time before reaping all possible beneficial effects. Authoritarianism involves rigid thinking about right and wrong based on one set of standards, a value placed on unquestioning obedience, beliefs about the importance of strict parental discipline, and a distrust of people who are different. Kagitcibasi (1978) concludes that this result supports the "assumption that adjustment to a different culture requires tolerance, flexibility, and open-mindedness, characteristics that do not fit with authoritarian tendencies [p. 149]."

Internal control

Indications of increased feelings of internal control were evident two years after cross-cultural experiences. People who believe in internal control perceive that life's outcomes can be shaped through individual effort. People who believe in external control, on the other hand, perceive that outcomes are due to luck, fate, or chance. Examining the measuring instrument again gives a good idea of what the concept entails. People are asked to read pairs of statements and to select the one which is closest to their own opinion (entire scale in Rotter, 1966).

- The average college student can do little to select the instructors and courses he wants. (external)
- With enough effort a student can select exactly the instructors and courses he wants. (internal)

Sojourners increase their feelings of internal control since they must face and cope with so many new situations. They cannot usually depend on others but, rather, must take responsibility themselves. Since most cope successfully (Abrams, 1978; Klineberg & Hull, 1979), they should experience greater feelings of self-reliance. Sojourners also expressed a decline in "religiosity." Kagitcibasi (1978) treated this finding separately, but a wiser approach is to integrate it with internal control. Although sample items were not given, it appears that only a small part of what *could* be called religiosity was actually measured. Opinions about the influence of religion vs. science and the impact of religion on one's life were tapped. While sojourners showed a decline on this measure, this may be another indicator of internal control rather than the importance of religion, broadly conceived, in their lives.

Achievement values

Since internal control includes feelings that people can influence their destinies through their own efforts, an obvious prediction is that achievement-oriented feelings would increase. Achievement (McClelland & Winter, 1971) refers to (a) setting a reasonable standard of success, not so high as to insure failure but not so low as to guarantee a trivial success; and (b) working toward that standard. The predicted increases were documented only on the later measures, again showing delayed effects. Earlier *declines* in achievement orientation may have been due to postschooling fatigue and a temporary disgust with work. Which of us has not felt this way at one time or another? It should be remembered that sojourners were attending schools in the United States and using a second or foreign language. After returning to Turkey, reacquainting themselves with family and friends, and becoming readjusted to everyday life, they undoubtedly had time to think about their experiences. Greater achievement orientation was one outcome. Achievement demands a realistic outlook on life since workable goals must be established. Alger (1965) found a similar effect among diplomats assigned to the United Nations. After leaving their U.N. posts and returning to their home countries, diplomats felt that they would be able to develop workable policies which would have a greater chance of effectively addressing world problems.

More speculative outcomes

In addition to his careful documentation of selected effects, Kagitcibasi (1978) gathered perceptions of how sojourners *thought* they had changed. While not definitive, the results suggest profitable lines for further inquiry.

> [People's] responses reflected general humanitarian tendencies; less emphasis on social, national, and religious differences, greater tolerance and understanding of people; greater skill, ease, and initiative in interpersonal relations; greater sense of responsibility; more self-control and self-knowledge; greater objectivity and flexibility in thinking, and tolerance of different points of view. It is not clear whether these reported changes were, in fact, the result of sojourn experience. However, the fact that the subjects *attributed* these changes to sojourner experience is important in itself [p. 153].

Other analysts have speculated on effects, and these should be subjected to scrutiny in the future. An excellent area for future research is the careful documentation of a sojourn's effects, and an examination of the following possibilities may provide a starting point.

Creativity

The development of creativity is an intriguing possibility. An individual may draw from experiences in different cultures and combine ideas into a creative synthesis. Creativity refers to new and original conceptualizations which are infrequently suggested by others. At the same time, creative solutions satisfy the demands of a specific problem or meet the demands of specific situations. Creativity is not bizarreness.

Many great artists have developed creative products after participating in a cross-cultural experience. Paul Gauguin lived for many years in Tahiti and later incorporated various images in his paintings. Anton Dvořak visited the United States, learned themes from American folk music, and included variations of them in his "New World Symphony." In fact, he was so skillful that he may have donated a theme which has entered the American folk tradition. The tune for "Going Home," a well-known black spiritual, may have been collected by Dvořak, or he may have written it. If the latter is the case, it shows that he was able to learn the new musical forms so well that he could make a contribution which is now considered traditional. Henry James wrote specifically about the experiences of Americans who chose to live for long periods of time in Great Britain. Mark Twain (as analyzed by McCormack, 1980) experienced life in Hawaii as a liberation from bonds that stifled his creative potential. Contrasts between

Hawaii and parts of the United States he knew allowed Twain to look upon his past with a fresh perspective. After his cross-cultural experience, he wrote his most successful novels.

More commonly, returning students have been able to incorporate their cross-cultural experience into coursework, especially the preparation of term papers and theses. They bring a novel perspective to their analyses which is bound to please professors accustomed to more parochial treatments. As another example, technical assistance advisers have increased long-term acceptance of innovations by combining ideas from their own and other cultures. In the Philippines, members of some rural communities are accustomed to presenting short plays to entertain each other. Technical assistance advisers have information, based on analyses done in their own countries, which they may want to communicate. Instead of passing out leaflets or using the mass media, one adviser wrote skits which incorporated the information and encouraged villagers to perform them during regularly scheduled entertainment periods.

Multiculturality

After an intense cross-cultural experience, people may be able to identify with cultures other than their own. In developing the concept of "multicultural man," Adler (1977) suggested that successful sojourners have a number of qualities which distinguish them from people tied to the culture into which they were born. Multicultural people (a) are adaptive when faced with difficulties and can interact in many situations regardless of the culture in which they find themselves; (b) are continually undergoing personal transitions since they are always finding new challenges in the different situations. This process, of course, can lead to discomfort since people will not always find a fit between themselves and new situations; and (c) can look at their own culture from the perception of an outsider. Again, this can sometimes be uncomfortable because of both the facts one finds and the sense of homelessness which an outsider can feel.

Multicultural people also share knowledge concerning a number of important ideas. According to my observations, successful sojourners can analyze these concepts objectively and can give examples from their own experience. Adler's (1977) three ideas provide a basis for discussion and even friendship formation among sojourners regardless of the country in which one's cross-cultural experience took place.

1. Every culture or system has its own internal coherence, integrity, and logic. Every culture is an intertwined system of values and attitudes, beliefs and norms that give meaning and significance to both individuals and collective identity.

2. No one culture is inherently better or worse than another. All cultural systems are equally valid as variations on the human experience.
3. All persons are, to some extent, culturally bound. Every culture provides the individual with some sense of identity, some regulations of behavior, and some sense of personal place in the scheme of things [p. 31].

To his credit, Adler did not stop at listing the positive aspects of multiculturality. He considered such negative outcomes as the inability to differentiate the important from the unimportant within a culture; a diffuseness of identity when sojourners react to various ideal conceptualizations of the individual; a loss of personal authenticity; becoming a gadfly or a dilettante; and mocking people who are perceived as unblessed with multiculturalness. In other parts of his analysis, however, Adler may have confused some clichés of the mid-1970s with substance. While discussing four case studies of multicultural people, he used terms like "considers the world to be his home," "lives an ascetic and 'feeling' style of life," and "still very much a disciple of his [Indian mystic] teacher [p. 33]." The 1980s will, undoubtedly, bring new clichés, every bit as boring, which must be carefully examined before substantive conclusions about a desirable quality such as multiculturality are made.

Analyzing related ideas, Lambert (1974) feels that culture contact programs can add to a person's repertoire of attitudes and skills. He analyzed bilingual education programs and developed the concepts of "additive bilingualism" and "additive biculturalism." He recognized the importance of the value which society places on the additional skills which the programs encourage.

. . . knowing Afrikaans and English in South Africa, Hebrew and English in New York and Israel, or French as well as English for English-speaking Canadian children would in each case be adding a second, socially relevant language to one's repertoire of skills. In no case would the learning of the second language portend the dropping or the replacement of the other as would typically be the case for French-Canadians or Spanish-Americans developing high-level skills in English. We might refer to these as examples of an *additive* form of bilingualism and contrast it with a more *subtractive* form experienced by many ethnic minority groups who because of national educational policies and social pressures of various sorts are forced to put aside their ethnic language for a national language [p. 31].

His arguments for additive biculturality are similar. When two or more cultures are valued within a society, people from one may feel motivated to learn the language of, and to pursue opportunities in, the other. In doing so, they add to their lives and, consequently, reap benefits from different parts of society. This conclusion is supported by the work of Kim (1978) who analyzed the experiences of Korean immigrants in Chicago. Kim studied the relation between the Korean community and other parts of society dominated by the white majority. Knowledge about, and interaction in, the dominant society did not interfere with people's feelings toward the ethnic community. People were able to retain loyalties toward both. Further, people who had friends in the dominant group were not seen as undesirable by other Koreans.

Cultural mediators

If people develop a multicultural orientation, they can act as guides for new sojourners. More generally, they can mediate between cultures by creating opportunities for monocultural individuals to communicate with counterparts in other countries. At times, this role is formalized, as with foreign student advisers on American campuses or simultaneous interpreters in multinational organizations. In other cases, the role is more informal. Evidence for the importance of informal mediators was provided by Bochner (1973) who interviewed long-term sojourners from Asia sponsored by the Fulbright-Hays program and the East-West Center. After returning home and establishing themselves in good jobs, people were often given the additional assignment of working with international visitors. They might act as interpreters, give an orientation to the organization, make sure the visitor was comfortable, and so forth. Employers undoubtedly felt that previous sojourners would be good mediators since they obviously had foreign language skills and could empathize with people from other cultures.

Cross-cultural researchers act as mediators since they incorporate knowledge about other cultures into general theory meant to explain human behavior. Historically, they have modified and improved theories, which were usually developed in one or a few parts of the world, by incorporating information from other cultures (Klineberg, 1980). Here, the mediation is between the general theory and behavior in other cultures, both of which are well known to the researchers. Technical assistance advisers also mediate in discovering the best ways to import another country's technology without damaging a culture.

Other speculative outcomes include those traits and skills, reviewed in chapter 3, which are predictive of success. Even though previous research and analysis has regarded certain qualities as desirable in the *selection* of people, they also may be developed during a sojourn. A linear type of model is undoubtedly an oversimplification: certain traits and skills are not the direct cause of successful sojourns, and successful cross-cultural experiences do not cause the development of other traits and skills. Rather, there are interactions and feedback loops, and an especially important consideration is the strengthening of qualities which are possessed prior to a sojourn. Hence, a number of qualities previously labeled (for convenience only) as "predictive" can also be considered by researchers interested in outcomes. In my view, prime qualities include strength of personality, empathy, problem-solving ability, language skills, knowledge of subject matter, and taking advantage of opportunities to learn.

RECOMMENDATIONS FOR INCREASING SOJOURNER SATISFACTION

Given the considerable knowledge or at least informed speculation about adjustment, coping, and positive effects, recommendations for increasing the probability of satisfying sojourns should be available. Indeed they are, and the target of recommendations has been administrators who have an influence on sponsored programs. Some of the best work in this area has been done by Herbert Kelman (with Steinitz, 1963; Kelman & Ezekiel, 1970) who worked with adult technical specialists, well established in their home countries, who were participants in an advanced training program in the United States. Based on my work with programs for cross-cultural researchers (Brislin, 1977; Triandis, 1980), I feel that his recommendations are worthy of careful study. Kelman and his colleagues found seven factors which related to sojourner satisfaction; I have reworded them slightly to form six guidelines. Recommendations for carefully prepared orientation programs and effective support services (e.g., housing, visas, money exchange) have been made several times throughout this book and will not be repeated here.

1. Relevance of the experience to the participant's specific professional concerns should be emphasized. Advisers can take steps to insure that participants communicate their background, concerns, goals, and needs. Often, this step demands the skills of an experienced facilitator since sojourners are sometimes extremely bashful about expressing themselves, especially if they have to communicate in their second or third language. Experience has demonstrated that sojourners want to feel individualized, not as part of a mass. An easy, inexpensive, and workable way of doing this is to encourage sojourners to talk about themselves. Efforts like this pay great dividends since they give status to sojourners (point 6, below) and begin the beneficial practice of encouraging personal contributions (point 3, below).

2. Sojourners should be advised of the opportunity for colleague-like re-

lationships with counterparts in the host country. As part of their efforts to prepare for the arrival of sojourners, advisers can often make arrangements for contacts between the visitors and potential colleagues. In a university setting, the colleagues might be American students who have spent time abroad, or faculty members who have studied in another country. Often, collegial relationships will emerge from such meetings. Perhaps I can make some speculations at this point, based on personal observations. There are many people who would be willing to spend a good deal of time with sojourners, but they *must be asked*. People enjoy being asked to help out on an important task and consider such requests a compliment. On the other hand, the social stigma associated with walking into an administrator's office and volunteering is just strong enough to keep them away. I recommend that administrators obtain lists of people who have had overseas experience and contact them personally, one by one. Lists could include students and faculty members who have studied abroad; the alumni of sponsored programs for adolescents, who have a surprising loyalty ten years after their sojourn; or businesspeople who have lived in other countries. The personal approach will be far more effective than the questionnaire-and-expression-of-interest method that I've seen in several organizations. The "yes" rate may be 50 percent, but from 10 calls there are now five people helping out.

3. The participants should be given opportunities to make personal contributions, and to help organize the program according to their desires. If participants want to make contributions, they should be encouraged to do so. Using the example of study programs, administrators might be able to design seminars which encourage input from participants. Other sojourners may want to contribute to other aspects of the program, such as its social life or its behind the scenes administration. Some programs allow sojourners to participate fully in the planning of certain segments such as trips, site visits, choice of material to be covered, and guest speakers who might be invited. Any opportunities of this type allow the expression of individual needs. In the type of discussion recommended under point 1, administrators can discover how (and if) the sojourner wants to contribute. It should be remembered that some participants will want to have "personal" input in terms of their contribution to a group with which they feel closely identified. Such a style of "contribution through a group" is common in Japan, for instance (Cathcart & Cathcart, 1976).

4. Choices in activities and arrangements, and opportunities to match choices with interests, should be available to sojourners. The *number* of choices available to sojourners in sponsored programs is not always a problem, although relevance to their home situation has been the target of criticism (Giorgis & Helms, 1978). Preliminary analyses of sojourners'

eventual needs can be made (Heisey, 1977) and options created. So-journers can then pick and choose among the possibilities to best meet their needs. Note that the general theme behind several of these recommendations is that sojourners will be most satisfied if they can personalize their programs and if they can be perceived as unique people by relevant others.

5. The participants should be given opportunities for informal social contacts with host nationals. Variations on this recommendation have been presented several times, yet its importance cannot be overemphasized (Klineberg & Hull ,1979). This principle is especially important during the early days of a program, before sojourners have had time to establish their own social networks. Arrangements do not have to be elaborate: very simple coffee hours or their cultural equivalent are appreciated. Program planners and advisers, who have well-established social relations with large numbers of people, can easily forget that sojourners may not have much to do after the formal program ends each day. Loneliness and bore-dom can then affect participants' learning the following morning when the formal program starts again. If administrators ask themselves, "Do participants have enough to do after the program ends each day, and on weekends?", they will have a good start toward including participants' social needs in the planning of a program.

6. The participants' national and personal status should be enhanced. If the preceding recommendations are taken into account, the issue of so-journers' feelings of status should not become a problem. Many people *can* face loss of status when living in another country. For instance, "college student" is a very high-status role in some countries, but it is not in the United States. Sad to say, many Americans are uncomfortable with people from other countries, and so they do not give very much attention to the visitors. The sojourners, understandably, interpret such behavior as insulting and status reducing.

Further, many people view themselves as representative of their country when traveling abroad, and so derogatory references to one's country are taken as personal affronts. If program planners build in opportunities for people to participate actively, and for people to report on the positive contributions of developments in their countries relevant to the program, feelings of status should be enhanced. One final recommendation, based on my personal experience, regards the negative aspects in these countries. Much can be learned from case studies of failure, corruption, poor or-ganization, and so forth, but examples of these should be put forward by people from the country in which the problem took place. If participants are secure with their status, their presentations of negative cases will cause no threat. Such material will be more profitably analyzed at later, rather than earlier, stages of a program since participants are more likely to be comfortable with their status at the later stages.

Points 5 and 6, concerned with social relations and status, have also received explicit attention from Klineberg and Hull (1979). They attempted to estimate the relative strength of the two factors and, while speculating that social relations is the more important, they admitted that their conclusion could not be thoroughly documented. Further, they argued that both factors are important and have a major effect on sojourner satisfaction and adjustment.

Based on my own experience with programs for cross-cultural researchers and professional educators, I agree with the importance of both factors. The final chapter focuses on other conclusions and speculations I have made based on organizing programs for sojourners, studying the literature, attempting to do research, and talking with others with similar interests and experiences.

SUMMARY

Given an understanding of traits and skills, groups, tasks, situations, and organizations, people's adjustment to other cultures can be analyzed. Adjustment is marked by people's satisfaction, perceived acceptance by hosts, ability to function during everyday activities without stress, and ability to complete assigned tasks.

The process of adjustment refers to *why* and *how* certain behaviors occurred rather than to *what* happened. While not downgrading the importance of the latter, it is essential to understand why people behave as they do in cross-cultural settings and how certain behaviors do or do not contribute to adjustment. Some analysts (e.g., Klein, 1977; Pool, 1965) have approached these issues by studying the processes of short-term adjustment experienced by people on brief sojourns. Others (Taft, 1977) have given greater attention to long-term problems of migrants or people from rural areas who relocate in cities. Knowledge of both short- and long-term processes is essential, especially since people on extended sojourns encounter the short-term problems during the early phases of the cross-cultural experiences.

Four short-term processes have been identified. People who use (1) instrumental adaptation have clear goals they want to accomplish. The sojourn is either a step toward those goals or is a temporary escape from a dedicated grind within one's own country. Other sojourners have a strong (2) social orientation and, consequently, involve themselves in the host culture. Adjustment problems stem from actual or perceived rebuffs from hosts. Some people, of course, effectively combine the instrumental and social orientations. In fact, many sojourners must make both types of adjustment since, in some countries, the ability to complete tasks is dependent upon cordial social relations. Another short-term process centers on the role of (3) ambassador for one's country. People who use this process are willing to share information about their countries but do not exchange intimate details which might lead to the formation of friendships. Social relations are more likely to be developed with fellow countrymen who happen to be living in the same area. When people's goals are blocked, they may adjust through (4) withdrawal. This reaction occurs when people desire cordial relations with hosts but fail to develop them, whether because of shyness, social ineptitude, or host rejection; and when people are unable to accomplish their task goals. Following withdrawal, the negative aspects of the host country are sometimes intensified in people's minds. Upon return to their home country, they may be very vocal in condemning programs for sojourners.

Whatever goals people have, they inevitably must cope with difficulties. While the view may once have existed that only poorly adjusted people have problems on a sojourn, this is no longer a commonly held opinion. Five coping strategies have been identified, and most sojourners use more than one depending upon their interpretations of a given situation. *Nonacceptance* means that people behave as they would in their own culture. With *substitution*, people learn appropriate responses practiced by hosts and behave likewise. If they *add*, people behave as they would at home in some situations and like hosts in others. In *synthesis*, people combine elements of behavior from both home and host cultures. Examples are easiest to see in material aspects of culture such as food or dress. Finally, *resynthesis* involves an original integration of ideas which are not found in either culture. No value judgment should be placed on the five strategies without extensive knowledge of context. While perhaps appearing at the top of a hierarchy, for instance, resynthesis will be rare. People simply do not have the time to develop original solutions for every problem they encounter. At times, the seemingly ethnocentric strategy of nonacceptance will be best. Businesspeople may accept or refuse to participate in kickback schemes based on the same considerations they would employ in their own country.

Some analysts have depicted the ups and downs of adjustment as a W-shaped curve. While compelling, and rivaling "culture shock" as a concept known to virtually all professionals concerned with cross-cultural experiences, the W-shaped curve has not been found in recent and carefully done empirical studies. Speculative reasons for its absence include the timing of data collection. Different people may experience a downswing in mood at *different times,* but a survey at any *one time* may yield an aggregate response interpretable as "neutral feelings." Or, perhaps the W-shaped curve is so well known that sojourners are prepared for the initial downswing in mood. Because of their expectations, the actual experience is not so severe.

As people cope with more and more situations and continue their sojourns, they may experience the processes collectively referred to as "long-term adjustment." Although "long" will differ from person to person, most analysts feel that sojourns of two or three years involve demands which require further analysis. Taft (1977) has identified four processes. *Cultural adjustment* refers to feelings of comfort in the host society as well as the smooth integration of personality and culture. *Identification* involves the acceptance of new reference groups and the subjective feelings that people "belong." There are also feelings that a person's own fate is linked with the host society and that sojourners and hosts have many shared concerns. *Cultural competence* involves knowledge of the local language or dialect and the ability to behave appropriately in different situations. As more and more is learned about the competencies which sojourners should have, preparations for cross-cultural experiences will become more sophisticated. *Role acculturation* centers around a sense of convergence between one's own attitudes and values and those held by hosts. Temporary sojourners who have every intention of returning home usually do not have to experience role acculturation to make a satisfactory or even excellent adjustment. Many migrants, on the other hand, will choose to accept host culture values and will reject those which were previously held. The perceived demand to reject old values is much less intense in pluralistic societies which tolerate or even encourage diversity. Aspects of pluralism which might be encouraged include different customs, beliefs about history, religious practices, skin colors, ethnic heritages, and the types of people who can make valued contributions.

Possibly, sojourners in pluralistic societies experience an easier adjustment since host norms allow for diversity in language, dress, and everyday behaviors. Evidence does exist that returned sojourners are better able to introduce new ideas which were learned in other cultures *if* administrators in the home country organizations encourage diversity.

The ability to contribute to organizations in one's home country constitutes a benefit stemming from cross-cultural contact. Others have been documented by Kagitcibasi (1978) in the single best study of a sojourn's effects. While there are methodological difficulties which are, perhaps, impossible to completely resolve, his results are well worth careful consideration. Sojourners increased in world-mindedness, becoming more accepting of and tolerant toward other peoples and more aware that solutions to important problems demand contributions which transcend national borders. They declined in authoritarianism, a complex concept which includes rigid thinking about right and wrong, obedience to superiors, and a distrust of people who appear different. These aspects of authoritarianism obviously do not lead to successful sojourns in cultures different from one's own. Sojourners also show an increase in internal control, or the belief that problems can be addressed through individual effort rather than left to fate or chance. Finally, sojourners increased in achievement orientation, another complex concept which incorporates hard and steady work toward a standard of success. Several of these factors were delayed, meaning that they were incorporated into people's behavior a year or two after the sojourn. Possibly, some positive effects demand that people have time to become reacquainted with their own culture and to reflect upon their cross-cultural experiences.

In addition to these empirical results, other analysts have suggested more speculative outcomes. Any one of these could become the focus of first-rate research in the future. Sojourners may increase in: (a) humanitarian tendencies; (b) self-control and self-knowledge; (c) greater objectivity and flexibility in thinking; (d) creativity, or ability to make new and original conceptualizations rarely suggested by others; (e) multiculturality, marked by an ability to adapt to many different situations in different cultures; (f) additive biculturalism, or knowledge of many roles appropriate to various situations. The term refers to the additional skills people learn and are later able to use as a function of cross-cultural contact. They may also (g) develop as cultural mediators, that is, people who can help monocultural individuals communicate with counterparts in other cultures.

Even if these effects are not as well documented as they should be, professionals have long believed they exist and have given attention to creating programs which maximize positive outcomes. Recommended guidelines include ensuring relevance to the participants' professional concerns; providing opportunities for the development of collegial relations; encouraging informal social contacts with hosts; and ensuring that participants' national and personal status are enhanced.

NOTES

1. One difficulty with using these items in future studies is their quaintness, even "out-of-dateness." Researchers will be wise to consider other items which reflect current international concerns. This was the decision made by Shaw and McClain (1979), who also documented increases in world-mindedness among American community leaders who sojourned in East Africa. Some of their items were:

- Without trade with developing countries, the U.S. would suffer considerable economic hardship. (agree)
- The U.S. is doing more than its fair share to help other countries grow and develop. (disagree)

In doing research, there is temptation to use already-existing scales rather than go through the extra effort of developing new measuring instruments. At times, this will be the correct decision since comparisons can then be made with the data gathered in previous studies. In addition, time and resources can then be invested in other aspects of the research project. At other times, however, problems with the original scale (e.g., quaintness, discussed above) will cause the research to be questioned. The methodological literature on cross-cultural studies has discussions of these issues (e.g., Brislin, 1976a).

11

Speculations About Cross-Cultural Interaction

In the first ten chapters I have tried to review and to analyze key concepts which should help in understanding cross-cultural interaction. While the final pages of a book might be a summary, I have tried to fulfill that desideratum at the end of each chapter. Assuming the basic concepts are now understood, I would like to devote this final chapter to speculations about the future. There are important emphases which should be considered in future research activities: issues in the application and dissemination of findings; the uses of research findings once they are widely known among professionals; and additional ideas about the importance of studying cross-cultural interaction. While it is difficult to shift from the research-based analyses of the first ten chapters to one's own speculations, the attempt is worthwhile. In graduate school, one of my professors told me: "After studying an area, you owe it to your readers to reflect upon important issues." That comment has remained in my mind as good advice.

FUTURE RESEARCH

Key research issues include applying the distinction between formative and summative evaluation; integrating theoretical ideas from the behavioral and social sciences; incorporating the points of view held by people from different cultures; and giving more attention to the disadvantages of programs which encourage cross-cultural contact.

Formative and summative evaluation

There are a few topics on which sufficient information exists and which, consequently, should not receive high priority in future research efforts. A prime example is research on the problems faced by people in their adjustment to another culture. Enough studies have documented difficulties in housing, food, loneliness, finances, and adjustment to other systems of rewards and punishments. The opinion that enough is known about these problems should not be interpreted as a slight to their importance. The problems are very real and very intense to the people who encounter them. Rather, the opinion should be taken as a recommendation for priorities. Study after study has documented that certain problems exist regardless of sojourn type. Much less is known, on the other hand, about *how* people adjust and what strategies might be learned from research on one type of cross-cultural encounter and later applied to another. Further, much less is known about the consequences of successful and unsuccessful adjustment or, more generally, about a sojourn's effects.

Scholars concerned with evaluating complex intervention programs such as Head Start, income maintenance, or health delivery make a distinction between formative and summative studies (Scriven, 1967). This may be a useful metaphor for thinking about cross-cultural interaction. "Formative" refers to how programs are developing and how people are relating to them. The focus is on the elements of a program as they exist at the time of evaluation. Attention is also given to the history which led to the present status and to possible outcomes if the program develops according to plans. One major aim is to give advice which might lead to improvements in both the short- and long-terms. At the formative stages, programs are open to modifications. Targets of attention might be how administrators can better help sojourners overcome problems; lines of communication between people; how people use various coping strategies at different times; how experienced sojourners might be more effectively utilized to orient newcomers; and how sojourners may sometimes contribute to their own problems.

"Summative" refers to judgments about a program's success or failure. Given certain criteria agreed upon by independent evaluators, administrators, and sojourners, studies center on whether or not the goals were met. Did sojourners learn what they expected to learn? Did they develop new skills? Did the cross-cultural interaction lead to desirable outcomes, such as greater flexibility in thinking, or to the development of mediators? Summative evaluations are what funders look for in asking the question, "Were the programs any good?" As mentioned in chapter 10, my prediction is that funders will increasingly ask about potential outcomes when making judgments concerning the support of a program. Even though planners obviously cannot have information about outcomes before a program is funded, they, ideally, can make informed predictions. If more studies (e.g., Kagitcibasi, 1978; Shaw & McClain, 1979) are done which document outcomes, planners will have enough information to field probing questions. In my opinion, increased support for cross-cultural programs will be dependent upon persuasive evidence for the presence of beneficial outcomes. Put another way, we will rise or fall on the basis of well-done summative studies. This emphasis is not meant to relegate formative studies to an undesirable, disreputable category. Especially valuable research could focus on how changes in formative aspects may increase the probability of desirable summative outcomes. Further, shared information concerning the formative evaluation efforts by others will allow planners to develop sharp, concise descriptions of effective program content. I believe it was Dr. David Livingstone who said that "We are made wise by our colleagues."

Integrating theoretical ideas from the behavioral and social sciences

Researchers seeking an approach likely to pay tremendous dividends might consider paying more attention to theoretical ideas developed within any of the behavioral and social sciences. The sojourn experience represents a major change in one's life. Consequently, any solid work on change may be a good source of ideas. Examples might be research on the stranger who moves into an area; desire for change shown by willingness to consult a professional therapist; and attempts to modify organizational structures so that goals can be more efficiently pursued. Perhaps this point, a very important one in my estimation, will be better communicated if some insights into the sojourn experience are examined. Guthrie (1975) analyzed the experiences of Peace Corps volunteers, but his insights are more widely applicable.

> An untold number of volunteers endured the anxiety of uncertainty until both they and their hosts became more predictable. This opened a new world, one in which it was possible to know something of the deeper feelings of another people and to communicate in both their spoken and unspoken languages. Those who achieved this transition have offered a number of beautiful statements of their feelings, statements which to paraphrase is to destroy. These experiences have an ineffable, religious quality about them. Many found that they could describe the depth of their emotions only in religious terminology, a terminology they had not previously used because they were not actively religious (see Szanton, 1966, pp. 51–53). In the same vein, those who were most articulate about the deep personal significance of their encounter observed that learning to cope with the mysteries of another society was inevitably stressful. They contended that those who said that they enjoyed every moment of it had really never come to grips with the meaning of meeting another people on their terms [p. 100].

Guthrie has identified parallels between the cross-cultural experience and (a) religious expression, (b) insights into feeling which normally remain unstudied, (c) stress, and (d) appreciation of the points of view held by others. These are not concepts which are useful only in cross-cultural studies. Rather, they are examples of ideas which, if better understood, could be central in the analysis of many problems people encounter in this fast-changing world. One of my goals has been to show how concepts developed from studies on one type of cross-cultural experience can help in understanding another. A goal for the future is to develop parallels between sojourn studies and research on any form of change, stress, or relations with others who somehow are "different." Attention to this goal has a very practical outcome. Communication among researchers concerned with various types of important personal experiences is enhanced, and sojourn studies will not be viewed as an odd specialty of relevance to only a small audience of like-minded, narrow professionals.

Studies on seemingly esoteric topics can also point to concepts which are useful in analyzing the sojourn experience. Participating in a vigorous exchange of ideas which began with the speculations of William James (1890), Maslach (1979) feels that the following conclusion about emotions is warranted.

> Subjects who reported negative feelings almost always provided an explanation for them, such as "I'm upset because I don't do well on tests," or "I'm annoyed because this guy keeps joking all the time." In contrast, subjects reporting positive or neutral emotions rarely indicated their cause and gave, instead, such nonexplanatory statements as "I don't know, it's just the way I normally feel." In line with the proposition by Jones and Davis (1965), it seems as if negative experiences are more likely to motivate a search for causal information. People want to know why they feel upset, frightened, or angry, perhaps because they want to control (and thus reduce) the future occurrence of such experiences. On the other hand, they are less motivated to know why they feel happy, pleased, or content, perhaps because they consider such feelings to be their normal baseline condition as opposed to a "deviant" response that demands explanation [p. 964].

If further research supports this idea, it should be very helpful in analyzing the experiences of sojourners. In chapter 5 and 10, I reviewed evidence that some sojourners focus on negative emotions and, consequently, are troublesome to others. The concept suggested by Maslach provides at least a partial explanation. Positive experiences require no self-examination, while negative experiences prompt a search for causes. While searching for answers, people may fail to take advantage of obvious aspects of the host culture which could lead to positive feelings. The concept may also help explain one of the most fascinating aspects of the cross-cultural experience. Why are *most* people so enthusiastic upon their return home? One reason may be that they inevitably encounter some negative experiences since they must cope with cultural differences. The negative emotions prompt a search for understanding, and this may yield the self-insights identified by Guthrie.

It should be noted that contributions can be made in more than one direction. Research done with the cooperation of sojourners can provide a test for theories of emotion, many of which were developed in artificial university laboratories. A criticism of laboratory studies is that since people can spend only limited amounts of time in them, they cannot participate in experiences which tap deep emotions. Since the sojourn experience is intense, it can provide a real-world test of theories developed to explain emotions.

Integrating points of view held by others

One goal of good programs is to increase the probability that hosts will offer a cordial welcome to sojourners. In fact, this is not only a goal but a fundamental necessity. Unless people in other cultures are willing to receive sojourners, people cannot participate in cross-cultural contact programs. An extremely important topic for future research, then, is to identify the causes of host acceptance and rejection.

An obvious way is to ask hosts about their experiences and to list their recommendations for improvement. I've found, however, that people have a difficult time answering questions which are at such a high level of generality. An alternative technique which appears to elicit very helpful responses (Brislin & Holwill, 1977) is based on reactions to writings about people's own cultures, or what is called "indigenous commentary." For years, researchers have traveled to, lived in, and described people's behavior in other cultures. If accurate, the resulting materials could provide first-rate input into orientation programs. Yet, what if they are wrong, or, at the very least, could be improved? Perhaps the circulation and use of less-than-desirable materials is one reason for decreasing sojourn opportunities in some countries (Warwick, 1980). Educated insiders read the materials, become upset, and do not support sojourn programs. Newcomers read the materials, behave according to recommendations, but make avoidable mistakes since the original research was faulty. In my experience, insiders do not necessarily lobby against programs for sojourners. But after interacting with poorly prepared visitors and reading poorly thought-out research reports, they simply do not push for such programs. They put their efforts in other worthy proposals which compete for their attention. Cross-cultural programs, then, die for lack of supporters.

The assumptions behind the indigenous commentary research were that people from a given culture, called "insiders," could provide very helpful insights after reading ethnographies. At the same time, they might be able to indicate why people are upset with *some* writings, and these reasons may lead to suggestions for improving cross-cultural relations. My conclusion is that these assumptions were proven true. The following comments were gathered in the research project which involved 105 insiders from 24 countries. The first two comments have not been previously published. The final two were used as examples in the report summarizing the research (Brislin & Holwill, 1977, pp. 22 and 23).

Insiders were especially skillful in bringing material up to date. After reading a report on his country's educational system, one respondent wrote:

> Since this was written, free education has been extended from six years to nine years. All the children can attend school without any entrance examination. Presently education is universal. The attendance rate in school was over 95% last year. One of every four people in the country is a student.

They were sensitive to the problem that sojourners sometimes generalize from very limited experiences in another culture:

> . . . even within the vicinity of the district centers, too many aspects of the real life existing there have been overlooked. Too many times, when visiting the neighboring islands, officials are confined to a single area where the true life of the natives is absent, and therefore officials return with the wrong idea of development in such a place.

They could verbalize the problem that people often impose preconceived points of view while working in another culture.

> My experience in the past has been that the scholars on Indian culture, or should I call them "intellectuals," having studied the cultural patterns of Indians in India go down to the colonies and try to relate all their hypotheses upon the people of ethnic Indian background. They go there with some preconceived notions or gestures, get highly excited, and jump to sweeping generalizations such as those put forth by the author in this article.

They also pointed to ways in which the products of sojourners, in this case researchers, could be of help.

> It appears that the book as a whole could help the native to understand the value of their culture in the phase of a fast changing period they are now facing. Furthermore, it could be used as a base in the preparation of a curriculum for the teaching of custom in the Junior Secondary School. It

is good reading material for people in my culture; better still for the older people if the book is translated into Fijian.

Use of the indigenous commentary technique has many advantages. It is inexpensive, based only on providing copies of materials and a method to record comments. Materials written about other cultures, which are often used in cross-cultural orientation programs, can be sharpened and brought up to date. At times, insiders will point to ideas which are worthy of follow-up investigations. Insiders are also paid a compliment since the person asking the questions obviously values their insights. Finally, if a number of books and articles can be identified as exemplary through this technique, such as the materials on Fiji which were gratefully received, they might be a worthy target of careful study. Perhaps there are identifiable aspects of the authors' work or work style which might form the basis of recommendations to new sojourners.

Greater attention to disadvantages

Although there are many benefits stemming from cross-cultural contact, there are also drawbacks. My impressions are that work on the former has overshadowed the latter and that there are understandable reasons for this bias. Almost all professionals involved in programs for sojourners are committed to defending them, and, consequently, they are much more interested in documenting positive rather than negative outcomes. This bias, however, can lead to tremendous difficulties. If program defenders are not prepared to answer sharp questions about possible drawbacks, they will not compete well in the funding arena.

Further, as more and more potential supporters travel and learn about other countries through journalistic presentations, they will simply not believe reports which focus on only positive aspects. I remember a painful seminar in which a researcher summarized positive observations about a rural village in a technologically underdeveloped country. The general tone of the presentation was that the village represented a near-utopia and that the rest of the world could learn from it. An audience member, who had also lived there, charged that the researcher was guilty of a badly biased romanticism. "How can you ignore the unsanitary living conditions, the in-group/out-group feelings based on class differences which existed long before contact with people from other countries, and the periods of hunger when nature interferes with their subsistence economy?" The researcher could not answer the questions effectively. While it may be comforting to believe that an alternative life style exists somewhere which could guide industrialized societies toward better policies, realistic concerns should force researchers to examine this concept carefully rather than to accept it uncritically. I was more sympathetic with the audience member than the researcher since I feel that overly romantic descriptions will eventually be labeled as dishonest and will encourage cutbacks in support for sojourn programs.

I have tried to speculate on drawbacks in several chapters. For instance, the dissatisfied and vocal returnee who contributes to staff burn-out was discussed in chapter 9. That presentation was based only on my observations, however, since detailed information on the issue does not exist. One reason for the positivity bias is that most people prefer to deal with the pleasant rather than the unpleasant. Given the opportunity to interview 100 enthusiastic returnees or 100 gripers, who can blame the researcher who prefers to interact with the former? Further, enthusiastic people are easier to schedule for interviews since they are eager to talk with someone about their insights.

Another drawback, identified by Shaw and McClain (1979), is that sojourners do not always behave as program organizers might desire. Fifteen community leaders from Findlay, Ohio, were offered a sojourn in East Africa. The program directors hoped that the leaders would return to Findlay and become active in encouraging other residents to increase their knowledge and concern about world events. While a great deal of post-sojourn effort took place, long-range developments were hampered since seven of the 15 participants moved from Findlay within three years after their experience in East Africa. Perhaps those who left became tired of the frequent requests for speaking engagements or could find little stimulation in Findlay after the broadening experience provided by the sojourn.[1] Shaw and McClain identified other difficulties, such as the lack of mechanisms to organize postsojourn activities. Their careful specification of problems allows other planners to benefit from their work and to anticipate trouble spots.

In addition to exercising caution about overly positive conclusions, researchers should also examine the occasional unwarranted criticism of sojourn programs. Some evidence exists that the longer people stay in another country, the more negative their views become toward hosts (Steinkalk & Taft, 1979; Triandis, 1972). When asked to comment on papers prepared by neophyte researchers, such as undergraduates in their first methodology course, I often see this finding supported by very flimsy evidence. I have long felt that the process is not a trend toward negative attitudes but, rather, a trend toward realism. As with any research reporting outcomes, processes, or effects, it is important to examine the sorts of items with which people agree or disagree since these judgments are the basis of the researcher's final conclusions. The following are items which could be used to measure attitudes toward citizens from a given country (Shaw and Wright, 1967). People would respond to items before and after their sojourn.

> (People from the country in which I lived:)
> 1. Show a high rate of efficiency in anything they attempt.
> 2. Can be depended upon as being honest.
> 3. Deserve much consideration from the rest of the world [p. 411].

Before their sojourn, people would respond on the basis of conventional wisdom. In addition, excitement about their forthcoming cross-cultural experience could easily be incorporated into their responses. After a long-term sojourn, however, they were likely to have a more realistic view. They would have, undoubtedly, observed a certain number of mistakes in project implementation and this led to slightly less positive responses to item number one. They saw the dishonesty and pettiness which are present in all societies, and, consequently, their postsojourn answer to item number two was less favorable. Could any sojourner living in the United States during the Watergate exposé era (1973–1974) return home without doubts about the honesty of America's leaders? These specific experiences will be reflected in answers to more general items like number three.

Programs which encourage the development of moderately positive but realistic attitudes are easier to defend than programs which promise the development of highly favorable attitudes toward the host country. Realism implies the possibility of joint effort toward workable solutions on issues which affect the host's and the sojourner's countries. It implies that people from different countries will be able to analyze problems and suggest policies which have a reasonable probability of implementation. Considerations such as self-interest, financing, stresses stemming from changes in the status quo, and enforcement are built into the suggestions. Positive attitudes, on the other hand, may be held about people who are charming and witty, but there is no guarantee that the attitudes can be put to any use. Another good research topic for the future is the relation between positive and realistic attitudes, as well as the advantages and disadvantages of each to people who are concerned with cross-cultural contact programs.

Encouraging the effective link to cross-cultural experiences

Progress in developing more effective cross-cultural contact programs is dependent upon the involvement of committed people. My observation is that committed people have had an intense cross-cultural experience. During a sojourn, so many emotions and attitudes are involved that people return with a very different outlook on life. Many of the effects have been discussed in various chapters: (a) loneliness while trying to establish new friendships; (b) the elation when problems of cultural differences are overcome; (c) confrontation with one's own culture after experiencing absences of concepts or material goods which have always been taken for granted; (d) a broadened outlook after observing problems in other societies; (e) a greater appreciation of other people who were previously regarded as out-group members; and (f) an understanding of cultural relativity, an idea which previously was something encountered only in anthropology texts.

As a result of these effects, returned sojourners have difficulties communicating with people who have not had any cross-cultural experiences. There is a temptation to label the latter as "parochial" or narrow-minded" since they seem unaware of problems which are deeply troubling to people in different parts of the world. Opportunities to involve others in cross-cultural programs, then, is made more difficult because there is no shared set of interests on which to build. A staff member of an organization devoted to providing opportunities for adolescents once asked me, "How can I explain to parents the sorts of experiences their children will encounter?" This query brings up a related problem: how can people who have not had a cross-cultural experience be expected to support additional efforts for making sojourn opportunities more generally available? Common sense suggests that the more people who are strongly committed and are willing to work toward common goals, the greater the probability of success. For instance, it would be highly desirable if various types of decision makers, such as legislators, business executives, and philanthropists, were interested in programs for sojourners. Yet, the question is similar to the one proposed by my colleague: how can people who have not experienced life in another culture understand its benefits? While the obvious answer would be to provide more people with opportunities for sojourns which would last two to three years, this approach is too expensive and too inefficient for widespread use. Further, the influential people who could benefit from a sojourn are often so committed to projects within their own countries that they are not interested in living elsewhere.

There is no good answer to the question, and attempts to answer it would provide exciting and important research directions for the future. Some people have attempted an approach which might be called the "compact encounter" method. Trifonovitch (1977b; Trifonovitch, Hamnett, Geschwind, & Brislin, 1978) created a community which had qualities typical of those found in other cultures. In this research, the community resembled a subsistence-level Pacific Island society. For two weeks, people from the continental United States lived in a rural part of Oahu, Hawaii, in an environment carefully planned to confront the inhabitants. All of them had agreed to participate in the research so that they might learn about other cultures. Trifonovitch asked himself, "What would sojourners living in an actual Pacific Island culture encounter which could challenge their previous conceptions about life?" The answers led to a number of situations which were created by the research team. Participants had to gather and prepare their own food. They made estimates of time by looking at the position of the sun and the stars. They provided their own entertainment since electronic media were not available. They saw animals, which had wandered around the community long enough to become pets, used as food. Evaluations to date have centered on participant acceptance, and this problem has by no means been solved. The same sorts of hostilities common in real sojourns were found, and they were more observable since people were together for the entire two weeks. There may not have been sufficient time for people to examine reasons for their hostilities and to reap the benefits of self-insight. Further, a community with a small but vocal collection of hostile individuals is not a pleasant place. One observation, however, has been noted by Trifonovitch and others (e.g., Klein, 1977), although *it* could be clarified by further research. People are much happier with their experiences long after their cross-cultural encounters. Months and even years after the research community was disassembled, Trifonovitch continued to receive positive letters and to record favorable recollections in face-to-face interviews. As would be expected, some who were most critical while in the community were the most grateful months and years later.

Various attempts should be encouraged which aim at developing some of the beneficial effects of cross-cultural contact. After careful evaluation, these might be packaged in ways which could be used by others. The transfer of concepts and materials from a research to an application phase brings up another set of issues which should receive serious attention.

APPLICATION OF RESEARCH FINDINGS

Assuming that research findings such as those identified in previous pages seem potentially useful, the next step is to package the findings in ways which permit effective dissemination. One way is to involve the talents of professionals who are well acquainted with a certain problem area. They could choose those research concepts which they feel are particularly useful and give examples or potential applications from the problem area.

For example, I stressed the importance of superordinate goals in the reduction of intergroup tension (chapter 7). While not using the term, Hirschman (1967) pointed to its usefulness in analyzing intergroup conflict in Uganda. During the establishment of organizations for the development of electric power systems, progress was threatened by long-standing friction among ethnic groups. Certain factors which I call superordinate goals, however, decreased the amount of actual conflict.

> While elements of such difficulties were certainly present, they were rather muted and, in fact, one felt or hoped that these organizations might act as training centers for coexistence and cooperation among different ethnic groups. [One reason was that] apart from the bill-collecting end of the business, both services require largely operation and maintenance of highly complex technical equipment so that the feeling of belonging to the same technical elite corps may here counteract ethnic antagonism [p. 47].

The basic question is whether or not giving labels to insights such as Hirschman's is helpful. I believe that it is. The labels allow efficient categorization and organization of ideas in people's minds. Specific examples designed for various specialties (e.g., business people, foreign student advisers, social workers assigned to helping immigrants) aid in assuring that the concepts will be clear and forceful. Use of the concepts as a common language allows professionals involved in various types of cross-cultural contact to communicate with each other. Further, learning a concept sometimes helps people interpret rather vague experiences which have long been poorly understood. I have had the opportunity to introduce some of the concepts presented through this book to university students who had previously participated in short-term sojourns. Many reported that "learning these principles allows me to organize and interpret my experiences." Colleagues at other universities have reported the same phenomenon among their students.

If concepts are applied to various specialties and compelling examples are developed for each, there still may be additional ways to disseminate the information more effectively. A highly speculative possibility is based on research findings reviewed in chapter 4. Recent theoretical investigations carried out by cognitive psychologists indicate that people think in terms of category prototypes, and judge possible category members by degree of similarity to the protoype. Once formed, people remember prototypes and similar elements (e.g., ideas, experiences, advice) much better than dissimilar elements. There may be prototypes in people's minds concerning these issues:

1. What is a successful sojourn?
2. What can professionals do to help sojourners?
3. When sojourners have tasks to accomplish, what factors help or hinder them?

I feel that this is a good area for consideration by researchers, especially those interested in the applied aspects of their disciplines. Prototypes could be identified, and suggestions for improvement could then be linked to them. If people indeed think in the manner described above, knowledge of their prototypes is essential. If unknown, then suggestions for improvement will not be assigned to their categorization system and, consequently be ignored or forgotten.

One of my hopes throughout this book is that concepts could be suggested which are close to people's prototypes. For instance, many professionals with whom I have spoken recognize the fact that sojourners go through a hostility phase during orientation programs. One reason the principle is not widely discussed in the published literature is that professionals attribute responsibility to themselves, wondering if they have developed a poor program. They are willing to discuss the concept only after I admit some of the flops with which I have been associated. By suggesting concepts close to people's prototypes concerning what happens during an orientation program, in this case a hostility phase, an important and widely known experience is brought out into the open. Reasons can then be identified, such as displacement of anxiety stemming from the uncertainty associated with a person's upcoming sojourn.

Further, the concepts derived from research findings can enrich the work of professionals. I have known people who abandoned work with sojourners because they felt staleness in their own programs. "How excited can one be about culture shock and the W-shaped curve year after year?", they ask me. One of my goals has been to suggest a smorgasbord of concepts from which different people can select according to their needs. By using the concepts and developing explanatory principles, professionals will be engaging in important, creative work which is intrinsically rewarding. The excitement resulting from seeing which concepts are useful in a program and which are not, and how materials can be improved to explain different concepts, will contribute toward attracting and retaining highly competent professionals.

Research findings can also be used by members of interest groups who wish to compete for a share of a society's resources. Members of various ethnic groups, for instance, have united around the common goals of bilingual education, training programs for the hard core unemployed, efforts to eliminate discrimination in hiring, and greater participation in desirable programs such as sponsored overseas study. Although I am not so naive as to believe that knowledge will set people free, I do feel that an awareness of potential intercultural communication difficulties increases the probability of developing successful action programs. If people from one cultural group recognize how others may react because of historical precedents, prejudicial attitudes, and the tendency to stereotype (chapters 2, 3, and 4), they can sometimes prepare their communications to nullify or even take advantage of preexisting conditions. They might make a point of engaging in stereotype-breaking activity, forcing others to pay attention. They might build upon the guilt feelings which members of the dominant group may hold because of past decisions and outrageous events. Or, they might make a point of emphasizing the similarities in goals held by people in different cultures and, subsequently, link their requests to the core set of commonly held ideas.

Another benefit is that concepts have less chance of being directed against a group if they are known to the potential human targets. I have observed a case in which members of several ethnic groups banded together to lobby for bilingual education programs. In attempting to minimize expenditures, people in charge of funding indicated a willingness to allocate funds to one of the ethnic groups. Presumably, the funders hoped that the bloc would be damaged if members of only one group left satisfied. But leaders of that seemingly favored group refused to accept the funds. They recognized that the funders wanted to break the coalition and the strength of a united effort. On the other hand, I have also observed cases in which the dominant group has preserved the status quo by encouraging members of different ethnic groups to bicker among themselves. So much time, effort, and even money is spent competing with out-groups that the real problem of unequal access to society's benefits is never effectively addressed.

As another example, people in power sometimes win in the long run by appearing to support the petitions of minority group members. In the late 1960s, members of various minorities within the United States demanded ethnic studies programs at various universities. Many well-entrenched administrators opposed them, sometimes on the basis of long-standing prejudices, but often on the basis of judgments concerning academic quality and the future of a program's graduates. They wondered if there was enough substantive knowledge to warrant a degree specialization; they were concerned about overlap with offerings in departments of sociology and anthropology; and they wondered how graduates could compete in the job market with a degree in ethnic studies. But instead of opposing programs openly and attracting intense flak, they appropriated funds knowing that the programs would die in a few years. According to a person appointed dean of an ethnic studies program at a prestigious university, opponents recognized a number of factors. They understood the cyclical nature of student interest in ethnic studies which, indeed, did decline in the mid and late 1970s. They also recognized the importance of productivity related to tasks (chapter 8), which, in some form, is always a criteria of success in a university. Consequently, they allowed students to participate in the selection of new faculty members. "Students chose faculty on the basis of how many beads people wore and how many ethnic references they would drop during a conversation," the dean told me.

"The student's choices were hired but, after the fuss died down, they were denied tenure. They could and did appeal, but criteria for tenure decisions are production-oriented and are rather cut-and-dried at most prestigious universities." If they had recognized these facts, concerned people could have developed policies to ensure long-range continuation of the ethnic studies program. Undoubtedly, this would have demanded attention to developing group-like ties with outsiders, and, perhaps, the concepts reviewed in chapter 6 would have been helpful.

DISSEMINATING RESEARCH FINDINGS

One of the most difficult problems researchers face is communicating their findings with people who might be able to use them. Discussions in the previous section on "applications" started with the assumption that potential users were eager to put research findings into practice. This willingness is by no means typical. More often, practitioners are unaware of potentially usable findings, unexcited by the possibility of interacting with researchers, or distrustful of the whole research enterprise.

Researcher-practitioner interaction

The problem of interaction between researchers and practitioners is a good starting point in analyzing the difficulties of dissemination. Researchers possess a set of values and use a jargon which are unfamiliar to most practitioners. The values include caution, the desirability of an unemotional perspective on problems, and appreciation by one's reference group of fellow researchers. Jargon includes terms to implement the values, such as "controls," "quasi-experimental designs," and "rejection rates of prestige journals." Consequently, when a practitioner does ask for advice regarding a decision which must be made immediately, (s)he finds little use in cautious statements like, "On the one hand, . . . on the other hand. . . ." To paraphrase slightly a comment made by President Truman about economists, practitioners must often dream about meeting one-handed researchers.

Many researchers are also hesitant to apply generalizations to the single case. Realizing that empirical relationships between variables are not perfect, researchers warn that mistakes will always be made when using generalizations. For instance, a number of traits which predict sojourner success were reviewed in chapter 3. Practitioners in charge of sponsored programs might ask, "Should this applicant be selected?" The researcher is more comfortable in saying, "I can give you the following information. People who have this applicant's measured traits tend to have a reasonable chance of success." But, since the practitioners have to make decisions about specific individuals in specific cases, they develop a noticeable impatience with the researcher's cautious generalities. To complicate the matter, the researchers are in a bind. If they give specific advice, they can be criticized for applying findings with known limitations. Colleagues can always charge that more information on a specific situation should be gathered before general principles are applied. Yet, the suggestion to practitioners that "more information is needed" provides little help if decisions have to be made within a short period of time.

The cautious statements are sometimes misattributed to emotional detachment and to a lack of concern with real problems. One reason is the failure to understand the difference between researchers' interests and the methodological approaches they must adopt in any given study. While interest must be intense to cope with the difficulties of research, methodological techniques which are widely accepted within the behavioral/ social sciences are mandatory. One purpose of the techniques is to protect conclusions from being contaminated by a researcher's own preferences. The protections and insistences on cautious interpretations, however, must seem like stalling tactics. I have heard a practitioner say, "If the problem is perceived as important, why can't researchers get their act together and come up with some solid recommendations?" Since practitioners rightfully place tremendous importance on their work, their attributions about researchers are damaging to interpersonal interactions.

Traits and competencies widely shared among members of different groups can also lead to communication difficulties. Although my observation may be biased since I interact more frequently with researchers than practitioners, it seems to me that members of the former are more willing to engage in self-criticism than the latter. Researchers admit that they often participate in investigations which have no immediate practical benefit and which can be understood only by like-minded colleagues. A significant number vigorously defend this approach by arguing that society benefits in the long run if researchers are allowed to pursue their own interests. A favorite example, almost reaching the status of a widely accepted script (chapter 4), is the development of penicillin. "How could Sir Arthur Fleming have written a grant proposal to justify his work with molds? There was no predictable benefit at the time he began his investigations." Researchers also admit to jumping on bandwagons when a topic area seems to be currently in style or when it is favored by grant-giving agencies. Many are not particularly good at communicating their results to others. A small, but nevertheless significant, number are not concerned with whether or not practitioners are able to use their findings.

Other results from self-examinations are even less flattering. After giving a presentation on preparation for a sojourn, an experienced researcher brought up a problem. "I realize that this issue is rarely discussed," he started, "but a major difficulty is the personality of some researchers. A significant number are so rigid, so determined to complete their projects, that they offend people. They make it difficult for other sojourners to be accepted by members of other cultures." The point is correct. My analysis is that researchers must possess determination and dedication to spend the necessary years on their formal education, to graduate from apprentice to leader roles, and to compete for limited space in professional journals. They must believe that what they are doing is worthwhile, and they must work tremendously hard to persuade colleagues that their findings are reliable and valid. Unfortunately, this dedication does lead to rigidity and insensitivity to others.

An influential theoretical idea (Witkin, 1977; Witkin & Berry, 1975) called "psychological differentiation" may shed additional light on the issue. People who develop highly analytical skills are individualistic and independent in their thinking and are less influenced by the environment in which they find themselves. In other words, they can ignore the total environment while focusing on one aspect for more detailed study. People who are less analytical are more influenced by their current environment. As discussed in chapter 6, the environment includes other people with whom one interacts. To benefit from the presence of others, these less analytical people are more sensitive to the contributions various people can make and probably have more highly developed social skills. The research profession, I believe, attracts people with analytical skills. Moreover, since practitioners most always work with many others in arranging for successful sojourns, they frequently possess less analytical but highly developed social skills.

Note that this distinction brings up another difficulty which could lead to ill feelings since the concept of analytical skills is value laden in most highly industrialized societies. Practitioners might be offended if this difference is discussed openly, even though researchers emphasize that it is a generalization to which there will be many exceptions. Witkin (1977) has insisted that value labels should not be placed on any distinctions his work might suggest. Analytical skills are useful at times, but so is social sensitivity. The positive value which *should* be applied is the tolerance and encouragement of plurality, as discussed in chapter 10.

More has been said about qualities of researchers which could lead to communication difficulties than about the qualities of practitioners. This imbalance reflects the state of people's thinking about the issue. Valuable studies could be done concerning the traits, competences, work styles, and situational demands of practitioners. With this additional knowledge as background, recommendations could be made for more effective researcher-practitioner interactions.

Advising decision makers

To be more effective in disseminating findings, researchers must make efforts to insure that executives have the information at the time of their deliberations. Since executives make so many decisions concerning a multitude of issues, they do not have time to study research findings which may *possibly* be useful at some later date. The alternatives being considered for any one decision at any one point in time become salient (chapter 4). If researchers can make their information available quickly and in a form which is easily usable, it has a good chance of being considered. If not, then decisions will be made nevertheless.

When he was chairman of the Senate Foreign Relations Committee, Senator William Fulbright held hearings on psychological aspects of foreign policy. He was concerned that decision makers in government had not taken advantage of the findings of anthropology and psychology in developing policies for foreign relations. Dr. Margaret Mead gave her recommendations relevant to this important issue. If the style of her remarks appears slightly less smooth than what is found in most of her writings, it must be remembered that the following is a transcription of oral testimony (Committee on Foreign Relations, 1969).

> I am initially going to take for granted, and this can be challenged and discussed, that the behavioral sciences have a great deal to offer if the situation is right. They have a great deal to offer if there are channels through which government will use their findings; to the extent that we can apply findings on the Soviet Union or on France or on China to national policy, we have to have somebody to listen. . . . This means we have to have, in an agency that is going to use these materials, very high level and respected people who can receive them, and this has not been the case. . . . The second point is that no behavioral science by itself can make a substantial contribution to public policy. In this I include also the social sciences, economics, political science, and history, which alone and without any help from the behavioral sciences, make one-sided and partial statements. . . . We discovered during World War II, and it is an English statement, but it applies equally here, "you cannot advise an adviser." You have to have access to people who have power to act either in Congress or in the executive branch, and not be out on the periphery somewhere [pp. 93–94].

Dr. Mead only hinted at a major reason why researchers cannot advise an adviser. The latter group of people are also frustrated that there are no clear and widely accepted channels along which information can be conveyed. Since the advisers themselves are looking for an audience, they are not always good targets for researchers who normally work outside of government and industry.

Important research needs to be done on how information can be better channeled so that it can be considered by decision makers. Topics might be:

1. the packaging of information to make it readily understandable and have the maximum impact possible.
2. encouraging researchers to consider the advantages and disadvantages of their recommendations rather than to assume the more common role of one-sided advocate. Decision makers have told me that researchers often appear biased and naive when they present only one side of a story.
3. methods for encouraging interdisciplinary collaboration and the integration of findings from the various behavioral and social sciences (mentioned by Dr. Mead).
4. ways of rewarding investigators who choose to engage in applied research. Currently, the norms in many academic disciplines dictate more recognition for basic than applied research.
5. related to the above, ways of rewarding those researchers who are able to communicate their findings to audiences of nonspecialists. Since job security and promotions usually depend upon publication for like-minded colleagues, young researchers receive no encouragement to become involved in applied investigations which would yield information useful to decision makers who do not happen to share the same specialized background.

MOTIVES, AND LESSONS FROM SUCCESS STORIES

My final suggestion for future research is to discover the motives of people who chose the profession of working with sojourners. Many problems have been mentioned: complaints; lack of understanding on the part of people who themselves have not had a cross-cultural experience; and the constant struggle to remain fresh when selecting, preparing, or coordinating new groups of sojourners. Because administrators do not understand the special problems of cross-cultural encounters, and because there is no interest group advocating greater support, professionals have an ambiguous status. While most observers have a vague idea that the professionals are doing worthwhile work, the lack of understanding means that cross-cultural matters are handled within marginal divisions of an organization. Examples are the foreign student advisers' offices on university campuses, training divisions in multinational corporations or the State Department, and the bilingual materials curriculum center within city or state departments of education. In addition, salaries are not particularly good for professionals in any of these positions. Yet very competent, intelligent people want to join professions such as those mentioned, and a single advertised opening yields hundreds of applicants. Given their willingness to enter the profession despite the problems, their motives must be strong. If these could be better understood, perhaps more effective ways of satisfying these motives could be developed so that people could continue to grow in their chosen careers.

My own motive is the enjoyment I experience upon observing a skilled professional help an obviously troubled sojourner or aid in interpreting peoples' cross-cultural encounters. I have been in foreign student advisers' offices when newly arrived, tired, confused sojourners were seeking help. The advisers normally set aside all other matters and begin to talk with the sojourners, sometimes dropping references to the people's home countries. Knowledge of the difficulties stemming from visas, housing, lack of food, and companionship allow the advisers to set up clear procedures so that the sojourners can satisfy immediate needs. The advisers ask the sojourners to return after these steps are taken, so that the details of registering at an unfamiliar university can proceed. Nothing is more gratifying than to see the difference on sojourners' faces before, compared to after, their interactions with a competent adviser. Similarly, I have been in the company of technical assistance advisers who had previously participated in a cross-cultural orientation program (e.g., Szanton, 1966). They have reported, "At the time, I thought all the presentations and discussions on cultural preparation were nonsense. But I can see their usefulness now, having experienced some of the events which were predicted in the program."

Occasionally, but I admit not regularly, some of the positive feedback is directed at my own work. After presenting information on the culture assimilator (chapter 4) to students in 1979, one came up after class and reported he was a volunteer in the Los Amigos de las Americas program during the summer of 1967. Consequently, he was included in the evaluation efforts to test the effectiveness of "culture assimilator" preparation for medical work in Honduras (Fiedler et al., 1971; O'Brien, Fiedler, and Hewlett, 1970). He said that, "After hearing your presentation, I remembered my experience and how the preparation probably helped my work in Honduras."

At times, learning about especially successful professionals gives insights into major historical questions. Interestingly, a question involving relations among ethnic groups during wartime, which has long intrigued me, was answered during the time I was preparing this volume. Why were there no internment camps established for Japanese-Americans in Hawaii after the Pearl Harbor bombings? As is now well known, 110,000 Japanese-Americans on the West Coast of the mainland United States were removed from their homes and transported to internment camps (Leighton, 1945).

However, 99.1 percent of the 160,000 Americans of Japanese Ancestry (AJA's) in Hawaii were left undisturbed. The question is especially puzzling since Hawaii was much closer to war action and to the Pacific military command than was the continental United States. Some answers to the question involve structural elements of society. The movement of 160,000 people would have been extremely difficult. Since the people were in relatively close proximity to each other, peaceful but firm resistance movements could have been established. Further, so many AJA's held responsible positions in Hawaii that replacement would have been nearly impossible during wartime.

Another reason, Smyser (1979) argues, was the presence of an individual who was especially competent in dealing with people from different cultural groups. Robert L. Shivers directed the Federal Bureau of Investigation office in Hawaii. After opening the FBI office in Honolulu in August 1939, Shivers saw that war with Japan was a possibility. He began to make inquiries into the loyalty of AJA's and concluded that they would pose no threat should war occur. Observers concluded that Shivers was especially skillful at minimizing personal biases so as to look at questions objectively. Even though he had been exposed to prejudice during his childhood in the Southern United States, he did not let past experiences with out-groups affect his personal relationships with AJA's. Shivers and his wife became very close to a young professional woman of Japanese ancestry who had lost her father and mother. The woman lived with the Shivers while establishing herself in a career, and her association developed into the closeness of a parent-daughter relation. A speculative possibility is that the close relationship brought out the same feelings of discovery and self-insight which are regularly experienced by sojourners. Shivers also developed social relations with various leaders of the Japanese-American community and established advisory groups to recommend courses of action should war with Japan become a reality.

Given this preparation, Shivers became very knowledgeable concerning the dynamics of the Japanese-American community. He designed a plan of action with the advisory group which the Army accepted.

> . . . the plan was vindicated when there was no sabotage or fifth column activity in Hawaii at the time of the Pearl Harbor attack. "Fortified with this fact, meaning the absence of sabotage [Shivers later wrote to a friend], we were able to stand up for what we thought was right against the opposition of, as you know, some high-placed officials" [Smyser, 1979, p. A20].

Because of his expertise, officers who assumed command after military rule was imposed continued to depend upon Shiver's advice. He and his co-workers simply had far more information on matters related to military intelligence than newly arrived officers could possibly possess. The community groups Shivers helped established continued to provide a liaison between the military and AJA's and ensured constant communication, the face-to-face interactions necessary to reduce stereotypes, and general goodwill. The community group, plus the presence of highly placed and well-informed people like Shivers who firmly opposed relocation, contributed to a network of trust which prevented a serious mistake.

This case study indicates that goodwill and intercultural sensitivity are not sufficient to prevent problems from occurring. Hard work and constant vigilance, such as the study of the AJA community and maintenance of the advisory group, were also essential.

My belief is that committed individuals can make important contributions to better intercultural relations. Any development in society which affects social relations demands the involvement of individuals who understand the ramifications of change and who can model appropriate interpersonal behaviors. In the case of massive changes such as those brought on by war, people are needed who can act as a counterpressure to hysterical forces which can destroy decency. In the case of positive changes such as increased budgetary expenditures for intercultural programs, knowledgeable people are needed who can use the money wisely. Whether the changes are due to legislation, revolution, or simply shifts in public opinion, committed individuals will always be necessary to make sense out of confusion, to point the way toward realistic accomplishments, and to mediate between competing groups desirous of the same economic benefits. In the important arena of relations among people from different cultures, a greater understanding of what happens to people as a result of cross-cultural contact will be an aid in guiding people toward more positive outcomes and in reducing the probability of negative results.

SUMMARY

Assuming that the concepts found in chapters 1 through 10 have been adequately presented, it may be useful to speculate on profitable directions for future research and analysis. While some readers may find that the exercise resembles an abandonment to fancy, others may find a notion which helps in their own thinking about the future.

In adopting the distinction between formative and summative evaluation, researchers give different sorts of advice and judgments depending upon the goals of their investigations. In formative evaluation, they can make recommendations for modification in ongoing programs. In summative evaluation, they make judgments regarding program success or failure, and these conclusions will often have an effect on the degree of support given to similar, newly developed programs. The link between the two concepts is that modifications in formative aspects may increase the probability of favorable outcomes as documented by the summative evaluation. For example, recommendations regarding increased communication between program administrators and participants may have an effect on sojourners' task accomplishments.

One of my goals has been to show how concepts developed from work with one type of cross-cultural experience have applicability to other types. Similarly, research on sojourners may contribute to an understanding of important personal experiences within any one culture. Since a sojourn represents an important change in one's life, insights may help in interpreting other changes such as entering a new profession during adulthood. Further, since cross-cultural experiences invoke strong emotions, a greater understanding of emotional behavior may result from careful research. The helpful contribution can also proceed in the other direction, with basic research yielding insight into cross-cultural experiences. Recent research on emotions (Maslach, 1979), for instance, has shown that people are more likely to seek explanations for negative rather than positive feelings. This may be a partial explanation for the hostility shown by some sojourners. A focus on negative emotions prevents positive aspects of the experience from coming to people's attention.

Some problems are so important that lack of attention can threaten the survival of sponsored sojourn programs. If the current lack of a cordial welcome to cross-cultural researchers in some parts of the world is considered to be a warning of future difficulties, then other types of sojourns are threatened. A very basic point is that sojourns are impossible without the cooperation of people in receiving countries. One way to learn more about reasons for nonacceptance is to integrate the opinions of hosts in program planning. Brislin and Holwill (1977), investigating reactions to cross-cultural researchers, found that hosts could give very helpful insights into reasons for acceptance and rejection. Their technique, which involves asking hosts to read and comment on the products prepared by researchers, could undoubtedly be used to investigate other types of sojourns.

As with any program which attracts committed and enthusiastic people, sojourns can be oversold. Future research should give greater attention to negative outcomes such as romanticism which blinds advocates to real problems. Currently, a positivity bias exists, and it is understandable. Most researchers and practitioners prefer to interact with 100 enthusiastic sojourners than 100 complainers. Yet, the latter people may be able to identify problems which demand greater attention from program administrators.

The sojourn has a tendency to create an in-group among the experienced and an out-group among nonparticipants. Most professionals who try to involve others in supporting sojourn programs find it difficult to communicate benefits to those who have not had a cross-cultural experience. While providing more sojourns for influential people is an obvious solution, this is too costly and inefficient for widespread use. Trifonovitch (1977) has attempted a "compact encounter" approach in which communities are designed which have a maximum impact on volunteer participants. Extending over a two-week period, various experiences are planned which ideally cause self-examination and self-insight. This approach is in need of careful assessment to determine its effectiveness.

In applying research findings so that they might be of use to practitioners, several possibilities are worthy of consideration. Practitioners might study the concepts presented in chapters 2 through 10 and develop examples for specific types of sojourns. Recent theoretical investigations indicate that people organize their thoughts around category prototypes. Examples are people's thoughts about "a successful sojourn" or "factors which help and hinder task accomplishment." New findings could be organized around people's already existing prototypes of these categories. Applications of the concepts can also *enrich* the work of practitioners. Rather than constant use of "culture shock," the "W-shaped curve," and a few others, use of multiple concepts can add freshness and excitement to their work. Practitioners can also make original contributions since effective techniques do not exist for communicating the importance and helpfulness of the concepts to sojourners.

To disseminate findings more effectively, researchers and practitioners will have to interact more frequently than they do at present. One approach which may improve matters involves documenting typical traits of researchers and the situations they face, and doing the same for practitioners. Once traits and problems are identified, guidelines might be developed to increase the probability of effective interaction. Ideally, there will be greater access in the future to people who might use research findings. Advising a collection of advisers has not proven fruitful; there must be access to actual decision makers.

Knowledge about the motives of people who chose to make a career in various cross-cultural professions is mandatory. Given this knowledge, rewards can be designed so that people's motives are satisfied. Consequently, they can continue to grow in their profession rather than stagnate or seek another career. My own motivations are enjoyment (a) from seeing the changes in obviously troubled sojourners after they have been helped by competent professionals, and (b) from helping people to interpret their cross-cultural experiences. Studying the work of successful professionals sometimes gives insights into major historical events, such as the contributions of Robert Shivers to the Japanese-American community in Hawaii during World War II. This case also shows that committed, sensitive people can make a difference in this complex and fast-changing world where the efforts of individuals sometimes seem unimportant and hopeless.

NOTE

1. The senior author of the study (W. Shaw, personal communication, March, 1980) indicated that the number of participants who left Findlay was startling. However, he could find no reasons which apply to all or even a small number of the seven who left. Rather, there were seven individual reasons involving changes in people's personal or professional lives.

References

Abelson, R. Script processing in attitude formation and decision making. In J. Carroll and J. Payne (Eds.), *Cognition and social behavior.* Hillsdale, N.J.: Lawrence Erlbaum Associates, 1976.

Abrams, I. The impact of Antioch education through experience abroad. Paper presented at the meeting of the International Studies Association, Washington, D.C., February 1978.

Adler, D., & Taft, R. Some psychological aspects of immigrant assimilation. In A. Stoller (Ed.), *New faces.* Melbourne and London: F. W. Cheshire, 1966.

Adler, P. The transnational experience: An alternative view of culture shock. *Journal of Humanistic Psychology,* 1975, *15*(4), 13–23.

Adler, P. Beyond cultural identity: Reflections upon cultural and multicultural man. In R. Brislin (Ed.), *Culture learning: Concepts, applications, and research.* Honolulu: University Press of Hawaii, 1977.

Adorno, T., Frenkel-Brunswick, E., Levinson, D., & Sanford, R. *The authoritarian personality.* New York: Harper, 1950.

Akter, T., & Pasinski, W. How to design an intercultural relations training course. Coronado, California: Human Resources Training Department, Naval Amphibious School, August 1973.

Albert, R., & Adamopoulos, J. An attributional approach to culture learning: The culture assimilator. *Topics in Culture Learning,* 1976, *4,* 53–60.

Alexander, A., Workneh, F., Klein, M., & Miller, M. Psychotherapy and the foreign student. In P. Pedersen, W. J. Lonner, and J. G. Draguns (Eds.), *Counseling across cultures.* Honolulu: University Press of Hawaii, 1976.

Alger, C. Personal contact in intergovernmental organizations. In H. Kelman (Ed.), *International behavior: A social psychological analysis.* New York: Holt, Rinehart, and Winston, 1965.

Allport, G. *The nature of prejudice.* Reading, Mass.: Addison-Wesley, 1954.

Althen, G. (Ed.) *Students from the Arab World and Iran.* Washington, D.C.: National Association for Foreign Student Affairs, 1979.

Amir, Y. Contact hypothesis in ethnic relations. *Psychological Bulletin,* 1969, *71,* 319–343.

Amir, Y., & Garti, C. Situational and personal influence on attitude change following ethnic contact. *International Journal of Intercultural Relations,* 1977, *1*(2), 58–75.

Amir, Y., Rivner, M., Bizman, A., & Ben-Ari, R. Contact between Israelis and Arabs and its effects: A theoretical and empirical evaluation. Manuscript submitted for publication, 1980.

Amuzegar, J. *Technical assistance in theory and practice: The case of Iran.* New York: Praeger, 1966.

Arensberg, C. M., & Niehoff, A. H. *Introducing social change: A manual for community development.* Chicago: Aldine-Atherton, 1971.

Arnold, C. Culture shock and a Peace Corps field mental health program. *Community Mental Health Journal,* 1967, *3* (1), 53–60.

Ashmore, R. The problem of intergroup prejudice. In B. Collins, *Social psychology*. Reading, Mass.: Addison-Wesley, 1970.

Baggozi, R., & Burnkrant, R. Attitude organization and the attitude-behavior relationship. *Journal of Personality and Social Psychology*, 1979, *37*, 913–929.

Bailyn, L., & Kelman, H. The effects of a year's experience in America or the self-image of Scandinavians. *Journal of Social Issues*, 1962, *18* (1), 30–40.

Barker, R. *Ecological psychology: Concepts and methods for studying the environment of human behavior*. Stanford, Calif.: Stanford University Press, 1968.

Barrett, G., & Bass, B. Cross-cultural issues in industrial and organizational psychology. In M. Dunnette (Ed.), *Handbook of industrial and organizational psychology*. Chicago: Rand-McNally, 1976.

Baty, R., & Dold, E. Cross-cultural homestays: An analysis of college student responses after living in an unfamiliar culture. *International Journal of Intercultural Relations*, 1977, *1*(1), 61–76.

Bauer, R., Pool, I., & Dexter, L. *American business and public policy: The politics of foreign trade*. New York: Atherton Press, 1963.

Bennett, E. Discussion, decision, commitment, and consensus in group decision. *Human Relations*, 1955, *8*, 251–274.

Bennett, J. Transition shock: Putting culture shock in perspective. *International and Intercultural Communication Annual*, 1977, *4*, 45–52.

Bennett, J. (Ed.) *The new ethnicity: Perspectives from ethnology* (Proceedings of the 1973 meetings of the American Ethnological Society). St. Paul, Minn.: West Publishing, 1975.

Bennett, J., Passin, H., & McKnight, R. *In search of identity: The Japanese overseas scholar in America and Japan*. Minneapolis: University of Minnesota Press, 1958.

Benoit, E. Economic steps towards peace. In Q. Wright, W. M. Evans, and M. Deutsch (Eds.), *Preventing World War III*. New York: Simon and Schuster, 1962.

Benson, P. Measuring cross-cultural adjustment: The problem of criteria. *International Journal of Intercultural Relations*, 1978, *2*(1), 21–37.

Berry, J. On cross-cultural comparability. *International Journal of Psychology*, 1969, *4*, 119–128.

Berry, J. Radical cultural relativism and the concept of intelligence. In L. Cronbach and P. Drenth (Eds.), *Mental tests and cultural adaptation*. The Hague: Mouton, 1972.

Berry, J. *Human ecology and cognitive style*. New York: Wiley/Halsted, 1976.

Berry, J. Psychological aspects of cultural pluralism: Unity and identity reconsidered. In R. Brislin (Ed.), *Culture learning: Concepts, applications, and research*. Honolulu: University Press ot Hawaii, 1977.

Berry, J. Social and cultural change. In H. Triandis and R. Brislin (Eds.), *Handbook of cross-cultural psychology*. Vol. 5. Boston: Allyn and Bacon, 1980.

Berscheid, E., & Walster. E. Physical attractiveness. In L. Berkowitz (Ed.), *Advances in experimental social psychology*. Vol. 7. New York: Academic Press, 1974.

Billig, M. *Social psychology and intergroup relations*. New York: Academic Press, 1976.

Bishop, G. Effects of belief similarity and dialect style on interracial interaction. Paper presented at the meetings of the American Psychological Association, Washington, D.C., September 1976.

Blaney, N., Stephan, C., Rosenfield, D., Aronson, E., & Sikes, J. Interdependence in the classroom: A field study. *Journal of Educational Psychology,* 1977, *69,* 121–128.

Blau, P., & Duncan, O. *The American occupational structure.* New York: Wiley, 1967.

Blom, G., Waite, R., & Zimet, S. Ethnic integration and urbanization of a first grade reading textbook: A research study. *Psychology in the Schools,* 1967, *4,* 176–181.

Bochner, S. *The mediating man: Cultural interchange and transnational education.* Honolulu: East-West Center, 1973.

Bochner, S. The mediating man and cultural diversity. In R. Brislin (Ed.), *Culture learning: Concepts, applications, and research.* Honolulu: University Press of Hawaii, 1977.

Bochner, S. Cultural diversity: Implications for modernization and international education. In K. Kumar (Ed.), *Bonds without bondage: Explorations in transcultural interactions.* Honolulu: University Press of Hawaii, 1979.

Bochner, S., & Perks, R. National role evocation as a function of crossnational interaction. *Journal of Cross-Cultural Psychology,* 1971, *2,* 157–164.

Boehringer, G., Zervolis, V., Bayley, J., & Boehringer, K. Sterling: The destructive application of group techniques to a conflict. *Journal of Conflict Resolution,* 1974, *18,* 257–275.

Bosmajian, H. *The language of oppression.* Washington, D.C.: Public Affairs Press, 1974.

Bottoms, A. Crime and delinquency in immigrant and minority groups. In P. Watson (Ed.), *Psychology and race.* Chicago: Aldine, 1973.

Brein, M., & David, K. Intercultural communications and the adjustment of the sojourner. *Psychological Bulletin,* 1971, *76,* 215–230.

Brewer, M. Perceptual processes in cross-cultural interaction. In D. Hoopes, P. Pedersen, and G. Renwick (Eds.), *Overview of intercultural education, training, and research.* Washington, D.C. (Georgetown University), SIETAR, 1977.

Brewer, M. Ingroup bias in the minimal intergroup situation: A cognitive–motivational analysis. *Psychological Bulletin,* 1979, *86,* 307–324.

Brewer, M., & Campbell, D. *Ethnocentrism and intergroup attitudes: East African evidence.* New York: Wiley/Halsted, 1976.

Brigham, J. Ethnic stereotypes. *Psychological Bulletin,* 1971, *76,* 15–35.

Brislin, R. Interaction among members of nine ethnic groups and the belief similarity hypothesis. *Journal of Social Psychology,* 1971, *85,* 171–179.

Brislin, R. Comparative research methodology. *International Journal of Psychology,* 1976, *11,* 215–229. (a)

Brislin, R. Methodology of cognitive studies. In G. Kearney and D. McElwain (Eds.), *Aboriginal cognition: Retrospect and prospect.* Canberra, Australia: Australian Institute for Aboriginal Studies, 1976. (b)

Brislin, R. Ethical issues influencing the acceptance and rejection of researchers who visit various countries. In L. Loeb-Adler (Ed.), *Issues in cross-cultural research. Annals of the New York Adacemy of Sciences,* 1977, *285,* 185–202.

Brislin, R. Structured approaches to dealing with prejudice and intercultural misunderstanding. *International Journal of Group Tensions,* 1978, *8*(1&2), 33–48.

Brislin, R. Orientation programs for cross-cultural preparation. In A. Marsella, R. Tharp, and T. Ciborowski (Eds.). *Current perspectives in cross-cultural psychology.* New York: Academic Press, 1979.

Brislin, R. The problems and prospects of cross-cultural studies as seen by experienced researchers. In L. Eckensberger, W. Lonner, and Y. Poortinga (Eds.),

Cross-cultural contributions to psychology. Amsterdam: Swets and Zeitlinger, 1979. (b)

Brislin, R. Expanding the role of the interpreter to include multiple facets of intercultural communication. *International Journal of Intercultural Relations,* 1980, *4,* 137–148.

Brislin, R., & Holwill, F. Reactions of indigenous people to the writings of behavioral and social scientists. *International Journal of Intercultural Relations,* 1977, *1*(2), 15–34.

Brislin, R., & Pedersen, P. *Cross-cultural orientation programs.* New York: Wiley/Halsted, 1976.

Brislin, R., & Van Buren, H. Can they go home again? (Reorientation programs for sojourners). *International Educational and Cultural Exchange,* 1974, *9*(4), 19–24.

Brodie, F. *Thomas Jefferson: An intimate history.* New York: Norton, 1974.

Bronfenbrenner, U. The mirror-image in Soviet-American relations. *Journal of Social Issues,* 1961, *55,* 253–260.

Brown, R., & Lenneberg, E. Studies in linguistic relativity. In H. Proshansky and B. Seidenberg (Eds.), *Basic studies in social psychology.* New York: Holt, Rinehart, and Winston, 1965.

Bruner, J. *On knowing: Essays for the left hand.* Cambridge, Mass.: Harvard University Press, 1962.

Bruner, J. *The relevance of education.* New York: Norton, 1971.

Bruner, J., Goodnow, J., & Austin, G. *A study of thinking.* New York: Wiley, 1956.

Bruner, J., & Perlmutter, H. Compatriot and foreigner: A study of impression formation in three countries. *Journal of Abnormal and Social Psychology,* 1957, *55,* 253–260.

Buchanan, W., & Cantril, H. *How nations see each other.* Urbana: University of Illinois Press, 1953.

Campbell. D. Social attitudes and other acquired behavioral dispositions. In S. Koch (Ed.), *Psychology: A study of a science.* New York: McGraw-Hill, 1963.

Campbell, D. Stereotypes and the perception of group differences. *American Psychologist,* 1967, *22,* 817–829.

Campbell, J., & Yarrow, M. Personal and situational variables in adaptation to change. *Journal of Social Issues,* 1958, *14,* 29–46.

Casino, E. Changing issues in the consultation process. Paper read at the 3rd Third World Conference, Omaha, Nebraska, October 1979.

Cathcart, D., & Cathcart, R. The Japanese social experience and concept of groups. In L. Samovar and R. Porter (Eds.), *Intercultural communication: A reader.* Belmont, Calif.: Wadsworth, 1976.

Christiansen, B. *Attitudes toward foreign affairs as a function of personality.* Oslo: University of Oslo Press, 1959.

Christie, R., & Cook, P. A guide to the published literature relating to the authoritarian personality through 1956. *Journal of Psychology,* 1958, *45,* 171–199.

Clark, K. Conversation with Kenneth B. Clark. *American Psychological Association Monitor,* 1979, *10*(9 & 10), 6.

Clarke, C. Influence of culture on the foreign student and counseling. In M. J. Baron (Ed.), *Advising, counseling, and helping the foreign student.* Washington, D.C.: National Association for Foreign Student Affairs, 1975.

Cleveland, H., & Mangone, G. (Eds.), *The art of overseasmanship.* Syracuse, N.Y.: Syracuse University Press, 1957.

Cleveland, H.; Mangone, G.; & Adams, J. *The overseas Americans.* New York: McGraw-Hill, 1960.

Coch, L., & French, J. Overcoming resistance to change. *Human Relations*, 1948, *1*, 512–532.

Coelho, G. *Changing images of America*. Glencoe, Ill.: Free Press, 1958.

Coelho, G. (Ed.) Impacts of studying abroad. *Journal of Social Issues*, 1962, *18*, 1–87.

Coelho, G. "Introduction" and personal growth and educational development through working and studying abroad. *Journal of Social Issues*, 1962, *18*, 1–6 and 55–67.

Collins, B., & Hoyt, M. Personal responsibility-for-consequences: On integration and extension of the "forced compliance" literature. *Journal of Experimental Social Psychology*, 1972, *8*, 558–593.

Committee on Foreign Relations. Psychological aspects of foreign policy (Hearings, June 20, 1969). Washington, D.C.: U.S. Government Printing Office, 1969.

Cook, S. Desegregation: A psychological analysis. *American Psychologist*, 1957, *12*, 1–13.

Cook, S. Motives in a conceptual analysis of attitude-related behavior. *Nebraska Symposium on Motivation*. Vol. 17. Lincoln: University of Nebraska Press, 1970, 179–235.

Cook, S., & Selltiz, C. Some factors which influence the attitudinal outcomes of personal contacts. *International Social Science Bulletin*, 1955, *7*, 51–58.

Cook, T., & Campbell, D. The design and conduct of quasi-experiments and true experiments in field settings. In M. Dunnette (Ed.), *Handbook of industrial and organizational psychology*. Chicago: Rand-McNally, 1976.

David, H. Involuntary international migration: Adaptation of refugees. In E. Brody (Eds.), *Behavior in new environments: Adaptation of migrant populations*. Beverly Hills: Sage, 1970.

David, K. Intercultural adjustment and applications of reinforcement theory to problems of "culture shock." *Trends*, 1972, *4*(3), 1–64.

Davis, D. *The problem of slavery in Western culture*. Ithaca, N.Y.: Cornell University Press, 1966.

DeLoria, V. *Custer died for your sins*. New York: Avon Books, 1969.

Detweiler, R. The categorization of the actions of people from another culture: A conceptual analysis and behavioral outcome. *International Journal of Intercultural Relations*, 1980, *4*, in press.

Deutsch, K., & Merritt, R. Effects of events on national and international images. In H. Kelman (Ed.), *International behavior: A social psychological analysis*. New York: Holt, Rinehart, and Winston, 1965.

Deutsch, M., & Collins, M. *Interracial housing: A psychological evaluation of a social experiment*. Minneapolis: University of Minnesota Press, 1951.

Deutsch, S., & Won, G. Some factors in the adjustment of foreign nationals in the United States. *Journal of Social Issues*, 1963, *19*(3), 115–122.

DeVos, G., & Hippler, A. Cultural psychology: Comparative studies of human behavior. In G. Lindzey and E. Aronson (Eds.), *Handbook of social psychology*. (2nd ed.) Vol. 4. Reading, Mass.: Addison-Wesley, 1969.

Dicken, C. Predicting the success of Peace Corps community development workers. *Journal of Consulting and Clinical Psychology*, 1969, *33*(5), 597–606.

Dickens, S., & Hobart, C. Parental dominance and offspring ethnocentrism. *Journal of Social Psychology*, 1959, *49*, 297–303.

Dinges, N. Interdisciplinary collaboration in cross-cultural social science research. *Topics in Culture Learning*, 1977, *5*, 136–143.

Dinges, N., & Brandon, P. A review of the literature on forced relocation. Paper presented at the meeting of the American Psychological Association, San Francisco, California, August 1977.

Dinges, N., & Duffy, L. Culture and competence. In A. Marsella, R. Tharp, and T. Ciborowski (Eds.), *Perspectives on cross-cultural psychology*. New York: Academic Press, 1979.

Doob, L. *Resolving conflict in Africa: The Fermeda workshop*. New Haven: Yale University Press, 1970.

Doob, L. Unofficial intervention in destructive social conflicts. In R. Brislin, S. Bochner, and W. Lonner (Eds.), *Cross-cultural perspectives on learning*. New York: Wiley/Halsted, 1975.

Doob, L., & Foltz, W. The Belfast workshop: The application of group techniques to a destructive conflict. *Journal of Conflict Resolution*, 1973, *17*, 489–512.

Doob, L., & Foltz, W. The impact of a workshop upon grass roots leaders in Belfast. *Journal of Conflict Resolution*, 1974, *18*, 237–256.

Downs, A. *Inside bureaucracy*. Boston: Little, Brown & Co., 1966.

Draguns, J. Mental health and culture. In D. Hoopes, P. Pedersen, and G. Renwick (Eds.), *Overview of intercultural education, training, and research*. Washington, D.C.: (Georgetown University) SIETAR, 1977.

Driver, M. *Conceptual structure and group processes in an inter-nation simulation. Part I: The perception of simulated nations*. Princeton, N.J.: Educational Testing Service, 1962.

Duijker, H., & Frijda, N. *National character and national stereotypes*. Amsterdam: North-Holland Publishing Co., 1960.

Dutton, D. Tokenism, reverse discrimination, and egalitarianism in interracial behavior. *Journal of Social Psychology*, 1976, *32*(2), 93–107.

Egbert, L.; Battit, G.; Welch, C.; & Bartlett, M. Reduction of postoperative pain by encouragement and instruction of patients. *New England Journal of Medicine*, 1964, *270*, 825–827.

Ehrlich, H. *The social psychology of prejudice*. New York: Wiley, 1973.

Ehrlich, H., & Van Tubergen, N. Social distance as behavioral intentions: A replication, a failure, and a new proposal. *Psychological Reports*, 1969, *24*, 627–634.

Endler, N., & Magnusson, D. *Interactional psychology and personality*. Washington, D.C.: Hemisphere Publishing, 1976.

Entwisle, D., & Webster, M. Expectations in mixed racial groups. *Sociology of Education*, 1974, *47*, 301–318.

Evan, W. Transnational forums for peace. In Q. Wright, W. M. Evan, and M. Deutsch (Eds.), *Preventing World War III*. New York: Simon and Schuster, 1962.

Ezekiel, R. The personal future and Peace Corps competence. *Journal of Personality and Social Psychology*, 1968, *8*(2, Pt. 2).

Fahvar, M., & Milton, J. (Eds.), *The careless technology: Ecology and international development*. Garden City, N.Y.: Natural History Press, 1972.

Fayerweather, J. *The executive overseas*. Syracuse, N.Y.: Syracuse University Press, 1959.

Feldman, J. Stimulus characteristics and subject prejudice as determinants of stereotype attribution. *Journal of Personality and Social Psychology*, 1972, *21*, 333–340.

Feldman, J., & Hilterman, R. Stereotype attribution revisited: The role of stimulus characteristics, racial attitude, and cognitive differentiation. *Journal of Personality and Social Psychology*, 1975, *31*, 1177–1188.

Feldman, J., & Hilterman, R. Source of bias in performance evaluation: Two experiments. *International Journal of Intercultural Relations*, 1977, *1*(2), 35–37.

Festinger, L. *A theory of cognitive dissonance.* Stanford, Calif: Stanford University Press, 1957.

Fiedler, F. Leader attitudes, group climate, and group creativity. *Journal of Abnormal and Social Psychology,* 1962, *65,* 308–318.

Fiedler, F. *A theory of leadership effectiveness.* New York: McGraw-Hill, 1967.

Fiedler, F.; Mitchell, T.; & Triandis, H. The culture assimilator: An approach to cross-cultural training. *Journal of Applied Psychology,* 1971, *55,* 95–102.

Finley, G. Collaborative issues in cross-cultural research. *International Journal of Intercultural Relations,* 1979, *3*(1), 5–13.

Fisher, C. Spring spending spree. In C. Peters and T. Adams (Eds.), *Inside the system.* New York: Praeger, 1970.

Foa, U., and Chemers, M. The significance of role behavior differentiation for cross-cultural interaction training. *International Journal of Psychology,* 1967, *2,* 45–57.

Foa, U., & Foa, E. *Societal structures of the mind.* Springfield, Ill.: Charles Thomas, 1974.

Fox, R.; Aull, C.; & Cimono, L. Ethnic nationalism and political mobilization in industrial societies. In E. Ross (Ed.), *Interethnic communication.* Athens, Ga.: University of Georgia Press. 1978.

Freedman, J., & Fraser, S. Compliance without pressure: The foot-in-the-door technique. *Journal of Personality and Social Psychology,* 1966, *4,* 195–202.

French, J. A formal theory of social power. *Psychological Review,* 1956, *63,* 181–194.

French, L. Missionaries among the Eastern Cherokees: Religion as a means of interethnic communication. In E. Ross (Ed.), *Interethnic communication.* Atlanta, Ga.: University of Georgia Press, 1978.

Frey, F. Cross-cultural survey research in political science. In R. Holt and J. Turner (Eds.), *The methodology of comparative research.* New York: Free Press, 1970.

Gallois, C., & Markel, N. Turn taking: Social personality and conversational style. *Journal of Personality and Social Psychology,* 1975, *31,* 1134–1140.

Gama, E., & Pedersen, P. Readjustment problems of Brazilian returnees from graduate studies in the United States. *International Journal of Intercultural Relations,* 1977, *1*(4), 46–59.

Gardner, R., & Lambert, W. *Attitudes and motivation in second learning.* Rowley, Mass.: Newbury House Publishers, 1972.

Gerard, H., & Miller, N. *School desegregation.* New York: Wiley, 1973.

Gergen, K. The significance of skin color in human relations. *Daedalus,* 1967, *96,* 390–407.

Gerver, D., & Sinaiko, H. (Eds.) *Language interpretation and communication.* New York: Plenum, 1978.

Giorgis, T., & Helms, J. Training international students from developing countries as psychologists: A challenge for American psychology. *American Psychologist,* 1978, *33,* 945–951.

Glaser, E., & Taylor, S. Factors influencing the success of applied research. *American Psychologist,* 1973, *28,* 140–146.

Glaser, W. The migration and return of professionals. Columbia University: Bureau of Applied Social Science, 1973 (also *International Migration Review,* 1974, *8*(2)).

Glaser, W. Improving communication in the technical cooperation relationship. *International Development Review,* 1975, *3,* 10–14.

Glaser, W. Experts and counterparts in technical assistance. In K. Kumar (Ed.), *Bonds without bondage: Explorations in transcultural interactions.* Honolulu: University Press of Hawaii, 1979.

Glenn, E.; Witmeyer, D.; & Stevenson, K. Cultural styles of persuasion. *International Journal of Intercultural Relations,* 1977, *1*(3), 52–66.

Gollin, A. *Education for national development: Effects of U.S. technical training programs.* New York: Praeger, 1969.

Gomez, H. Comments. In D. Korten (Ed.), *Population and social development management: A challenge for management schools.* Caracas, Venezuela: Instituto de Estudios Superiores de Administración, 1978.

Goodenough, W. *Cooperation in change.* New York: Russell Sage, 1964.

Gough, H. *Manual for the California Psychological Inventory.* Palo Alto, Calif.: Consulting Psychologists Press, 1964.

Goulet, D. Notes on the ethics of developmental assistance. In K. Kumar (Ed.), *Bonds without bondage: Explorations in transcultural interactions.* Honolulu: University Press of Hawaii, 1979.

Greenfield, M. Our ugly–Arab complex. *Newsweek.* Dec. 5, 1977, *90,* 110.

Gudykunst, W. Intercultural contact and attitude change: A review of literature and suggestions for future research. *International and Intercultural Communication Annual,* 1977, *4,* 1–16.

Gudykunst, W.; Hammer, M.; & Wiseman, R. An analysis of an integrated approach to cross-cultural training. *International Journal of Intercultural Relations,* 1977, *1*(2), 99–110.

Guillotte, J. Ethnic communication circuits and noise in a rural community in Tanzania. In E. Ross (Ed.), *Interethnic communication.* Athens, Ga.: University of Georgia Press, 1978.

Gullahorn, J., & Gullahorn, J. An extension of the U-curve hypothesis. *Journal of Social Issues,* 1963, *19*(3), 33–47.

Gumperz, J. The conversational analysis of interethnic communication. In E. Ross (Ed.), *Interethnic communication.* Athens, Ga.: University of Georgia Press, 1978.

Gurin, P., & Epps, E. *Black consciousness, identity, and achievement.* New York: Wiley, 1975.

Guskin, A. Tradition and change in a Thai university. In R. Textor (Ed.), *Cultural frontiers of the Peace Corps.* Cambridge, Mass.: MIT Press, 1966.

Guthrie, G. Cultural preparation for the Philippines. In R. Textor (Ed.), *Cultural frontiers of the Peace Corps.* Cambridge, Mass.: MIT Press. 1966.

Guthrie, G. A behavioral analysis of culture learning. In R. W. Brislin, S. Bochner, and W. J. Lonner, *Cross-cultural perspectives on learning.* New York: Wiley/Halsted, 1975.

Guthrie, G., and Zektick, I. Predicting performance in the Peace Corps. *Journal of Social Psychology,* 1967, *71,* 11–21.

Hackman, J., & Oldham, G. Motivation through the design of work: Test of theory. *Organizational Behavior and Human Performance,* 1976, *16,* 250–279.

Hall, E. *The silent language.* Garden City, N.Y.: Doubleday, 1959.

Hall, E. *The hidden dimension.* Garden City, N.Y.: Doubleday, 1966.

Hall, E. *Beyond culture.* Garden City, N.Y.: Anchor, 1976.

Hall, E. Learning the Arabs' silent language. *The Bridge,* 1980, *5*(1), 5–6, 31–34.

Hamilton, D., & Gifford, R. Illusory correlation in interpersonal perception: A cognitive basis of stereotypic judgments. *Journal of Experimental Social Psychology,* 1976, *12,* 392–407.

Hammer, M.; Gudykunst, W.; & Wiseman, R. Dimensions of intercultural effectiveness: An exploratory study. *International Journal of Intercultural Relations,* 1978, *2*(4), 382–393.

Harding, J.; Proshansky, H.; Kutner, B.; & Chein, I. Prejudice and ethnic relations.

In G. Lindzey and E. Aronson (Eds.), *Handbook of social psychology.* (2nd ed.) Vol. 5, Reading, Mass.: Addison-Wesley, 1969.

Handlin, O. *The uprooted.* Boston: Little-Brown, 1951.

Harding, R., & Looney, G. Problems of Southeast Asian children in a refugee camp. *American Journal of Psychiatry,* 1977, *134*(2), 407–411.

Hare, B. R. Racial and socioeconomic variations in preadolescent area specific and general self-esteem. *International Journal of Intercultural Relations.* 1977, *1*(3), 31–51.

Harmon, R. *The art and practice of diplomacy: A selected and annotated guide.* Metuchen, N.J.: The Scarecrow Press, 1971.

Harper, R.; Wiens, A.; & Matarazzo, J. *Nonverbal communication: The state of the art.* New York: Wiley, 1978.

Harris, D.; Gough, H.; & Martin, W. Children's ethnic attitudes: II. Relationship to parental beliefs concerning child training. *Child Development,* 1950, *21,* 169–181.

Harris, J. A science of the South Pacific: Analysis of the character structure of the Peace Corps volunteer. *American Psychologist.* 1973, *28,* 232–247.

Harris, J. Identification of cross-cultural talent: The empirical approach of the Peace Corps. In R. Brislin (Ed.), *Culture learning: Concepts, applications, and research.* Honolulu: University Press of Hawaii, 1977.

Harris. M. History and significance of the emic/etic distinction. *Annual Review of Anthropology,* 1976, *5,* 329–350.

Harris, P., & Moran, R. *Managing cultural differences.* Houston: Gulf Publishing, 1979.

Harvey, J.; Ickes, W.; & Kidd, R. (Eds.) *New directions in attribution research.* New York: Wiley/Halsted, 1976.

Harvey, O.; Hunt, D.; & Schroder, H. *Conceptual systems and personality organization.* New York: Wiley, 1961.

Heclo, H. *A government of strangers.* Washington, D.C.: Brookings Institution, 1977.

Heenan, D., & Perlmutter, H. *Multinational organization development.* Reading, Mass.: Addison-Wesley, 1979.

Heisey, D. A Swedish approach to international communication. In R. Brislin (Ed.), *Culture learning: Concepts, applications, and research.* Honolulu: University Press of Hawaii, 1977.

Helms, M. Discussion: Ethnicity and the state. In L. Ross (Ed.), *Interethnic communication.* Athens, Ga.: University of Georgia Press, 1978.

Herman, S. *Israelies and Jews: The continuity of an identity.* New York: Random House, 1970.

Hermann, M. Some personal characteristics related to foreign aid voting of Congressmen. Unpublished master's thesis, Northwestern University, 1963.

Higginbotham, H. Culture and the role of client expectancy in psychotherapy. *Topics in Culture Learning,* 1977, *5,* 107–124.

Higginbotham, H. Cultural issues in providing psychological services for foreign students in the United States. *International Journal of Intercultural Relations,* 1979, *3,* 49–85(a).

Higginbotham, H. Comments on cognitive behavior modification. In R. Brislin, Orientation programs for cross-cultural preparation. In A. Marsella, R. Tharpe, and T. Ciborowski (Eds), *Current Perspectives in Cross-Cultural Psychology.* New York: Academic Press, 1979(b).

Hiller, H. The organization and marketing of tourism for development: An argument for the necessity of intervention in the market place. In R. Brislin (Ed.),

Culture learning: Concepts, applications, and research. Honolulu: University Press of Hawaii, 1977.

Hirschman, A. *Development projects observed.* Washington, D.C.: Brookings Institution, 1967.

Ho, D. Psychological implications of collectivism: With special reference to the Chinese case and Maoist dialectics. In L. Eckensberger, W. Lonner, and Y. Poortinga (Eds.), *Cross-cultural contributions to psychology.* Amsterdam: Swets and Zeitlinger, 1979.

Hoffman, J. Identity and intergroup perception in Israel. *International Journal of Intercultural Relations,* 1977, *1*(3), 79–102.

Holsti, O. The belief system and national images: A case study. *Journal of Conflict Resolution,* 1962, *6,* 244–252.

Homans, G. *The human group.* New York: Harper, 1950.

Ickis, J. Comments. In D. Korten (Ed.), *Population and social development management: A challenge for management schools.* Caracas, Venezuela: Instituto de Estudios Superiores de Administración, 1978.

Ilić, S.; Jha, C.; Sawe, J.; & Sokirkin, A. Report on the use of experts and consultants in the United Nations. United Nations (Geneva): JIU/Rep/73/3, 1973.

Inkeles, A., & Smith, D. *Becoming modern.* Cambridge, Mass.: Harvard University Press, 1974.

Irvine, S., & Carroll, W. Testing and assessment across cultures: Issues in methodology and theory. In H. Triandis and J. Berry (Eds.), *Handbook of cross-cultural psychology.* Vol. 2. Boston: Allyn and Bacon, 1980.

Irwin, M.; Klein, R.; Engle, P.; Yarbrough, C., & Nerlove, S. The problem of establishing validity in cross-cultural measurements. In L. Loeb–Adler (Ed.), Issues in cross-cultural research. *Annals of the New York Academy of Sciences,* 1977, *285,* 308–325.

Isaacs, H. *Emergent Americans: A report on "Crossroads Africa."* New York: John Day, 1961.

Jacob, B., & Jacob, P. The diplomacy of cross-national collaborative research. In K. Kumar (Ed.), *Bonds without bondage: Explorations in transcultural interactions.* Honolulu: University Press of Hawaii, 1979.

James, W. *The principles of psychology.* New York: Dover, 1950 (originally published in 1890).

Janis, I., & Mann, L. *Decision making.* New York: Free Press, 1977.

Janis, I., & Smith, M. Effects of education and persuasion on national and international images. In H. Kelman (Ed.), *International behavior: A social psychological analysis.* New York: Holt, Rinehart, and Winston, 1965.

Jones, E. The rocky road from acts to dispositions. *American Psychologist,* 1979, *34,* 107–117.

Jones, E., & Davis, K. From acts to dispositions: The attribution process in person perception. In L. Berkowitz (Ed.), *Advances in experimental social psychology.* Vol. 2. New York: Academic Press, 1965.

Jones, E.; Kanouse, D.; Kelley, H.; Nisbett, R.; Valins, S.; & Weiner, B. (Eds.) *Attribution: Perceiving the causes of behavior.* Morristown, N.J.: General Learning Press, 1972.

Jones, J. *Prejudice and racism.* Reading, Mass.: Addison-Wesley, 1972.

Jones, R., & Ashmore, R. The structure of intergroup perception: Categories and dimensions in views of ethnic groups and adjectives used in stereotype research. *Journal of Personality and Social Psychology,* 1973, *25,* 428–438.

Jones, R., & Burns, W. Volunteer satisfaction with in-country training for the Peace Corps. *Journal of Applied Psychology,* 1970, *54*(6), 533–537.

Jones, R., & Popper, R. Characteristics of Peace Corps host countries and the behavior of volunteers. *Journal of Cross-Cultural Psychology,* 1972, *18*(1), 68–87.

Kagitcibasi, C. Cross-national encounters: Turkish students in the United States. *International Journal of Intercultural Relations,* 1978, *2*(2), 141–160.

Kahneman, D., & Tversky, A. On the psychology of prediction. *Psychological Review,* 1972, *80,* 237–251.

Kanouse, D., & Hanson, L. Negativity in evaluation. In E. Jones, D. Kanouse, H. Kelley, R. Nisbett, S. Valins, and B. Weiner (Eds.), *Attribution: Perceiving the causes of behavior.* Morristown, N.J.: General Learning Press, 1972.

Kashoki, M. Indigenous scholarship in African universities: The human factor. (Paper prepared in advance for participants in Burg Wartenstein Symposium No. 78). New York: Wenner-Gren Foundation for Anthropological Research, 1978.

Katz, D. The functional approach to the study of attitudes. *Public Opinion Quarterly,* 1960, *24,* 164–204.

Katz, D. Nationalism and strategies of international conflict resolution. In H. Kelman (Ed.), *International behavior: A social psychological analysis.* New York: Holt, Rinehart, and Winston, 1965.

Katz, I. Negro performance in interracial situations. In P. Watson (Ed.), *Psychology and race.* Chicago: Aldine, 1973. (a)

Katz, I. Alternatives to a personality-deficit interpretation of Negro underachievement. In P. Watson (Ed.), *Psychology and race.* Chicago: Aldine, 1973. (b)

Katz, J. The effect of a systemmatic training program on the attitudes and behaviors of white people. *International Journal of Intercultural Relations,* 1977, *1*(1), 77–89.

Kelley, H. Attribution theory in social psychology. In D. Levine (Ed.), *Nebraska symposium on motivation.* Vol. 15. Lincoln, Nebraska: University of Nebraska Press, 1967.

Kelley, H. Attribution in social interaction. In E. Jones, D. Kanouse, H. Kelley, R. Nisbett, S. Valins, and B. Weiner (Eds.), *Attribution: Perceiving the causes of behavior.* Morristown, N.J.: General Learning Corporation, 1972.

Kelman, H. Changing attitudes through international activities. *Journal of Social Issues,* 1962, *18*(1), 68–87.

Kelman, H. Social-psychological approaches to the study of international relations: Definition of scope. In H. Kelman (Ed.), *International behavior: A social psychological analysis.* New York: Holt, Rinehart, and Winston, 1965.

Kelman. H. Social-psychological approaches to the study of international relations: The question of relevance. In H. Kelman (Ed.), *International behavior: A social psychological analysis.* New York: Holt, Rinehart, and Winston, 1965.

Kelman, H., & Bailyn, L. Effects of cross-cultural experience on national images: A study of Scandinavian students in America. *Journal of Conflict Resolution,* 1962, *6,* 319–334.

Kelman, H., & Ezekiel, R. *Cross-cultural encounters.* San Francisco: Jossey-Bass, 1970.

Kelman, H., with Steinitz, V. The reactions of participants in a foreign specialists' seminar to their American experience. *Journal of Social Issues,* 1963, *19*(3), 61–114.

Kern, K. Immigration and the integration process. In A. Stoller (Ed.), *New faces.* Melbourne and London: F. W. Cheshire, 1966.

Kessen, W. (Ed.) *Childhood in China.* New Haven: Yale University Press, 1975.

Kidder, L. The inadvertent creation of a neocolonial culture: A study of Western sojourners in India. *International Journal of Intercultural Relations,* 1977, *1*(1), 48–60.

Kiev, A. Psychiatric disorders in minority groups. In P. Watson (Ed.), *Psychology and race.* Chicago: Aldine, 1973.

Kim, Y. Inter-ethnic and intra-ethnic communication: A study of Korean immigrants in Chicago. *International and Intercultural Communication Annual,* 1977, *4,* 53–68.

Kim, Y. A communication approach to the acculturation process: A study of Korean immigrants in Chicago. *International Journal of Intercultural Relations,* 1978, *2*(2), 197–224.

Kipnis, D. *The powerholders.* Chicago: University of Chicago Press, 1976.

Kiste, R. *The Bikinians.* Menlo Park, Calif.: Cummings, 1974.

Klein, M. Adaptation to new cultural environments. In D. Hoopes, P. Pedersen, and G. Renwick (Eds.), *Overview of intercultural education, training, and research.* Washington, D.C.: (Georgetown University) SIETAR, 1977.

Klein, M., Alexander, A., Tseng, K., Miller, M., Yeh, E., Chu, H., & Workneh, F. The foreign student adaptation project: Social experiences of Asian students in the U.S. *International Educational and Cultural Exchange,* 1971, *6*(3), 77–90.

Klineberg, O. Life is fun in a smiling, fair-skinned world. *Saturday Review,* February 16, 1963, pp. 75–78, 87.

Klineberg, O. *The human dimension in international relations.* New York: Holt, Rinehart, and Winston, 1964.

Klineberg. O. Historical perspectives: Cross-cultural psychology before 1960. In H. Triandis and W. Lambert (Eds.), *Handbook of cross-cultural psychology.* Vol. 1. Boston: Allyn and Bacon, 1980.

Klineberg, O., & Hull, F. *At a foreign university.* New York: Praeger, 1979.

Kluckhohn, F., & Strodtbeck, F. *Variations in value orientaitons.* Evanston, Ill.: Row, Peterson, 1961.

Kroeber, A., & Kluckhohn, C. *Culture.* Cambridge: Papers of the Peabody Museum, 1952, *47,* No. 1.

Kumar, K. (Ed.) *Bonds without bondage: Explorations in transcultural interactions.* Honolulu: University Press of Hawaii, 1979. (a)

Kumar, K. Indigenization and transnational cooperation in the social sciences. In K. Kumar (Ed.), *Bonds without bondage: Explorations in transcultural interactions.* Honolulu: University Press of Hawaii, 1979. (b)

Kutner, B.; Wilkins, C.; & Yarrow, P. Verbal attitudes and overt behavior involving racial prejudice. *Journal of Abnormal and Social Psychology,* 1952. *47,* 649–652.

LaFrance, M., & Mayo, C. Cultural aspects of nonverbal communication: A review essay. *International Journal of Intercultural Relations.* 1978, *2*(1), 71–89.

Lambert, R., & Bressler, M. *Indian students on an American campus.* Minneapolis: University of Minnesota Press, 1956.

Lambert, W. Culture and language as factors in learning and education. In F. Aboud and R. Meade (Eds.), *Cultural factors in learning and education.* Bellingham, Wash.: Western Washington University, 1974.

Lambert, W., & Klineberg, O. *Children's views of foreign peoples.* New York: Appleton-Century-Crofts, 1967.

Lambert, W., & Tucker, R. *Bilingual education of children: The St. Lambert experiment.* Rowley, Mass.: Newbury House, 1972.

Lampe, P. The importance of ethnicity in ethnic studies programs. *International Journal of Intercultural Relations,* 1979, *3,* 175–185.

LaPiere, R. Attitudes and actions. *Social Forces*, 1934, *13*, 230–237.

Lee, L. Is social competence independent of cultural context? *American Psychologist*, 1979, *34*, 795–796.

Leighton, A. *The governing of men*. Princeton, N.J.: Princeton University Press, 1945.

Lesser, S., & Peter, H. Training foreign nationals in the United States. In R. Likert and S. Hayes (Eds.) *Some applications of behavioral research*. New York: UNESCO, 1957.

Levine, R. Socialization, social structure, and intersocietal images. In H. Kelman (Ed.), *International behavior: A social psychological analysis*. New York: Holt, Rinehart, and Winston, 1965.

LeVine, R., & Campbell, D. *Ethnocentrism*. New York: Wiley, 1972.

Levinson, D. Authoritarian personality and foreign policy. *Journal of Conflict Resolution*, 1957, *1*, 37–47.

Lockyear, F. Factors affecting non-sponsored students from Iran. In G. Althen (Ed.), *Students from the Arab World and Iran*. Washington, D.C.: National Association for Foreign Student Affairs, 1979.

Lopez, T. Cultural pluralism: Political hoax? Educational need? *Journal of Teacher Education*, 1973, *24*, 277–278.

Lott, J. Migration of a mentality: The Filipino community. *Social Casework*, 1976, *57*(3), 165–172.

Macomber, W. *The angels game: A handbook of modern diplomacy*. New York: Stein and Day, 1975.

Mahoney, F. Success in Somalia. In R. Textor (Ed.), *Cultural frontiers of the Peace Corps*. Cambridge, Mass.: MIT Press, 1966.

Malpass, R., & Salancik, G. Linear and branching formats in culture assimilator training. *International Journal of Intercultural Relations*, 1977, *1*(2), 76–87.

Marr, P. Social, cultural, and religious problems of adjustment for Arab students from the fertile crescent and gulf. In G. Althen (Ed.), *Students from the Arab World and Iran*. Washington, D.C.: National Association for Foreign Student Affairs, 1979.

Marsella, A.; Kinzie, J.; & Gordon, P. Ethnic variations in the expression of depression. *Journal of Cross-Cultural Psychology*, 1973, *4*, 435–458.

Maslach, C. The client role in staff burn-out. *Journal of Social Issues*, 1978, *34*(4), 111–124.

Maslach, C. Negative emotional biasing of unexplained arousal. *Journal of Personality and Social Psychology*, 1979, *37*, 953–969.

McCauley, C., & Stitt, C. An individual and quantitative measure of stereotypes. *Journal of Personality and Social Psychology*, 1978, *36*, 929–941.

McClelland, D., & Winter, D. *Motivating economic achievement*. New York: Free Press, 1971.

McConahay, J., & Hough, J. Symbolic racism. *Journal of Social Issues*, 1976, *32*(2), 23–45.

McCormack, W. Problems of American scholars in India. *Asian Survey*, 1976, *16*, 1064–1080.

McCormack, W. The effect of leaving the field: Mark Twain's voyage to Hawaii. Manuscript completed, 1980, publication forthcoming, preprints available (International Education, U. of California, Berkeley).

McGuire, W. The nature of attitudes and attitude change. In G. Lindzey and E. Aronson (Eds.), *Handbook of social psychology*. (2nd ed.) Vol. 3. Reading, Mass.: Addison-Wesley, 1969.

McGuire, W. The concepts of attitudes and their relations to behaviors. In H. Sinaiko and L. Broedling (Eds.), *Perspectives on attitudes assessment: Surveys and their alternatives*. Arlington, Virginia: Office of Naval Research, 1975.

Merton, R. *Social theory and social structure*. Glencoe, Ill.: The Free Press, 1957.

Mestenhauser, J. *Learning informally with foreign students*. Minneapolis: University of Minnesota (Foreign Students Adviser's Office), 1974.

Mestenhauser, J., & Barsig, D. Foreign students as teachers: Learning with foreign students. Publication No. P00478. Washington, D.C.: National Association for Foreign Student Affairs, 1978.

Milburn, T. Conflict in cross-cultural interaction. In D. Hoopes, P. Pedersen, and G. Renwick (Eds.), *Overview of intercultural education, training, and research*. Washington, D.C.: (Georgetown University) SIETAR, 1977.

Milgram, S. *Obedience to authority*. New York: Harper & Row, 1974.

Miller, G., & McNeil, D. Psycholinguistics. In G. Lindzey and E. Aronson (Eds.), *Handbook of Social Psychology*. (2nd ed.) Vol. 3. Reading, Mass.: Addison-Wesley, 1969.

Miller, H. The effectiveness of teaching techniques for reducing colour prejudices. *Liberal Education*, 1969, *16*, 25–31.

Mirvis, P., & Seashore, S. Being ethical in organizational research. *American Psychologist*, 1979, *34*, 766–780.

Mischel, W. Predicting the success of Peace Corps volunteers in Nigeria. *Journal of Personality and Social Psychology*, 1965, *1*(5), 510–517.

Mischel, W. Toward a cognitive social learning reconceptualization of personality. *Psychological Review*, 1973, *80*, 252–283.

Mishler, A. Personal contact in international exchanges. In H. Kelman (Ed.), *International behavior: A social-psychological analysis*. New York: Holt, Rinehart, and Winston, 1965.

Molina, J. Cultural barriers and interethnic communication in a multiethnic neighborhood. In E. Ross (Ed.), *Interethnic Communication*. Athens, Ga.: University of Georgia Press, 1978.

Morris, R. National status and attitudes of foreign students. *Journal of Social Issues*, 1956, *12*, 24–25.

Morris, R. *The two way mirror: National status in foreign student adjustment*. Minneapolis: University of Minnesota Press, 1960.

Murillo-Rohde, I. Family life among mainland Puerto Ricans in New York City slums. *Perspectives in Psychiatric Care*, 1976, *14*(4), 174–179.

Murray, P. *Proud shoes: The story of an American family*. New York: Harper & Row, 1978.

Myer, R. Initial findings from a survey of LDC alumni from U.S. universities. Paper delivered at the Conference on International Education, Washington, D.C., February 1979.

Myrdal, G. *An American dilemma: The Negro problem and modern democracy*. New York: Harper, 1944.

Newcomb, T. Autistic hostility and social reality. *Human Relations*, 1947, *1*, 69–86.

Newcomb, T.; Turner, R.; & Converse, P. *Social Psychology*. New York: Holt, 1965.

New York Times, "Seven students cleared in death during hazing face discipline." January 20, 1975, p. 60.

New York Times, "Six students are suspended in college hazing death." September 19, 1975, p. 34.

Nicolson, H. *Diplomacy*. (2nd ed.) London: Oxford University Press, 1960.

Nurcombe, B. *Children of the disadvantaged.* Honolulu: University Press of Hawaii, 1974.

Oberg, K. Culture shock and the problem of adjustment to new cultural environments. Washington, D.C.: Department of State, Foreign Service Institute, 1958.

O'Brien, G., & Plooij, D. Development of culture training manuals for medical workers with Pitjantjatjara aboriginals. The relative effect of critical incident and prose training upon knowledge, attitudes, and motivation. In G. Kearney and D. McElwain (Eds.), *Aboriginal cognition: Retrospect and prospect.* Canberra, Australia: Australian Institute of Aboriginal Studies, 1976.

O'Brien, G.; Fiedler, F.; & Hewlett, T. The effects of programmed culture training upon the performance of volunteer medical teams in Central America. Seattle: University of Washington, Organizational Research, 1970.

Osgood, C. *An alternative to war or surrender.* Urbana, Ill.: University of Illinois Press, 1962.

Osgood, C. Cross-cultural comparability in attitude measurement via multilingual semantic differentials. In I. Steiner and M. Fishbein (Eds.), *Current studies in social psychology.* New York: Holt, Rinehart, and Winston, 1965.

Osgood, C. Explorations in semantic space: A personal diary. *Journal of Social Issues,* 1971, *27*(4), 5–64.

Osgood, C. Objective indicators of subjective culture. In L. Loeb-Adler (Ed.), Issues in cross-cultural research. *Annals of the New York Academy of Science,* 1977, *285,* 435–450.

Osgood, C. From Yang and Yin to "And" or "But" in cross-cultural perspective. *International Journal of Psychology,* 1979, *14,* 1–35.

Osgood, C., May, W., & Miron, M. *Cross-cultural universals of affective meaning.* Urbana, Ill.: University of Illinois Press, 1975.

Osgood, C., Suci, G., & Tannenbaum, P. *The measurement of meaning,* Urbana, Ill.: University of Illinois Press, 1957.

Oskamp, S. Social perception. In L. Wrightsman, *Social psychology in the seventies.* Monterey, Calif.: Brooks/Cole, 1970.

Parkinson, C. *Parkinson's law and other studies in administration.* Boston: Houghton Mifflin, 1957.

Pearson, R. Cross-cultural value conflict: Limiting the conception of multicultural education. *International Journal of Intercultural Relations,* 1977, *1*(2), 88–98.

Pedersen, P. Personal problem solving resources used by University of Minnesota foreign students. *Topics in Culture Learning,* 1975, *3,* 55–65.

Pedersen, P. The triad model of cross-cultural counselling. *Personnel and Guidance Journal,* October 1977.

Pedersen, P. The triad model: A cross-cultural coalition against the problem. In R. Corsini (Ed.), *Innovative psychotherapies.* New York: Wiley, 1980.

Pedersen, P., Lonner, W., & Draguns, J. (Eds.), *Counseling across cultures.* Honolulu: University Press of Hawaii, 1976.

Perlmutter, H. Some characteristics of the xenophilic orientation. *Journal of Abnormal and Social Psychology,* 1956, *52,* 130–135.

Peter, L., & Hull, R. *The Peter Principle.* New York: William Morrow, 1969.

Pettigrew, T. Personality and socio-cultural factors in intergroup attitudes: A cross-national comparison. *Journal of Conflict Resolution,* 1958, *2,* 29–42.

Pincus, C. In a Jerusalem Ulpan. *Topics in Culture Learning,* 1977, *5,* 61–71.

Pool, I. What American travellers learn. *Antioch Review,* 1958, *18,* 431–446.

Pool, I. Effects of cross-national contact on national and international images. In

H. Kelman (Ed.), *International behavior: A social-psychological analysis.* New York: Holt, Rinehart, and Winston, 1965.

Price-Williams, D. A study concerning concepts of conservation of quantities among primitive children. *Acta Psychologica,* 1961, *18,* 297–305.

Pruitt, D. An analysis of responsiveness between nations. *Journal of Conflict Resolution,* 1962, *6,* 5–18.

Pruitt, D. Definition of the situation as a determinant of international action. In H. Kelmn (Ed.), *International behavior: A social-psychological analysis.* New York: Holt, Rinehart, and Winston, 1965.

Pruitt, F. The adaptation of African students to American society. *International Journal of Intercultural Relations,* 1978, *2*(1), 90–116.

Pushkin, I., & Veness, T. The development of racial awareness and prejudice in children. In P. Watson (Ed.), *Psychology and race.* Chicago: Aldine, 1973.

Rabbie, J., & Horowitz, M. Arousal of ingroup-outgroup bias by a chance win or loss. *Journal of Personality and Social Psychology,* 1969, *13,* 269–277.

Rabinowitch, E. *The dawn of a new age: Reflections on science and human affairs.* Chicago: University of Chicago Press, 1964.

Randolph, G.; Landis, D.; & Tzeng, O. The effects of time and practice upon culture assimilator training. *International Journal of Intercultural Relations,* 1977, *1*(2), 105–119.

Raspberry, W. Reading, writing, and dialect. *The Washington Post,* August 1, 1979, p. A21.

Reychler, L. *Patterns of diplomatic thinking: A cross-national study of structural and social-psychological determinants.* New York: Praeger, 1978.

Rich, A. L. *Interracial communication.* New York: Harper & Row, 1974.

Rich, A., & Ogawa, D. Intercultural and interracial communication. In L. Samovar and R. Porter (Eds.), *Intercultural communication: A reader.* (2nd ed.) Belmont, Calif.: Wadsworth, 1976.

Richmond, A. Race relations and behaviour in reality. In P. Watson (Eds.), *Psychology and race.* Chicago: Aldine, 1973.

Riordan, C. Equal-status interracial contact: A review and revision of the concept. *International Journal of Intercultural Relations,* 1978, *2*(2), 161–185.

Ritterband, P. The determinants of motives of Israeli students studying in the United States. *Sociology of Education,* 1969, *42,* 330–349.

Roberts, A., & Rokeach, M. Anomie, authoritarianism, and prejudice: A replication. *American Journal of Sociology,* 1956, *61,* 355–358.

Robinson, J., & Snyder, R. Decision-making in international politics. In H. Kelman (Ed.), *International behavior: A social-psychological analysis.* New York: Holt, Rinehart, and Winston, 1965.

Rogers, C. Communication: Its blocking and its facilitation. *Etc.: Review of General Semantics,* 1952, *9,* 83–88.

Rokeach, M. *The open and closed mind.* New York: Basic Books, 1960.

Rosch, E. Human categorization. In N. Warren (Ed.), *Studies in cross-cultural psychology.* Vol. 1. London and New York: Academic Press, 1977.

Rosenberg, M. Images in relation to the policy process: American public opinion on cold-war issues. In H. Kelman (Ed.), *International behavior: A social psychological analysis.* New York: Holt, Rinehart, and Winston, 1965.

Rosenblith, J. A replication of "Some roots of prejudice." *Journal of Abnormal and Social Psychology,* 1949, *44,* 470–489.

Ross, E. Interethnic communication: An overview. In E. Ross (Ed.), *Interethnic Communication.* Athens, Ga.: University of Georgia Press, 1978.

Ross, L. The intuitive psychologist and his shortcomings: Distortion in the attribution process. In L. Berkowitz (Ed.), *Advances in Experimental Social Psychology.* Vol. 10. New York: Academic Press, 1977.

Rotter, J. Generalized expectancies for internal vs. external control of reinforcement. *Psychological Monographs,* 1966, *80* (Whole No. 609).

Ruben, B. Human communication and cross-cultural effectiveness. *International and Intercultural Communication Annual,* 1977, *4,* 95–105.

Ruben, B., & Kealey, D. Behavioral assessment of communication competency and the prediction of cross-cultural adaptation. *International Journal of Intercultural Relations,* 1979, *3*(1), 15–47.

Rummel, R. International transactions and conflict: Polarities or complements? In K. Kumar (Ed.), *Bonds without bondage: Explorations in transcultural interactions.* Honolulu: University Press of Hawaii, 1979.

Rusk, D. Parliamentary diplomacy-debate versus negotiation. *World Affairs Interpreter,* 1955, *26,* 121–138.

Ryan, W. *Blaming the victim.* New York: Pantheon Books, 1971.

Samovar, L., & Porter, R. (Eds.) *Intercultural communication: A reader.* (2nd ed.) Belmont, Calif.: Wadsworth, 1976.

Sampson, D., & Smith, H. A scale to measure world-minded attitudes. *Journal of Social Psychology,* 1957, *45,* 99–106.

Sanford, N. The roots of prejudice: Emotional dynamics. In P. Watson (Ed.), *Psychology and race.* Chicago: Aldine, 1973.

Sanua, V. Immigration, migration, and mental illness: A review of the literature with special emphasis on schizophrenia. In E. Brody (Ed.), *Behavior in new environments.* Beverly Hills: Sage Publications, 1970.

Sarbin, T., & Allen, V. Role theory. In G. Lindzey and E. Aronson (Eds.), *Handbook of social psychology.* (2nd ed.) Vol. 1. Reading, Mass.: Addison-Wesley, 1968.

Satia, J. Comments. In D. Korten Ed.), *Population and social development management: a challenge for management schools.* Caracas, Venezuela: Superiores de Administración, 1978.

Sawyer, J., & Guetzkow, H. Bargaining and negotiation in international relations. In H. Kelman (Ed.), *International behavior: A social psychological analysis.* New York: Holt, Rinehart, and Winston, 1965.

Schwartz, F. The foreign student and interpersonal relationships. In M. Baron (Ed.), *Advising, counseling, and helping the foreign student.* Washington, D.C.: National Association for Foreign Student Affairs, 1975.

Schwarzwald, J., & Yinon, Y. Symmetrical and asymmetrical interethnic perception in Israel. *International Journal of Intercultural Relations,* 1977, *1*(1), 40–47.

Scott, F. *The American experience of Swedish students.* Minneapolis: University of Minnesota Press, 1956.

Scott, W. Rationality and non-rationality of international attitudes. *Journal of Conflict Resolution,* 1958, *2,* 8–16.

Scott, W. Psychological and social correlates of international images. In H. Kelman (Ed.), *International behavior: A social psychological analysis.* New York: Holt, Rinehart, and Winston, 1965.

Scriven, M. The methodology of evaluation. In R. Stake (Ed.), *AERA Monograph Series on Curriculum Evaluation.* Vol. 1. Chicago: Rand-McNally, 1967.

Seelye, H., & Wasilewski, J. Toward a taxonomy of coping strategies used in multicultural settings. Paper presented at the meetings of the Society for Intercultural Education, Training, and Research, Mexico City, March 1979.

Selltiz, C.; Christ, J.; Havel, J.; & Cook, S. *Attitudes and social relations of foreign students in the United States.* Minneapolis: University of Minnesota Press, 1963.

Selltiz, C., & Cook, S. Factors influencing attitudes of foreign students toward the host country. *Journal of Social Issues,* 1962, *18,* 7–23.

Sewell, W., & Davidsen, O. The adjustment of Scandinavian students. *Journal of Social Issues,* 1956, *12,* 9–19.

Sewell, W., & Davidsen, O. *Scandinavian students on an American campus.* Minneapolis: University of Minnesota Press, 1961.

Shaw, M., & Wright, J. *Scales for the measurement of attitudes.* New York: McGraw-Hill, 1967.

Shaw, W., & McClain, E. *The Findlay story.* Dayton, Ohio: Charles Kettering Foundation, 1979.

Sherif, M. Superordinate goals in the reduction of intergroup tension. *American Journal of Sociology,* 1958, *63,* 349–356.

Sherif, M. *In common predicament: Social psychology of intergroup conflict and cooperation.* New York: Houghton Mifflin, 1966.

Simon, H. *Administrative behavior: A study of decision-making processes in administrative organizations.* New York: Macmillan, 1957. (a)

Simon, H. *Models of man: Social and rational.* New York: Wiley, 1957. (b)

Simon, R., & Alstein, H. *Transracial adoption.* New York: Wiley, 1977.

Simpson, G., & Yinger, J. Techniques for reducing prejudice: Changing the situation. In P. Watson (Ed.), *Psychology and race.* Chicago: Aldine, 1973.

Smith, H. Do intercultural experiences affect attitudes? *Journal of Abnormal and Social Psychology,* 1955, *51,* 469–477.

Smith, L. Teaching English in Asia: An overview. In R. Brislin (Ed.), *Culture learning: Concepts, applications, and research.* Honolulu: University Press of Hawaii, 1977.

Smith, M. B. (Ed.) Attitudes and adjustment in cross-cultural contact: Recent studies of foreign students. *Journal of Social Issues,* 1956, *12* (entire issue).

Smith, M. B. Explorations in competence: A study of Peace Corps teachers in Ghana. *American Psychologist,* 1966, *21,* 555–556.

Smith, M. B. *Social psychology and human values.* Chicago: Aldine, 1969.

Smith, M. B.; Fawcett, J. T.; Ezekiel, R.; & Roth, S. A factorial study of morale among Peace Corps teachers in Ghana. *Journal of Social Issues,* 1963, *19*(3), 10–32.

Smith, M. E. The case of the disappearing ethnics. In E. Ross (Ed.), *Interethnic communication.* Athens, Ga.: University of Georgia Press, 1978.

Smyser, A. He saved island AJAs from mass internment. *Honolulu Star-Bulletin,* December 6, 1979, pp. A20–21.

Social Science Institute. *Racial attitudes.* Social science source document no. 3. Nashville, Tenn.: Social Science Institute of Fisk University, 1946.

Spaulding, S., & Flack, M. *The world's students in the United States.* New York: Praeger, 1976.

Spector, P. Troop-community training. Paper presented at the NATO conference on "Special training for multilateral forces," Brussels, Belgium, July 1969 (reviewed in Brislin & Pedersen, 1976).

Stagner, R. Egocentrism, ethnocentrism, and altrocentrism: Factors in individual and intergroup violence. *International Journal of Intercultural Relations,* 1977, *1*(3), 9–29.

Star, S.; Williams, R.; & Stouffer, S. A note on Negro troops in combat. In S. Stouffer, A. Lumsdaine, M. Lumsdaine, R. Williams, M. Smith, I. Janis, S. Star, & L. Cottrell (Eds.), *The American Soldier: Combat and its aftermath.* Vol. 1. Princeton, N.J.: Princeton University Press, 1949.

Steinkalk, E., & Taft, R. The effect of a planned intercultural experience on the attitudes and behaviors of the participants. *International Journal of Intercultural Relations,* 1979, *3,* 187–197.

Stephan, W., & Rosenfield, D. Effects of desegregation on racial attitudes. *Journal of Personality and Social Psychology,* 1978, *36,* 795–804.

Stifel, L. Comments. In D. Korten (Ed.), *Population and social development management: A challenge for management schools.* Caracas, Venezuela: Instituto de Estudios Superiores de Administración, 1978.

Stouffer, S.; Lumsdaine, A.; Lumsdaine, M.; Williams, R.; Smith, M.; Janis, I.; Star, S.; & Cottrell, L. *The American Soldier: Combat and its aftermath.* Princeton, N.J.: Princeton University Press, 1949.

Sue, D., & Sue, S. Counseling Chinese-Americans. *Personnel and Guidance Journal,* 1972, *50,* 637–644.

Sue, S., & Sue, D. Chinese-American personality and mental health. *Amerasia Journal,* 1971, *1,* 36–49.

Szanton, D. Cultural confrontation in the Philippines. In R. Textor (Ed.), *Cultural frontiers of the Peace Corps.* Cambridge, Mass.: MIT Press, 1966.

Taft, R. *From stranger to citizen.* London: Tavistock, 1966.

Taft, R. Migration: Problems of adjustment and assimilation in immigrants. In P. Watson (Ed.), *Psychology and race.* Chicago: Aldine, 1973.

Taft, R. Coping with unfamiliar cultures. In N. Warren (Ed.), *Studies in cross-cultural psychology.* Vol. 1. London and New York: Academic Press, 1977.

Tajfel, H. Cognitive aspects of prejudice. *Journal of Social Issues,* 1969, *25,* 79–97.

Tajfel, H. The roots of prejudice: Cognitive aspects. In P. Watson (Ed.), *Psychology and race.* Chicago: Aldine, 1973.

Talbot, L. Ecological consequences of rangeland development in Masailand, East Africa. In M. Farvar and J. Milton (Eds.), *The careless technology: Ecology and international development.* Garden City, N.Y.: Natural History Press, 1972.

Tapp, J.; Kelman, H.; Wrightsman, L.; Triandis, H.; & Coelho, G. Continuing concerns in cross-cultural ethics: A report. *International Journal of Psychology,* 1974, *9,* 231–249.

Taylor, D., & Jaggi, V. Ethnocentrism and causal attribution in a South Indian context. *Journal of Cross-Cultural Psychology,* 1974, *5,* 162–171.

Taylor, S., & Fiske, S. Salience, attention, and attribution: Top of the head phenomena. In L. Berkowitz (Ed.), *Advances in experimental social psychology.* Vol. 11. New York: Academic Press, 1978.

Taylor, S.; Fiske, S.; Etcoff, N.; & Ruderman, A. Categorical and contextual bases of person memory and stereotyping. *Journal of Personality and Social Psychology,* 1978, *36,* 778–793.

Tendler, J. *Inside foreign aid.* Baltimore, Md.: Johns Hopkins University Press, 1975.

Textor, R. *Cultural frontiers of the Peace Corps.* Cambridge, Mass.: MIT Press, 1966. (a)

Textor, R. Introduction. In R. Textor (Ed.), *Cultural frontiers of the Peace Corps.* Cambridge: MIT Press, 1966(b).

Thayer, C. *Diplomat.* New York: Harper, 1959.

Thibaut, J., & Kelley, H. *The social psychology of groups.* New York: Wiley, 1959.

Thomas, W., & Znaniecki, F. *The Polish peasant in Poland and America.* Boston: Gorham, 1918–1920. 5 vols.

Thomson, C., & English, J. Premature return of Peace Corps volunteers. *Public Health Reports*, 1964, *79*, 1065–1073.

Triandis, H. Exploratory factor analyses of the behavioral component of social attitudes. *Journal of Abnormal and Social Psychology*, 1964, *68*, 420–430.

Triandis, H. *The analysis of subjective culture.* New York: Wiley, 1972.

Triandis, H. *Interpersonal behavior.* Monterey, Calif.: Brooks/Cole, 1977. (a)

Triandis, H. Subjective culture and interpersonal relations across cultures. In L. Loeb-Adler (Ed.), Issues in cross-cultural research. *Annals of the New York Academy of Sciences*, 1977, *285*, 418–434. (b)

Triandis, H. Theoretical framework for evaluation of cross-cultural training effectiveness. *International Journal of Intercultural Relations*, 1977, *1*(4), 19–45. (c)

Triandis, H. Preface. In H. Triandis and W. Lambert (Eds.), *Handbook of cross-cultural psychology.* Vol. 1. Boston: Allyn and Bacon, 1980.

Triandis, H., & Davis, E. Race and belief as determinants of behavioral intentions. *Journal of Personality and Social Psychology*, 1965, *2*, 715–727.

Triandis, H.; Loh, W.; & Levin, L. Race, status, quality of spoken English, and opinions about civil rights as determinants of interpersonal attitudes. *Journal of Personality and Social Psychology*, 1966, *3*, 468–472.

Triandis, H.; Lonner, W.; Lambert, W.; Berry, J.; Heron, A.; Brislin, R.; & Draguns, J. (Eds.), *Handbook of cross-cultural psychology.* Boston: Allyn and Bacon, 1980.

Trifonovitch, G. Culture learning/culture teaching. *Educational Perspectives*, 1977, *16*(4), 18–22. (a)

Trifonovitch, G. On cross-cultural orientation techniques. In R. Brislin (Ed.), *Culture learning: Concepts, applications, and research.* Honolulu: University Press of Hawaii, 1977(b).

Trifonovitch, G.; Hamnett, M.; Geschwind, N.; & Brislin, R. Experiential cross-cultural training. Paper delivered at the combined meetings of the Nineteenth International Congress of Applied Psychology and the International Association for Cross-cultural Psychology, Munich, Germany, August 1978.

Trubowitz, J. *Changing the racial attitudes of children.* New York: Praeger, 1969.

Tseng, W.; McDermott, J.; & Maretzki, T. *Adjustment in intercultural marriage.* Honolulu: University Press of Hawaii, 1977.

Turner, J. Social comparison and social identity: Some prospects for group behavior. *European Journal of Social Psychology*, 1975, *5*, 5–34.

Useem, J., & Useem, R. *The Western educated man in India.* New York: Dryden Press, 1955.

Useem, J., & Useem, R. The interfaces of a binational third culture: A study of the American community in India. *Journal of Social Issues*, 1967, *23*(1), 130–143.

Van Zandt, H. How to negotiate in Japan. *Harvard Business Review*, Nov.–Dec. 1970, pp. 45–56.

Verma, G. Some effects of curriculum innovation on the racial attitudes of adolescents. *International Journal of Intercultural Relations*, 1977, *1*(3), 67–80.

Vroom, V. Industrial social psychology. In G. Lindzey and E. Aronson (Eds.), *Handbook of social psychology.* (2nd ed.) Vol. 5. Reading, Mass.: Addison-Wesley, 1969.

Waite, R. Further attempts to integrate and urbanize first grade reading textbooks: A research study. *Journal of Negro Education*, 1968, *37*, 62–70.

Walsh, J. The Mexico-United States border problem: A culturo-legal perspective. Paper delivered at the meetings of the Society for Intercultural Education, Training, and Research, Mexico City, March 1979.

Warwick, D. The politics and ethics of cross-cultural research. In H. Triandis and

W. Lambert (Eds.), *Handbook of cross-cultural psychology*. Vol. 1. Boston: Allyn and Bacon, 1980.

Watson, J., & Lippitt, R. *Learning across cultures: A study of Germans visiting America*. Ann Arbor: University of Michigan, Institute for Social Research, 1955.

Watson, P. (Ed.) *Psychology and race*. Chicago: Aldine, 1973 (a).

Watson, P. Introduction. In P. Watson (Ed.), *Psychology and race*. Chicago: Aldine, 1973. (b)

Watson, R. Investigations into deindividuation using a cross-cultural survey technique. *Journal of Personality and Social Psychology*, 1973, *25*, 342–345.

Watt, D., & Walker, K. *The experiment in international living: Letters to the founder*. Brattleboro, Vt.: The Experiment Press, 1977.

Weldon, D.; Carlston, D.; Rissman, A.; Slobodin, L.; & Triandis, H. A laboratory test of effects of culture assimilator training. *Journal of Personality and Social Psychology*, 1975, *32*, 300–310.

White, R. Images in the context of international conflict: Soviet perceptions of the U.S. and the U.S.S.R. In H. Kelman (Ed.), *International behavior: A social psychological analysis*. New York: Holt, Rinehart, and Winston, 1965.

White, S., & Mitchell, T. Job enrichment versus social cues: A comparison and competitive test. *Journal of Applied Psychology*, 1979, *64*, 1–9.

Whorf, B. *Language, thought, and reality: Selected writings*. Cambridge, Mass.: MIT Press, 1956.

Wicker, A. Attitudes vs. actions: The relationship of verbal and overt behavioral responses to attitude objects. *Journal of Social Issues*, 1969, *25*(4), 41–78.

Wicker, A. Processes which mediate behavior-environment congruence. *Behavioral Science*, 1972, *17*, 265–277.

Williams, R. *Strangers next door: Ethnic relations in American communities*. Englewood Cliffs, N.J.: Prentice-Hall, 1964.

Wispe, L. (Ed.) Positive forms of social behavior. *Journal of Social Issues*, 1972, *28*(3) (entire issue).

Witkin, H. Theory in cross-cultural research: Its uses and risks. In Y. Poortinga (Ed.), *Basic problems in cross-cultural psychology*. Amsterdam: Swets and Zeitlinger, 1977.

Witkin, H., & Berry, J. Psychological differentiation in cross-cultural perspective. *Journal of cross-cultural psychology*, 1975, *6*, 4–87.

Wright, Q.; Evans, W.; & Deutsch, M. (Eds.) *Preventing World War III*. New York: Simon and Schuster, 1962.

Wrightsman, L. *Social psychology in the seventies*. Monterey, Calif.: Brooks/Cole, 1972.

Yarrow, M.; Campbell, J.; & Yarrow, L. Acquisition of new norms: A study of racial desegregation. *Journal of Social Issues*, 1958, *14*(1), 8–28.

Yeh, E.; Miller, M.; Alexander, A.; Klein, M.; Tseng, K.; Workneh, F.; & Chu, H. The American student in Taiwan. *International Studies Quarterly*, 1973, *17*, 359–371.

Yinger, J., & Simpson, C. Techniques for reducing prejudice: Changing the prejudiced person. In P. Watson (Ed.), *Psychology and race*. Chicago: Aldine, 1973.

Young, A. Interview, in *Playboy*, July, 1977; summarized in *Newsweek*, June 20, 1977, p. 34.

Yousef, F. Communication patterns: Some aspects of nonverbal behavior in intercultural communication. In E. Ross (Ed.), *Interethnic communication*. Athens, Ga.: University of Georgia Press, 1978.

Zaidi, S. Adjustment problems of foreign Muslim students in Pakistan. In R. Brislin,

S. Bochner, and W. Lonner (Eds.), *Cross-cultural perspectives on learning.* New York: Wiley/Halsted, 1975.

Ziffer, W. Missionary pre-service training—some observations: Part I. *International review of Missions,* 1969, *58*(230), 195–203.

Zimbardo, P. The human choice: Individuation, reason, and order versus deindividuation, impulse, and chaos. In W. J. Arnold and D. Levine (Eds.), *Nebraska symposium on motivation, 1969.* Lincoln: University of Nebraska Press, 1970.

Zimbardo, P. Pirandellian prison. *New York Times Magazine,* April 8, 1973; also *International Journal of Criminology and Penology,* 1973, *1,* 69–97.

Zimbardo, P. *Shyness.* Reading, Mass.: Addison-Wesley, 1977.

Zubrzycki, J. The immigrant family: Some sociological aspects. In A. Stoller (Ed.), *New Faces.* Melbourne and London: F. W. Cheshire, 1966.

Author Index

Abelson, R., 89
Abrams, I., 261, 274, 277, 295
Adamopoulos, J., 101
Adams, J., 8, 54, 207
Adler, D., 118, 123
Adler, P., 13, 157, 293, 297, 298
Adorno, T., 35, 50
Akter, T., 10
Albert, R., 101
Alexander, A., 160
Alger, C., 14, 16, 189, 222, 264, 265, 270, 274, 295
Allen, V., 29, 112
Allport, G., 73, 88, 98, 172, 177, 180
Althen, G., 209
Alstein, H., 17
Amir, Y., 10, 14, 171, 172, 173, 174, 180, 187, 192
Amuzegar, J., 209
Arensberg, C., 9
Arnold, C., 113
Aronson, E., 184
Ashmore, R., 45, 50, 187
Austin, G., 73

Bagozzi, R., 193
Bailyn, L., 126
Barber, R., 146
Barsig, D., 215, 238
Bartlett, M., 134
Battit, G., 134
Baty, R., 10, 174
Bauer, R., 127, 136, 222
Ben-Ari, R., 14
Bennett, J., 130, 160
Benson, P., 54, 61, 63, 67, 112
Berry, J., 60, 83, 204, 282, 289, 290, 324
Berscheid, E., 27

Birren, F., 53
Bishop, G., 66
Bizman, A., 14
Blaney, N., 184
Blau, P., 249
Blom, G., 36
Bochner, S., 4, 122, 160, 179, 288, 299
Bosmajian, H., 71
Bottoms, A., 159
Brandon, P., 10
Bradley, H., 125
Brein, M., 282
Bressler, M., 31, 58
Brewer, M., 7, 72, 76, 78, 111
Brislin, R., 7, 9, 13, 42, 48, 54, 60, 66, 82, 83, 101, 107, 128, 131, 137, 147, 151, 156, 178, 185, 194, 210, 224, 230, 235, 239, 288, 293, 300, 307, 312, 313, 317, 330
Brodie, F., 26
Brown, R., 30
Bruner, J., 125
Burnkrant, R., 193

Campbell, D., 7, 77, 80, 141, 293
Campbell, J., 190
Carlston, D., 194
Carroll, W., 256
Casino, E., 235
Cathcart, D., 167, 301
Cathcart, R., 167, 301
Chein, I., 35
Chemers, M., 102
Christ, J., 176
Christie, R., 50
Chu, H., 160
Clark, K., 190, 291
Clarke, C., 160

Cleveland, H., 8, 54, 131, 207
Coch, L., 240
Coelho, G., 210
Collins, B., 23
Collins, M., 10, 14, 181, 186, 187
Converse, P., 78
Cook, S., 15, 50, 146, 174, 176, 185, 293

David, K., 66, 178, 282
Davis, D., 26
Davis, E., 47
Davis, K., 89, 95
De Loria, V., 25
Detweiler, R., 56
Deutsch, M., 10, 119, 121, 181, 186, 187, 262
De Vos, G., 160
Dexter, L., 127, 222
Dickens, S., 35
Dinges, N., 10, 237, 285
Dold, E., 10, 174, 175
Doob, L., 171, 177
Downs, A., 234
Draguns, J., 158, 161, 162, 163, 170
Driver, M., 86
Duffy, L., 285
Duncan, O., 249
Dutton, D., 46

Egbert, L., 134
Ehrlich, H., 9, 11, 30, 31, 35, 36, 57, 60, 74, 78, 117, 125, 154
Endler, N., 52
Engle, P., 83
Entwisle, D., 194
Epps, E., 195
Etcoff, N., 73
Evans, W., 262
Ezekiel, R., 63, 147, 202, 203, 207, 212, 224, 274, 300

Fahvar, M., 13
Feldman, J., 80, 98
Festinger, L., 23
Fiedler, F., 61, 101, 104, 165, 166, 327
Finley, G., 9, 54, 59, 60, 61

Fisher, C., 234
Fiske, S., 73, 78, 92, 98
Flack, M., 8, 54, 114
Foa, E., 164
Foa, U., 102, 103, 164
Foltz, W., 171
Fraser, S., 71
Freedman, J., 71
French, J., 28, 240
French, L., 242
Frenkel-Brunswick, E., 11, 50
Frey, F., 60
Frijda, N., 44

Gallois, C., 66
Gama, E., 16, 123, 132, 216
Garti, C., 173
Gerard, H., 10, 14, 182
Gergen, K., 32
Gerver, D., 9, 214
Geschwind, N., 317
Giorgis, T., 301
Glaser, E., 262
Glaser, W., 179, 184, 204, 206, 217, 220, 221, 230
Glenn, E., 152, 153, 205, 241
Gomez, H., 258
Goodenough, W., 9, 192
Goodnow, J., 73
Gordon, P., 160
Gough, H., 35, 140
Goulet, D., 219
Greenfield, M., 37
Gudykunst, W., 54, 63, 83, 172, 176, 184, 187
Guetzkow, H., 65, 128, 166, 184, 207, 264
Guillotte, J., 121
Gullahorn, J. T., 15, 124, 279, 280
Gullahorn, J. E., 15, 124, 279, 280
Gumperz, J., 67, 68, 97
Gurin, P., 195
Guthrie, G., 9, 52, 100, 201, 222, 237, 310

Hackman, J., 212
Hall, E., 65, 126, 293

Hammer, M., 54, 63, 83
Hamnett, M., 212, 317
Handlin, O., 22
Hanson, L., 96
Harding, J., 35, 50
Harding, R., 66, 112, 135, 146
Hare, B., 57, 173, 190, 195
Harmon, R., 8
Harper, R., 65
Harris, J., 8, 35, 52, 54, 57, 201, 202
Harris, P., 270
Harvey, J., 12
Harvey, O., 55
Havel, J., 176
Heclo, H., 208, 239, 259
Heenan, D., 246, 265, 272
Heisey, D., 218, 219, 226, 302
Helms, J., 301
Hermann, M., 57, 120
Hewlett, T., 327
Higginbotham, H., 66, 159, 161, 170, 252
Hiller, H., 9
Hilterman, R., 80, 98
Hippler, A., 160
Hirschman, A., 318, 319
Ho, D., 20, 39
Hobart, C., 35
Hoffman, J., 75, 120
Holsti, O., 82
Holwill, F., 107, 224, 312, 313, 330
Homans, G., 12, 110
Horwitz, M., 77
Hough, J., 28, 46
Hoyt, M., 23
Hull, F., 261, 263, 272, 274, 277, 280, 281, 295, 302, 303
Hull, R., 8, 243
Hunt, D., 55

Ickes, W., 12
Ickis, J., 258
Ilić, S., 234
Inkeles, A., 216, 270
Irvine, S., 256
Irwin, M., 83
Isaacs, H., 126

Jackson, J., 190
Jacob, B., 211, 231, 237
Jacob, P., 211, 231, 237
Jaggi, V., 94
Janis, I., 77, 87, 89, 110, 133
Jha, C., 234
Jones, E., 73, 89, 91, 93, 95, 107
Jones, J., 27, 94, 141
Jones, R., 124, 146

Kagitcibasi, C., 16, 125, 292, 293, 294, 295, 296, 305, 309
Kahneman, D., 92
Kanouse, D., 12, 73, 96
Kashoki, M., 54, 112, 122, 216, 221, 288
Katz, D., 42, 43, 194, 242, 262, 263
Katz, I., 94, 95, 164, 194
Katz, J., 180
Kealey, D., 52, 54, 55, 56, 57, 62, 70, 71, 150, 210
Kelley, H., 12, 73, 99, 100, 123
Kelman, H., 126, 189, 210, 238, 261, 274, 300
Kern, K., 118
Kessen, W., 39
Kidd, R., 12
Kidder, L., 80, 149, 150, 207, 232
Kiev, A., 161
Kim, Y., 109, 112, 124, 299
Kinzie, J., 160
Kipnis, D., 28, 149
Kissinger, H., 261
Kiste, R., 10
Klein, M., 54, 57, 160, 273, 276, 303, 318
Klein, R., 83
Kleinjans, E., 223
Klineberg, O., 8, 32, 36, 37, 50, 60, 261, 263, 272, 274, 277, 280, 281, 295, 299, 302
Kluckhohn, C., 5
Kluckhohn, F., 125
Korzeny, F., 214
Kroeber, A., 5
Kumar, K., 58, 112, 220
Kutner, B., 35, 141

La France, M., 66
Lambert, R., 31, 58, 60
Lambert, Wallace, 63, 284, 298
Lambert, William, 37, 60
Lampe, P., 290
Landis, D., 86
LaPiere, R., 141, 142
Lee, L., 285
Leighton, A., 10, 23, 118, 182, 327
Lenneberg, E., 31
Lesser, S., 87
Levin, L., 74
LeVine, R., 74, 77, 171, 188
Levinson, D., 11, 50
Lippitt, R., 294
Lockyear, F., 179
Loh, W., 74
Lonner, W., 161, 170
Looney, G., 66, 112, 113, 135, 146
Lopez, T., 257
Lott, J., 95
Luckiesh, M., 32

McCauley, C., 81
McClain, E., 117, 293, 306, 309, 315
McClelland, D., 53, 295
McConahay, J., 28, 46
McCormack, W., 209, 296
McDermott, J., 17
McGuire, W., 41, 87, 193
McNeil, D., 11, 30
Macomber, W., 247
Magnusson, D., 52
Mahoney, F., 229
Malpass, R., 73, 83, 104
Mangone, G., 8, 54, 207
Mann, L., 89, 133
Maretzki, T., 17
Markel, N., 66
Marr, P., 82
Martin, W., 35
Maslach, C., 251, 253, 311, 330
Matarazzo, J., 65
May, W., 33
Mayo, C., 65
Mead, M., 325, 326
Merritt, R., 119, 121

Merton, R., 220
Mestenhauser, J., 213, 214, 215, 238
Milburn, T., 184
Milgram, S., 49
Miller, G., 11, 30
Miller, H., 173
Miller, M., 160
Miller, N., 10, 14, 173, 182
Milton, J., 13
Miron, M., 33
Mirvis, P., 286
Mischel, W., 52
Mishler, A., 151
Mitchell, T., 101, 212, 213, 484
Moran, R., 8, 270
Morris, R., 274
Murillo-Rohde, I., 23, 64, 118, 148
Murray, P., 190
Myer, R., 291
Myrdal, G., 26

Nerlove, S., 83
Newcomb, T., 78
New York Times, 49
Nicolson, H., 8, 21, 54, 56, 58, 61, 139
Niehoff, A., 9
Nisbett, R., 12, 73
Nurcombe, B., 60

Oberg, K., 13, 155, 157
O'Brien, G., 171, 194, 327
Ogawa, D., 177
Oldham, G., 212
Osgood, C., 32, 33, 34, 41, 262
Oskamp, S., 95

Parkinson, C., 243
Pasinski, W., 10
Pearson, R., 242, 257
Pedersen, P., 7, 13, 16, 54, 101, 123,
    128, 131, 132, 151, 156, 160,
    162, 170, 178, 215, 236, 239,
    288
Perks, R., 160
Perlmutter, H., 246, 265, 272
Peters, H., 87
Peter, L., 243

Pettigrew, T., 195
Piaget, J., 256
Pincus, C., 121, 145, 235
Plooij, D., 171, 194
Pool, I., 9, 118, 126, 127, 143, 222, 272, 273, 276, 303
Popper, R., 124, 146
Price-Williams, D., 256
Proshansky, H., 35
Pruitt, D., 86, 128, 205
Pruitt, F., 112, 115, 116, 122, 232, 290
Pushkin, I., 35

Rabbie, J., 77
Rabinowitch, E., 184
Randolph, G., 86, 194
Raspberry, W., 190
Reychler, L., 8, 16
Rich, A., 177
Richmond, A., 98, 144, 148, 184, 249, 291
Riordan, C., 88, 172, 177, 180, 189, 195
Rissman, A., 195
Ritterband, P., 13, 146, 147
Rivner, M., 14
Roberts, A., 36
Robinson, J., 57, 246
Rogers, C., 65
Rokeach, M., 36
Rosch, E., 89, 104
Rosenberg, M., 21, 194
Rosenblith, J., 35
Rosenfield, D., 184, 189, 192
Rosenfield, W., 54, 57, 118, 171, 181
Ross, L., 92, 93
Rotter, J., 294
Ruben, B., 52, 54, 56, 57, 59, 70, 71, 150, 210, 221
Ruderman, A., 73
Rummel, R., 191
Rusk, D., 264
Ryan, W., 252

Salancik, F., 73, 83, 104
Sampson, D., 294

Sanford, N., 11, 50, 76
Sanua, V., 120, 159, 161
Sarbin, T., 29, 112
Sawe, J., 234
Satia, J., 269
Sawyer, J., 65, 128, 166, 184, 207, 264
Schroder, H., 55
Schumann, H., 150
Schwartz, F., 160
Scott, W., 55, 69, 75, 82
Scriven, M., 309
Seelye, H., 277, 278
Selltiz, C., 146, 174, 176, 185
Shaw, W., 117, 293, 294, 306, 309, 315, 316, 332
Sherif, M., 120, 183, 184
Shivers, R., 328, 329, 331
Sikes, J., 184
Simon, H., 89
Simon, R., 17
Simpson, C., 99, 140, 145, 180, 181, 187, 191
Sinaiko, H., 9, 214
Slobodin, L., 194
Smith, D., 216, 270
Smith, H., 126, 294
Smith, L., 254
Smith, M., 77, 87, 110, 130, 285
Smyser, A., 328
Snyder, R., 57, 246
Sokirkin, A., 234
Spaulding, S., 8, 54, 114
Spector, P., 193
Stagner, R., 59, 196
Steinitz, V., 300
Steinkalk, E., 9, 315
Stifel, L., 258
Stitt, C., 81
Stephan, W., 36, 54, 57, 118, 171, 181, 184, 189, 192
Stevenson, K., 152
Stouffer, S., 10
Strodtbeck, F., 125
Suci, G., 33
Sue, D., 160, 162
Sue, S., 160, 162

Szanton, D., 68, 100, 101, 157, 222, 310, 327

Taft, R., 9, 15, 16, 23, 54, 59, 62, 79, 112, 118, 123, 124, 135, 145, 156, 160, 282, 284, 303, 305, 315
Tajfel, H., 77, 196
Talbot, L., 83, 85
Tannenbaum, P., 33
Tapp, J., 210, 286
Taylor, D., 94
Taylor, S., 73, 78, 81, 92, 98, 174, 262
Tendler, J., 232, 240, 248, 254, 288
Textor, R., 9, 63, 124, 145, 156, 229
Thayer, C., 21, 54, 58, 111, 139, 237, 241
Thibaut, J., 123
Triandis, H., 5, 6, 9, 43, 47, 72, 74, 96, 101, 142, 154, 185, 194, 210, 300, 315
Trifonovitch, G., 280, 317, 318, 331
Trubowitz, J., 183
Tseng, K., 160
Tseng, W., 17
Tucker, R., 63
Turner, J., 76
Turner, R., 78
Tversky, A., 92
Tzeng, O., 86

Useem, J., 126, 162
Useem, R., 126, 162

Valins, S., 12, 73
Van Buren, H., 131, 137
Van Tubergen, N., 154
Van Zandt, H., 202, 209
Veness, T., 35
Verma, G., 164, 173
Vroom, V., 236, 240

Waite, R., 36
Walker, K., 9
Walsh, J., 24, 25

Walster, E., 27
Warwick, D., 312
Wasilewski, J., 272, 277, 278
Watson, J., 294
Watson, P., 28, 47, 142
Watt, D., 9
Webster, M., 195
Weiner, B., 12, 73
Welch, C., 134
Weldon, D., 194
White, R., 59, 81
White, S., 212, 213
Whorf, B., 11, 30
Wicker, A., 146, 193
Wiens, A., 65
Wilkins, C., 141
Williams, R., 144, 207, 291
Wilson, J., 165
Wilson, K., 235
Winter, D., 53, 295
Wiseman, R., 54, 83
Wispe, L., 49
Witkin, H., 324
Witmeyer, D., 152
Workneh, F., 160
Wright, Q., 262, 294, 316
Wrightsman, L., 141, 210

Yarbrough, C., 83
Yarrow, M., 141, 190
Yarrow, L., 190
Yeh, E., 160
Yinger, J., 99, 140, 145, 180, 181, 187, 191
Young, A., 48, 167
Yousef, F., 153, 178

Zaidi, S., 171
Zektick, I., 52, 201, 237
Ziffer, W., 17
Zimbardo, P., 49, 142, 276
Zimet, S., 36
Zubrzychi, J., 22, 112, 113
Zumwalt, E., 239

Subject Index

Abilities, 39, 270; see also Skills

Acceptance by hosts, 271

Accountability, 254, 255

Acculturation, 226, 286–288, 305

Achievement need, 53, 94, 139, 142, 226, 295

Acquaintance potential, 185–186, 198

Active processing of information, 71, 73–108, 311

Activity dimension of connotation, 33–34

Additive processes, 227, 298–299, 306

Adjustment, 10, 14, 17, 54, 55, 67, 86, 106, 107, 109, 111–117, 122, 145, 147, 159, 169, 245, 271–307, 309

   long term, 4, 87–88, 132, 271, 282–292, 304–305

   short term, 87–88, 132, 269–279, 304

   stages of, 4, 117, 125, 279–283

   time, 15

Adjustment function of attitudes, 42

Administrators, role of, 4, 10, 14, 17, 20, 45, 82, 85, 86, 106, 150, 165, 167, 171–199, 214–215, 217–218, 226, 228–270, 300–303, 305, 320, 327

Adolescents, programs for, 10, 119, 146, 237, 250, 259, 272–279, 292, 317

Adoption, interracial, 17, 113, 263

Advisers to sojourners, 82, 91, 92, 116, 125, 128, 186, 214–215, 230, 239, 251, 254, 255–257, 265, 267, 280, 300–303, 325–327

Affective reactions, 41, 110, 158, 316

Affirmative action, 1, 98–99, 108, 130–131, 177, 197

Afghanistan, 51

Africa, 26, 115, 122, 171, 176, 188–189

Aggression, 142–143

Alcohol, 67

Altruism, 49–50

Ambassador effect in sojourns, 275–276, 304

Ambiguity, 55–56, 105, 219–221, 258, 267; see also Tolerance for ambiguity

Ambivalence, 120

American dilemma, 26

Americans, 80, 90, 96–97, 102–104, 124, 127, 130, 146, 167

Anonymous relations, 141–144, 168, 221–222, 227

Anxiety, 158, 194, 310

Application of research findings, 262, 318–328, 330

Appropriateness of behavior, 271

Arranged interethnic contact, 10

Arab countries, 14, 37, 102–105, 152–153, 171, 176, 192

Arms length prejudice, 47, 100

Asia, 58, 102, 147, 354–355

Assertive attitudes, 195–196, 199

Assimilation, 23, 116–119, 135, 282, 289, 291

Attention, 145–146, 174, 222, 246, 258

Attitudes, 15, 30, 34–36, 37, 39, 40–51, 86–89, 111, 118, 124, 128, 153, 171, 173–175, 183, 195–197, 271, 275, 282, 284, 286–287, 289, 316

Attractiveness, 123

Attribution, 12, 73–74, 91–105, 115, 124, 131–132, 138, 161–162, 163–165, 169–170, 320

Australia, 16, 171

Authoritarianism, 36, 49, 50–51, 69, 175, 294

Authority, 243–245, 305

Autistic hostility, 78

Background factors, 173–178, 197, 224; see also History

Baseline ratings, 92

Behavior change, 193–194, 199

Belief similarity, 77, 105

Belongingness, sense of, 114–115, 124

Benefitting from cross-cultural expenses, 54, 62, 70, 165, 224

Big cities, 146

Bilingual education, 242–243, 253, 268, 298–302, 306, 322

Black Americans, 26–30, 34–35, 42, 45, 51, 66, 76, 94, 98, 111, 116, 118, 136, 148, 171, 174, 178, 180, 189, 195, 290–291

Black as a concept, 31–32, 37

Brain drain, 110, 168, 216–219, 226

Branching format, 104

Brazil, 16, 113, 123

Broad mindedness, 100, 127, 147, 317; see also Tolerance

Budgeting, role of, 195, 198, 259

Bureaucracy, 56, 70, 103, 192, 207, 209, 211, 221, 225, 228–270

Burnout, 251–253, 267, 277

Business people, 1, 2, 8, 14, 53, 54, 90, 91, 127, 136, 171–199, 207, 209, 222, 246, 247, 273, 278, 279, 304

Busing, 176

Busy work, 243

Case studies of organizations, 229–231

Categorization, 43–44, 67, 68–69, 72–91, 105–106, 108, 172, 273, 281, 319–320, 331; see also Stereotypes

Category width, 56–57

Catholic-Protestant relations, 38, 171

Cautions about contact, 15

Caveats about intergroup contact, 172–173

Change programs, 88, 156, 190, 261, 297; see also Cross-cultural orientation programs

Changes due to cross-cultural contact, 15, 87–88, 125, 131, 141, 193–196, 199, 310, 329–330

Channeling, 190–191, 198, 264–265, 269

Chicanos, 9, 182

Children of immigrants, 23–24, 109, 117–120

Chinese, 32, 39, 141–142, 163–164, 238

Choice as a variable, 289, 290, 301

Citizen involvement, 21

Civil rights, 1, 26, 29–30, 36

Climate, 138, 168

Climate regarding contact, 178–179

Cognitive processing, 72; see also Thinking processes

Collaboration, 206, 209, 210, 215, 227, 326

Collective action, 39, 287

Colonization of America, 20

Color connotations, 31–32

Colorful events, 175–176, 192–193

Comfort during cross-cultural contact, 5, 28–30, 38, 42, 50, 56, 86, 88, 111, 122, 178, 182–183, 187, 194, 198, 265, 279, 282, 297

Commitment to a country, 23–24, 127, 233

Common effect, 96–97

Communications channels, 25, 31, 81, 167, 213, 214, 253, 255–266, 269, 275

Communication skills, 63, 64–66, 70, 140, 164, 167, 171, 194, 203, 214, 323, 326, 329

Compact encounter method, 317–319, 331

Comparison level, 122–123, 194, 203

Comparison of cultures, 89–91

Competence, 284–286, 305

Compounds as housing, 124, 232–233
Conative component of attitudes, 41
Concepts, 64, 104
Conceptual development, 2, 16–17, 309–312, 319–320, 330–331
Conditions at time of contact, 175–176
Confirmation of thinking, 80
Confrontation between groups, 116–119, 129–131, 136–137, 151–152, 168, 187, 317
Congressmen, 57
Connotation of words, 32–35
Consequences for people, 150–151, 169
Consequences of categorization, 79–91, 268
Consistency of traits, 51–54
Constituencies, 248
Constraints, 145, 252, 255
Contact: key variables which influence outcomes, 14, 118, 171–199, 266
Contradictions, 249–251
Contrast cultures, 158
Controversy, 88
Contributions to community, 145–146
Control of others, 244, 254; see also Power
Conversational currency, 65
Coping, 54, 129, 137, 138, 139, 155–156, 166, 169, 188, 272, 277–279, 295, 306
Cordial relations, 107, 109, 139, 150, 154, 167, 170, 171, 205–206, 235, 237, 275, 312, 330
Counterpart role, 221, 226–227
Courage, 58
Creativity, 147, 166, 255, 278, 288, 296–297, 306
Criteria; see Measurement
Critical incidents, 101–105, 106
Cross-cultural contact, 10, 29, 52, 60, 72, 99, 101, 119, 133, 136, 156, 171–199
 advantages of, 3, 15, 25, 54, 76, 109, 125–128, 143, 228, 258–266, 271, 292–300, 305–306

disadvantages of, 129–134, 142–143, 149, 297–299, 314–316, 330
outcomes, 4, 15, 73, 90, 117, 119, 149, 179, 187, 193–196, 219–221, 254, 309, 310
problems with, 4, 29, 36, 200–227
reasons for increases, 1, 24
types of, 8–10
Cross-cultural experiences, 17, 54, 104, 117, 134, 184, 204, 230, 240, 269, 296
 everyday; see Everyday encounters
 interpretation of, 17, 104, 125, 159, 327–328, 331
Cross-cultural orientation programs, 1, 4, 7, 53, 63, 65–67, 82, 83, 100–105, 107, 128, 131–134, 145, 151, 159, 170, 177–178, 191, 194, 236, 239, 251–253, 258, 261, 267, 281, 300–303, 312, 320; see also Organized attempts at change
Cruelty, interpersonal, 49–50
Cultural relativity, 104, 297, 317
Cultural assimilator, 101–105, 106
Culture, definition of, 3, 4, 48, 51
Culture shock, 12–13, 137, 138, 155–161, 169–170, 178, 280, 304
 advantages of, 12, 157–158
 disadvantages of, 12–13, 158–161
 mundane qualities, 157
 symptoms, 156
Cyprus, 51
Deadline orientation, 264, 269
Decision making, 89, 106, 111, 145, 152–153, 162, 209, 239–241, 257–258, 267, 288, 325–326, 331
Deindividuation, 142–144
Descriptions of situations, 140–141
Deviance, 125, 126, 136, 311
Differences as basis for categorization, 72, 93, 100, 105, 119, 138, 151–155, 177, 267
Differentiation, 103, 324–325

Diplomats, 2, 8, 13, 14, 16, 21–22, 54, 56, 58, 108, 111, 126, 128, 129, 134–135, 139, 155, 164, 164–165, 170, 184, 205, 207, 221–222, 231, 237, 239, 241–242, 247, 260, 262–265, 270, 274

Discovering key information, 209

Discrimination, 41, 43, 72, 78, 136, 140–142, 144, 172–173, 193

Discipline; see Parental discipline

Discussion, 183

Dissemination of information, 261–262, 322–326, 331

Dominant majority, 116, 177

East Africa, 83–85

Economic factors, 1, 17, 89, 130, 150, 171, 179, 231–232, 261, 262, 271–272, 283, 319

Education, influence of, 30, 35, 36–38, 45, 121, 130, 136; see also School, influence of

Egalitarianism, 100–101

Ego defensive function of attitudes, 42–43

Elite in foreign policy, 21–22, 38

Emics-etics, 83–86, 106, 155, 240

Emotions, 311–312, 316–317, 330

Empathy, 59, 65, 67, 70, 188–189, 246, 252, 300

Energy, 122, 176

Entertaining visitors, 234–235, 259, 268

Environment, 123, 145–146, 149, 167, 324

Equal status contact, 89, 178, 180, 197–198

Equipment, 214, 218, 246, 248–249, 254–255, 393

Escape, motive of, 274

Ethnicity, 2, 10, 24, 36, 75, 88, 99, 130–131, 178, 289, 298, 305, 320, 321–322

Ethnocentrism, 76, 246, 304; see also Prejudice; Stereotypes

European parliament, 213, 260, 263

Evaluation, 33–34, 98–99, 142, 144, 164–165, 243, 253–254, 292–293, 308–310, 329–330, 331; see also Measurement

Events, role of, 173

Everyday encounters, 43, 71, 91, 111, 114, 127, 132, 156–157, 159, 163, 167, 177, 193, 204, 249, 265, 277–279, 285

Expansion of reference groups, 127, 136–137

Expectations, 130, 162, 204–206, 211, 225, 252

Experiences of sojourners, 122, 145, 146, 204, 225; see also Sojourners

Experiental learning, 467–499; see also Role playing, 317–319

Expertise demanded, 222–223

Expressive behavior, 158–159, 222–223

External events, 119, 138–139

Externalization, 76–77

Extremity of attitudes, 173–175

Face-to-face rejection, 141–142

Facilitators, 182–183, 198

Factors under administrative control, 179–199

Failure, 253–255

Familiar and unfamiliar, 48, 74–75, 89, 105, 137, 145, 151–152, 167–168, 194

Families, 109, 131, 146–147, 176, 216–217, 277, 286, 290, 293, 295

Favorable relations, 88, 163–165, 166, 171, 188, 269

Feedback, 62, 158

Feelings, 138, 147, 157, 159, 187, 188–189, 299; see also Attitudes

Fellow countrymen, 133, 160–161, 162, 169–170, 275–276

Field-home office distinction, 246–247, 266

First impressions, 59

Flexibility, 297, 306

Fluid groups, 130–131

Followingup opportunities, 40

Foot-in-the-door technique, 71

Forced contact, 174–175

Forced relocation, 10, 14, 178–179, 182–183

Foreign alliances, 20, 38

Foreign relations, 21, 22, 38, 127, 128

Foreign service institute, 249, 251–252

Foreign service officers; see Diplomats

Foreign students, 1, 2, 108, 273; see also Overseas students

Formation of new reference groups, 120–131

France, 32, 146

Fraternity initiations, 49

Freedom to move, 121

Friendship, 110, 115–116, 117, 124, 134, 143, 153, 154, 160, 182, 184, 188, 217, 253, 266, 270, 274–275, 299; see also Groups

Fringe benefits, 150

Frustration, 137, 138, 156, 158, 169, 220, 245, 273

Functions, 42–44, 73, 75–76, 105

Funding, 199, 212, 217, 219, 227, 229, 232–234, 241, 242–243, 245, 254, 255, 267, 268, 269, 272, 309, 322

Fundamental attribution error, 93, 101

Future, 1–2, 329

Generalizations, 152, 180–181, 313, 322

Generation gaps, 23, 118–119, 130–131

Germany, 87–88

Goals of sojourns, 54–55, 135, 138–139, 172, 183–185, 198, 230, 236, 241–243, 256, 273–274, 287, 290, 295

Good-bad distinction, 34, 41, 169

Government support, 176, 217, 234, 262–264, 268, 325, 385–387

Great Britain, 20, 67, 146, 164

Greece, 6, 86, 96, 151

Grinds, 203, 273

Groups, 3, 10–11, 11–12, 24, 39, 109–137, 165–168, 248, 276, 284

membership groups, 109, 110–120, 135–136

reference groups, 109, 111–131, 133–135, 182–184, 216–218, 226, 283

Groups in situations, 14, 171–199

Guest workers, 17

Habits, 62

Hawaii, 147

Helping relations, 128–129, 137, 161, 171, 206, 248, 267, 313

Hindis, 94

History, 10, 11, 18–39, 177, 197, 209, 237, 284

Home country, 126–127, 135–136

Home stay programs, 9, 175

Host culture, 123–124, 148–149

Host nationals, 62, 71, 86–87, 91–92, 103–104, 107, 109, 145, 146, 154, 203, 204–206, 217, 223–224, 231, 265, 271, 284

Hostility, history of, 177, 185, 208, 280, 320

Housing regulations, 232, 233, 268, 283

Human Relations Area Files, 142, 209

Human relations, 13, 291, 305–306

Humor, 280, 290

Hungary, 159

Identification, 35–36, 50, 124, 246, 248, 266, 283–284, 297, 305

Ideology, 120–121, 136, 242

Ignorance of international concerns, 21–22

Images, 5, 55, 81, 89–90, 92, 101, 108

Immigrants, 1, 2, 9, 13, 17, 18–20, 22–24, 54, 64, 93, 95, 112, 116, 120–121, 124, 129–130, 148, 159–160, 178–179, 217–218, 226, 230, 282, 284, 285, 287, 299

Imposition on one's point of view, 18, 24–28, 38, 90, 100, 224, 297–298, 310, 313

India, 31, 58, 67, 80, 126, 149–150, 232, 313

Indigenous commentary technique, 312–314

Indiscriminate use of categories, 88–89

Individual differences, 51–52, 157

Individual level factors, 10–12, 259

Individualism, 19–20, 38, 39, 71, 119, 139, 204

Individuation, 142–144, 168

Industry, 54

Information processing, 72, 80–82, 95–96, 104, 106, 111, 122, 127–128, 134, 172, 194, 209–210, 224, 261, 265, 270, 326

Ingroup-outgroup distinction, 7, 50, 51, 74, 76–77, 79, 81–82, 94, 105, 120, 127, 228, 233, 246, 330
    advantages of, 7, 69
    disadvantages, 7; see also Prejudice

Inhibited growth, 129

Instability, 99–101

Institutional support, 191–192, 213–214; see also Organizations

Institutionalization of discrimination, 144

Integration, 289

Intelligence, 54, 60–61, 70, 95, 121, 175, 252

Interests, 66–67, 117, 183

Intergroup relations, 171–199; see also Cross-cultural contact

Internal control, 294, 306

International relations, 24, 25–26, 38, 125–126, 266

Interpreters, language, 9, 14, 64, 213–214, 226

Intervening, 281–282, 314–315

Intimate contact, 17, 47, 100–101, 114–115, 154, 187–188, 198, 217, 302, 306

Iran, 51

Ireland, 51, 176

Isomorphic attribution, 101, 106

Israel, 14, 120–121, 136, 146, 152, 171, 174–175, 176, 192, 235, 249, 283

Italy, 32

Japan, 20, 53, 84, 133, 167, 182–183, 202, 254–255, 278, 290, 327–329, 331–332

Jealousy, 208, 258–259

Jewish people, 32, 40, 42, 51, 81, 88, 95, 111, 120–121, 171, 176, 249

Jim Crow, 29

Job enlargement, 212–213, 219, 226

Job performance, 27, 42–43, 68, 75, 80, 93, 98–99, 132, 164–165, 171, 200–227, 237, 243, 263, 267, 283, 288, 321; see also Task

Judgments about others, 74, 89–90, 91–92, 107, 117, 132, 139, 162, 165, 286, 288, 297–298, 310

Justification of behavior, 25

Kenya, 171

Knowledge function of attitudes, 43, 299

Knowledge increase and categorization, 80–81, 107

Knowledge of subject matter, 41, 59, 63–64, 70, 75, 128, 158, 184, 196–197, 199, 218, 221, 227, 277, 279, 284–285, 299, 300

Korea, 112, 299

Ku Klux Klan, 28, 143, 176

Language, 11, 19, 30–34, 38, 63–64, 67–68, 74, 84, 91, 93–94, 109, 113, 143, 147, 153, 158, 254–255, 257, 268, 274, 282, 284–285, 287, 295, 298–299

Language skills, 53, 70

Laos, 107

Latin America, 65, 232, 235

Leader-member relations, 236–239, 240

Leadership, 165–168, 211–212, 215, 226, 328–330

Learning, 4, 101, 126, 128, 147, 157–159, 162, 215, 319

Legal changes and legal factors, 1, 111, 135, 171, 176, 196, 209, 218, 231, 250, 254; see also Affirmative action

Lena Horne-Harry Belafonte effect, 99

Lessons from studies on intergroup contact, 172–199

Linear format, 103–104

Linking of cultures, 83–86

Listening, 60

Localitis, 247–248, 266

Loneliness, 100, 110, 122, 146, 157, 169, 273, 317

Loyalty, 58

Managing cross-cultural contact, 171–200, 209–212, 244–245, 263–265

Manifest destiny, 24

Marginality, 125–126

Marriage, intercultural, 17, 217

Marshall Islands, 48

Masai culture, 85, 151

Mass media, 30, 36–38, 130, 144, 176, 179, 190, 297

Match of images, 90, 106

Measurement, 33–34, 45–46, 84, 140–141, 174–175, 201–204, 224, 280–281, 291–294, 305, 306, 307, 316

Mediators, 12, 299, 306

Melting pot, 18, 27, 289

Mental health, 159–163, 282

Mexico, 25, 29, 257

Middle-class in United States, 18, 257

Mid-East, 102

Migrant workers, 17

Mikado, 126

Military personnel, 9

Military forces, 262–263, 291, 328–329

Minority status, 2, 197, 290

Missionaries, 17, 205

Mistakes during sojourn, 271

Misunderstanding, spiraling of, 213

Mobility, 66, 121–122, 266, 290

Models, 5, 118, 147–148, 168, 182

Money, 121, 136, 178, 229–230, 231–232, 238–239, 244

Monism, 271, 286–289, 290

Morale, 248, 253

Motivation, 110–111, 128, 138, 157–158, 169, 187–188, 199, 273, 274–276, 283, 327–330, 331

Multiculturality, 297–299, 306

Multidimensionality, 55, 271

Multinational corporations, 11, 147–148, 213–214, 264, 270, 272; see also Business people

Muslims, 94

Myths, 18

Narrow mindedness, 100, 111

Nationality, 2, 87, 99, 107, 115–116

Native Americans, 9, 24–25, 29, 51

Nazi atrocities, 40, 49, 51, 111

Negativity, 96, 251, 276–277, 302, 311, 315, 330

Negotiation, 13, 15, 65, 152–153, 165–167, 169–170, 184, 207–208, 209, 219, 222–223, 241–242, 262–263, 278

Neighborhood desegregation, 1, 2, 14, 93, 98, 171, 174, 181–182, 186, 207

Networks, 3, 114–115, 146, 248

Niche, 13, 146–147, 168

Non-development of prejudice, 195–196, 200

Non-judgmental, 59

Non-verbal behavior, 65, 107, 132–133, 214

Norms, 10, 11, 17, 29, 75, 107, 110–111, 131–132, 134, 139, 143–145, 151, 154–155, 173, 178, 205–206, 209, 220, 250, 270, 276

North America, 6, 65, 80

Number of preconceptions, 172–175

Number of people, 139, 168

Observable behaviors, 286

Oil resources, 2, 22, 25, 177, 261

Openness-closedness of thinking, 55, 62, 199, 294; see also Tolerance

Organizational factors, 10–11, 14, 39, 135, 189, 191–193, 197–199, 228–271, 292, 306

   advantages of, 14, 211–212, 260–266, 269–270, 288, 318–319

Organizational factors (*cont.*)
disadvantages of, 243
goals of, 202, 215
Organized attempts at change, 37, 44, 46, 215
Orientation programs; see cross-cultural orientation programs
Other people as situational variable, 141–142, 168–169
Outgroups, 7, 11, 38, 41, 43, 46, 57, 72, 183–184, 317; see also Ingroup-outgroup distinction; Prejudice; Stereotypes
Overadministration, 243–245
Overlapping group ties, 188–189, 198
Overmanning, 145–146, 168, 185–186
Overseas students, 1, 2, 8, 13, 14, 54, 63, 78, 82, 90, 92, 96–97, 102, 111–112, 146, 154, 159–160, 169, 179, 185–186, 200–201, 205, 206, 209, 214–215, 226, 230, 231, 233, 238, 253–255, 256, 280, 285, 287–288, 297, 302
Oversimplification of issues, 37
Pacific, 102, 147, 235, 317–319
Pakistan, 171
Palestine, 120
Parental discipline, 11, 16, 30, 34–36, 38, 50, 118
Parents, influence of, 118–120, 182, 317
Parkinson's law, 243
Participative decision making, 239–241, 261, 268, 270
Patience, 56
Patrons, 59
Patter, 59, 111
Peace Corps, 9, 54, 63, 100, 112–113, 124, 129, 144–145, 147, 150, 157, 201–203, 205, 207, 212, 220, 222, 225, 229, 231, 237, 246, 249, 258, 286, 438, 459
Perception, 27–28, 60, 93–94, 97, 100, 124, 159, 211, 246, 252, 271, 283, 285–286
Personal growth, 129, 301, 310

Personality, 39, 50, 51–52, 54–62, 71, 140, 245, 259, 282–283; see also Traits
Peter principle, 243
Philippines, 68, 95, 152, 155, 201–202, 222, 297
Physical attractiveness, 27, 59, 89, 202
Physical distance, 246
Physical symptoms, 156, 160, 169
Planning, 210
Pleasant experiences, role of, 183
Pluralistic attitudes, 271
Plurality, 4, 257, 271, 282, 286–292, 305
Point of view of others, 127–128, 312–314; see also Sensitivity
Political factors, 1, 14, 59, 153, 171, 237, 248, 258–259, 267
Policy making, 21–22, 25, 38, 127, 152–153, 164–165, 177–178, 191, 207–209, 229, 233, 239, 247, 255–256, 264, 266–267, 291, 316, 321
Potency, 33–34
Power, 28, 34, 64, 116, 142, 148–150, 165–166, 168, 191, 207–209, 225, 247, 258–259
Precision, 61
Prediction of overseas performance, 202–203, 224–225
Prejudice, 11, 26–28, 40–48, 55, 60, 69, 73, 118, 141, 164, 176, 194–196, 233, 320
forms of, 45–49, 78
functions of, 42–44
Preparedness for contact, 177–178
Pressures on organizations, 245–259
Prisons, 49
Private behavior, 153
Problem solving, 100, 109, 161–163, 165–167, 184, 218, 223, 229, 252, 255–256, 261–264, 269, 299, 331
Process in adjustment, 272–303, 446
Productivity, 212, 245

Professionals concerned with cross-cultural contact, 7–8, 184, 185–186, 203–204, 224, 237, 248, 251, 255–256, 272, 308, 314, 317, 320, 322–327, 331–332

Program planning, 45, 88, 131–134, 208, 221, 233, 271, 320

Projection, 76–77

Proper behavior, ideas about, 6, 12, 110, 111, 135

Prototypes, 89, 319–320

Provincialism, 247, 266

Psychological links, 83

Public behavior, 147, 153, 260–261, 265, 279

Publicity, 222, 234, 251, 259, 264, 269, 275

Puerto Rico, 148, 161

Qualities of others, 77–78, 121, 225

Question asking, 60

Race relations, 164–165; see also Cross-cultural contact

Racism, 26–27, 45–46, 88, 145, 176

Reactive attitudes, 195

Reaffirmation, 126–127, 136

Real likes and dislikes, 47–48

Recommendations made by sojourners, 223–224, 227

Red-neck racism, 45–46

Red tape, 230

Reference group change, 119–131, 198, 216

Refugees, 1, 66, 112–113, 120–121, 135, 146–147, 257, 264, 327–329; see also Immigrants

Regulations in an organization, 228, 231–236

Reinforcing activities, 66–67

Reintegration, 117, 122, 125, 129, 131–134, 136–137

Relations with others, 54–55, 58–59, 65–66, 70, 91, 114, 166–167, 235, 274–275, 276, 289, 290, 296, 300–301

Relevance, 108, 226, 300; see also Hedonic relevance

Reliability, 61

Religious commitment, 115, 120–121, 287, 288, 295, 310–311

Reorganization, 260

Reports to Administrators, 233–234

Researchers, 9, 54, 60, 83, 84–85, 112, 121, 144, 147, 167, 184–185, 205, 210–213, 218, 220, 222, 225, 230, 231, 237–238, 246, 255–256, 268, 299, 306, 311, 321–326, 331

Resources; see Rewards in situations

Responsibility, 242–245

Return to home country, 109–110, 117–118, 122, 123–124, 131–134, 136–137, 159–160, 257–258, 280, 284, 285, 288–289, 291, 295, 299, 305, 311, 315

Rewards in situations, 164–165, 170, 222, 226, 236–238, 253, 268, 325–326

Rigidity, 35–36, 53, 62, 86, 98, 118, 119, 172–173, 197, 285

Role playing, 128, 133, 205

Role shifting, 59–60, 127–128, 226

Roles, 29–30, 38, 59–60, 128, 133–134, 137, 145, 148, 165–167, 203, 215, 219, 226, 283, 286–288, 305

Romanticism, 257, 314, 330

Sabbaticals, 128

Saliency, 78–79, 87, 105–106, 108, 115, 223

Satisfaction on sojourns, 64, 123, 147, 212, 245, 270, 271, 300–303

Satisficing, 89, 106–107

Scandanavian, 126

Scapegoat, 28

Schemata, 104

School desegregation, 2, 54, 118, 136, 156, 171, 176, 179, 182–183, 184, 189, 192, 194, 207, 239, 249, 256

School, influence of, 19, 23, 36–38, 111, 117–118, 135, 144, 176, 197–198, 242, 284

School textbooks, 36–37, 38

Scripts, 89, 91–92, 108
Selection of sojourners, 202–204, 206, 210, 229, 246, 248, 299, 321–322
Self esteem, 58, 77, 94, 101, 110, 189–190, 198, 257, 284, 295
Self image, 58, 77, 79, 94, 105, 115, 155, 169, 173, 252, 274, 296, 297, 306, 311, 324
Self interest, 164, 170
Self sufficiency, 22–23
Selflessness, 59
Semantic differential, 32–35
Sensitivity, 48, 120, 207–209, 225, 252, 278, 313, 331
Shared fate, 124
Shifting reference groups, 110, 117–120, 126–134, 136
Similarities, 60, 77, 105, 187, 208
Situations, 10, 12–13, 50, 52–53, 56, 78, 91, 93, 97–98, 107–108, 137–170, 207, 221, 245, 255, 267, 285, 297
    difficulties of analyzing, 140
    related to acquaintance potential, 185; see also Groups in situations
Skills, 40, 51–53, 63–69, 70–71, 121, 123, 158, 166, 167, 204, 215, 218, 221, 223, 226, 268, 277–279, 286, 324–325; see also Abilities
Slavery, 26–29, 34
Sociability, 40, 59, 61, 165, 274–275, 304, 324
Social class, 2, 196
Social distance, 75, 154–155, 232, 302
Social ineptness, 30, 96, 142, 159, 193, 199, 201–202, 304
Socialization, 23–24, 69
Sojourner, 8, 15, 54, 81, 87, 88, 91, 97, 101, 104–106, 107, 114, 117, 126, 133, 137, 143, 146–147, 148–150, 153, 169, 200, 214, 219, 223; see also Cross-cultural contact

Sponsored programs, 229–230, 271
Spouses, 109
Status, 59–60, 89, 102–103, 121, 136, 142, 168, 181, 206–207, 214, 215, 223, 225, 238–239, 270, 274–275, 292, 302, 306
Status-quo, defense of, 19, 46
Stereotypes, 12, 37, 40–49, 55, 60, 69–70, 71, 73, 78, 80–81, 97–99, 105, 108, 152, 167, 176, 180–181, 191, 198, 225, 313
Strength of personality, 54, 57–58, 70
Stress, 4, 15, 86–87, 92, 109, 122, 133, 167, 169, 170, 289
Structure of language, 30–32
Structure of situations, 144, 168, 259
Study abroad; see Overseas students
Style of living, 9, 17
Subjective culture, 5
Subordination, 28, 215
Success on sojourns, 54, 56, 66–67, 72, 158, 173, 201–202, 221, 224, 235, 253–257, 295, 300, 319, 326–330
Summer camps, 10, 184–185, 189
Superordinate goals, 120, 184–185, 198, 239, 241, 256, 262, 266, 270, 319
Support groups, 23, 110, 112–117, 124, 134–135, 146, 150, 181–182, 189, 190, 198, 217, 261, 265, 312; see also Groups
Support services, 238–239, 269
Survival mechanism, 34
Sweden, 218–219, 226
Symbolic demands, 242
Symbolic racism, 46
Synthesis, 277, 304
Taking advantage of opportunities, 63, 66–67, 70, 300, 301
Task completion, 63–64, 68–69, 70–71, 138, 146, 165–168, 170, 200–221
Task orientation, 40, 54, 61–63, 70, 139, 150, 273–274, 276
Tasks, 10–11, 13–14, 84–85, 145–146, 165–168, 179, 200–227, 321

Teachers, role of, 186; see also School, influence of

Technical assistance advisors, 2, 9, 17, 54, 62, 71, 85–86, 112, 123–124, 132, 166, 178, 179, 200, 207, 209, 218–219, 220–224, 231, 244, 246, 267, 273, 285, 287–288, 297, 327

organizational factors, 236–270

stages of their work, 166

Technological development of countries, 200–227, 232, 244, 247, 269, 270, 275, 286

Television, 37–38

Tension, 129, 166, 176, 177, 185, 197

Tension reduction, 260–261, 262

Tests, 162, 311; see also Measurement

Thailand, 258

Theory, use of, 310–312

Therapy, 161–163

Thinking processes, 72–107, 126, 152–153, 173, 216, 255, 311, 329, 331

Third culture, 170

Time, 86, 89, 114–115, 116, 124, 129, 137, 145, 168, 179, 192, 209, 234–235, 246, 253, 256, 260, 261–264, 268, 271, 279–283, 303–304, 305

Tokenism, 46, 98–99

Tolerance, 35–36, 40, 53, 54–55, 57, 70, 72, 100, 104, 115, 118, 122, 125, 129, 144, 154, 176, 182, 189, 195, 197, 260, 269, 288, 290, 291, 295

Tolerance for ambiguity, 55

Tourism, 1, 9, 108, 143, 194

Training during sojourn, 218–219, 226

Trait-situation distinction, 93–96, 245

Traits, 30, 39, 40–49, 51–63, 69–70, 71, 78, 80, 94, 95–97, 105, 107, 122, 244, 292, 331

Transfer of skills, 57, 62, 107, 187, 210, 221, 228, 285

Transition between cultures, 88, 145, 160, 162, 205, 235–236, 242, 269, 273, 297–298, 310; see also Cross-cultural orientation programs

Translation, 33, 213–214

Translators, 9, 114

Travel, 127

Treaties, 25

Truk, 48

Trust, 205

Turkey, 16, 292–300

Turning inward, 20–21

Ulpan, 121, 145, 235

Uncertainty, 255–256, 267–268, 310; see also Ambiguity

Undermanning, 145, 186

Understanding others, 78, 168, 329–330

Unfamiliar situations, 155–156

United Nations, 26, 48, 152–153, 189, 213, 262, 263, 269, 274, 288

United States, 81, 87, 124, 127, 146, 152–153, 154–155, 167, 181, 191, 230

Universals, 7–8, 33

University curriculum, 218–219

Using one's talents, 40, 63, 67–68, 70, 123, 147, 291, 301

U.S.S.R., 81, 82, 152–153

Values, 39, 43, 100, 111, 114, 126, 146, 149, 239, 257–258, 282, 286–287, 290

Venezuela, 258

Vietnam, 21, 51, 135, 146

Vividness, 92, 108, 280

Vocabulary items, 32

Volunteers, 174, 178, 189, 197, 215, 237, 250, 258, 267

W-shape curve, 279–283, 304

Well-mannered indifference, 178

Westward movement, 24

White America, 95, 98, 111, 116, 118, 136, 141–142, 171, 178, 195, 290

Whiteness as a concept, 32–33, 36, 37

Whorfian hypothesis, 30–31
Withdrawal, 276–277, 304
Women in professions, 250–251
Work, 61, 90, 98–99, 123, 128, 130,
　　132, 144, 146, 147, 154, 164,
　　200–227, 229, 231–232, 233,
236, 259, 264, 273, 295, 329;
　see also Tasks
Working through negative conse-
　quences, 133–134, 242
World Bank, 249, 251
World-mindedness, 294, 305, 307

About the Author

Dr. Richard Brislin is a research associate at the Culture Learning Institute, East-West Center, in Honolulu, Hawaii. His first cross-cultural experiences were his high school years in Anchorage, Alaska, and undergraduate study on the island of Guam. After graduating from the University of Guam in 1966, he attended graduate school at the Pennsylvania State University (Ph.D. in Psychology, 1969). Since coming to the East-West Center in 1972, he has directed programs for international educators and cross-cultural researchers. Each program has been approximately four months in length, with participants from Asia, the Pacific, and the United States working together to increase their expertise in cross-cultural studies. One of these programs overlapped with a conference to develop the *Handbook of Cross-Cultural Psychology* (1980: Dr. Harry Triandis, senior editor), of which Dr. Brislin is a co-editor. His other books are *Cross-Cultural Research Methods* (1973, with W. Lonner and R. Thorndike); *Cross-Cultural Perspectives on Learning* (1975, co-edited with S. Bochner and W. Lonner); *Cross-Cultural Orientation Programs* (1976, with P. Pedersen); *Translation: Applications and Research* (an edited collection, 1976); and *Culture Learning: Concepts, Applications, and Research* (an edited collection, 1977). During the 1978–1979 academic year, he was a visiting professor at the School of Foreign Service, Georgetown University. His hobbies include collecting materials related to the American circus, and performing in a string band devoted to disseminating music from the Southern Appalachian mountain region of the United States.